Mismanaging Mayhem

Mismanaging Mayhem

How Washington Responds to Crisis

Edited by James Jay Carafano
and Richard Weitz

The Changing Face of War

PRAEGER SECURITY INTERNATIONAL
Westport, Connecticut • London

Library of Congress Cataloging-in-Publication Data

Mismanaging mayhem : how Washington responds to crisis / edited by James Jay Carafano
and Richard Weitz.
    p. cm. — (The changing face of war, ISSN 1937–5271)
  Includes bibliographical references and index.
  ISBN-13: 978–0–313–34892–1 (alk. paper)
  1. Interagency coordination—United States—History. 2. Crisis management—United
States—History. 3. Emergency management—United States—History. 4. United States—
Foreign relations administration. I. Carafano, James Jay, 1955- II. Weitz, Richard.
  JK411.M57 2008
  351.73—dc22   2007035288

British Library Cataloguing in Publication Data is available.

Library of Congress Catalog Card Number: 2007035288
ISBN: 978–0–313–34892–1
ISSN: 1937–5271

First published in 2008

Praeger Security International, 88 Post Road West, Westport, CT 06881
An imprint of Greenwood Publishing Group, Inc.
www.praeger.com

Printed in the United States of America

The paper used in this book complies with the
Permanent Paper Standard issued by the National
Information Standards Organization (Z39.48-1984).

10 9 8 7 6 5 4 3 2 1

For the men and women who serve the nation—past, present, and future

Contents

Introduction **Mismanaging Mayhem: Interagency Operations Past and Future** 1
James Jay Carafano and Richard Weitz

Chapter 1 **End of Days: Responding to the Great Pandemic of 1918** 6
John Shortal

Chapter 2 **Word Warriors: Information Operations during World War II** 27
Nicholas Evan Sarantakes

Chapter 3 **Marketing Freedom: Cold War, Public Diplomacy, and Psychological Warfare** 46
Carnes Lord

Chapter 4 **After Disaster: Recovering from the 1964 Alaskan Earthquake** 66
Dwight A. Ink

Chapter 5 **Winning Hearts and Minds: The Vietnam Experience** 89
Richard W. Stewart

Chapter 6   Crisis! What Crisis?: America's Response
              to the Energy Crisis   113
              Ben Lieberman

Chapter 7   Breaking Ranks—Breaking Rules:
              The Iran-Contra Scandal   130
              Alex Douville

Chapter 8   Interagency Paralysis: Armed Intervention
              in Bosnia and Kosovo   149
              Vicki J. Rast

Chapter 9   Fighting in Financial Foxholes: America
              and the Asian Financial Crisis   172
              Rozlyn C. Engel

Chapter 10   "Interagency Overseas": Responding to the
              2004 Indian Ocean Tsunami   192
              Gary W. Anderson

Chapter 11   In the Wake of the Storm: The National
              Response to Hurricane Katrina   211
              John R. Brinkerhoff

Chapter 12   Interagency Problems and Proposals:
              A Research Review   235
              Richard Weitz

Index   273

About the Editors and Contributors   291

Mismanaging Mayhem: Interagency Operations Past and Future

Introduction   James Jay Carafano and Richard Weitz

Between the unshakable ideas that government is the root of all evil and the answer to all problems stands the reality of governing. Governing is hard. When life and liberty stand at risk, applying everything official Washington can do to keep the nation safe, free, and prosperous can be even more perilous.

The United States government has more than 2 million civilian employees. Five out of six work out of sight of the national capital. They are joined by almost 3 million in uniform around the world and a Congress backed by a staff of over twenty thousand on Capitol Hill. Counting them all together makes Washington a bigger employer than any corporation. The men and women that serve in the executive and legislative branches comprise a vast enterprise—carrying out mundane duties, responding to crises, forging new visions, correcting past mistakes. Over the course of history, sometimes they have made America a better place—sometimes their efforts have gone horribly wrong.

Coordinating the work of departments, agencies, staffs, and Congress—and then harmonizing action with state and local governments, the private sector (including everything from commercial companies to the Red Cross), and foreign partners ranging from other countries to international organizations like the United Nations and European Union—is often called "interagency operations." Conducting them well is a challenge. The Departments of Defense, State, Homeland Security, and Treasury, as well as the FBI, CIA, and other government agencies, have different capabilities, budgets, cultures, operational styles, and congressional oversight committees. They even operate under different laws. Getting multiple agencies and departments organized on battlefields, after disasters, and during times of crisis can be as frustrating as "herding cats." As a result, the history of getting government agencies to cooperate is replete with stories of courage, heartbreaking tragedy, and blundering incompetence. The purpose of the book is to shed light on why managing interagency operations has proven especially difficult for the U.S. government.

To meet the dangers of the twenty-first century, interagency operations will be more important than ever, yet few Americans understand the troubling history of Washington's failures and the pressing needs for reform. *Mismanaging Mayhem* is an unprecedented effort at crafting a sober history of government's most pressing problem: working together when lives are on the line.

The stories told here examine some of the nation's darkest moments and most exhilarating victories, from dealing with the great flu epidemic of 1918, to responding to natural disasters at home and abroad, to fighting wars and rebuilding countries. They document how government bureaucracies have tried to work together over time to keep Americans safe and secure. These histories are remarkable not only for the lessons they offer on the difficulties of improving interagency operations but also for suggesting some surprising insights on the tumultuous legacy of when Washington took charge.

- Government policies contributed to the influenza pandemic of 1918.
- During World War II, winning political battles mattered more than winning the war of ideas.
- In the course of the Cold War, some agencies thought their most important job was to criticize the United States.
- If the president had not acted with dispatch after the 1964 Alaskan earthquake, the whole state might have been evacuated.
- America largely won the battle for "hearts and minds" in Vietnam.
- Congress and the White House helped create the "energy crisis."
- Iran-Contra operations cut through bureaucratic red tape, but they undermined the presidency in the process.
- Suffering from the "Somalia Syndrome," interagency squabbling worsened humanitarian suffering in Bosnia and Kosovo.
- Washington's initial response exacerbated the Asian financial crisis.
- Although a UN official criticized American tsunami relief as "too little, too late," the U.S. response was, in fact, an exemplary success.
- Contrary to media reporting, the Federal Emergency Management Agency led an effective response immediately after hurricane Katrina in the most devastated areas.

Mismanaging Mayhem tells the untold stories of how and why government agencies worked together to make things better—or worse.

Although many of the revelations in the case studies are surprising, the collective lessons of interagency history are even more insightful. Perhaps the most fundamental truism they suggest is that there is nothing wrong with the underlying principles of American governance. Some contend that interagency operations can never work effectively because our form of government values competing centers of power over unified purpose and effort. These studies suggest the opposite. Constitutional "checks and balances" that divide federal power between the executive, legislative, and judicial branches are essential for good governance. This division entails not only sharing responsibility within and among the branches of government but also ensuring accountability and transparency in the act of governing. Shortcutting, circumventing, centralizing, undermining, or obfuscating constitutional responsibilities is not an effective means for making interagency operations or democratic government work better.

Respecting the principle of federalism is also vital. Embodied in the U.S. Constitution, the imperatives of limited government and federalism give citizens and local communities the greatest role in shaping their lives. The Tenth Amendment declares that "powers not delegated to the United States by the Constitution, nor prohibited by it to the States, are reserved to the States respectively, or to the people." In matters relating to their communities, local jurisdictions and individuals have the preponderance of authority and autonomy. This just makes sense: the people closest to the problem are the ones best equipped to find the best solution.

Nevertheless, Washington can do much better. The U.S. government has a long-standing problem integrating the elements of national power. The case studies, covering a span of nine decades of American history, offer examples of interagency successes and failures. Despite the differences, some themes appear again and again.

- Government undervalues individuals. Human capital refers to the stock of skills, knowledge, and attributes resident in the workforce. Throughout its history Washington has paid scant attention to recruiting, training, exercising, and educating people to conduct interagency operations. Thus, at crucial moments, success or failure often turned on the happenstance of whether the right people with the right talents happened to be in the right job. Rather than investing in human capital before a crisis, Washington plays Russian roulette.
- Washington lacks the lifeline of a guiding idea. Doctrine is a body of knowledge for guiding joint action. Good doctrine does not tell individuals what to think, but it guides them in how to think—particularly, how to address complex, ambiguous, and unanticipated challenges when time and resources are both in short supply. The greater the scale of an operation, the more decentralized execution matters, the more essential sound doctrine becomes. Throughout its history, government has had very little that merits the label of "interagency doctrine." When its doctrine was taught and practiced, it made a difference. When not, chaos won.
- Process cannot replace people. At the highest levels of government, no organizational design, institutional procedures, or legislative remedy proved adequate to overcome poor leadership and combative personalities. Presidential leadership is particularly crucial to the conduct of interagency operations. Over the course of history, presidents have had significant flexibility in organizing the White House to suit their personal styles. That is all for the best. After all, the purpose of the presidential staff is to help presidents lead, not to tell them how to lead. Likewise, congressional leadership, especially from the chairs of congressional committees, is equally vital. There is no way to gerrymander the authorities of the committees to eliminate the necessity for competent, bipartisan leadership that puts the needs of the nation over politics and personal interest. In the end, no

government reform can replace the responsibility of the people to elect officials who can build trust and confidence in government; the responsibility of officials to select qualified leaders to run the government; and the responsibility of elected and appointed leaders to demonstrate courage, character, and competence in time of crisis.

In the case of interagency operational failures, history does often repeat itself, most especially when the issues of investing in human capital, establishing interagency doctrine, and focusing on strategic leadership remain unaddressed.

The fact that in some instances interagency collaboration works better than in others suggest the possibility for effective systematic reforms. *Mismanaging Mayhem* is also instructive for framing the challenge of implementing reforms. The case studies suggest that it is a mistake to think of the interagency processes as a uniform, one-size-fits-all activity that requires uniform, one-size-fits-all changes. Rather, the interagency process can be divided into three distinct components.

At the highest level stands the process of making interagency policy and strategy. These are the tasks largely accomplished in government office buildings inside the Washington beltway by the White House and heads of federal agencies, in cooperation and consultation with the Congress. They are largely responsible for deciding how all the elements of national power (including military force, diplomacy, economic might, and power of information) will be used to get things done. They decide the ends (what must be done), the means (what will be used), and the ways (how it will be done) for achieving national objectives. History suggests that over the course of modern history this has, in fact, become the strongest component of the interagency process. When results fall short, as for example in the case studies of the Iran-Contra scandal and the interventions in Bosnia and Kosovo, failure can often be traced to people and personalities more than process. Improving performance at the highest level of interagency activities should properly focus on the qualities and competencies of executive leadership, as well as getting leaders the quality information they need to make informed decisions.

Operational activities stand on the second rung of the interagency process. These activities comprise the overarching guidance, management, and allocation of resources for implementing the decisions made in Washington. Managing the response to the pandemic of 1918 and rebuilding after the Alaskan earthquake both offer examples of organizing government campaigns to implement government policy. Arguably, it is at this level of government where Washington's record is most mixed. Outside the Pentagon's combat command structure (which has staffs to oversee military operations in different parts of the world), the U.S. government has few established mechanisms with the capability to oversee complex contingences over a wide geographical area. Processes and organizations are usually established ad hoc. Some are successful; some are dismal failures.

The third component of interagency activities is in the field where the actual work gets done: rescuing people stranded on rooftops, handing out emergency supplies, administering vaccines, supervising a contractor. Here, success and failure usually turn on whether government has correctly scaled the solution to fit the problem. Most overseas interagency activities are usually conducted by a "country team" supervised by ambassadors and their professional staffs. Likewise, inside the United States, state and local governments largely take care of their own affairs. When the problems are manageable, as in the case of coordinating tsunami relief within individual countries, these approaches work well. On the other hand, when the challenges swell beyond the capacity of local leaders to cope, as the case studies of pacification programs in Vietnam and the response to hurricane Katrina illustrate, more robust support mechanisms are required. Arguably, what is most required at the level of field activities is better doctrine and more substantial investments in human capital (preparing people to do to the job before the crisis).

In addition to the insights provided by the historical case studies, *Mismanaging Mayhem* includes a review of contemporary research and literature relevant to interagency operations. An extended essay addressing everything from emergency response to intelligence operations summarizes the recommendations of over a hundred papers, books, and studies. This chapter offers a one-stop shop for an introduction into the plethora of issues and proposals made by scholars on how to master the challenge of herding cats. The case studies provide a context for judging the value of their insights. Taken together, the history of interagency operations and the many proposals made to guide the way forward offer the foundation for a national discussion on the next steps for interagency reform.

The editors and authors of *Mismanaging Mayhem* brought a depth of experience and expertise to the task of writing the unwritten history of interagency operations. Many have both extensive academic credentials and a wealth of real-life operational experience. All freely contributed their time and talents, recognizing that their only reward would be advancing the cause of making government serve its citizens better.

1
Chapter

End of Days: Responding to the Great Pandemic of 1918

John Shortal

From 1918 to 1919, an influenza pandemic struck the United States in three successive waves. This pandemic was the most destructive in the history of the world. The United States suffered six hundred seventy-five thousand deaths out of a population of 105 million. The American government not only failed to mount an effective, coordinated response to the crisis, but Washington's policies exacerbated the outbreak and undermined the war effort.

In 1918, the United States was a nation at war. The president and his principal advisors were preoccupied with the battle for France. Government censorship prevented the press from unreservedly covering the influenza pandemic. No one was appointed to deal with the emergency. Washington never developed a strategy to coordinate the national, state, and local response to the pandemic. No surveillance and tracking system was developed to identify trends and movement patterns of the pandemic. No quarantine or containment procedures were planned, developed or implemented at the direction of the central government. The volume of sick and dying overwhelmed the health care system.

Despite the social disruption and economic loss caused by the disease, Washington failed to learn and implement effective responses and countermeasures between the successive influenza waves. The federal government never developed a communications and outreach plan to educate the public and the health care community regarding the nature of the disease and the actions required to protect citizens. If a pandemic similar to that of 1918–19 were to strike the United States today, and the U.S. government responded in a similar manner, 90 million people would fall ill, 45 million would receive out patient care, 10 million would be hospitalized, and 2 million would die.

FIRST WAVE

The first known cases of influenza were reported in rural Haskell County, Kansas in late January and early February 1918 by Dr. Loring Minier, a country doctor, whose practice covered hundreds of square miles. Dr. Minier began to notice that several patients, in small towns and isolated farms, exhibited common symptoms usually associated with influenza. The patients all had chills, high fevers, dry coughs, body aches, headaches, sore throats, and stuffy noses. However, he noticed that this strain of the influenza virus was different. It was especially virulent and lethal.

As cases mounted, the nature of the outbreak disturbed Minier most. This virus killed young adults, the strongest and healthiest members of society. Normally, this group had the best chance of surviving a disease. Minier was so concerned that he took the extraordinary step of reporting the virus to the U.S. Public Health Service. These officials neither offered advice nor assistance nor acted on the information.[1]

Throughout February 1918, the volume of influenza patients overwhelmed Minier's small practice. By mid-March, however, the disease seemed to have run its course. There were no new cases. People returned to school and work. The disease had burned itself out in rural Haskell County—at least that was what Minier thought.

Between late February and early March, three young men from Haskell County left home for Camp Funston, Kansas.

In March 1918, Camp Funston was the second-largest training facility for the United States Army with fifty-six thousand new recruits. The facility was growing so rapidly that a hospital had not yet been built. There were not enough barracks for all the soldiers. Many were quartered in tents. They lacked heating fuel and warm clothes. Nature did not help. The especially harsh winter of 1917–18 was a perfect breeding ground for disease.[2]

The army camps proved to be particularly effective incubators for the flu virus. Influenza is caused by a virus that attacks the upper respiratory tract—nose, throat, and, in some cases, the lungs. The influenza virus spreads from one person to another through airborne particles, which are expelled from the lungs when the infected person coughs or sneezes. The virus enters the body through the nose or mouth. Influenza can also be picked up simply by touching a surface that has been contaminated by someone with the disease. It takes between one and four days for a person to develop symptoms of influenza. However, a person can be contagious before they start to show symptoms. The disease spreads very quickly through the masses in a crowded environment and cold weather enables the virus to exist for longer periods outside the body.

On March 4, 1918, a few days after the soldiers from Haskell County arrived at Camp Funston, the first case of influenza was reported. Within three weeks, more than 1,100 soldiers were admitted to the hospital and thousands more received treatment at the numerous infirmaries at the camp. The symptoms lasted two to three days. Then the men recovered.

The army did not consider notifying the U.S. Public Health Service nor did they quarantine the post. The soldiers, sick and healthy, were loaded onto trains and shipped to other camps. In a few short weeks, the movement of soldiers on railroads and rivers spread the influenza virus across the country. The influenza interrupted the training and preparation for combat at twenty-four of the army's thirty-six major installations.[3]

A World at War

In the last week of March 1918, the United States entered its second year of the war. That month, the German army launched a great offensive. In a desperate search for a decisive victory on the Western Front, the high command planned to drive a wedge between the British and French armies and defeat them before American forces could reach the battlefield in large numbers. Attacking on a fifty-mile front, the German army advanced forty miles in eight days, took seventy thousand prisoners, and inflicted two hundred thousand casualties. By the first week of April, German artillery shelled Paris.[4]

The allies, exhausted by four years of war, clamored for the arrival of American soldiers. The United States government, trying to be a good ally, mobilized the nation. Civilians poured into the cities in search of work in the defense industry. Ports swelled with sailors and merchant seamen. Soldiers packed railroad cars headed for the overseas embarkation docks on the East Coast. There, they transferred to troopships and shipped for France. The influenza went with them.

Urban centers along the eastern seaboard proved especially fertile breeding locations for the disease. The influenza virus struck the large urban centers as swiftly and as aggressively as it had the military installations. From March to April, the plague decimated thirty of the largest fifty cities and nearby military camps, disrupting commerce in its wake.[5] In Detroit, in March 1918, a total of 1,066 employees of the Ford Motor Company contracted the influenza virus and were sent home from work.

The pattern at the Ford plant was illustrative of the outbreak's course. On March 1, ten people reported sick with influenza. On March 27, the number of cases increased to fifty-four. On March 28, the number jumped to 145. From March 29 to April 8, the Ford Plant averaged 168 sick people per day. On April 9, the number decreased to sixty-five and continued to decline everyday until May 8, when the epidemic ended.[6] Again, as on the military installations, many fell ill, but few died.

As the wave of influenza appeared suddenly and dissipated quickly, it received little notice. In fact, one historian noted, "The spring epidemic is not even mentioned in the index of the 1918 volumes of *The Journal of the American Medical Association*." Influenza was not a reportable disease; only influenza-related deaths were registered with the various public health departments, which most doctors ascribed to uncomplicated cases of pneumonia.[7] The U.S. government, myopically focused on the war effort, paid scant attention.

While the outbreak waned, the Allies' desperation for American reinforcements swelled. The British prime minister, Lloyd George, sent a telegram to the

American secretary of war, Newton Baker, on March 29. In the telegram he wrote, "I have cabled to President Wilson asking him to . . . send men over to France with the utmost speed to make good losses . . . before this fighting is over, every man may count."[8] In April 1918, one hundred twenty thousand soldiers were shipped from ports on the U.S. East Coast to France. That was just the beginning. In the next seven months, the strength of the American army in France increased to 1,878,714 men. Unfortunately, as recorded in a popular song of the time, these American replacements brought the influenza "over there."

The first reported cases of the virus in France occurred at the port of Brest, during the first week of April. Almost 40 percent of the American army disembarked at the French port. From Brest, influenza quickly spread to the French army. It struck Paris by the end of the month. The British army was hit particularly hard in mid-April. In the British First Army alone, tens of thousands got sick and thirty-six thousand were hospitalized. The British Second and Third Armies were similarly affected. By the middle of June, the civilian population of England was also suffering from influenza.[9]

Flu did not take sides in the war. The German army was also hit hard by the disease. In fact, after the war, General Erich Ludendorff, commander in chief on the Western Front, blamed influenza for the failure of the spring offensive. The pattern was identical in all countries and in all armies in the spring of 1918; few died, but many got deathly ill.

Europe was not alone. The U.S. Navy helped spread the disease around the world. In April, the USS *North Carolina* in Norfolk, Virginia reported one hundred cases. In Rochefort, France, the USS *May* had 25 percent of the crew sick with influenza. The USS *Oregon* at Mare Island, California recorded two-thirds of its crew, amounting to 450 men, ill. In Santiago, Chile, the Seventh Regiment of the Marines reported a mild epidemic. In May, the pandemic picked up speed. The USS *Birmingham* at Gibraltar had seventy-eight cases. The USS *Chester* at Plymouth, England, reported 20 percent of the crew ill. The USS *Nashville* at Bizerti, Africa, reported that 47 percent of its crew fell ill while traveling from Gibraltar. Influenza traveled with the fleet to China, Russia, Hawaii, and the Azores.[10]

On land, the pandemic quickly spread through Europe from England, France, and Germany to Portugal, Greece, Denmark, Norway, Holland, Spain, and beyond. It also jumped to Bombay and New Zealand. In the spring, despite its ability to spread like wildfire, the first wave of influenza remained relatively mild. It moved rapidly, incapacitating large numbers, but did not result in a high mortality rate. The number of worldwide deaths in the first wave was estimated to be in the tens of thousands.[11]

In the summer of 1919, as influenza traveled around the world, America remained virtually flu free. Then, across the globe as it had in the United States, the outbreak subsided. In France, the British military authorities were so sure that the influenza attack was over that they officially declared an end on August 10. The pandemic, however, was far from over.

Understanding Influenza

In order for the influenza virus to become a pandemic strain, it must accomplish three tasks. It must first enter the human body and germinate. Second, it must be harmful to humans and third, be easily transmittable among populations. In the fall of 1918, the influenza virus accomplished all three tasks. The result for the United States, and the entire world, was the worst pandemic in history.

The influenza virus, like any virus, is constantly mutating. However, unlike other viruses, when the influenza virus mutates, it usually causes only slight changes in hemagglutin and neuraminidase. Hemagglutin is a protein that is adept at binding the virus to the cell that is being infected. Hemagglutin is most likely to bind to the respiratory tract. Once the virus docks with a cell, it invades the cell and dumps virus RNA into the cell's reproductive system, producing millions of new viruses. Neuraminidase spreads the new viruses from cell to cell. It takes approximately ten hours from the time the virus docks with the cell, until the new viruses (between one thousand and ten thousand) exit and begin invading new cells.[12]

This mutation of hemagglutin and neuraminidase happens just often enough to help the virus avoid detection by the body's immune system. The immune system can only fight a virus if it can see it. This is a critical characteristic of the influenza virus; its shape-shifting confuses the immune system. Changes to the surface of the virus, deter the human body from producing antibodies which could attack it. This minor mutation of the hemagglutin and neuraminidase is called antigen-drift. This antigen-drift is slow and recurrent. It was the major cause of new influenza outbreaks each year.[13]

The influenza virus alters much faster than other viruses. That is why vaccines for influenza are different from those for other diseases. Unlike polio, smallpox, measles, and the mumps, scientists must constantly update the vaccination serum to protect against the current strain of the influenza virus.[14]

Periodically, the influenza virus makes a transformation that is so drastic and sudden that the human immune system cannot identify the new virus. Dr. Anthony S. Fauci, director of the National Institute of Allergy and Infectious Diseases at the National Institutes of Health, explains, "Antigen shift is the reason that we must update influenza vaccines annually."[15] The antigen-shift that occurred in 1918 caused the pandemic.

SECOND WAVE

In the late summer of 1918, after traveling the globe, the influenza virus returned to the United States. The influenza outbreak in August and September bore no resemblance to the virus from the previous spring. This influenza virus had changed. As it had passed from person to person around the world, the virus had become a much more deadly and efficient killer.

In the second wave of the 1918–19 influenza pandemic, the United States government continued to focus on the war effort and ignored the health crisis posed by the pandemic. No one stepped forward to take charge, and the government in Washington left state and local officials to deal with the pandemic on their own. This wave of influenza killed tens of millions around the world.

They called the 1918 influenza, the "Spanish sickness." In the spring of 1918, only neutral nations admitted the existence of an influenza pandemic. Stories of the disease's path, particularly in the Spanish press, were the only reports the public received on the existence of influenza pandemic. Meanwhile, censorship in France, Britain, Germany, and the United States masked the real facts about the course of the disease. Neither side wanted the enemy to have an advantage or to know their secrets and plans. This reticence also prevented citizens from knowing the truth.[16]

The second wave of the influenza pandemic first manifested itself in three distant locations: the port cities of Freeport, Sierra Leone; Brest, France; and Boston, United States. The spread of the pandemic's second wave through the United States coincided with the U.S. Army's commencement of major offensives in France. On September 10, 1918, the United States Army attacked the Germans at St. Mihiel. That same month the Americans launched the Meuse-Argonne offensive. One historian called the Meuse-Argonne offensive "the most ambitious military effort in history." Six hundred thousand soldiers and four thousand artillery pieces participated in the attack. Many of the soldiers moved sixty miles to reach their attack positions.[17]

In cable after cable in September 1918, General Pershing, the American commander in France, wired the army chief of staff, General Peyton C. March, for more troops. At one point General Pershing said, "We do not have the troops necessary to replace even our ordinary casualties . . . I cannot plan future operations intelligently without knowing that I will have at hand the means necessary to carry them out. If our calls cannot be met because of insurmountable difficulties, I ask that I be so informed." Press censorship was so pervasive that even General Pershing did not fully grasp the effect of the influenza on the American army's ability to provide reinforcements.

One week later General March telegrammed General Pershing to tell him the truth about the situation in the United States. The American government did not want the Germans to know that tens of thousands of soldiers were sick.[18]

More than General Pershing's planning was hampered by the secrecy which resulted from censorship. The rigid control of the press, and the way the United States government organized for World War I, had a highly deleterious effect on the country's response to the influenza pandemic.

President Woodrow Wilson set the tone for the American government. In March 1917 he told a newspaper editor that "to fight you must be brutal and ruthless, and the spirit of ruthless brutality will enter into every fiber of our national life, infecting congress, the courts, the policeman on the beat, the man on the street."[19] With the plague now undermining the war effort, Washington started to pay attention.

Organized for Disaster

President Wilson selected extraordinary men to help him mobilize the nation for war, such as Secretary of Treasury William Gibbs MacAdoo, a man of unusual energy and ingenuity. MacAdoo developed a plan to finance the war by selling war bonds, raising half of the $33 billion required to fund American participation in the war. Wilson also established the War Industries Board in 1917, with Bernard Baruch, a wealthy New York stockbroker, as director. In a few short months, Baruch, wielding little more authority than his charisma, drive, and influence, increased industrial production by 20 percent. The president appointed Herbert Hoover as the director of the National Food Administration. Hoover also proved innovative and inspirational. He was so successful in persuading farmers to increase production that the United States not only fed its own civilian and military population, but supplied much of the food consumed by the allies as well. Hoover also ran the Fuel Board, responsible for conserving oil and coal for the war effort. Together with the secretary of war, Newton Baker, and the secretary of the navy, Josephus Daniels, Wilson had enlisted the best and the brightest to rapidly and successfully mobilize for war.

Initial efforts by Wilson and his team served to hamstring, rather than enhance, the government's pandemic response. At the height of the first influenza wave, at the administration's request, Congress passed the Sedition Act of 1918. The Sedition Act made disloyalty a crime. This act, coupled with the Espionage Act of 1817, made it illegal to obstruct the draft or to oppose the Liberty loan plan introduced to fund the war. The law made disloyalty to the war effort a crime punishable by $10,000 and twenty years in jail. The U.S. courts interpreted this act very loosely. For example, Judge Van Valkenburgh defined freedom of speech as "criticism which is . . . friendly to the government, friendly to the war, and friendly to the policies of the government."[20]

The United States government also created several organizations to fight dissent and detect disloyalty, including the American Protective League, which boasted one hundred thousand volunteers.

The national Council of National Defense and its state chapters incorporated a vast network of volunteers and advisors, including one hundred eighty-four thousand people employed by local law enforcement agencies. Its two main local agencies were the Loyalty Bureau and the Public Safety Committee. Both these organizations also had a dark side. They encouraged Americans to spy on each other and report acts of disloyalty or pacifism. The resulting atmosphere of intolerance and distrust hampered rather than facilitated cooperation between the federal government, states, and local communities.

Local efforts to enforce patriotism sometimes devolved into acts of political revenge or outright lawlessness. In Arizona, members of a gun-toting vigilante group called the Citizens Protective League, arbitrarily rounded up twelve hundred local labor and antiwar activists and shipped them out of state with warnings never to return. Government officials did nothing. The *Los Angles Times* declared the league's initiative "a lesson that the whole of America would do well to copy."[21]

The federal government also created the Committee on Public Information, under the direction of George Creel, charged with generating support for the war. The committee had the power to punish anyone who published anything negative about the war. The committee told editors that if they had any doubt about an article to be published, they should submit it to the committee for review. Journalists could be punished by the Department of Justice for printing anything viewed as unpatriotic. The post office had the legal authority not to distribute any publication considered subversive. Editors remained wary of publishing reports that could be remotely viewed as disloyal or critical of the war effort.

An Unhealthy Response

Government worked at cross purposes. While most of Washington focused on harnessing the nation for war and suppressing any news that might distract Americans from that task, the few officials directly responsible for dealing with the health crisis did little. The Public Health Service, under the direction of Surgeon General Rupert Blue, was the government agency responsible for directing the response to the influenza pandemic in the fall of 1918. Unlike Wilson's other war managers, Blue had been appointed by President Howard Taft. He was not part of the president's inner circle. Additionally, although Blue had built a career as a "plague fighter," battling malaria, typhoid fever, and bubonic plague, he proved incapable of leading an effective response to the public health disaster that was about to engulf the American landscape.

Before the war, the U.S. Public Health Service was a small organization that consisted of quarantine stations responsible for inspecting incoming ships, the Marine Hospital, and a small Hygienic Laboratory. Upon becoming president, Wilson expanded the authority of the service to pursue studies of the "diseases of man and the conditions affecting the propagation and spread thereof."[22] The president, however, did not greatly increase the funding or authority of the Public Health Service. When the war broke out, Blue commanded 180 public officials and 44 quarantine stations. This was the federal government's entire force to combat the oncoming plague. The situation was similarly grim at the local level. State public health departments were neither efficient nor well funded. The commissioner of health in the state of Washington summed up the quality of the nation's public health departments when he said that his subordinates were inadequately paid "and their policy is to do as much as the pay justifies."[23]

Blue did not possess the strength of character, energy, or ingenuity of either MacAdoo, Hoover, or Baruch. In the first week of September as influenza spread from Boston to the rest of the United States, the surgeon general did not direct the state public health departments to gather any data on the early cases of influenza. There was no method of tracking the movement of the virus. No early warning system existed, nor was a structure developed to identify and treat the populations that were most severely affected by the disease.

When the second wave came, the Public Health Service did nothing. The surgeon general did not attempt to quarantine ships transporting American soldiers and sailors. A strict maritime quarantine of any major U.S. port was out of the question. Quarantine would disrupt the flow of troops and supplies to the Western front. Colonel S. M. Kennedy, chief surgeon of the port of New York, said, "We can't stop this war on account of Spanish or any other kind of influenza."[24] As a result, returning veterans spread the disease throughout the country.

The government's greatest failure was deciding not to inform the American public about the true nature of the threat. The health service did nothing to prepare local communities for the pandemic. Service staff did not communicate a need for local preparedness, nor did it disseminate information to alert the public of the nature of the disease and the actions required to protect their health. Instead, they chose not to coordinate with other federal agencies and not hurt the war effort in any way. In fact, the service did more than remain silent; it suppressed the truth.

As one historian said, "In 1918, Departments of Public Health were often referred to as Departments of Public Assurance." Leaders made statements like, "If normal precautions are taken, there is nothing to fear." A Chicago public health official said, "Worry kills more people than the disease itself." In Bronxville, New York, the *Review Press and Reporter* reported, "Fear kills more than the disease and the weak and the timid often succumb first." In reality, the lack of public countermeasures, encouraged by indifferent government pronouncements, fueled the spread of the disease.[25]

On September 25, 1918, influenza was reported in twenty-six states. Senior medical officials from the army, navy, and Red Cross met in Washington to develop a strategy for the pandemic and to identify ways they could help individual states to cope with the disease. Neither Blue nor any other representative of the Public Health Service attended the meeting. Surgeon General Blue was afraid of disrupting the war effort and vacillated throughout the month of September.[26]

Crucible of the Crisis

Philadelphia was hit hardest by the flu. In the absence of a strategy or guidance from the federal government, local officials reacted slowly. Their lethargic response cost thousands of lives. In 1918, Philadelphia had a permanent population of 1.7 million, not including three hundred thousand workers who had migrated to the city in order to work in the defense establishment. The city was woefully unprepared for the pandemic's arrival. Medical facilities were seriously understaffed because of the war. Twenty-six percent of doctors and an even higher percentage of nurses had gone to serve in the military. At the same time, 75 percent of the medical and surgical staffs were deployed overseas.[27]

On September 18, 1918, the first cases of flu appeared at the Philadelphia Navy Yard. Nevertheless, city public health officials did not even record incidents of the disease. Day by day, the number of sick and dying grew exponentially. On September 21, the Board of Health finally made influenza cases reportable. At the same time, however, the Philadelphia public health director, Wilmer Krusen, announced that "no epidemic prevails in the civilian population at the present time."[28] War bond marches even continued. Two hundred thousand people gathered along a two-mile route in downtown Philadelphia, as sailors, soldiers, marines, and Boy Scouts paraded by.

Influenza spread like wildfire throughout the city. Three days after the parade 117 people died of influenza. On October 4, the University of Pennsylvania newspaper, the *Daily Pennsylvanian*, reported 636 new cases of influenza and 139 deaths. On that day, the Board of Health closed all public places including schools, churches, and theaters.[29] By then, it was too late.

As the number of dead and dying increased, so did fear and anxiety. The people of Philadelphia had no information on what was happening. The censorship of the media, and lack of knowledge about influenza, resulted in a total inability to properly react to the pandemic. The population of the city simply did not know what to do and who to turn to for advice. The pharmacies were stripped of all medicine in the first days of the outbreak, forcing people to rely on home remedies—"goose-grease poultices, sulfur fumes, onion syrup, and chloride of lime." The newspapers had advertisements from swindlers preying on people's fears and needs. The ads promised relief: "Sick with influenza? Use Ely's Cream Balm. No more snuffling. No struggling for breathing."[30]

What Philadelphia needed, in October 1918, to survive was strong leadership. The federal government did not provide it. Neither did the governor. The Board of Health did not have the staff, the leadership experience or economic and political influence necessary to control the spread of the pandemic. The mayor and City Hall should have stepped up and coordinated relief efforts, but they did not. As one historian said, "In Philadelphia, the City Hall was a source of favors more than of leadership."[31] Leadership for the city of Philadelphia came from an ad hoc arrangement of diverse organizations. In Pennsylvania, George Wharton Pepper headed the state chapter of the defense council. In Philadelphia, the council was directed by Judge J. Willis Martin. The Peppers and Martins were connected to the oldest and most distinguished families in the city. They both had significant political and economic clout. Judge Martin's wife directed Emergency Aid, which was Philadelphia's most important private social agency. On October 7, Pepper, Martin and the heads of dozens of private organizations met at the headquarters building of Emergency Aid. The meeting included many women from Philadelphia's most prominent families, the principal informal leaders in the city. They formed an ad hoc committee that had ready access to money and was prepared to spend it to coordinate the fight against influenza. Almost every organization in Philadelphia, political, social, economic, and religious, volunteered to partner with this committee to help in the crisis.[32]

The National Response

The situation in Philadelphia was not unique. Rather, it was indicative of a pattern that reoccurred in every major U.S. city. Local efforts to combat the outbreak occurred independently. The politicians, the media, and even the public health officials believed that the war was the priority. Therefore, financing the war through liberty bonds, work at shipyards and war industries, moving troops from smaller posts to larger posts and then on to ports of embarkation on the East Coast took precedence over battling the pandemic. President Wilson never made a public statement about influenza.[33] Washington never made a serious effort to mount a nationally coordinated campaign to combat the pandemic.

The government never deviated from its single-minded focus on the war effort. As one historian noted, "The relief effort for influenza victims would find no assistance in the Food Administration or the Fuel Administration or the Railroad Administration. From neither the White House nor any other senior administration post would there come any leadership, any attempts to set priorities, any attempt to coordinate activities, any attempt to deliver resources."[34] Lack of coordination was not the result of indifference; it emanated from Wilson's single-minded determination to prosecute the war in France.

Ironically, Washington policies exacerbated the greatest threat to the American war effort. In many large cities industries suffered from acute absenteeism due to influenza. Basic services—sanitation, law enforcement, fire fighting, and postal delivery—were greatly disrupted. Absenteeism also interrupted transportation, communication, health care, and food supplies.

In the fall of 1918, accurate information about influenza was critically necessary. Washington completely failed to meet that need. Neither civic leaders nor doctors knew vital facts about the disease, such as its spread patterns and the rate of infection. This information was needed by both the medical community, to fight the disease, and the public to ease panic. Despite the desperate need for authoritative information, Washington did very little. Initially, the Public Health Service was reluctant to make any statement about the disease for fear of being perceived as disloyal to the war effort. Public health officials waited almost a month before saying anything. In fact, the first public announcement made by the Public Health Service, on September 13, 1918, was to say that the "Bureau has no information on the nature of the disease."[35]

Furthermore, the service did not have a system in place to track the disease nor to keep the medical community and public informed. There was no system of reporting new cases of the disease that connected the federal, state, and local governments. The surgeon general waited until the crisis was upon him to respond. He was slow to react even then. In October, he finally directed the states and municipal health departments to submit weekly reports on influenza. However, by that time, doctors were so overworked that, in many cases, they identified preexisting conditions, rather than influenza, as the cause of death. The overworked health departments could not analyze the data because of the volume of deaths reported at the peak of the crisis.

Initially, the surgeon general did not direct any action that would isolate or quarantine the spread of the disease. In October, he finally directed public health officials to close all public places. Unfortunately, local public health officials did not have the power to implement this order. Some communities embraced the public health measures to control influenza. Others resisted because they were inconvenient, burdensome, or went against the community values, such as closing schools or churches.

The surgeon general published 6 million pamphlets to educate local health departments and the general public about the dangers of influenza. Unfortunately, they arrived too late to be of use. The Public Health Service also created a Volunteer Medical Service Corps, which maintained lists of doctors available to help with influenza. But again, the surgeon general waited to implement this until October 1918. By that time, the disease had already seized the country, and medical professionals were in short supply.[36]

Likewise, the Red Cross created a national committee to coordinate with the surgeon general and the armed forces. The Red Cross and the Public Health Service agreed to a division of labor. The service would locate, assign, and pay physicians. The Red Cross agreed to supply nurses and pay their salaries and expenses; provide emergency hospital supplies, resources, and personnel to state and local health departments; and distribute official statements by the Public Health Service on prevention and treatment.[37]

In less than two months, the Red Cross recruited almost fifteen thousand women to reinforce the overwhelmed medical communities. These women included trained nurses, practical nurses, nurse's aides, and women who had taken the Red Cross home hygiene course. They assisted in military hospitals and camps, troop ships, civilian hospitals, and in private homes throughout the United States. The Red Cross also directed every local chapter to organize its own committee on influenza. Volunteers surveyed the local hospitals, identified personnel and supply requirements and then coordinated the allocation of nurses and the procurement of needed medical supplies. In many cases, they set up makeshift hospitals.[38]

Once efforts were fully under way, the ad hoc partnership between the Red Cross, the Public Health Service and the military proved effective. The Red Cross initially provided $575,000 to recruit nurses and other medical support personnel. Eventually, the Red Cross spent $2 million of its own budget to fight the influenza pandemic. In addition to much-needed funding, the Red Cross provided health care professional support and vital logistical support to local communities and hospitals in need.[39]

Red Cross funding proved critical in the fight against influenza in the fall of 1918. The money quickly found its way to local officials. The Public Health

Service, on the other hand, continued to have acute cash-flow problems. With an annual budget of only $3 million, the service had barely sufficient resources to pay for its annual operations.

Eventually, Congress appropriated $1 million for the Public Health Service's fight against the influenza pandemic. Republican leader Henry Cabot Lodge captured the feeling prevalent in Congress when he said, "If the disease is not arrested, it may spread to every part of the country. Already it has affected our munitions plants. Its ravages may be more severe unless we grapple with it now, and we cannot do it without money."[40] Still, even with a flush of funds, the Public Health Service was not as successful as the Red Cross in securing doctors or nurses. The pay was insufficient and the service waited until the epidemic was in full force, and the available doctors committed, before trying to recruit them. After the service's recruiting mission largely failed, the surgeon general had to return $115,000 of the appropriated funds.[41]

The Military Response

The influenza pandemic had a critical impact on the war effort. The number of sick U.S. soldiers arriving in France overwhelmed the army medical staff. Pershing's staff requested additional medical personnel and supplies and for soldiers to be quarantined for one week prior to embarkation. The acting surgeon general of the army, Charles Richard, noted in a message to the army chief of staff that "if infected troops continue to arrive in France it will add greatly to the burden already heavy of caring for sick and noneffectives with the present shortage of medical personnel and equipment."[42] General Richard was not overstating the case. On September 18, 1918, the hospitals and convalescent camps of the Allied Expeditionary Forces (AEF) held 66,738 men. Two weeks later the number was up to 84,856. By November 7, 190,564 military personnel had fallen ill with influenza.[43]

General Richard recommended "that all troop movements overseas be suspended for the present, except as demanded by urgent military necessity." The army rejected the idea and the army's Medical Department appealed directly to President Wilson. The army chief of staff, General Peyton March, told the president that troop shipments should not be stopped for any reason. He emphasized to the president the "psychological effect it would have on a weakening enemy to learn that the American divisions and replacements were no longer arriving."[44] The president deferred to General March.

In the United States, the volume of sick soldiers virtually halted all training at military installations. The man in charge of the Selective Service, Major General Enoch Crowder, realized that sending more soldiers into the camps would only exacerbate the situation. On his own authority, Crowder canceled the draft for the month of October. His decision prevented one hundred forty-two thousand men from reporting to military installations overwhelmed by influenza. This act and the million dollars appropriated by the Congress were among the very few positive decisions made by the federal government during the influenza pandemic.[45]

Over the course of the outbreak, army medical officers and military scientists learned a good deal about how the virus was transmitted and how to treat the victims. They also discovered, however, that other than ruthless quarantine and isolation, there was little that could be done to stem the spread of infection.

Even within the military, some of the most effective responses to the disease originated not from the War Department but from decisions by individual officers in the field. The commander of Camp Colt, Pennsylvania, a young officer, Dwight Eisenhower, led one of the most successful efforts. The medical staff segregated the sick from the rest of the camp and Eisenhower ordered a daily round of inoculations against infectious diseases (such as smallpox and typhoid) and medical examinations for all personnel. After a week, the epidemic was contained. Only 150 people had died. Eisenhower's response had so impressed the War Department that he was ordered to send members of his medical staff to other posts in order to train their medical personnel.[46]

By the end of November 1918, the second wave ended. This wave was much deadlier than the first. The most surprising aspect was who died. This wave struck the young and healthy. In most communicable disease outbreaks this group has the lowest mortality rate, since they generally have the most robust immune systems. This was not the case in the second wave. Fifty percent of those who died were in the twenty- to thirty-year age group.[47]

THIRD WAVE

The virus mutated again and returned in December 1918. This latest outbreak peeked in January and February of 1919, though it persisted until April. Although less lethal than the second wave, the flu that swept the country in 1919 remained deadly.

Again, the outbreak severely impacted both military and civilian communities. The United States Army, which had almost 4 million men at the peak of the war, quickly demobilized to two hundred thousand by 1920. The third wave arrived after the campaign in Europe had ended; thus it was not overshadowed by the need to maintain morale and secrecy. Neither the press nor Congress, however, took any interest in this wave of the pandemic. Few lessons learned from the second wave were applied to the latest outbreak.[48]

After the war, the United States maintained an army to occupy Europe, including a cadre of two hundred forty thousand to police parts of western Germany. In the first three months of 1919, almost thirteen thousand soldiers were sick from influenza. The postwar medical establishment proved only marginally effective in fighting the latest outbreak of the disease.

In February 1919, an Alabama senator presented a resolution to Congress requesting that funds be appropriated so that the U.S. Public Health Service could study influenza. The senator wanted the U.S. Public Health Service to investigate the cause of the disease and find a way to eliminate it in the future. The secretary of war, Newton Baker, endorsed this resolution because he believed that studying

influenza and related diseases was the "most urgent [issue] confronting public
health authorities today." However, in 1920, the Congress only approved one-
tenth of the money requested, five hundred thousand of the $5 million. Even
when the war was over, the American government still had little interest in the
Spanish flu.[49]

AFTER THE DISASTER

The impact of the influenza pandemic was immense. In the United States, six
hundred seventy-five thousand people died out of a population of 105 million.
Worldwide the loss has been estimated between 20 to 50 million. In raw numbers,
the disease killed more people than any other in human history. Yet, despite the
enormous loss of life, little attention was paid to reflecting on the federal government's failure to launch a coordinated response. As historian Alfred Crosby noted,
there are several reasons for this. First, the disease struck quickly, caused massive
damage in a short period of time, and moved on. Second, it did not kill anyone
famous or powerful. Its victims were predominantly in the prime of their lives,
twenty to thirty years old, the same age as those who had died in the war. Third,
when it dissipated, it did not leave anyone scarred or disfigured like polio, cancer
or syphilis. Fourth, it impacted everyone equally, young and old, rich and poor,
Germans and Americans. Fifth, no institution or organization (political, economic,
or military) changed because of the disease. Most Americans viewed the three
waves as a consequence of the war.[50]

In retrospect, it should have been clear that the requirement for effective
interagency operations was axiomatic. The influenza outbreak demonstrated that,
by their nature, public health crises adversely impact every aspect of life and can
never be dealt with in isolation. Any public health crisis will likely demand a cooperative response from all elements of government. And any major activity,
whether it be fighting a war or responding to a natural disaster, will require us to
grapple with significant health issues.

The often synergistic relationship between large-scale activity and public
health crises also illustrated that major interagency challenges frequently do not
present themselves sequentially. Governments frequently find that they have to
deal with crises simultaneously. Concentrating on one to the exclusion of others
is unacceptable and can have disastrous consequences. In addition, the larger the
scale and complexity of the operation, the less likely it is that leaders can rely on
a "textbook response" to guide them on how to best organize and respond to the
unknowns and ambiguities, competing demands, and multiplicity of factors that
might complicate their efforts.

There is no question that the response of the Wilson administration was
completely inadequate. Ironically, Wilson understood the value of integrating
government activities to work toward a common goal. After all, he organized the
war effort with singular determination, concentrating not only on diplomatic and
military tasks but also on harnessing the home front for war. Indeed, raising,

organizing, and deploying the AEF was a remarkable achievement, considering that before 1918 the U.S. military was small, widely dispersed, and thoroughly ill-equipped to fight modern wars.

In responding to the pandemic of 1919, however, Wilson failed to recognize that an interagency response was required. Washington never mounted an integrated effort. The federal government lacked an overall policy to guide operations. Without the lifeline of a guiding idea, agencies often found themselves working at cross purposes, or worse striving for a common goal (i.e., winning the war) but ignoring one of the greatest threats to achieving the objective, a debilitating illness that sapped more manpower than the enemies' bombs and bullets.

Washington floundered because it lacked a clear policy or doctrine that provided an overall principle by which to manage the crisis. In 1918, Rupert Blue had the responsibility of ensuring public health, but he had neither the influence, nor the authority, nor the resources to carry out his mandate. He did not have access to the president that Hoover, Baruch, MacAdoo, or Baker enjoyed. Blue was incapable of impressing upon the president the seriousness of the pandemic. The president turned to other senior leaders for advice regarding the crisis, as illustrated by his deferral to the army chief of staff, in the pandemic's second wave.

Outside dealing with the business of war, the White House lacked the capacity to conduct integrated policy planning and crisis decision making at the highest levels. The executive office of the president was small and there was no equivalent to today's National Security Council.

Left to devise policy on his own, Blue did not make any decisions in the first wave. Between waves, he took no action to learn from the previous pandemic. In the second wave, he had the opportunity to quarantine the disease when it first erupted. He also could have attempted to stop the Fourth Liberty Loan drive, but again he vacillated. In fact, the surgeon general tried too hard not to disrupt the war effort, and acted only after the pandemic had spread.

The deeply flawed response to the pandemic also demonstrated the value of shared situational awareness in responding to a crisis, not only for informing top-level decision makers but also for distributing knowledge to empower decentralized coordination and execution at the local level. In short, what leaders responding to the pandemic lacked was a means to get the right information to the right person at the right time to do the right thing. This shortfall was particularly glaring with regard to the lack of surveillance and reporting, a form of situational awareness particularly vital to dealing with the spread of communicable disease.

In 1918, there was no system in place to track the movement of influenza. There was no method in place for the medical community to share information between countries. The lack of an established reporting and surveillance system combined with the paranoid desire to obscure the details of the disease to maintain support for the war destroyed any hope for cooperation between nations or communities. Without the free flow of information regarding the disease, the national leaders and medical community in the United States did not know where or when the virus would strike. Additionally, there was no advance notice on the identity or nature of the illness.

The surgeon general did not require that the medical community report new cases of influenza in 1918. Even after the loss of life and disruption of industry in the first wave, the Public Health Service made no attempt to track or report on influenza. This action was only taken after the disease had erupted all along the East Coast in the second wave, when it was too late to save lives. The service did not have a system to coordinate information from local community leaders, physicians and nurses, hospital administrators and public health officials. Failure to classify influenza as reportable and the lack of a coordinating system across federal, state, and local levels meant that there was virtually no early warning system or initial response to the pandemic.

Public Health Service officials had no way to detect the introduction of new cases into the United States. Once the disease had erupted in America, they could not track its movement from one community to another. They could not monitor the pandemic's impact on a community—number sick, hospitalized, or dead. They could not identify trends in the disease and target populations that were seriously affected and appropriately direct resources to help.

The response to the 1918 pandemic also demonstrated that the larger the scale and complexity of the operation, the greater the need for decentralized execution that relies heavily on the individuals closest to the crisis to identify problems and develop and implement solutions. War censorship, however, made effective information sharing impossible. Washington lacked all means to conduct open communication between the federal government and state and local officials, as well as the medical community and the general public. Censorship of the press and the loose interpretation of the Sedition Act led to reluctance on the part of key leaders to inform the medical community, and the general public, about the nature of the pandemic. Physicians in local communities had no information on influenza. The influenza they encountered in 1918–19 was unlike anything they had seen before. They were looking for answers about basic medical treatments, prioritization recommendations for the ill, medications to use and where to send people for care. Unfortunately, in 1918, the little information that was known was slow to arrive.

Open communication with the general public is essential to reduce anxiety and fear, and to enlist support for emergency measures. During the pandemic of 1918–19, with millions of people sick, the government and the media were silent on the disease. This silence did not engender trust in the decisions of public health officials. The public must be educated on any threat it faces. For example, in October 1918, when the surgeon general finally closed all public gathering places, the civic response to this measure was mixed. Some communities supported it and others felt the measure was oppressive and resisted. In some cities, churches were closed, but bars were kept open. There was disagreement in various communities on the necessity of closing schools or churches. In San Francisco, when public health officials tried to get people to wear gauze masks, they encountered criticism: civil libertarians opposed compulsory behavior; business owners protested that trade would be hurt; Christian Scientists objected to the disregard of personal liberties.[51]

The need for effective decentralized execution was nowhere more apparent than in meeting the challenge of surging medical capacity to deal with the overwhelming number of influenza cases. When the pandemic hit in 1918, hospitals in both the civilian and military communities were quickly overwhelmed. There simply were not enough beds, staff, and medical supplies to treat all patients adequately. The hospital administrators experimented with a variety of techniques to deal with the volume of patients. They extended work hours, assigned student doctors and nurses to duties, discharged the least sick, and accepted only the most severe cases. They set up tents, used armories, schools, and churches to treat the overflow of patients. This scenario occurred in virtually every large urban center around the country.[52] Even within the military, decentralized execution and innovation, such as the response at Camp Colt, proved the most effective at dealing with the acute care crisis.

There was a tremendous shortfall in capacity even though most people struggled with the disease at home, and not in the hospitals. In many cases family members did the best they could to treat the sick without medicine or a cure. Societal expectations have changed since 1918. Today people do not stay at home and rely on their family for health care as they did in 1918. Unfortunately, hospitals are no better prepared to handle a surge today then they were in 1918. In 2006, Dr. Thomas Ingelsby of the University of Pittsburgh Medical Center for Biosecurity said that "an epidemic comparable to that of 1918 would require 197% of hospital beds, 461% of intensive care unit beds, and 198% of all available respirators. The gap between our need for surge capacity in urban areas and our current resources is staggering."[53] Today the situation is exacerbated by the financial situation hospitals are operating in. Managed-care demands to reduce costs, and cuts in government reimbursement, have forced hospitals to take beds off-line and to depend on just-in-time staff and supplies. Today even minor changes to projected patient loads cause serious problems. A pandemic on the 1918–19 scale would quickly overwhelm the current capacity. Thus, the need for local, decentralized solutions will be vital should such a disaster strike.

Likewise, in responding to the pandemic of 1918, finding sufficiently trained health care providers proved a daunting task. The government and the U.S. Public Health Service was not successful in identifying physicians to assist in the crisis. Most of the qualified doctors and health care professionals were in the military. However, the Red Cross did a superb job, on no notice, of finding fifteen thousand nurses and assistants. The time to develop lists of potential health care responders is before, not after, a pandemic strikes. In 1918, it was necessary to take anyone with medical training, including medical students, and retirees. In 2006, Dr. John Bartlett of Johns Hopkins University said the critical need will be for hospital providers skilled in "primary care, infection control, emergency medicine, pulmonary-critical care, and infectious diseases; nurses, respiratory

therapists, pharmacists and support personnel."[54] As in 1918, all of these will be short supply.

Implementation of effective containment and quarantine often proved a matter of local innovation and adaptation. In 1918, Commander John Poyer, the governor of American Samoa, ordered a strict quarantine of the islands. This was a bold move, which the governor made because he observed the devastating affect that the influenza virus had on the New Zealand administered western Samoa. No ships, including mail transports, were allowed to enter or leave American Samoa. No vessels from western Samoa, which had the flu, were allowed to land in American Samoa until ten days after the last case of influenza was reported there. In essence, the governor completely isolated American Samoa from the outside world. It worked, and American Samoa remained influenza free.[55] In other isolated locations, containment and quarantine were likewise successful in halting or slowing the spread of the pandemic.

In 1918, the surgeon general did not have the power to enforce quarantine nationwide, and did not even recommend it, until it was too late. Even if Blue had such authority it is difficult to imagine how it could have been effectively coordinated and implemented on a national scale. More likely, effective quarantine and isolation would have to come for decentralized, cooperative efforts. In the future, national leaders will have to educate the American people on the importance of this, in order to gain their willing support.

A pandemic on the scale of 1918 would be catastrophic to any country. Dr. Jeffery Taubenberger said that "even with modern antiviral and antibacterial drugs, vaccines, and prevention knowledge, the return of a pandemic virus equivalent in pathogenicity to the virus of 1918 would kill (more than) 100 million people world wide."[56] A national health policy that can be explained, understood, and implemented at the local level will have to be a crucial part of any effective response. This response will have to have a strong interagency character. A pandemic will require everyone's support to cope with the illness, social disruption, and economic loss that it is bound to cause. This strategy should include public and private partnerships with the government as well. While interagency response for a pandemic is essential, such an approach could serve as model for responding to any complex, large-scale contingency operation.

NOTES

1. John Barry, *The Great Influenza: The Epic Story of the Deadliest Plague in History* (New York: Viking Press, 2004), 93.

2. Ibid., 95.

3. Alfred Crosby, *America's Forgotten Pandemic: The Influenza of 1918* (New York: Oxford University Press, 1989), 19; Joseph Stiler, *The Medical Department of the United States Army,* vol. IX, *Communicable and Other Diseases* (Washington, DC: U.S. Government Printing Office, 1928), 132–33.

4. Richard Stewart, *American Military History,* vol. 2, *The United States Army in a Global Era, 1917–2003* (Washington, DC: U.S. Government Printing Office, 2005), 29.

5. James Armstrong, "Philadelphia, Nurses, and the Spanish Influenza Pandemic of 1918," *Navy Medicine* 92, no. 2 (March–April 2001): 16.

6. U.S. Navy, *Annual Reports of the Navy Department for the Fiscal Year 1919* (Washington, DC: U.S. Government Printing Office, 1920), 2423.

7. Crosby, *Forgotten Pandemic*, 18.

8. *United States Army in the World War, 1917–1919*, vol. 2, *Policy Forming Documents of the American Expeditionary Forces* (Washington, DC: U.S. Army Center of Military History, 1988), 263.

9. Barry, *Epic Story*, 182. *United States Army in the World War, 1917–1919*, vol. 12, *Reports of the Commander-in-Chief, AEF, Staff Sections and Services* (Washington, DC: U.S. Army Center of Military History, 1988), 312–53.

10. U.S. Navy, *Annual Report 1919*, 2424.

11. Barry, *Epic Story*, 311.

12. Goldsmith, *Influenza*, 16–18.

13. Ibid.

14. Ibid.

15. Department of Health and Human Services, Doctor Anthony S. Fauci, Testimony to the Committee on Appropriations, Subcommittee on Foreign Operations, Export, Financing, and Related Programs, United States House of Representatives, March 2, 2006. See also Connie Goldsmith, *Influenza: The Next Pandemic* (Minneapolis: Twenty-First Century Books, 2007), 16–18.

16. Barry, *Epic Story*, 171 and 180.

17. Ibid. Alan Millett and Peter Maslowski, *For the Common Defense: A Military History of America* (New York: The Free Press, 1984), 355.

18. In *The United States Army in the World War*, vol. 2, Telegram, General March to General Pershing, October 10, 1918, p. 625; Telegram General Pershing to General March, October 2, 1918, pp. 618–19.

19. Harris Meiron and Susie Harris, *The Last Days of Innocence: America at War 1917–1918* (New York: Random House, 1997), 283; Barry, *Epic Story*, 121.

20. Ronald Schaeffer, *America in the Great War: The Rise of the Welfare State* (New York: Oxford University Press, 1991), 17.

21. Thomas Fleming, *The Illusion of Victory: America in World War* (New York: Basic Books, 2003), 139.

22. Crosby, *Influenza*, 19; Barry, *Epic Story*, 309; William Holcomb, "The U.S. Public Health Service Commissioned Corps: A Need for Engineers," *Military Medicine* (December 2003).

23. Crosby, *Influenza*, 19.

24. Ibid., 31.

25. John Barry, "Pandemic Influenza—Past, Present, Future: Communicating Today Based on the Lessons from the 1918–1919 Influenza Pandemic," at the Workshop Proceedings for the U.S. Department of Health and Human Services Centers for Disease Control and Prevention, in Washington, DC, October 17, 2006; Barry, *Epic Story*, 336.

26. Barry, *Epic Story*, 311.

27. Eileen Lynch, "The Flu of 1918," *Pennsylvania Gazette*, 1998, 3, at http://www.upenn.edu/gazette/1198/lynch.html; James Armstrong, "Philadelphia, Nurses, and the Spanish Influenza Pandemic of 1918," *Navy Medicine* 92, no. 2 (March–April 2001): 2.

28. Barry, *Epic Story*, 204–5.

29. Lynch, "Flu of 1918," 3.

30. Ibid., 3.

31. Crosby, *Influenza*, 79.

32. Barry, *Epic Story*, 323–24.

33. Jim Duffy, "The Blue Death," *Johns Hopkins Public Health*, Fall 2004, 3, cited in http://www.jhsph.edu/publichealthnews/magazine/archive/Mag_Fall04/prologues/index.html.

34. Barry, *Epic Story*, 302.

35. Ibid., 310.

36. Ibid., 316; Gary Gernhart, "A Forgotten Enemy: PHS's Fight Against the 1918 Influenza Epidemic," *Public Health Reports* 117, November/December (1999): 559–61.

37. "The Influenza Pandemic of 1918 and the Red Cross Response," cited in http://www.redcross.org/museum/history/influenza.asp.

38. Ibid.

39. Ibid.

40. Crosby, *Influenza*, 52.

41. Barry, *Epic Story*, 319.

42. Carol Byerly, "The Politics of Disease and War: Infectious Disease in the United States Army during World War I" (dissertation, University of Colorado, 2001), 240.

43. *U.S. Army in World War I*, vol. 12, 146–47.

44. Byerly, *Politics of Disease*, 255; Peyton March, *The Nation at War* (Garden City: Doubleday, Doran and Company, 1932), 359–60.

45. Barry, *Epic Story*, 303.

46. Carlo D'Este, *Eisenhower: A Soldier's Life* (New York: Henry Holt, 2002), 134–35.

47. Goldsmith, *Influenza*, 34; Stiler, *Medical Department*, 86–89.

48. Byerly, *Politics of Disease*, 328.

49. Ibid., 328–29.

50. Crosby, *Influenza*, 321–23.

51. Ibid.

52. Monica Schoch-Spana, "Hospitals Full-Up: The 1918 Influenza Pandemic," *Public Health Reports* 116, Supplement 2 (2001): 33.

53. John Bartlett, "Planning for Avian Influenza," *Annals of Internal Medicine* 145, no. 2 (July 18, 2006), cited in http://www.annals.org/cgi/content/full/145/2/141.

54. Ibid.

55. Crosby, *Influenza*, 234–40.

56. Jeffery Taubenberger and David Morens, "1918 Influenza: The Mother of All Pandemics," *Emerging and Infectious Diseases* 12, no. 1 (January 2006), cited in http://www.cdc.gov/ncidod/EID/vol12no)!/05-0979.htm.

2
Chapter

Word Warriors: Information Operations during World War II

Nicholas Evan Sarantakes

Before December 7, 1941, Americans stood deeply divided over whether the United States should get involved in another "war to end all wars." That changed the instant news crackled from the radio reporting the surprise attack on Pearl Harbor. With the nation committed to the fight against the Axis powers, Washington wanted to make sure that Americans would continue to believe they were fighting the "good war" throughout the difficult years and sacrifices that lay ahead. What resulted was an unprecedented effort to influence public opinion in the United States and around the world.

War information became a war priority. At the outbreak of the American involvement in World War II, a number of different federal agencies, cabinet departments, and military services conducted information operations. There was a good deal of overlap. The necessity of working together became quickly apparent. That proved no easy task. For better or worse, and it was generally for the worse, leaders in Washington often defined what was best for their bureaucracy as also being what was in the interest of the nation at large, and conversely what threatened their institutions endangered the well-being of the nation as a whole. Bitter confrontations on matters large and small were hallmarks of Washington's effort to get the word out.

IN THE DAYS AFTER PEARL HARBOR

Americans entered into the war with conflicting attitudes toward propaganda and official information agencies. On the one hand, they were suspicious. Much of this hostility was based on experience. During World War I, President Woodrow Wilson established the Committee on Public Information to serve both as a propaganda and censorship agency. Headed by George Creel, a journalist by profession, the committee had the job of helping to unify the country in support of the war. Creel called it "the world's greatest adventure in advertising." Under Creel the government launched an unprecedented wartime information campaign that proved both effective and controversial.[1]

Creel's programs proved adept at both whipping up support for administration policies and fueling anti-German sentiment. After the war, however, as memories of victory faded, on reflection Americans resented government manipulation. Postwar controversies including the contentious debate over Wilson's failed efforts to gain support for the Versailles Treaty and the League of Nations soured many on Washington's wartime promises. Some contemporary historians even blamed administration propaganda for dragging the United States into the war in the first place.[2] As a result, on the eve of war the American public was divided, skeptical, and mistrustful of government involvement in information operations.

On the other hand, as the troubles in Europe and Asia widened and it became apparent that U.S. troops would soon be entering the fray, the hometown appetite for information became insatiable. "Dissatisfaction with the government's handling of war news began right at the start, with Pearl Harbor; and various aspects of that episode repeated themselves in others that were to follow," recalled Elmer Davis, the director of war information.[3] Americans wanted the facts. They wanted a lot—and they wanted it fast.

During World War I, Creel's committee had issued press releases for the Departments of State, War, and the Navy. Not wanting to again cede a monopoly on managing the news, over the course of the interwar period, many government agencies and the military services established their own press offices so they could tell their own story. In addition, as World War II loomed Washington established a number of new ad hoc agencies that focused on information as part of their mission. These included the Office of Facts and Figures (OFF), the Foreign Information Service (FIS), Office of the Coordinator of Information (COI), the Office of Civilian Defense, Office of Government Reports, Office of Censorship, Division of Information of the Office of Emergency Management, Coordinator of Inter-American Affairs, and the Coordinator of Information in the State Department. Over the length of the war several of these agencies came and went. Some merged into others. Some were simply abolished.

The history of these short-lived information agencies is instructive. The OFF, which lasted only nine months, offers a case in point. On October 21, 1941, President Franklin D. Roosevelt signed Executive Order 8922, establishing the OFF. Roosevelt appointed Archibald MacLeish, the Pulitzer Prize winning poet and the Librarian of Congress, to head the new organization.

MacLeish believed the United States had embarked on a moral crusade in a war forced on the world by Nazi aggression, "a revolution aimed at the destruction of the whole authority of excellence which places law above force, beauty above cruelty, singleness above numbers." MacLeish insisted that OFF not market propaganda—that was what the Nazis did. OFF would be different, better. MacLeish pursued what he dubbed the "strategy of truth," providing news information that was honest and true.[4]

Despite MacLeish's zeal for the fight, during the brief existence of OFF the agency accomplished next to nothing. MacLeish, while an exceptionally talented writer, was not a particularly adept administrator. Still, his reputation as a high-profile, deeply ideological, and partisan New Dealer did help attract a number of talented writers, journalists, publicists, advertising executives, and lawyers to the agency. Even though OFF comprised less than three hundred people the agency played an important role as a proving ground for propagandists. Many of the staff went on to influential positions in official Washington in areas related to war news. They would become avid advocates for an idealistic approach to information operations.

The COI, under the leadership of William "Wild Bill" Donovan, a World War I Medal of Honor recipient and successful Wall Street lawyer, also played a notable role in early war information programs. Long before Pearl Harbor and the establishment of COI, Donovan had established a personal relationship with the president. Roosevelt held Donovan in high regard and gave him a number of informal diplomatic missions. While working with British officials, Donovan developed an interest in intelligence operations, including secret propaganda, often called psychological warfare. He came to favor covert operations and deceptive practices that ran counter to the "strategy of truth" approach that MacLeish favored.

Donovan was pushing for the creation of a national intelligence agency that could perform a number of different missions. One of these functions would be information warfare. In July 1941, Roosevelt established the Office of the Coordinator of Information with Donovan as the COI director. The Foreign Information Service became a subagency. Donovan intended to use the FIS to spread propaganda and manipulate foreign audiences. He also tapped the Pulitzer prize–winning playwright Robert E. Sherwood to run FIS. Sherwood had been a presidential speechwriter, and by recruiting him, Donovan hoped to further win over the support of Roosevelt and his inner circle.[5]

THE OLD GUARD

War brought a whole host of new agencies to official Washington and these various bureaus soon found themselves in fierce competition with established bureaucracies, particularly the War and Navy Departments. It took months and months to sort out the various differences in missions and responsibilities. While the military services eventually became avid practitioners of providing war information, they were initially dismissive of its value. In fact, initially the army and navy wanted to limit the amount of news they made available out of concern that it might prove useful to the enemy. To preserve operational security, the service's initial impulse was to tell Americans and the world as little as possible.

In the days after Pearl Harbor, with scant information coming from the armed services, Americans took their war news from where they could get it. The best source was the Axis powers. As the Japanese pushed the United States and the European colonial powers out of Asia, they were only too eager to share the news of their exploits. The result was a public relations disaster. "It was not unnatural that the American public, unable to mistake the general trend of events in those first disastrous months, should have come to the conclusion that while the Japanese radio might exaggerate the damage inflicted on us," Davis wrote, "its news was far more dependable than that issued by our own army and navy."[6] The enemy had won the first round.

The military was not entirely blind to the importance of providing the American public war news. Public affairs officers plied reporters with news about the exploits of individual soldiers, sailors, marines, and airmen. There were, however, limitations to the value of these stories as they gave little indication of progress in the war. "These doubtless gave a momentary lift to public morale," Davis observed, "but they also created an impression that things in general were going far better for us than they really were, and the eventual let down was all the worse." When the armed forces did reveal operational news, they often blundered the opportunity. "The War Department's releases on the fall of Bataan," Davis wrote, "were full and candid; but with only a few days of preparation they came as a shock to a public which had come to believe from the general tenor of the news from Bataan, that our forces there might hold out forever."[7]

Another factor that complicated early information work was that the services found themselves as much at war over COI as they were with the enemy. Donovan gave Sherwood a fairly wide berth in hiring personnel for the FIS. Sherwood's partisanship was equal to that of MacLeish. Sherwood felt New Dealers who shared his vision about pursuing liberal, Wilsonian ideals, would make ideal advocates for contrasting American values, institutions, and principles with totalitarianism. The FIS not only raised charges of partisan politics, other agencies including the State Department, the FBI, the Coordinator of Inter-American Affairs, and the Bureau of the Budget questioned the utility of the organization, arguing it was nothing more than a costly duplication of services that other agencies were already providing.

Even within COI controversy ran rampant. Donovan tried to sidestep criticism over FIS politics by having his office placed under the military. A World War I veteran and officer in the National Guard, he was comfortable working in a military setting. Sherwood and the staff of FIS, however, were not. Many were academics, writers, journalists, actors, and publishers with professional backgrounds that made them accustomed to a good deal of liberty in their work environments, quite different from the well-disciplined, hierarchal structure of the War and Navy Departments.

Donovan also differed over the COI's plan to "weaponize" propaganda. Sherwood's vision for the agency was much closer to MacLeish's "strategy of truth." "Democracies have a good story to tell," Sherwood argued, "We stick to the truth, for we believe the truth is on our side. . . . The American image overseas would suffer, if we emulated Axis methods and resorted to lies and deceit."[8] The FIS director was determined to keep the service away from the military. Sherwood began using his contacts at the White House to lobby for either the separation of his organization from Donovan's or the abolition of the COI altogether, spreading its components to other parts of the government.

In June 1942, Roosevelt split the squabbling factions, signing an executive order creating the Office of War Information (OWI) which merged OFF and FIS. Meanwhile, the COI became the Office of Strategic Services (OSS), the main spy agency for the United States during the war.

MISSION IMPOSSIBLE

In Washington organizations with some type of mission related to information operations came into being in haphazard fashion. No one, though, was trying to define the purpose of these various bureaus and departments in relation to one another. The individuals leading OWI, for example, had their own ideas on what their agency should do to contribute to winning the war, ideas they had developed without serious consultation with the armed forces. Even within OWI there were disagreements over the focus of their effort. Some thought OWI a propaganda tool, a news bureau, a foreign press service, a think tank, or a psychological warfare command. Much of this confusion resulted from the fact that OWI had absorbed a number of agencies that each had been created for different purposes.

As OWI struggled with its identity crisis, the armed services, the OSS, the State Department, and a number of other federal entities embarked on their public affairs campaigns. They too had their particular takes on the proper focus and priorities for public information policy. Almost all of these organizations would challenge the OWI for leadership of U.S. government information operations at one time or another.

To make matters worse, OWI, the OSS, the army, and other federal agencies all lacked any doctrine that described the purpose, scope, or elements of war information. The lack of doctrine had a crippling effect. As historian Clayton D. Laurie argued, "The struggle to influence the thoughts and behavior of friends and foes alike made World War II a contest of ideologies as well as arms."[9] Yet, the United States lacked a common framework that described the role of war information in an ideological struggle. Washington faced a unique challenge that did not bother their Axis opponents—defining the difference between government-supplied information and propaganda.

One of the reasons there was no doctrine was that many people saw defining tasks and methods as an issue of minor importance. Clayton R. Koppes and Gregory D. Black in their study of the American film industry in World War II noted that propaganda was "a bit like pornography—hard to define but most people think they know it when they see it."[10] In the end, there was a general belief that the issue would work itself out as people figured out what worked and what did not. That did not prove to be the case. As the war progressed, differences on these matters grew. The OWI and OSS became embroiled in a number of disputes on doctrine and definitions, which were really efforts to explain the differences between information, propaganda, and psychological warfare. This war of words held great significance because their interpretation would define missions and responsibilities and prescribe the allocation of resources.

In the first months after America's entry into the war, people in Washington proved better at explaining what they were not going to do, rather than what they hoped to achieve. U.S. policies, officials insisted, would not copy the coercive and manipulative actions of Nazi propagandists like Joseph Goebbels. New York mayor Fiorello LaGuardia, who for a period headed the Office of Civilian Defense, offered a case in point. Reporters proved skeptical of the office's domestic information mission, which they assumed was just a fancy way to say propaganda. "There are three reasons why it is not," La Guardia countered. "The first is that we don't believe in this country in artificially stimulate high-pressure, doctored nonsense, and since we don't, the other two reasons are unimportant."[11] MacLeish in his brief tenure as OFF director was equally adamant, stressing that the United States would pursue a policy of only telling the honest facts. Arthur Krock of the *New York Times* countered that "if OFF pipes out the undiluted, uncolored facts, it will be the first government information bureau to do that."[12] Nevertheless, Washington officials continued to insist that war information in democracies differed fundamentally in character from propaganda machines of totalitarian states.

Ultimately three different doctrines emerged. The OWI stuck to its "strategy of truth," a highly ideological approach that saw the war as a continuation of the New Deal at home and abroad. Sherwood and MacLeish remained its two strongest advocates. Within OWI, Sherwood headed overseas operations focusing on foreign affairs. MacLeish addressed domestic policy matters.

Advocates of the "strategy of truth" were also rejecting disinformation and insisting on honest reporting of facts which included an overt identification of the source providing the information. "Sherwood believed," Clay Laurie writes that it "was a tool capable of uplifting, of educating, of enlightening the world to the high ideals, virtues, and aims of Americans." Still, Laurie notes that while Sherwood wanted to avoid using falsehood, FIS reported the truth highly selectively.[13] Service reports simply omitted damaging and embarrassing information. Sherwood, MacLeish and their subordinates saw no hypocrisy in this selective use of the truth nor ever considered that such reporting might undermine the credibility of FIS.

The OSS took a different approach. Donovan wanted nothing to do with domestic operations, though he believed like Sherwood and MacLeish, that war information should not be politicized. Donovan, however, had a different goal in mind. He wanted to conduct information operations against the enemy that weakened their will. Donovan envisioned using war information as part of an aggressive propaganda campaign.

While the OSS gathered and provided analysis of intelligence as its first and primary mission, Donovan thought of information operations as the "arrow of initial penetration," followed by sabotage and supplying resistance organizations. All of these efforts would soften up regions before conventional military operations got under way. Losing FIS represented a blow to his grand strategic scheme. The OSS chief believed that the FIS could have made a real contribution to the war effort if it had been willing to sow dissension in Germany and encourage revolts against Nazi occupation. Still, since this was a niche that the OWI and the army failed to fill, Donovan planned to use the OSS to fill the void with its own deception and misinformation operations.

The U.S. Army opted for yet another approach, concentrating on psychological warfare intended to be truthful, largely apolitical, and focused on immediate tactical needs, like undermining enemy morale on the battlefield and getting individual soldiers to surrender. The army also planned an information campaign to bolster the morale of the troops with its own newspapers, magazines, and movie reels.

Despite the vast amount of resources and people under the command of the army, the service started at a huge disadvantage compared to ad hoc agencies like the COI, OWI, and OFF. During the interwar period, the army had allowed its expertise in information operations to lapse. By 1941 only one officer who had any experience in propaganda efforts remained in the Military Intelligence Division of the General Staff.

Not only did the army enter the war with scant expertise, the commitment of the senior leadership to war information was conflicted. General George C. Marshall, chief of staff of the U.S. Army, was tentative at first in his support. He was slow to see the value of war information, but became a major proponent as the war progressed.[14]

MUDDLED FROM THE START

Although information operations eventually demonstrated their importance to the war effort, that value was far from apparent in the months after Pearl Harbor. In large part, the slow start resulted from the organizational chaos created by establishing new organizations with overlapping and conflicting missions.

Confusion and confrontation were nowhere more apparent than in the relationship between OWI and the White House. Many in the agency saw the war as the ideological struggle that the president had described in his public remarks. The administration, however, often sacrificed idealism for practicality and expediency. Government policies required that the OWI ignore the less than democratic rule of the British in India and reflect the ambiguity of official U.S. policy toward Charles de Gaulle's Free French movement and the Vichy regime of Henri Philippe Pétain that collaborated with the Nazis. Such compromises bothered OWI officials to no end.

The biggest crisis came after the allies invaded North Africa and encountered strong resistance from the colonial French garrisons. The controversy that followed over the "Darlan deal"—when after an armistice General Dwight Eisenhower left the French commander, the collaborator Admiral Jean-Francois Darlan, in charge—sparked a public relations controversy of the first order.

Darlan had been the number two man in Pétain's state and commander in chief of the French armed services. At the time of the invasion he was in North Africa only through happenstance—he was visiting his gravely ill son. Darlan promised to order French units to stop fighting. In return, Eisenhower recognized Darlan's authority in French North Africa. As a result, the repressive laws of the Vichy regime remained in place, individuals imprisoned for resisting the Nazi domination of France stayed in their jail cells, and anti-Semitism continued to be official French policy despite the American occupation of the region.

After the Americans assaulted the beaches, the press assaulted Eisenhower. In its first major combat operation in the West, the United States had compromised with a Fascist leader. Many of the liberal propagandists of the OWI were angry at what they thought was a betrayal of American principles and attempted to use public information as a way to shape, define, and even reverse policy. The deal also outraged the American public. The storm of protest that followed caught Eisenhower off guard. Blaming the messenger for the message, the general then made what his biographer Stephen E. Ambrose calls a "blunder." Eisenhower imposed strict censorship on political news.[15]

Personnel from OWI challenged military officials and took steps on their own to undermine the Darlan deal. Some gathered information on the continued repression of political dissidents under Darlan's regime and then gave it to war correspondents headed home. Others destroyed French radio and press facilities that belonged to the Vichy regime or its supporters.

Fortunately for Eisenhower his younger brother, Milton, was the number two man in the OWI. Davis sent Milton to Algeria to meet with his brother and end the crisis. Milton convinced his brother to end restrictions on war information and encourage visits to the theater by columnists and reporters from major news outlets. The crisis only really ended when a French royalist assassinated the admiral.

The bungling of the Darlan affair between the army and OWI should have come as no surprise given the origin of the young agency. Roosevelt had never really been interested in establishing an all-powerful information bureau as Wilson had done during World War I. He only created OWI in response to domestic critics who decried the lack of war information. This ambiguity was clearly reflected in the agency's charter. "It was the clear purpose of Executive Order 9182 to give OWI full control of the information policies of all departments and agencies," Davis noted, but then added, "while leaving most of the production of information in the agencies themselves."[16] In setting up the agency, Roosevelt chose a compromise that would appease his critics, but satisfy his own wishes, creating an agency that was responsible for everything, but controlled almost nothing.

ORGANIZING FOR VICTORY

At the outset, OWI, OSS, and the army all disagreed on the appropriate division of roles, missions, and priorities. Even within OSS rivalries over the control and scope of information warfare activities raged. Nevertheless, as the war progressed the roles and missions of federal entities were sorted out. Five reasons eventually prompted a rethinking of government policies:

1. The Office of War Information cleaned house. The purge included many people within the domestic branch of the OWI, who like MacLeish, wanted to define what American was fighting for on their own political terms. They wanted to address substantive issues presenting the American people with the information that they thought was relevant and would lead to policies they supported. In essence, they wanted OWI to become a policy-making shop. MacLeish realized this approach would engender controversy, but he persisted. "If OWI takes a position on issues as bitterly controversial as those here involved it will be attacked as OFF was attacked." He also believed: "I submit, however, that if OWI is not pre-pared to take a position on these fundamental issues it may suffer in other and more fatal though less painful ways."[17] When he lost this debate, MacLeish resigned his position and focused on his duties as Librarian of Congress. Shortly after MacLeish left, a number of writers resigned in a mass protest. They quit over new policies that former advertising executives who had joined OWI were implementing. These new ideas would have the agency focus more on selling the war than in explaining it to the public. "There is only one issue—the deep and fundamental one of the honest presentation of war information," they declared in a statement they released to the press. "We are leaving because of our conviction that it is impossible for us, under those who now control our output, to tell the full truth. No one denies that promotional techniques have a proper and powerful function in telling the story of the war. But as we see it, the activities of OWI on the home front are now dominated by high-pressure promoters who prefer slick salesmanship to honest information."[18] Sherwood was eventually forced out as well. As a result, the overseas branch shifted more toward objective news and information.
2. Congress got involved. While the OWI settled on its new direction, Congress proved reluctant to accept an approach that amounted to launching a government advertising campaign. Objecting to the notion of selling policies to the American public, Congress cut funding for the domestic branch of OWI.
3. The war intervened. With U.S. troops beginning to go into harm's way, the armed forces were hard pressed to keep news from the public. The Navy Department took the lead. During the campaign for control of Guadalcanal a new approach on war information emerged. After weeks of bitter fighting, it was unclear whether the Marine Corps and navy were going to emerge victorious. The sea services adopted a new policy of frank discussion. Deciding it was better to steel Americans for another defeat, public affairs officials and commanders openly talked about the perilous conditions American personnel faced in the campaign.[19]
4. The army made a decision. Although Donovan led a civilian agency, he had proved more willing to work in cooperation with the military. The Joint Chiefs of Staff and the service secretaries preferred working with him over the OWI. Eventually, Donovan returned to active duty in the army and was promoted to the rank of major general. Together the OSS and the armed services outmatched OWI at political infighting. On March 9, 1943, Roosevelt signed Executive Order 9312 defining the foreign information activities for both OWI and OSS. While

the document declared that the Office of War Information would plan, develop, and execute all phases of "foreign propaganda activities involving the dissemination of information," this mission proved far less than a bureaucratic victory. This agency had to coordinate its activities with the military in theaters of operation, and could do nothing without the concurrence of the armed forces. In addition, Donovan and the OSS also claimed that disinformation and subversion were not propaganda, disputing the power of the executive order, which led to another round of bitter disputes over doctrine. That dispute led to another round of heated debate over doctrinal definitions. For the rest of the war, the army used its authority to co-opt OWI teams and direct their activities toward apolitical, tactical efforts.[20]

5. War information started to show results. As the personnel detailed to these operations began to have tangible, measurable success, attitudes changed. When information operations efforts actually proved useful in the field they gained greater acceptance with both military and civilian leaders. In turn, the military provided more resources and asserted more authority over war information activities.[21]

THE WAR OF IDEAS

While the armed forces and the OSS gained prominence in managing information operations overseas, the bureaucratic battle at home continued without any reprieve. In 1943, Congress nearly eliminated the OWI's domestic functions and other departments moved in to fill the void. Over the next two years, the Department of the Treasury attempted to seize control of domestic information operations with five war bond campaigns. The purpose of these drives was to encourage the American people to invest in the war effort and counter inflation. These campaigns proved highly successful. In the second drive, for example, 61,279 radio announcements appeared on local and regional radio stations during this three week effort. A total of 171 programs participated, mentioning the drive in some fashion during its three week run.

During the campaigns, Secretary of the Treasury Henry Morgenthau, Jr., insisted on themes that emphasized how he saw the nature of the war as much as the imperative of buying war bonds. Morgenthau intended to use the domestic public relations efforts that accompanied the campaigns to redefine foreign policy toward Germany, wishing to impose harsh peace conditions and break up the German state. He thought he had the backing of the president. In fact, while Roosevelt's views toward the German people had hardened, he had not decided to adopt Morgenthau's harsh postwar policies. Davis countered the Treasury Department's effort to dominate war information policy by screening the speeches of top officials and refusing to approve remarks that endorsed the Morgenthau Plan. Roosevelt complicated matters when he encouraged Morgenthau to believe the secretary would play a prominent role in postwar policy making, but then used another agency to undermine the efforts on the part of the Treasury Department. In reality, Roosevelt had only encouraged Morgenthau in order to make his own proposals seem more balanced and reasonable.[22]

Treasury's assault on OWI's authority was not unique. In 1943, the Department of State also moved into the realm of domestic information efforts. With Secretary of State Cordell Hull's approval, Undersecretary of State Edward Stettinius, Jr. began a reorganization of the department. One of the features of this effort was the creation of new bureaus that would help American diplomats gauge and shape public opinion on foreign policy matters. In January of 1944, Stettinius created the Office of Public Information. That same year the State Department got into the radio business with a series called "The State Department Speaks" in which senior officials of the department would discuss important foreign policy issues.

When Stettinius became secretary at the end of the year, following Hull's resignation, he decided to create a new position to supervise these activities: assistant secretary for public and cultural relations. He appointed Archibald MacLeish.

This position was MacLeish's third in the realm of information policy, and unlike the other two, this new post gave him a real opportunity to make policy. During his confirmation hearings, he told the Senate Foreign Relations Committee: "It would not be too much to say that the foreign relations of a modern state are conducted quite as much through the instruments of public international communication as through diplomatic representatives and missions." Under questioning, he added, "This would be the job of making known to the American people as fully as can be done within the necessary limits of this kind of work the facts they require to make up their minds."[23] New Dealers were going to get a new chance. In the end, however, he proved no more successful than OWI in using information to shape policy.

OVER THERE AND OVER HERE

While agencies warred in Washington for control over domestic information operations, the military also became more directly involved in affecting public opinion. The most famous of these efforts was the *Why We Fight* films series. General George C. Marshall, U.S. Army chief of staff, worried about turning a group of individualistic citizens into a professional, well-disciplined army. He believed the War Department could do this job, but these new recruits needed to know and understand why the United States was fighting this war. The general enlisted Hollywood for the job of getting the message out. He personally gave film director Frank Capra, a major in the Signal Corps, the mission of making the *Why We Fight* series. Marshall hoped the films would be a tool to bolster morale and explain to soldiers the reasons for the war.

Capra played a prominent role in the army's effort to use movies as an instrument of war information. He remembered the general saying, "They will prove not only equal, but superior to totalitarian soldiers, *if*—and this is a large if, indeed—they are given answers as to *why* they are in uniform, and *if* the answers they get are *worth* fighting and dying for." He then explained what he wanted: "Now, Capra, I want to nail down with you a plan to make a series of documented, factual-information films—the first in our history—that will explain to our boys in the Army *why* we are fighting and the *principles* for which we are fighting."[24] The result was a film series that was a model of both good propaganda and film making. The first franchise in the series, *Prelude to War*, won an Academy Award. The films were screened in the United States and around the world for both military and civilian audiences. Capra was promoted twice and left the service as a colonel. The promotions were well earned; Hollywood gave the army a dominant role in the war information campaign.

JUGGLING PAILS OF WATER

Despite changes and reorganization and the military's increasingly prominent role, throughout the war one of the greatest challenges proved to be the number of agencies with conflicting responsibilities, and the absence of any mechanism forcing them to work together. Overlapping areas of responsibility and convoluted lines of authority were, in fact, characteristic traits of Franklin D. Roosevelt's administrative style. "A little rivalry is stimulating, you know. It keeps everybody going to prove that he is a better fellow than the next man," the president explained once.[25] The president actually never provided clear moral, ideological, or policy guidance on matters involving war information and propaganda. While there was arguably some merit in Roosevelt's interest in promoting competition between federal agencies, his approach also created a good deal of conflict, usually resulting in bitter turf wars between bureaucracies that increased in intensity in direct proportion to the lack of attention that the White House offered.

Davis appeared to have the authority to end this feuding when he came into office with a mandate to coordinate both information policies and the release of public information—but that view was misleading. He could use his power to some degree, and could block public officials, like Morgenthau, from making speeches when they strayed too far from the president's wishes. The vagueness of his authority over federal agencies, however, made it difficult for him to either enforce policy decisions or broker compromises.

The lack of a clear role and mission was the central shortcoming of OWI and its failure to play a pivotal role in affecting interagency coordination over war information. A number of indicators showed the diminished status of OWI, and were reflective of an ineffective bureaucratic organization.

As the war lengthened and government grew, office space in Washington, D.C. was at a premium. The offices of the OWI ended up being located two miles from downtown. Davis argued that this location made a significant difference, particularly as it attempted to perform its news agency mission: "accordingly the Agency lost some of its effectiveness."[26] To make matters worse, the overseas branch worked out of New York. Davis never had a firm control over that part of the agency.

Leadership proved another reoccurring problem for OWI. Personnel were selected for their reputations as writers, rather than as administrators and managers.

Davis and Sherwood both admitted they had no administrative experience. MacLeish proved not much better.

Funding was perhaps the most critical measure of support. While OWI and OSS received the lion's share of budgets for war information, in practice their budget clout was limited. As the war progressed, the armed forces increasingly used their authorities to set priorities for what had to be done.

As the war lengthened for reasons large and small it became increasingly difficult for Davis to exert any authority. George Creel, Wilson's information czar during World War I warned Davis that he was trying to "make the best of things as you have found them. Such a course is possible when things are fairly good, but when things are downright bad, nothing is more fatal than an amiable effort to make the best of them."[27] In the end, Creel predicted that the OWI director would never be able to manage the government bureaucracy the way he had done. "I am more sorry than I can say that your control over Army, Navy and State is not real in any sense of the word," Creel warned, "while you may think you have established an arrangement that will permit a free flow of news, just wait until an issue arises."[28] He was right. Davis came to take this view as his own before the end of the war. "We tried coordination by conference and agreement; the results were fairly good but not good enough; and it required an unreasonable amount of time and effort to get any results at all."[29] The real problem he faced is that he had no power to enforce coordination. "It took experience to teach us that you are not going to get much conformity," Davis lamented, "unless you can fire the man who does not conform."[30]

WORKING WITH OTHERS

Congress played an extremely important role in U.S. information policies—principally in a negative manner. Two factors motivated the legislators—partisan interest and concerns over First Amendment civil liberties. Most people tend to forget that Congress remained hostile to the Roosevelt Administration. Although Democrats controlled both chambers of the legislature throughout the war, the mid-term elections of 1942 went against the administration. Republicans nearly gained control of both the House and the Senate. Combined with conservative members of the South, enemies of the New Deal were effectively in control.[31]

Over the course of the war Congress gutted a number of New Deal agencies, including the OWI. The House Appropriations Committee cut the OWI's domestic budget by nearly 40 percent. The House voted to abolish its domestic branch altogether. In the end, conference committee settled on $2,750,000 which was a cut of roughly 70 percent. As Davis noted this figure was configured to avoid "the odium of having put us out of business, and carefully not enough to let us accomplish much."[32]

Some of the antipathy toward OWI was just party politics. Political opponents worried that the agency would service the political interests of the Roosevelt administration. There were, however, also legitimate concerns. One of the tenets of democracy was that an informed public was a critical element in public life and that the job should belong to news outlets in the private sector. The existence of OWI challenged that concept. Domestic information could easily become manipulative propaganda, designed to sell a government policy to the people rather than simply a process the government used to inform the people on how it was implementing the will of the electorate.

Davis was stoical about the inherent problems of informing a democracy. "Perhaps this was inevitable," he lamented.[33] Nevertheless, the attacks demoralized the agency. One of Sherwood's deputies observed later, "OWI never fully recovered here at home from the damage done to its prestige by Congress and by certain elements of the Press."[34] Davis believed that creating an OWI oversight committee in the Congress might have helped. "Such a committee or committees," he wrote, would have given "the agency the benefit of continuing Congressional advice, and could help dispel the often absurd misunderstandings that prevailed in our time."[35] Both houses considered but rejected the proposal believing there were too many committees already in Congress.

The OWI not only failed to engage with Congress, it had also limited support from the White House. Throughout the war, other agencies heads and cabinet secretaries enlisted the prestige of the president by having important announcements involving them released through the White House. In contrast, the president generally kept OWI at arm's length, seriously undermining Davis's role as war information manager. In retrospect, Davis concluded, "the most authoritative and important war information will always be found in the speeches, statements, and press conferences of the President; a man who serves as his adviser on these matters, and on occasion as his spokesman, may actually be the most important information official of the government."[36] Unlike Wilson, however, Roosevelt never conferred such power on a single individual or agency.

The fourth estate also resisted efforts to centralize and coordinate government information policies. "OWI was generally in disfavor with much if not most of the press," Davis noted.[37] Individual reporters and editors resisted government encroachment on their activities, arguing such actions ran counter to their interests and civil liberties. At the same time, producers and studio executives in Hollywood believed they knew better than some government bureaucrat back in Washington what the American public wanted. Not only did they resist taking direction from OWI, the media grew increasingly irritated over the agency's failure to delivery on its promise of providing fast, factual and relevant war information. Reporters expected Davis to pry news out of the Washington bureaucracy. They quickly became disillusioned. Some accused OWI of fostering complacency or deliberately withholding bad news. They also resented Davis' aloofness. He rarely visited the National Press Club or socialized with his former colleagues. He was more than willing to criticize the professional performance of reporters, a practice that earned him a good deal of hostility and was largely counterproductive. "The next Director of War Information had bet-ter realize that criticism is a one way street," Davis observed.[38]

MISMANAGING CHAOS

When Davis wrote his final report, he reflected on the skills that some future information agency head would need. There is a clear sense of exasperation in his comment: "He should also possess the varied abilities of a lobbyist, a traffic policeman, and the impresario of an opera company, you would have a pretty good Director of War Information."[39] The OWI director's wish list underscored that absent either a centralized governance structure or an overall intent and common body of knowledge and procedures to guide decentralized decision making and coordination, the effectiveness of interagency cooperation rested solely on the personality and skills of individual leaders.

Indeed, leadership, both good and bad, did much to shape the character of war information operations. Many of the people that became involved in war information, for example, were extremely dedicated, talented, and resourceful, motivated by good old-fashioned patriotism. Writers, editors, publishers, direc-tors, and film producers—people involved in the media of either news or entertainment—wanted to use their skills and experiences from their civilian careers in service to their country. Many helped Capra make the *Why We Fight* films for no cost and no profit. On the other hand, some people put their careers ahead of public service. They were willing to make films to help the war effort, but were equally determined, if not more so, to make sure that this work did not pre-vent them from making theatrical productions or cut into their profit margins.[40]

The military also had some negative incentives in place when it came to the media. Officers always looked at public affairs positions as being, according to one observer, "at best a blank in their careers." Working with the media was a less than desirable assignment, sometimes even professionally dangerous. "A serious mistake could ruin him. Naturally this encourages a tendency to play safe or what seems to be safe."[41] As a result, war information duties did not always attract skilled and talented officers and noncommissioned officers. One of the many reasons that the army had little influence early on in propaganda efforts was the fact that it assigned unqualified officers to positions of com-mand. These individuals believed their jobs were to serve as caretakers of civil-ian operations rather than as leaders. As a result, civilian propagandists from OWI and the OSS that served as part of army-controlled organizations had no real reason to heed military officials.

Institutional culture also affected the practice of leadership. Newly invented agencies like OWI and OSS had an institutional culture that matched its institu-tional history, which is to say there was rather little. Instead, the views and deci-sions of leaders and staff reflected the professional practice in their civilian careers—advertising, journalism, and academia. In contrast, in the military the thought of making honest information widely available to the public during the course of the war ran counter to the initial impulses of good military operations. As Walter Cronkite, then of United Press International, observed, "The United States military was as unprepared for handling the requirements of the press as it was for meeting the enemy."[42] Where war information was concerned the military had to learn new leadership skills.

The military eventually learned how to come to terms with its public affairs responsibilities. The Navy Department, for example, which had pioneered a more open approach to public information, saw positive advantages of this policy. Secretary of the Navy Frank Knox, a newspaper publisher before entering government service, started the practice by having battlefield commanders brief reporters in Washington. Following his death, Knox's successor, James V. Forrestal, took the initiative even further. At his first press conference, Forrestal announced that he wanted "to tell what the Navy was doing and let the facts speak for themselves without embroidery." To foster openness, the new secretary personally instructed Captain Harold "Min" Miller to go to the headquarters of Admiral Chester Nimitz and improve press coverage of the navy. Miller did an impressive job of providing logistical support to news reporters. The result was that reporters ended up favoring the navy and Marine Corps in their coverage of the Pacific campaign.[43]

In the end, leadership made a world of difference in formulating and implementing war information policies. Essentially publicists and propagandists needed, for lack of better words, a patron. This was true at all levels. The *Stars and Stripes* newspaper succeeded only because Eisenhower believed a hometown paper away from home was needed to sustain the morale of his troops. Marshall's personal support for Capra was critical for the director in making the *Why We Fight* series, and even then he faced a good deal of internal opposition within the army. "The war information films were made in spite of the heavy-handed opposition of entrenched colonels," Capra recalled in his memoirs. In the field, theater commanders warmed up to propaganda aimed at the enemy when they saw that it could deliver useful military results like inducing the surrender of enemy combatants. "I don't know much about psychological warfare," Eisenhower admitted, "but I want to give it every chance."[44]

The need for a patron existed at the national level as well. George Creel and Woodrow Wilson had a close relationship in World War I. Davis and Roosevelt did not. Davis had been offered an opportunity to meet with the president on a daily basis to discuss war news, but he turned down the idea, believing that Roosevelt's time was too valuable. That decision was a huge mistake.

WINNING THE GOOD WAR

War information amassed a mixed record in helping to win the war by undermining the enemy's resolve while steeling Americans for the sacrifices of a protracted and difficult conflict. In the field, at the tactical level there is some evidence to suggest that information operations, when well organized and integrated, proved effective. In the Pacific, official Japanese army documents showed that propaganda was becoming a real concern to Japanese officers and that they had to spend time explaining to their men why American propaganda was false. Diaries show that local issues like the lack of food, the poor quality of their weapons, and the weak leadership of their officers were themes that hit a real chord with the average Japanese soldier. The Philippines campaign offered a particular case in point. Despite the widespread perception then and now that Japanese fought to the last man, ten thousand men surrendered in the Philippine Islands. There were a number of instances where whole units conceded defeat and turned themselves over to the Americans. The ratio of Japanese that became POWs to those that died was 1:100 at the beginning of the American invasion. In July of 1945, the last month of the campaign, the ratio was down to 1:7 for an overall average of 1:26. Debriefings with many of these prisoners confirmed that they had surrendered due to psychological warfare efforts.[45]

On the other hand, there is little evidence that propaganda had much impact at the operational or strategic levels. Donovan's hope of undermining the enemy's will ahead of the invading troops proved to be nothing more than just that—a dream. There were resistance organizations in the nations of Europe, Asia, and the Pacific, but they were quite small. It seems the average citizen of an Axis occupied nation attempted to make the best of the onerous and distasteful circumstances in which they found themselves.[46]

The record of information operations on domestic audiences is even more ambiguous. Support for the war remained consistently high from Pearl Harbor to VJ-Day. The role that war information played in maintaining American morale and acceptance of administration policy remains a subject of continuous study and a lot of controversy.

POSTWAR POSTMORTEM

There is little question that the word warriors of World War II spent as much time fighting with each other as they did in generating effective war information. It is difficult to assess whether a more effective interagency effort would have produced better operations or results. It is easy, however, in retrospect to identify the sources of interagency competition that limited intergovernmental cooperation.

Roosevelt's penchant for creating conflict between various agencies in order to foster competition, prompt initiative, and give himself freedom to operate, certainly contributed to the difficulty of sorting out the roles and missions of traditional organizations and the fledgling agencies established to manage war information. Additionally, the president showed little interest in propaganda activities and psychological warfare. He preferred to rely on his own rhetorical skills and more traditional political means to advocate for administration policies.

In the absence of strong, centralized management there was little else to foster cooperative efforts among the plethora of agencies peddling war information. Lack of common doctrine, shared-institutional values, common goals and strategies, and congressional diffidence crippled efforts to build strong relationships, trust and confidence, and cooperative programs. Where progress occurred in promoting effective war information programs, it usually resulted from the individual efforts of committed, energetic, imaginative, and resourceful leadership.

NOTES

1. Allan Winkler, *The Politics of Propaganda: The Office of War Information, 1942–1945* (New Haven: Yale University Press, 1978), 1–3.

2. See, for example, James Duane Squires, *British Propaganda at Home and in the United States from 1914 to 1917* (Cambridge, Harvard University Press, 1935); H.C. Peterson, *Propaganda for War: The Campaign against American Neutrality, 1914–1917* (Norman, University of Oklahoma Press, 1939).

3. Elmer Davis, edited by Ronald T. Farrar, *Report to the President* (Austin, TX: Association for Education in Journalism, 1968), 6–14.

4. Clayton D. Laurie, *The Propaganda Warriors: America's Crusade against Nazi Germany* (Lawrence: University Press of Kansas, 2006), 64–65.

5. Ibid., 76–79.

6. Winkler, *Politics of Propaganda*, 44–46; Davis, *Report to the President*, 15–18.

7. Davis, *Report to the President*, 15.

8. Laurie, *Propaganda Warriors*, 88–103.

9. Ibid., 3.

10. Clayton R. Koppes and Gregory D. Black, *Hollywood Goes to War: How Politics, Profits and Propaganda Shaped World War II Movies* (New York: Macmillan, 1987), 49.

11. Ibid., 55–56.

12. Ibid., 56.

13. Laurie, *Propaganda Warriors*, 93–95.

14. Ibid., 144–48.

15. Stephen E. Ambrose, *Eisenhower*, vol. 1, *Soldier, General of the Army, President-Elect* (New York: Simon and Schuster, 1983), 209–15; Winkler, *Politics of Propaganda*, 85–89.

16. Davis, *Report to the President*, 82.

17. Winkler, *Politics of Propaganda*, 62–64; Sydney Weinberg, "What to Tell America: The Writer's Quarrel in the Office of War Information," *Journal of American History* 55, no. 1 (June 1968): 73–89.

18. Winkler, *Politics of Propaganda*, 62–64. See also Weinberg, "What to Tell America," 73–89.

19. Richard B. Frank, *Guadalcanal: The Definitive Account of the Landmark Battle* (New York: Random House, 1990), 330–33.

20. Laurie, *Propaganda Warriors*, 168–69.

21. Allison B. Gilmore, *You Can't Fight Tanks with Bayonets: Psychological Warfare against the Japanese Army in the Southwest Pacific* (Lincoln: University of Nebraska Press, 1998), 67–68.

22. Steven Casey, *Cautious Crusade: Franklin D. Roosevelt, American Public Opinion, and the War against Nazi Germany* (New York: Oxford University Press, 2001), 157–60.

23. U.S. Congress, Senate, Committee on Foreign Relations, Nominations, *Department of State, Hearings 78th Congress, 2d session, On Nominations of Joseph C. Grew to be Undersecretary of State, Nelson A. Rockefeller to be Assistant Secretary of State, Archibald MacLeish to be Assistant Secretary of State, Julius C. Holmes to be Assistant Secretary of State, James C.*

Dunn to be Assistant Secretary of State, December 12 & 13 1944 (Washington, DC: U.S. Government Printing Office, 1944), 31–33.

24. Frank Capra, *The Name above the Title: An Autobiography* (New York: Da Capo Press, 1971), 327; see also Leland Poague, ed., *Frank Capra Interviews* (Jackson: University of Mississippi Press, 2004), 60.

25. Winkler, *Politics of Propaganda*, 20.

26. Davis, *Report to the President*, 11.

27. Winkler, *Politics of Propaganda*, 36.

28. Ibid., 35.

29. Davis, *Report to the President*, 83.

30. Ibid., 82.

31. Thomas Fleming, *The New Dealer's War: Franklin D. Roosevelt and the War within World War II* (New York: Basic Books, 2001), 156–61.

32. Winkler, *Politics of Propaganda*, 70–71.

33. Davis, *Report to the President*, 79.

34. Laurie, *Propaganda Warriors*, 179.

35. Davis, *Report to the President*, 80.

36. Ibid., 83.

37. Ibid., 80.

38. Steven Casey, *Cautious Crusade: Franklin D. Roosevelt, American Public Opinion, and the War against Nazi Germany* (New York: Oxford University Press, 2001), 75–76; see also Davis, *Report to the President*, 82; Donald A. Ritchie, *Reporting from Washington: The History of the Washington Press Corps* (New York: Oxford University Press, 2005), 62–63; Koppes and Black, *Hollywood Goes to War*, 63.

39. Davis, *Report to the President*, 84.

40. Randy Roberts and James S. Olson, *John Wayne: American* (New York: The Free Press, 1995), 250–56; Koppes and Black, *Hollywood Goes to War*, 57.

41. Davis, *Report to the President*, 25.

42. Walter Cronkite, *A Reporter's Life* (New York: Alfred A. Knopf, 1996), 81.

43. Townsend Hoopes and Douglas Brinkley, *Driven Patriot: The Life and Times of James Forrestal* (New York: Random House, 1992), 190–93.

44. Laurie, *Propaganda Warriors*, 164. See also Capra, *Above the Title*, 340; Winkler, *Politics of Propaganda*, 112–48; Herbert Mitgang, *Newsmen in Khaki: Tales of a World War II Soldier Correspondent* (Dallas, TX: Taylor Trade Publishing, 2004), x, 36.

45. Gilmore, *You Can't Fight Tanks with Bayonets*, 146–64.

46. Philip Snow, *The Fall of Hong Kong: Britain, China, and the Japanese Occupation* (New Haven: Yale University Press, 2003); Mark Mazower, *Inside Hitler's Greece: The Experience of Occupation, 1941–44* (New Haven: Yale University Press, 1995); Robert O. Paxton, *Vichy France*, 2nd revised ed. (New York: Columbia University Press, 2001). For a dissenting view about the French experience, see John Sweets, *Choices in Vichy France: The French under Nazi Occupation* (New York: Oxford University Press, 1986).

Marketing Freedom: Cold War, Public Diplomacy, and Psychological Warfare

Carnes Lord

World War I was Washington's first information war. But the excesses of the Creel Committee, particularly its extensive domestic role, created a powerful backlash, reinforcing Americans' distaste for government-managed information. The United States did not respond to the intensive and increasingly sophisticated propaganda and political warfare efforts of the totalitarian regimes in the 1920s and 1930s. That changed with the coming of World War II. After victory, however, America wanted to get back to normal. Washington largely dismantled the institutions of information warfare that had been created in the course of that struggle, notably the Office of War Information and the psychological warfare elements of the War Department and the Office of Strategic Services (OSS). The Voice of America (VOA) nearly suffered a similar fate.

The coming of the Cold War changed things once again. From 1947 to 1948, a clear and present danger from the Soviet Union and international Communism emerged. The first Soviet atomic test in 1949, and the outbreak of war in Korea in June 1950, made the threat appear even more imminent. Washington responded. Congress reauthorized State Department information programs through the Smith-Mundt Act of 1948, though the law prohibited distributing domestic propaganda. Several veterans of the psychological warfare apparatus from World War II assumed key positions on the White House staff, ensuring that the ideological struggle was acknowledged as a vital field of Cold War competition. The State Department's Policy Planning staff and its influential director, George Kennan, entered the fray. The Cold War's ideological war was underway.

AN EVOLVING ARSENAL OF IDEAS

Both continuity and change characterize the American approach to psychological operations and public diplomacy over the course of the Cold War.[1] The United States showed a fundamental consistency in roles and missions, but also goals, emphasis, tactics, resources, and modalities of interagency cooperation. The period 1949–53 proved the formative era for U.S. psychological-political policies and institution-building in the postwar era. With minor adjustments, newly created organizations like Radio Free Europe/Radio Liberty (RFE-RL) and the United States Information Agency (USIA) remained in place until the fall of the Wall.[2] How government employed the instruments of information operations, however, changed during the course of the Cold War.

With Washington's rediscovery of the ideological tool came a determination to avoid the lies and deception of classic Nazi and Soviet propaganda. Especially as America entered what might be called the "Hot" Cold War (1948–53), however, it was also recognized that an ambitious and aggressive American approach was required. In June 1953 the high-level Jackson Committee, at the request of President Dwight D. Eisenhower, produced a top secret report concluding that "international information activities" should be the leading edge in a comprehensive and aggressive strategy for confronting the Soviet global challenge.[3] One model was that pioneered by wartime OSS Chief "Wild Bill" Donovan, and in the process of reincarnation in the successor Central Intelligence Agency (CIA), under which such activities were a tool of covert subversion and "political warfare" that included assistance to foreign political parties, "election operations," and financial subvention of foreign newspapers and magazines. Also needed, though, was an intensified effort in the more traditional information areas such as radio broadcasting and educational and cultural exchange, a gap that Eisenhower decided to fill in 1953 by creating the USIA. Because he was schooled in psychological warfare at the highest level of command in World War II, Eisenhower believed in the value of information warfare and proved an avid supporter of going on the offensive in the war of ideas.

The president's campaign was short-lived. Soviet dictator Josef Stalin died in March 1953. Eisenhower extended diplomatic feelers offering the new Soviet leadership a more cooperative relationship. In 1955, he experimented with various early arms control overtures. At the same time, the growth of Soviet military capabilities, particularly in atomic weapons, also raised second thoughts about the wisdom of undertaking political warfare operations intended to stimulate popular uprisings in Eastern Europe. Additionally, State Department officials argued the Soviet Union and its satellites were less vulnerable to Western subversion than previously thought. Provocative measures risked savage internal repression as well as prompting military action against Western Europe.

In 1956, during the Hungarian Revolution, widespread publicity given to Radio Free Europe Hungarian-language broadcasts allegedly encouraged violent resistance against Soviet occupying forces marked a clear turning point. The United States did virtually nothing in response to the Soviet military intervention crushing the revolution. U.S. inaction severely discredited U.S. propaganda that talked of "rolling back" Soviet power in Eastern Europe.

Although "rollback" was never formally accepted as American policy, it did reflect the spirit of American psychological warfare during the early Cold War period. The new strategy of "containment" of the Soviet threat called for a different approach, which would eventually become known as "public diplomacy." Acknowledging that Communist domination of Russia and Eastern Europe would not be easily shaken off, American policy makers shifted toward a lower key, longer-range strategy, with greater emphasis on the "cultural" as distinct from the political or informational dimension of the war of ideas. Information programs would emphasize the positive character of the American way of life. This shift, already evident in Eisenhower's second term, had the secondary effect of pushing public diplomacy increasingly to the margins of administration policy.

Partly in reaction to this perceived neglect, Eisenhower's successor John F. Kennedy placed renewed emphasis on public diplomacy programs. Kennedy appointed well-known journalist Edward R. Murrow as USIA director, inaugurating an imagined brief "golden age." Murrow enjoyed direct access to the president and a reserved seat at meetings of the National Security Council. Kennedy appeared to embrace Murrow's dictum that USIA should be in on the takeoffs of policy, not just its crash landings. Public diplomacy should have a significant role in shaping national policy in light of the requirements of projecting American influence abroad.[4]

In reality, however, little changed. If anything, the Kennedy and Johnson administrations saw the estrangement between public diplomacy and policy deepen. Government radio programs like the Voice of America, for example, saw their central mission increasingly as providing "objective" or "balanced" reporting of news on the model of American and other Western commercial broadcasters. Public diplomacy programs and personnel increasingly distanced themselves from psychological or political warfare activities and the organizations associated with them. Public information programs developed strong institutional cultures committed to the autonomy of their organizations and resistant to any taint of association with intelligence or military requirements. Indeed, at the end of this evolution (in the early to mid-1970s), these programs tended increasingly not to consider themselves instruments of U.S. policy at all, and to view as illegitimate any true operational oversight of their activities by policy officials.

The attitude of officials managing public diplomacy programs mirrored wider changes brought on by the Vietnam War. Upheavals in American political culture were reflected in a national media that became increasingly critical of the war. The media's newly adversarial attitude complicated the task of the official information agencies.

Other factors also contributed to diminishing the importance and eroding the legitimacy of overseas communications programs. The policy of détente toward the Soviet Union inaugurated by President Richard M. Nixon and his national security adviser Henry Kissinger, with its emphasis on the centrality of arms control and the imperative of reducing the risk of superpower nuclear war, seemed to call for an end to classic confrontational Cold War propaganda campaigns. Communism as such should no longer be openly opposed by American government spokesmen, nor should the United States challenge the legitimacy of the Soviet empire. Kissinger in particular had little use for the information agencies.[5]

The Carter administration gave public diplomacy a new lease on life. The administration's "human rights" agenda offered a more politically palatable approach to ideological conflict with the Soviets. Carter wanted American foreign policy to emphasize promoting human rights and individual liberties across the globe, paying attention to diverse issues from apartheid in South Africa to dictatorships in Latin America. Carter's presidency also oversaw a reorganization of USIA (including renaming it the U.S. International Communications Agency).

At the same time, Carter's National Security Adviser, Zbigniew Brzezinski, pushed public diplomacy to adopt a more distinctly anti-Soviet line. In the wake of the American defeat in Vietnam, Soviet geopolitical adventurism around the world expanded into Africa and Latin America, culminating with the invasion of Afghanistan in 1979. Brzezinski sought to contrast Soviet military aggression with America's defense of human rights.

The administration's message, however, was at best mixed. The president famously congratulated the American people for having gotten over its "inordinate fear of Communism." Meanwhile, as the Soviets continued an arms buildup in Western Europe, modernized their nuclear arsenal, and funded insurgencies and terrorism around the world, the United States criticized regimes pushing back against Soviet expansion for their less than fully democratic practices. As a result, American public information programs frequently found themselves working at cross purposes.

When Ronald Reagan entered the White House in 1981, another significant shift occurred. Reagan held a very different view on the use the psychological-political instruments of national power. More attuned to the importance of words and ideas in politics than any American leader since Eisenhower and Kennedy, Reagan placed renewed emphasis on psychological operations and public diplomacy.

Reagan also had a mission for the government's informational instruments— to help win the Cold War once and for all. He intended to end a decade of détente-oriented policies toward the Soviet bloc, and embark on a major military buildup. Reagan used language about the Soviet Union and Communism that had not been heard from an American president since the Korean War, if then. He provided America's public diplomacy organizations with an infusion of resources and a new mandate to reengage in ideological struggle with the Soviets as part of a comprehensive strategy designed—like that of the Jackson Report thirty years earlier—to challenge the very basis of Soviet power.

For the first time since the mid-1950s, public diplomacy was again seen as a weapon of political warfare designed to subvert the Soviet system—to effect political change within the Soviet bloc by an aggressive information strategy designed to encourage democratic and liberal forces and constrain the ability of the Soviet leadership to project power or influence beyond its borders. Few expected this strategy to have an impact within the short span of Reagan's tenure. They were wrong.

There is every reason to conclude that American public diplomacy and psychological operations at the end of the Cold War measurably hastened the fall of the Soviet Union and the dissolution of the Communist world. In the end, ideas made a difference.[6]

Presidential policies mattered. The conduct of psychological operations and public diplomacy waxed and waned significantly over the course of the Cold War. Major changes occurred in how the government used informational instruments and how effectively agencies cooperated and collaborated in supporting national policies. Presidential leadership, rather than organizational innovation or restructuring roles and responsibilities, proved the determining factor. At the same time, the constraining influences of American political culture proved very difficult even for presidents to overcome. In combination with powerful tendencies toward bureaucratic autonomy and parochialism, these have consistently handicapped the performance of the American government in the psychological-political arena.

BEHIND CLOSED DOORS

In understanding how the interagency process responded to presidential leadership, the role of the CIA is still the most problematic. Much remains unknown even today about the agency's activities in this area, particularly in the crucial early period of the Cold War. Reflecting the legacy of William Donovan, founder of the wartime OSS, nonattributable or "black" propaganda operations were from the beginning an important feature of CIA "covert action," as it later came to be called. These included most significantly clandestine radio broadcasting, press placements, and clandestine support of political or cultural activities. The best known CIA-sponsored media during the Cold War came from the Congress for Cultural Freedom supporting the European-oriented *Encounter* magazine.[7]

In general, CIA operations were conceived as part of a larger set of techniques frequently referred to as "political warfare." The first, and one of the most successful, cases was the CIA intervention in the Italian elections of 1948. These operations helped keep the Italian Communist Party from taking power by mustering support for electoral opponents.[8]

Indeed, some government programs that eventually became purely public information agencies started out principally as political warfare tools. When the CIA created Radio Free Europe (1949) and Radio Liberty (1952), it did so as part of a larger effort to mobilize émigrés from the East Bloc for political and sometimes actual warfare against the Communists.

Occasionally, use of psychological-political instruments virtually alone could have important strategic effects. In 1954, an agency-run broadcasting station facilitated a CIA-engineered overthrow of the Arbenz regime in Guatemala.[9] Such successes, however, proved to be the high water mark for CIA-led operations. Black propaganda, especially after the Hungarian fiasco, gradually assumed a much reduced role in CIA covert operations. The agency lost interest in the radios and their control of these stations became little more than nominal.

In the wake of Watergate, the CIA virtually abandoned political warfare. Following the sustained assault on the intelligence community and covert action in particular by Congress and the media in the 1970s as well as the deliberate devaluation of covert action by the Carter administration, its capabilities in this area by all accounts had dwindled to the point of insignificance by the end of the decade.[10]

CIVILIAN-MILITARY DIVIDE

Eisenhower witnessed firsthand the constant friction between psychological warfare practitioners in the OSS and within the uniformed military. While he acknowledged the controversies, Eisenhower's education and experience led him to believe that military and civilian operations should be kept in separate spheres so that military activities did not become "politicized." Though Eisenhower reenergized the government's psychological warfare programs during his tenure, he never sought to close this divide and military and civilian activities remained un-bridged through most of the Cold War.

As during World War II, psychological warfare as practiced by the military tended to be organized in a straightforward fashion to support military goals and objectives, not political ones. Unlike the OSS, the military had little interest in what today is often referred to as "regime change."[11]

The military, however, also included some mavericks attracted to the political dimension of warfare. It is telling that the reestablishment of a special warfare capability in the army in the early 1950s occurred under the umbrella term *psychological warfare*. Success was achieved in the 1950s in the Philippines, where Air Force colonel (later general) and CIA operative Edward Lansdale helped Defense Minister (later president) Ramon Magsaysay devise a sophisticated counterinsurgency strategy with an important communications component. The campaign effectively defeated the Communist-inspired Huk rebellion.[12]

The Vietnam War provided by far the largest arena for American military "psychological operations" (PSYOP) of the Cold War era, sparked in part by President Kennedy's personal interest in promoting special warfare forces.[13] The army's 4th Psychological Operations Group was fully deployed throughout the military regions of the Republic of Vietnam for much of the war, supported by elements of the 7th Psychological Operations Group based in Okinawa.

In an almost unprecedented example of interagency cooperation, the army participated in the Joint United States Public Affairs Office (JUSPAO), a unique hybrid organization that brought together U.S. Information Service (USIS) civilians and uniformed military personnel under the direction of the USIA head of post, working out of the embassy in Saigon. Perhaps the best known and most successful PSYOP operation of the war was the Chieu Hoi ("Open Arms") program, which induced defections from Viet Cong insurgents and the North Vietnamese army to the South Vietnamese government. Other USIS programs targeted urban residents, rural villagers, and housewives.

With the collapse of the American effort in Vietnam, the army turned its back on unconventional conflict of any sort and allowed its PSYOP and other special warfare capabilities to atrophy. The Pentagon's primary focus returned to the challenge of fighting a war against the Red Army in an all-out European conflict. Little was done, however, to reorient army PSYOP to support this focus. At the strategic level, virtually no thought seems to have been given to using U.S. government radio broadcasting assets already available in Europe as a psychological-political tool in the event of crisis or an outbreak of hostilities there, in spite of the very evident vulnerabilities the Soviets faced in controlling and utilizing the forces of their reluctant Warsaw Pact allies.[14]

In the 1980s, presidential policies intervened once again. Institutional rebuilding of military PSYOP was a significant component of the Reagan administration's larger effort to revitalize U.S. psychological-political capabilities. The Defense Department drew up a "master plan" for the improvement of PSYOP doctrine, training, equipment, and force structure in the army and air force.[15] Progress made in all these areas laid the groundwork for the very extensive and generally successful employment of PSYOP assets by the United States in later conflicts in Panama (1989) and the Persian Gulf (1990–91).[16]

Moreover, a new office was created within the Pentagon for what may be called defense public diplomacy. This involved activities such as the declassification and publication of intelligence data on Soviet bloc military capabilities (notably in the form of an annual document entitled *Soviet Military Power*), sponsorship of defense-related conferences abroad, and the countering of hostile propaganda and disinformation efforts. The latter supported a larger and unusually fruitful interagency effort involving the State Department and USIA.

DOCTRINAL DISSONANCE

The informational instrument of national power offers enormous opportunities for advancing national interest at modest cost. For all the constraints facing it, the Reagan administration demonstrated the efficacy of psychological-political instruments when supported by sound policy and strong leadership. On the other hand, the problems in utilizing informational instrument effectively in the era that spanned Stalin and the Soviet collapse proved profound. Obstacles to efficiency and effectiveness were deeply rooted not only in the organization and conduct of the government, but in American political culture itself. What the nation did not have during the Cold War (as it had lacked during the world wars as well) was a common doctrine setting out basic goals and prescribing acceptable practices and procedures.

There was, and arguably remains today, a fundamental confusion if not outright disagreement among practitioners as to whether the public diplomacy programs should act as disinterested providers of information, or rather should seek to project American influence through the proactive shaping of information and through other forms of psychological-political action.

Advocates of an "informational" approach implicitly or explicitly reject the idea that government public diplomacy programs should serve as a strategic tool of American foreign or national security policy. As for the question of who is to decide what legitimately constitutes "information," their implicit response is that it should not be the government at all but rather the commercial media, or (in the case of cultural programs) the nation's cultural and academic authorities.

By contrast, those who view public diplomacy as one of several tools for the projection of strategic influence regard the informational approach as intellectually incoherent. An instrument of national power, they argue, exists to serve the nation. In addition, they contend that in the long run government programs that serve no clearly definable government purpose are politically unsustainable, with intractable problems with regard to accountability, control, and return on investment.

This fundamental lack of clarity over the public diplomacy mission frustrated efforts of agencies to develop a generally agreed vision, sense of purpose, body of principles, or set of doctrines. In June 1953, the newly created United States Information Agency commissioned a study of the "operating assumptions" that guided the work of American propaganda personnel, intended to identify and describe "areas of ignorance, confusion, or internal contradiction" that needed further investigation.[17] This originally five-volume study was delivered to USIA director Theodore Streibert in November 1954, whereupon it was promptly classified on grounds of political sensitivity and locked away for the next twenty years.[18]

A study along similar lines conducted in 1964 argues that USIA has been prevented from implementing the goals formally set for it by the Executive Branch and Congress in part because of its "inability to clarify its basic operating assumptions," including "whether it is to function as an information or propaganda instrument."[19]

Lack of effective doctrine was not just a civilian problem, but plagued the military and intelligence community as well. Military PSYOP always found it difficult to articulate its distinct role apart from covert operations and public diplomacy. Even today, doctrinal definitions of PSYOP continue to be expansive, to the degree that it is difficult to distinguish it from civilian-originated public diplomacy. Indeed, the military PSYOP community has tended to assimilate PSYOP to the "information" model of public diplomacy, though practitioners still generally accept that their core mission involves the projection of "influence" to a target audience.

The lack of defining doctrine has had a particularly significant impact on the operations of the Voice of America. Formally part of USIA after 1953, VOA has nevertheless always maintained considerable autonomy within the larger organization and early developed its own institutional culture and outlook. The key doctrinal expression of this outlook is the so-called "Charter" of the Voice, drawn up in 1959 and enshrined in legislation in 1976.[20] This short document has three provisions. VOA would:

1. "serve as a consistently reliable and authoritative source of news. VOA news will be accurate, objective, and comprehensive";

2. "represent America, not any single segment of American society, and will therefore present a balanced and comprehensive projection of significant American
thought and institutions";
3. "present the policies of the United States clearly and effectively, and will also
present responsible discussion and opinion on those policies."

These guidelines, for the most part unexceptionable, were fundamentally
inadequate as operational doctrine, and did nothing to establish clarity about
VOA mission and objectives. While acknowledging a role relating to U.S. policy,
they leave unexplained what it might mean to present policy "effectively," or what
the parameters of "responsible" discussion of policy are. The main thrust of the
guidelines appears to be to validate the "information" approach to public diplomacy. In fact, from the beginning they served as a bureaucratic device to protect
the agency from unwanted outside interference in what are claimed to be professional journalistic decisions.

Another area rife with doctrinal confusion related to defining the audience
for information programs. Whether elites or masses should constitute the
primary audience for these programs is the key issue here, involving complex
issues of priorities and tradeoffs that have never been fully resolved within USIA
in particular. As a result, information efforts during the Cold War tended to
occupy a middle ground (between, for example, the elite-oriented British model
and the mass-oriented Soviet model) that compromised effectiveness with both
audiences.[21]

Finally, there remained the perennial issue of whether USIA should be merely
an implementer of foreign policy or have a role in making policy. The
most authoritative statement appeared in a memorandum drafted during
Kennedy administration. The agency director described his mission as twofold:
"influencing public attitudes in other nations," and "advising the President, his
representatives abroad, and the various Departments and Agencies on the implications of foreign opinion for present and contemplated U.S. policies, programs
and official statements."[22] USIA did have opinion polling and media analysis
capabilities that could support such a mission. They were routinely made available
to the State Department and other policy agencies. There is, however, little evidence that any USIA director served in a senior policy advisory role. Indeed, with
few exceptions, including Murrow in the Kennedy administration, Carl Rowan
under President Johnson, and Charles Wick serving Reagan, USIA directors have
had little direct relationship with their presidents.

In the mid-1970s, the Stanton Commission undertook a review of international information programs. Commissioners identified the core missions of
public diplomacy as: education and cultural affairs, general information, policy
information, and policy advice. The report concluded that for these activities to
be well integrated with foreign policy they needed to be merged with the State
Department. Commissioners recommended abolishing USIA and establishing a
new agency combining the information and cultural functions of USIA with the
State Department's Education and Cultural Affairs (ECA) bureau.

The report also proposed creating a new office within the department to administer all programs articulating and defending foreign policy. It recommended that VOA be made an independent federal agency. Though not implemented at the time, the Stanton Commission study laid the intellectual groundwork for changes in the 1990s, notably, the merger of the USIA with the State Department and the creation of an autonomous broadcasting entity under a Broadcasting Board of Governors.[23]

The Reagan White House also made an attempt to bring coherence to public diplomacy doctrine. In March 1984 it issued National Security Decision Directive (NSDD) 130, "International Information Policy." This directive described public diplomacy as "a key strategic instrument for shaping fundamental political and ideological trends around the globe on a long-term basis and ultimately affecting the behavior of governments." In an effort to counter the "information" model and the influence of commercial journalism on public diplomacy, it made clear that the fundamental purpose of international information programs was to "affect foreign audiences in ways favorable to U.S. national interests."[24]

All of this, however, had little visible impact; indeed, VOA leadership actively resisted the message of NSDD 130.[25] In fact, VOA continues to assert its traditional autonomy. In 1999, President William J. Clinton merged USIA into the State Department, thus effectively separating the radios from any direct policy oversight. American international broadcasting officials in recent years have gone so far as to deny that broadcasting is a form of "public diplomacy" in any sense.

IMPACT OF INFORMATION

Government not only lacked a doctrine for coordinating the tools of psychological operations and public diplomacy, it only poorly understood the challenge of integrating informational tools with the other elements of national power. Indeed, some of America's greatest ideological triumphs resulted from the incidental effects of other government programs or the private sector. For example, the American "reeducation" effort in occupied Germany and Japan, carried out largely by the army, was in fact arguably the single most important and successful use of the psychological-political activity carried out by the United States in the course of the entire Cold War.[26]

The European Recovery Plan, more popularly known as the Marshall Plan for then secretary of state George C. Marshall, offers another case in point. The plan provided for American technical and financial assistance for European economies recovering from the devastation of World War II. The Marshall Plan had a significant public relations component. Indeed, the Paris-based staff that carried them out had a budget far larger than that of the entire State Department information bureau.[27]

The issue of nuclear weapons and nuclear war is a particularly interesting dimension of Cold War psychological-political conflict and deserves special comment. From the 1950s onward, growing public awareness of the potentially apocalyptic effects of a nuclear exchange between the United States and the Soviet Union offered a tempting field for psychological exploitation, while at the same time the emerging notion of "deterrence" as the primary mission of nuclear weapons plainly depended on perceptions and beliefs of national leaders that might themselves be subject to deliberate manipulation.

Of all American presidents of this era, Eisenhower was perhaps the most attuned to these questions. The great diplomatic offensives on nuclear issues launched by the United States on his initiative virtually at the height of the Cold War—"Atoms for Peace" and "Open Skies"—were consciously conceived by the president as campaigns of psychological warfare designed to win the moral high ground for the United States rather than as serious efforts to reach negotiated agreements with the Soviet Union.[28]

Two other strategic foci of American public diplomacy in the 1960s and 1970s should also be mentioned. Following the spectacular success enjoyed by the Soviet space program with the launch of Sputnik in 1956, space exploration and technology became an area of intense competition. USIA and NASA engaged in a sustained collaborative campaign to promote U.S. space achievements during this period. Also of interest are USIA's extensive activities in support of the bicentennial celebration of American independence in 1976. Among other things, this gave a decisive impetus to the creation of American studies programs in academic institutions around the world.[29]

During the Reagan era, a concerted effort was made to relocate public diplomacy as a whole within the larger strategic framework of administration policy toward the Soviet bloc. The Reagan administration moved to exploit military and arms control issues much more systematically than had been done by any administration since that time. This first emerged in the unprecedented publicity given by the U.S. government to the history of Soviet violations of arms control agreements. In 1982–83, the United States and the Soviet Union waged a major propaganda battle over the deployment of American intermediate-range nuclear forces in Western Europe, geared at influencing European public and political opinion. The decisive American victory in this contest was in retrospect a milestone in the endgame of the Cold War in the 1980s.

The relationship between the government and the private sector in carrying out overseas information programs also proved significant. Often the resources of commercial enterprises, like Hollywood, and nongovernmental organizations, such as faith-based groups, exceeded the capacity of the government to reach and influence audiences.

In some cases nongovernmental groups held greater credibility with target audiences than government officials. Because direct personal interaction is often the most effective way to convey messages and change hearts and minds, it is unsurprising that private sector entities with a significant presence in a region played an important role in shaping perceptions of Americans and U.S. policies.

A related effect sometimes called "political action," resulted from a mixture of traditional diplomacy and public diplomacy involving direct interactions with well-defined political or social groups (women, students, labor unionists, religious leaders, scientists, and the like), and the activities of nongovernmental organizations. Throughout the Cold War, political action played a significant role. The support of the AFL-CIO, an American umbrella worker's union, for the Solidarity Movement in Poland was one example.

An array of Cold War defense-related activities also had important psychological-political impact, though they were generally not designed for that purpose and are neglected in most discussions of the subject.[30] The first and probably most significant of these was Armed Forces Network (AFN), the global radio and television broadcasting system of the Defense Department (founded in 1942). While their purpose was to serve American troops stationed abroad, these stations soon developed a large foreign listenership, attracted by a steady diet of popular music, nonpropagandistic news programming (taken wholesale from the commercial American media), and the opportunity to develop English language skills. By the 1960s, AFN estimated it had an audience of more than twenty million Europeans.

The American military also funded an array of programs involving the education and training of foreign military officers, often in military educational institutions (such as the various service war colleges) in the United States.[31] These experiences proved instrumental in cultivating positive attitudes toward the United States and developing personal ties with American counterparts in an elite group of foreign officers who frequently went on to occupy senior leadership positions in their countries.

U.S. military forces, especially the navy, conducted "presence" missions overseas involving port visits, joint exercises with foreign militaries, and other forms of what might be called military diplomacy. The armed forces also carried out a variety of disaster relief, humanitarian assistance, and civic action programs around the world that served to cultivate general goodwill toward the United States and its armed forces. While the military efforts, as well other government initiatives, commercial enterprises, and nongovernmental groups made notable contributions to winning the Cold War of ideas, remarkably there was little effort and few successes in linking them to the government's formal information operations.

INSTITUTIONAL FRICTION

Lack of an overarching conceptual framework of the sort conceptualized in doctrine exacerbated the conflicting bureaucratic cultures of the agencies involved in psychological operations and public diplomacy. These institutional conflicts proved intractable, even when Washington attempted to address them by reorganizing federal entities.

USIA and the State Department always had a troubled relationship. The State Department tended to resist public diplomacy missions, disparage their importance, and question the competence of practitioners. Prior to 1953, international information and education/cultural affairs functions were lodged in State but were poorly integrated and largely ignored by senior foreign service officers and departmental leadership. When Congress created USIA, the State Department was generally content to leave the agency largely to its own devices.

The education/cultural affairs function remained within State's Education and Cultural Affairs (ECA) bureau for the next twenty-five years, when it would be absorbed by a reorganized U.S. International Communications Agency (the name was changed back to USIA in 1982); it operated in relatively self-contained fashion in both institutional homes. Some predicted that relationships would change once State became the lead agency for public diplomacy following the disestablishment of USIA in 1999. That proved not to be the case.[32]

Relations between the State Department and Executive Office of the White House remained perennially troubled as well, even after the National Security Act of 1947 created the National Security Policy to draft interagency policies to guide the integration of the elements of national power. The White House, while more sympathetic to the public communication function, tends to orient itself primarily to a domestic audience.

Part of the reason for this arms-length attitude on the part of both the State Department and the White House was the potential political sensitivity of psychological-political activities. It was a lesson learned early in the Cold War. Senator Joseph McCarthy's anti-Communist crusading in the early 1950s targeted information bureaucracy in the State Department. The incident contributed to the reluctance of Secretary of State John Foster Dulles to retain the information function in the department.

When the Jackson Committee surveyed American psychological-political capabilities, it recommended, in spite—or rather precisely because—of the importance it placed on them. Jackson proposed the creation of an Operations Coordinating Board (OCB) that would function as the implementing arm of the National Security Council. Eisenhower approved, also insisting the OCB staff have expertise on psychological warfare.[33]

In retrospect, the decision did not improve matters. The OCB lacked strong and consistent leadership on psychological-political operations. Following the demise of the OCB at the beginning of the Kennedy administration, there was essentially no staff support or mechanism for coordinating public diplomacy and policy at the White House level until the first Reagan term. In January 1983, Reagan promulgated National Security Decision Directive (NSDD) 77, "Management of Public Diplomacy Relative to National Security," establishing an interagency Special Planning Group under the chairmanship of the president's National Security Adviser, and four subordinate groups chaired formally by senior agency or White House officials.[34]

The Special Planning Group met very infrequently. At the working level, the committees that were created were primarily planning bodies, except for the Public Affairs Committee, which for a period handled operational coordination of the White House with public affairs officials in the agencies on a daily basis. The

International Broadcasting Committee also played a quasi-operational role at times in coordinating diplomatic initiatives concerning new broadcasting facilities abroad, as well as in a major interagency effort to devise ways to counter Soviet jamming of U.S. international radio broadcasts.

The NSDD 77 interagency structure brought USIA as a full partner into the interagency national security process for the first time. Administration actions on several other fronts complemented this. In particular, the State Department's role in public diplomacy was significantly enhanced; senior Foreign Service officers were assigned this account under the direct supervision of the undersecretary for political affairs, Lawrence Eagleburger. A key strategic direction of State's activities centered on "Project Democracy," launched by the president's Westminster speech to the British parliament of June 1982, which would lead in the following year to the creation of the National Endowment for Democracy, a new agency to serve as a catalyst and source of assistance to democratic development abroad.

Efforts were also made to revamp the management and operations of the U.S. overseas radio broadcasting organizations and bring them into closer alignment with administration policy. In the case of Radio Free Europe/Radio Liberty, changes were made in the governing legislation of these stations that enhanced control of them by the presidentially appointed Board for International Broadcasting, and thereafter major personnel changes were effected at senior management levels.

State and NSC staff officers worked together to review the strategic issue of language priorities for international broadcasting and initiated substantial changes in this area at both RFE-RL and VOA. At the same time, review was undertaken of the technical needs of the radios, which led to a major reorientation and modernization of the long-neglected and underfunded transmitter and relay sites in Europe and elsewhere on which they depended, as well as to an initiative to counter Soviet jamming of U.S. broadcasts. These efforts included a significant diplomatic component facilitated by the State Department and coordinated through the NSDD 77 International Broadcasting Committee. Decisions were also made at the policy level to create new broadcasting entities (Radio Marti and "Radio Free Afghanistan") in support of the administration's regional and grand strategies.

MANAGING CRISIS

The United States government experimented with various approaches and organizational mechanisms over the course of the Cold War for dealing with the special requirements of crisis situations. In early Cold War crises, notably the Suez Crisis of 1956, the U-2 shoot-down incident of 1960, and the Bay of Pigs invasion of 1961, it is evident that USIA was not a factor.[35] During the Hungarian Revolution of 1956, as noted earlier, Washington seems not to have realized the potential sensitivity of RFE broadcasts until it was too late.

The formal interagency crisis management committees of the 1970s and 1980s trace their ancestry to the "ExCom"—the crisis management interagency body of Cuban Missile Crisis fame. One of the few clear cases of public diplomacy considerations directly influencing the formulation of policy occurred during this crisis, reflecting the presence on the ExCom of USIA senior leadership.

In the 1970s, little seems to have been done to institutionalize mechanisms or procedures to ensure that USIA and the radios would be fully integrated into the interagency decision-making process and capable of rapid transition to a crisis mode of operating.

In the 1980s the Reagan administration created for the first time a Crisis Management Center in the White House, with a permanent staff and elaborate formal procedures for interagency coordination across precrisis, crisis, and post-crisis phases.[36] The existence of this staff element contributed materially to the success of U.S. crisis information efforts in response to the Chernobyl incident and the KAL 007 shoot-down episode.

THE HILL

It is probably fair to say that over the years Congress played a less than help-ful role. In the early Cold War, the State Department's information programs and the Voice of America were key targets of abuse at the hands of Senator McCarthy and his notorious staff aides. For the most part, Congress has shown little interest in or understanding of USIA or the radios; accordingly, these organizations have been chronically underfunded and exposed to abrupt and ill-considered budget cuts. And where Congress has intervened, it has tended to do so opportunistically and in order to pick ideological bones.

Public diplomacy falls under the jurisdiction of the Senate Foreign Relations Committee and the House Foreign Affairs Committee, but lacks a subcommittee of its own; generally speaking, no more than one or two members or staff on either com-mittee have been even broadly knowledgeable on the subject. This has, however, had the effect of enhancing the power of the few who do care about it, sometimes with very adverse consequences for rational management of the public diplomacy account.

The Senate Foreign Relations Committee today undoubtedly wields more power over the international broadcasters than does the Executive Branch—a fact not generally appreciated. It should also be noted that Congress rarely holds hear-ings on this subject, and has not passed an authorization bill for the relevant agen-cies for more than twenty years. There has not been a significant set of hearings on public diplomacy in general for thirty years.[37]

Those who care about public diplomacy in Washington, not surprisingly, tend to be found in the world of journalism. They are part of an "iron triangle" formed by congressional staffers, journalists, and ex-journalists working in the public diplomacy agencies, who collaborate to publicize alleged failings or misdeeds of these organizations in order to bring pressure to bear on an administration from Capitol Hill to do something about them.

This pattern was particularly in evidence during the 1980s, in what amounted to a constant guerrilla war against the Reagan administration's public diplomacy reforms waged under the energetic leadership of a single staff member of the Senate Foreign Relations Committee.[38] But it has earlier roots as well. In the 1970s, for example, the staff of the Board for International Broadcasting tended to use the New York and Washington media to publicize supposed lapses in the broadcasting practices of RFE-RL as a way of bringing pressure to bear on the radios' largely independent management.

THE PEOPLE IN PUBLIC DIPLOMACY

Public diplomacy required an unusual mix of skills not normally found within government, including language ability and talents of a high order, a good generalist education and knowledge of the world and current affairs, writing ability, presentational skills, the ability to function effectively under severe time pressures, and perhaps above all, creativity. Neither Congress nor any administration ever adequately addressed the challenge of building a workforce with the necessary abilities and attributes.

In the aftermath of World War II, public diplomacy organizations tended to be staffed by a mixture of émigrés or defectors, academics, intellectuals, artists or writers, journalists, public relations or advertising executives, and intelligence analysts. As time went on, however, many of these people would lose their primary identity and become career bureaucrats. In the case of USIA, the major fault line in terms of the agency's personnel makeup was that separating the creative element (mainly journalists or academics) from the managerial element (mainly foreign service officers).

The tensions between the constituents of the public diplomacy community were not always unhealthy, but they sometimes caused difficulties that damaged worker morale. At RFE-RL, an additional complicating factor was that managers tended to be Americans where the workers were frequently foreigners who held very different ideas about both the substance and approach to follow in their broadcasting programs.

Recruitment of talented persons was never easy, and became progressively less so as their prestige gradually declined over the course of the Cold War. It soon became quite clear that USIA employees would always be lightly regarded within the State Department and elsewhere in the national security bureaucracy, and their function seen as one of only marginal importance for American interests in the world. As for the Foreign Service element in the agency, it was also clear that diplomats with an interest in or talent for public diplomacy were generally not those destined to rise to the top of their profession.

One of the most massive problems the United States faced throughout the Cold War in staffing the relevant agencies to support psychological-political activities was the poor and indeed virtually nonexistent state of education and training in this area—a problem that persists today.[39] Even in the world of government-sponsored training, public diplomacy has been at best a marginal presence. The Foreign Service Institute has only recently included significant offerings on the subject, mostly geared to preparing ambassadors and other senior officers to face the rigors of the media.

TEAM EFFORT BLUES

Throughout the Cold War psychological operations and public diplomacy were inherently interagency in nature, requiring some degree of coordination between the State Department, the information agencies, particularly USIA, the Department of Defense, the Central Intelligence Agency, and the White House. Unique obstacles to coordination, relating principally to the time pressures involved in international communications as well as to the perceived need of protecting the autonomy of news-reporting entities within the government, were inherent as well. In practice, impediments to integration overcame the necessity to cooperate. Even where formal coordinating mechanisms existed, their effectiveness left much to be desired.

In the initial phase of the Cold War, there was considerable intellectual and organizational confusion as American policy makers attempted to reinvent psychological-political warfare. As a result, Washington built the weapons it needed to fight the war of ideas but shunted them off into separate spheres of government. Treating psychological-political activities as a functionally distinct area of staff or interagency work isolated them from the mainstream of national security policy making. That perhaps was the greatest limitation of the conduct of information operations throughout the Cold War.

Psychological-political activities by their nature do not lend themselves to centralized command and control. Indeed, efforts to centralize or consolidate organizations and responsibilities had scant positive impact on the conduct of operations.

The fundamental problem faced throughout the Cold War was the absence of robust staff elements involved in the planning and execution of these activities in the major departments, especially State and Defense, as well as the pressures internal to the culture of the information agencies to distance themselves from the policy process. This situation in turn reflected the underlying problem—the absence of a clearly articulated missions and supporting doctrine, as well as glaring deficiencies in professional education and training.

NOTES

1. For a historical overview, see Paul A. Smith, *On Political War* (Washington, DC: National Defense University Press, 1989).

2. Wilson P. Dizard, Jr., *Inventing Public Diplomacy: The Story of the U.S. Information Agency* (Boulder, CO: Lynne Rienner, 2004). See also Thomas C. Sorensen, *The Word War: The Story of American Propaganda* (New York: Harper and Row, 1968); John W. Henderson, *The United States Information Agency* (New York: Praeger, 1969); Alvin A. Snyder, *Warriors of Disinformation: American Propaganda, Soviet Lies, and the Winning of the Cold War* (New York: Arcade, 1995); Richard T. Arndt, *The First Resort of Kings: American Cultural Diplomacy*

in the 20th Century (Washington, DC: Potomac Books, 2005); Alan L. Heil, Jr., *Voice of America: A History* (New York: Columbia University Press, 2003); Arch Puddington, *Broadcasting Freedom: The Cold War Triumph of Radio Free Europe and Radio Liberty* (Lexington: University Press of Kentucky, 2000).

   3. For an overview of the period, see Gregory Mitrovich, *Undermining the Kremlin: America's Strategy to Subvert the Soviet Bloc, 1947–1956* (Ithaca: Cornell University Press, 2000).

   4. See "Winning the Cold War: The U.S. Ideological Offensive," Hearings before the Subcommittee on International Organizations and Movements, Committee on Foreign Affairs, House of Representatives, 88th Cong., 1st and 2nd Sess. (Washington, DC: U.S. Government Printing Office, 1963–64).

   5. In one revealing incident, Kissinger aide Helmut Sonnenfeldt told a group of American diplomats in 1975 that it lay in the American national interest to foster a more "organic" relationship between the Soviet Union and its East European satellites, as a way to remove dangerous irritants in the U.S.-Soviet relationship. Walter Isaacson, *Kissinger: A Biography* (New York: Touchstone Books, 1992), 664–65. For the impact of such thinking within the radios at the time, see George Urban, *Radio Free Europe and the Pursuit of Democracy: My War within the Cold War* (New Haven: Yale University Press, 1997), 76–82.

   6. Carnes Lord, "The Past and Future of Public Diplomacy," *Orbis* (Winter 1998): 49–72.

   7. Peter Coleman, *The Liberal Conspiracy: The Congress for Cultural Freedom and the Struggle for the Mind of Postwar Europe* (New York: The Free Press, 1989).

   8. See, for example, Robert T. Holt and Robert W. van de Velde, *Strategic Psychological Operations and American Foreign Policy* (Chicago: University of Chicago Press, 1960), 159–205.

   9. John Ranelagh, *The Agency: The Rise and Decline of the CIA* (New York: Simon and Schuster, 1986), 264–69.

   10. The impact of CIA director Stansfield Turner's notorious purge of the clandestine service in this regard should not be underestimated; it marked the passing of the generation of CIA officers that had grown up in the milieu of the high Cold War. For a recent history of CIA covert action incorporating much new material, see John Prados, *Safe for Democracy: The Secret Wars of the CIA* (Chicago: Ivan R. Dee, 2006). Although Prados claims to have integrated psychological warfare operations fully in his account, what he has to say in this area is often sketchy or inaccurate.

   11. For an overview of OSS and army activities, see Clayton D. Laurie, *The Propaganda Warriors: America's Crusade against Nazi Germany* (Lawrence: University Press of Kansas, 1996).

   12. Alfred H. Paddock, Jr., *U.S. Army Special Warfare: Its Origins* (Washington, DC: National Defense University Press, 1982); Cecil B. Currey, *Edward Lansdale: The Unquiet American* (Washington, DC: Brassey's, 1998). See also Richard G. Stilwell, "Political-Psychological Dimensions of Counterinsurgency," in Frank L. Goldstein and Benjamin F. Findley, Jr., eds., *Psychological Operations: Principles and Case Studies* (Maxwell AFB, Alabama: Air University Press, 1996), 319–32.

   13. Vietnam operations discussed here are detailed in Benjamin F. Findley, Jr., "US and Vietcong Psychological Operations in Vietnam," in Goldstein and Findley, *Psychological Operations*, 233–41.

   14. In spite of the existence of a pro forma Memorandum of Understanding between the Board for International Broadcasting and USEUCOM, as of 1981 (as the author can

attest from personal knowledge), no planning had been done to protect RFE-RL headquarters in Munich or other assets throughout Western Europe from Soviet interference or attack, or to evacuate the radios' personnel to a safer location. See also Henry S. Rowen, "Political Strategies for General War: The Case of Eastern Europe," in Frank R. Barnett and Carnes Lord, *Political Warfare and Psychological Operations: Rethinking the U.S. Approach* (Washington, DC: National Defense University Press, 1989), 169–97.

15. For a detailed account, see Alfred H. Paddock, Jr., "Military Psychological Operations," in Barnett and Lord, *Political Warfare*, 45–65.

16. See Dennis P. Walko, "Psychological Operations in Panama during Operations Just Cause and Promote Liberty," and Frank L. Goldstein and Daniel W. Jacobowitz, "PSYOP in Desert Shield/Desert Storm," in Goldstein and Findley, *Psychological Operations*, 249–77, 341–56.

17. Leo Bogart, *Premises for Propaganda: The United States Information Agency's Operating Assumptions in the Cold War* (New York: The Free Press, 1976), vii.

18. Ibid., xxi.

19. Ronald I. Rubin, *The Objectives of the U.S. Information Agency: Controversies and Analysis* (New York: Praeger, 1966), 10. See also Robert F. Delaney, "Psychological Operations in the 1970's: A Program in Search of a Doctrine," in Ronald De McLaurin et al., eds., *The Art and Science of Psychological Operations: Case Studies of Military Application* (Washington, DC: Department of the Army, 1976), 1–15.

20. P.L. 94-350. See Heil, *Voice of America*, 64–65, 152–77.

21. The confusion is effectively captured in Rubin, *The Objectives of the U.S. Information Agency*, 47–61.

22. Excerpts in Henderson, *The United States Information Agency*, 66–68.

23. Panel on International Information, Education, and Cultural Relations, *International Information, Education, and Cultural Relations: Recommendations for the Future* (Washington, DC: Center for Strategic and International Studies, 1975). For the history of this and similar such studies, see Lois W. Roth, "Public Diplomacy and the Past: The Search for an American Style of Propaganda (1952–1977)," *The Fletcher Forum* (Summer 1984): 353–96.

24. Quoted in Christopher Simpson, *National Security Directives of the Reagan and Bush Administrations* (Boulder, CO: Westview, 1995), 393–97.

25. As the author, the principal drafter of this document, can personally attest.

26. Dizard, *Inventing Public Diplomacy*, 40.

27. Ibid., 47–48.

28. Kenneth A. Osgood, "Form before Substance: Eisenhower's Commitment to Psychological Warfare and Negotiations with the Enemy," *Diplomatic History* 24 (Summer 2000): 405–33.

29. See the discussion in Dizard, *Inventing Public Diplomacy*, 109–17.

30. Dizard, *Inventing Public Diplomacy*, 34–37.

31. See "The U.S. Ideological Effort: Government Agencies and Programs," study prepared for the Subcommittee on International Organizations and Movements, Committee on Foreign Affairs, House of Representatives, 88th Cong., 1st Sess. (Washington, DC: US Government Printing Office, January 1964), 36.

32. See Carnes Lord, *Losing Hearts and Minds? Public Diplomacy and Strategic Influence in the Age of Terror* (Westport, CT: Praeger, 2006), 73–82.

33. "Report of the President's Committee on International Information Activities, June 30, 1953," in *Foreign Relations of the United States, 1952–1954*, vol. 2 (Washington, DC: United States Government Printing Office, 1984), pt. 2, p. 1796; for the PSB and OCB,

see further pp. 1853–57. OCB retained a six-person staff for "information and education projects" (out of a total of about forty). John Prados, *Keepers of the Keys: The National Security Council from Truman to Bush* (New York: William Morrow, 1991), 73–75.

34. Simpson, *National Security Directives,* 265–67.

35. See, for example, Rubin, *The Objectives of the U.S. Information Agency,* 142–50.

36. Ronald H. Hinckley, "National Security in the Information Age," *The Washington Quarterly* (Spring 1986): 125–39.

37. "Public Diplomacy and the Future," Hearings before the Subcommittee on International Operations of the Committee on International Relations, House of Representatives, 95th Cong., 1st Sess. (Washington, DC: U.S. Government Printing Office, June 1977).

38. Peter Galbraith (later U.S. ambassador to Croatia), operating with top cover but, to put it mildly, little substantive guidance from Senators Claiborne Pell (D-RI) and Edward Zorinsky (D-NE). The lack of Washington experience of USIA director Charles Z. Wick made him particularly vulnerable to Galbraith's interventions, which tended to focus on alleged administration efforts to "politicize" the public diplomacy agencies by using them to advance a conservative agenda.

39. For the early Cold War, see Rubin, *The Objectives of the U.S. Information Agency,* 173–82.

After Disaster: Recovering from the 1964 Alaskan Earthquake

Dwight A. Ink

It was Good Friday. Washington headed home for the weekend. Then, without notice, the most severe earthquake ever recorded in North America struck Alaska. The quake severely impacted much of its population, devastating the economy. Engineers surveying the damage concluded the situation was hopeless. Critical facilities could not be rebuilt during the short Alaskan construction season. Most of the affected population would have to be moved to the lower forty-eight. Despite these dire predictions, an unprecedented response that combined insightful support from Washington political leaders and unorthodox management strategies developed by government career professionals entrusted with directing the rebuilding averted catastrophe.

NORTH! TO ALASKA

Alaska had achieved statehood only five years before the earthquake struck. Alaska's pre-oil economy was very fragile. Tourism stood at a small fraction of what exists today. The state's finances remained so anemic that questions had been raised during the debate on granting statehood as to whether Alaska was yet prepared to take on the fiscal responsibilities required for sustaining sovereignty. As a result, President Lyndon B. Johnson considered establishing some type of federal economic commission to help Alaska develop plans and financing for much-needed economic development. Arguably, no state in the Union stood less prepared to take on the burden of a catastrophic natural disaster.

In Washington, President Johnson was preoccupied with completing a difficult transition after the assassination of President John F. Kennedy, a transition that involved very sensitive relationships with former Kennedy appointees. Johnson grappled with trying to secure political support for moving forward with his ambitious social agenda, much of which had been envisioned by Kennedy, while also developing his candidacy for the fall presidential election. At the same time, the civil rights battle reached its climax, and long-neglected urban neighborhoods had become tinderboxes, ready to explode. Johnson also found himself devoting more and more attention to the Vietnam conflict. Nor could he neglect the Cold War, complex nuclear issues, and tensions in Europe. The president had his hands more than full. Then the earth shook.

Without warning, a horrendous earthquake struck Alaska on March 27, 1964. Measuring 9.2 on the Richter scale, and lasting between three and four minutes, it had a devastating impact. The ground rose or sank at least five feet over most of an expanse exceeding fifty thousand square miles, where roughly two-thirds of the Alaskan population lived. The quake had a particularly devastating effect on fishing, the base of the Alaskan economy. Most fishing boats were destroyed or severely damaged, and the canneries were knocked out. The quake also altered the geography of the coastal landscape. Small boat harbors were now either too shallow for most boats, or were too deep for the breakwaters to protect the boats from the autumn storms. Exporting anything also proved impossible. The terminus of the Alaskan railroad had vanished into the water, as had parts of neighborhoods and business districts in Anchorage and other towns. Highways had buckled, bridges collapsed, and air transportation was seriously disrupted.

The earthquake changed forever the habitat of many native Alaskans who lived along the coast. Shorelines changed in many places. Several towns found that at high tide they now stood partially under water. The town of Homer was located on a spit of land that had become partially submerged. Geologists feared that the spit had become so vulnerable to erosion from future storms that it would disappear altogether. Given its precarious situation, officials debated whether it made sense to provide public funds to help rebuild at all. The Valdez waterfront also disappeared, raising alarming questions about whether the town's future safety was so in doubt that it did not warrant rebuilding. Many communities found water and sewer lines not just broken, but pulverized. Thousands of homes and businesses were destroyed or damaged beyond repair. Few Alaskans had earthquake insurance, largely because it was prohibitively expensive.

Remarkably, given the devastation to transportation networks and critical infrastructure, the initial emergency response by community groups and the federal government to help local governments provide food and water, medical assistance, and shelter to residents throughout the state was swift and effective. Prospects for the longer-term recovery required to sustain a viable state, however, were an entirely different matter. The future appeared grim.

CRISIS RESPONSE

Alaska proved fortunate in having a large military presence at the time of the earthquake. Civilian communications were completely disrupted, but within minutes of the earthquake, the Command Post of the Alaskan Military Command at Anchorage became a command center through which communications were established between Alaska and Washington and between state and city Civil Defense Headquarters in south-central Alaska. Since they were involved in an immediate humanitarian crisis, the military believed they had inherent authority to act. They did not wait for formal requests for assistance or obtain clearances before dispatching assistance.[1]

The Military Affiliate Radio System went into operation on emergency power less than one hour after the earthquake, and maintained a twenty-four-hour schedule for several weeks. Military signal personnel helped civilian companies restore communication service. Military water trailers supplied water to the greater Anchorage area within three hours after the earthquake. Within forty-eight hours, the military flew water purification units in from Fort Lewis, Washington. At dawn a large airlift began in which seventeen C-123 transport planes carried relief supplies and equipment to Seward, Valdez, Kodiak, and other more isolated communities. That same morning Fort Richardson, Alaska, opened four field mess halls that operated around the clock. Elmendorf Air Force Base provided similar emergency food service. Emergency housing for about five thousand people was arranged the evening of the quake. At the same time, the military responded to local phone and radio requests by assigning troops to assist in security and travel control. The navy distributed generators, pumps, medicine, sleeping bags, and other items desperately needed in Kodiak.[2]

On the morning of March 28, Governor William A. Egan requested that the president declare a major disaster under the authority of P.L. 81-875. Several hours later Johnson acted, designating Alaska a federal disaster area. Under the direction of Edward A. McDermott, the Office of Emergency Planning (OEP, the forerunner of the Federal Emergency Management Agency—FEMA) moved quickly to work with other agencies and local governments to help meet the initial response requirements of food and shelter, as well as providing limited funding for some emergency repairs. The OEP performed its task of coordinating emergency support well. Other federal agencies soon joined in. The Federal Aviation Agency, for example, began immediately to assess the damage and direct repairs of state and municipal airports. The federally owned Alaskan Railroad also began to undertake repairs. The Bureau of Public Roads, the Departments of Health, Education, and Welfare, Labor, Agriculture, and Commerce, and the Coast Guard also moved quickly to provide emergency help.[3]

Despite the crippling impact of the earthquake on local resources, many local government personnel turned in wonderful emergency performances, and the work of several civic organizations, such as the Red Cross and Salvation Army, was impressive.[4] Contributing significantly to a surprisingly effective initial response was the initiative shown by individual Alaskans. They were unusually creative in finding ways to cope with disaster, and not easily discouraged.[5]

IN GOOD FRIDAY'S WAKE

Earthquakes present engineering recovery complexities beyond those found in hurricanes or other natural disasters.[6] Property lines shift, and ground elevations change abruptly. Earthquakes cause considerable hidden structural damage not readily identified or evaluated. The behavior of underlying soils in the event of future earthquakes is difficult to ascertain. At times, as was true in Alaska, deep soil tests are required to determine where it is safe to rebuild. For example, in Anchorage, treacherous Bootleggers Cove Clay lay buried well under the surface, and when saturated, it reacted to the motions of an earthquake like a layer of grease above which the overburden slid unevenly toward the ocean, carrying whole neighborhoods with it. Drilling rigs from the Nevada atomic energy test sites had to be slowly barged up the ocean to Alaska for much of the soil testing before rebuilding decisions could be made in the areas that might be vulnerable to future earthquakes.

Economic issues associated with the earthquake's aftermath also proved overwhelming. In addition to the body blow to the fishing-based economy, inflation worries loomed over reconstruction planning. Inflation had been a perennial problem in Alaska, where competition for reconstruction and support services could spark an unrelenting bidding war. Widespread fears persisted that the economic pressures of the recovery operations would send inflation skyrocketing. The loss of projected state and local tax revenue, combined with large emergency expenditures, threatened to leave state and local governments without the funds to continue essential services.[7]

Rapid reconstruction, while threatening to overheat the local economy, was desperately needed to help keep Alaskans employed. Some in the crippled fishing industry could survive at least temporarily by finding reconstruction jobs, but only if reconstruction moved rapidly enough and left them with enough money to remain in the state during the winter months.

Making this dilemma truly acute was the knowledge that the short Alaskan construction season made prospects for completing the most critical construction during the first year extremely dim. Failure to do so would have meant that about a third of the Alaskan population would likely enter winter without water or sewage facilities and with inadequate shelter, their jobs gone, and rising inflation. In this event, most would have had no choice but to abandon the state, with highly uncertain prospects for their return, raising a serious question as to whether Alaska could still function as a state.

UNORTHODOX RECOVERY

Within twenty-four hours of the earthquake, it had become clear that the existing machinery at all three levels of government could not begin to cope with the complexity, magnitude, and urgency of the physical and economic recovery faced by Alaska. All the heroic emergency efforts of the first responders could not hide the painful fact that much of the state was in a shambles and its economy ruined. Strong federal leadership would have to be brought into play very quickly for Alaska to survive as a viable state. Alaskan recovery would require organization and operating approaches never used before.

Departing in dramatic fashion from the usual approaches to organizing disaster recoveries, several days after the earthquake Johnson appointed much of his cabinet as the Federal Reconstruction and Development Planning Commission for Alaska.[8] This temporary commission was to cooperate with the state in developing plans for both reconstruction and economic development.

Johnson then took the unprecedented step of appointing a powerful senator, Clinton Anderson of New Mexico, as chair of the Commission. Anderson was a strong political ally of Johnson, and his earlier experience as secretary of agriculture gave him a much better grasp of the executive branch than most senators have. In addition, he had experience with relief programs during the 1930s and with the post–World War II international food emergency. Further, Anderson was a member of the Senate's Interior and Insular Affairs Committee, where he had conducted hearings on Alaskan statehood.

Other initial members of the Commission appointed by Johnson were the secretary of defense, the secretary of the interior, the secretary of agriculture, the secretary of commerce, the secretary of labor, the secretary of health, education, and welfare; the administrators of the Federal Aviation Administration, the Housing and Home Finance Agency, and the Small Business Administration; the chairman of the Federal Power Administration; and the director of the Office of Emergency Planning. Although not a formal member of the Commission, the director of the Bureau of the Budget participated in the Commission meetings and played a very important role. Nearly every other agency of government eventually became involved, including the Department of State.

Participation by all the significant agencies in the federal, state, and local governments created a remarkably complicated interagency and intergovernmental mechanism. Without professional management advice from the Bureau of the Budget, strong commission leadership, skilled coordination, and highly innovative engineers and managers, it is difficult to conceive how Alaskan recovery efforts could have been effectively coordinated. The response lacked any recovery plans, doctrine, or policies to guide their efforts. Instead, Johnson relied on experienced political and career leaders, and empowered them to act quickly in a decentralized manner without red tape.

Decisive presidential leadership made the difference. By establishing a cabinet commission, Johnson demonstrated his personal commitment to recovery and reconstruction. The decision by the president not only galvanized action, it demonstrated how strong national leadership at the outset can reduce the potential drain on the president's crowded schedule later on as work proceeds.

LEADING THE CROWD

Anderson gave remarkably strong policy leadership, but a senator should not be placed in a position of directing executive operations. Therefore, Johnson appointed an experienced career official to serve as executive director. The assignment went to the author, serving at the time as assistant general manager of the Atomic Energy Commission (AEC).[9] As the number three operating AEC official, his AEC role at the time included the expediting and troubleshooting elements of a typical chief operating officer, combined with responsibility under both Republican and Democratic administrations for liaison with the White House, Congress, and the press. Experience gained from this combination of duties proved to be very useful in the role of executive director who reported to both Senator Anderson and the president.

Mindful of his senatorial role, Anderson was careful not to inject himself into operations, leaving the executive director free to manage day-to-day activities. As for the president, Johnson was too busy with other executive issues to try to manage Alaskan recovery, but he did follow events closely, both because of his personal concern and because he recognized the political cost of failure.

As the commission staff exerted every effort to help the departments expedite their work and make sure the departments received credit for their achievements, they received tremendous support from the department heads. The staff's role as a facilitator of operations helped greatly in the occasional situation where its authority had to be exerted to break through a bottleneck or address a jurisdictional question. Backed by the authority of the president, the commission had a rare opportunity to facilitate rapid policy and operational decision making, encouraging an impressive level of cooperation among the scores of federal agencies that were involved.

The executive director—serving as a career professional and thus not perceived as aspiring to political office, appointed for only a temporary position (thought to be about six months), and with a very small staff detailed from various organizations—could move very quickly without raising significant concerns about impinging on departmental jurisdictional concerns. In addition, with Anderson serving as the public face of the reconstruction, the executive director and the commission staff could operate with a relatively low profile, concentrating on operations rather than public relations.

An important factor in the success of the executive director position was the role played by one of Johnson's assistants, Lee White. White offered insights into how to work with the Johnson administration, including a great deal about Johnson's personal preferences in how he wished to interact with the staff of the Executive Office of the President at the White House, such as the type of reporting the president wanted. White also helped create the impression that the executive director was close to the president and had ready access to him. Neither was the case, but White was in a position to provide presidential access should it be needed. Indeed, interagency cooperation proved so effective that there was never a case where the president needed to be involved with operational problems or decisions.

It was Anderson, not the executive director, who was the president's confidante, the person on whom he was relying to save Alaska. It was clear that someone close to the president, in this case Anderson, was needed to make this rather informal organizational arrangement function as a cohesive team. And it was also essential that someone, in this case the executive director, be fully equipped professionally to lead the operations and develop whatever new management strategies might be required for success.

Frank DiLuzio, Anderson's assistant, helped ensure that the work of the chairman and the executive director proceeded in tandem. DiLuzio proved very effective at (a) convincing people that the executive director, in fact, had the full confidence of Anderson and the president, and did speak for them; and (b) helping the chairman herd needed legislation through a divided Congress.

The Bureau of the Budget (BOB) management staff, headed by Harold Seidman, also played an important role. BOB designed the simple, but powerful, federal machinery that Johnson quickly set in motion (except for the unprecedented feature of having a senator chair the cabinet committee, which was Johnson's personal idea). During the months the temporary commission was in existence, the BOB staff was of tremendous help in making sure that the departments understood the nature of the special unorthodox arrangements and gave full support to the commission staff.[10] This organization staff arm of the president no longer exists.

COMMISSION STAFF

The commission provided the political leadership, and developed the recovery policies, required under Johnson's executive order. The staff, headed by the executive director, conducted the commission's day-to-day operations.

All staff members were detailed from agencies involved in the recovery except for several from congressional committees. The director, deputy director, two secretaries, and three engineers were the only ones serving full time. The other seventeen provided various levels of part-time service, largely as liaisons with their home agencies. These members visited Alaska but spent more of their time in Washington, helping the executive director and their own leadership draw upon agency resources to ensure rapid execution.

The commission worked with a very small staff because its role was not to perform recovery work, but to mobilize, energize, and coordinate agency personnel throughout the federal government. The federal agencies were the ones doing the work in cooperation with state and local public and nongovernmental groups.

With the exception of the secretaries, the full-time staff members spent most of their time in Alaska, while the larger part-time staff operated more from Washington. Typically, the executive director would fly to Alaska for about ten days, going from community to community, and then return to Washington for a week to brief Anderson and White House staff, consult with agency heads and their liaisons, and discuss Alaskan needs with key members of Congress. When the executive director was in Washington, the deputy executive director would be in Alaska to ensure continuity between the efforts going on in the field and the support provided in Washington by federal entities. The staff was the action arm of the president and the commission, as well as an oversight group for monitoring agency reconstruction performance.

The commission staff was fully operational less than two weeks after the disaster. In part, this quick reaction was possible because it was temporary.

Equally important, since they were operating out of the White House under the Executive Office of the President, there were fewer bureaucratic obstacles to overcome. Time was not devoted to the customary drafting, debating, and clearing of roles and legal authorities for these structures that otherwise would have had to take place before becoming operational. None of these temporary groups possessed legal authority per se, relying instead on commission policies and the authority each member of the group had by virtue of his agency membership.

Indeed, the executive director had no specific legal authority. Yet, because he was executive director of a cabinet commission and because he reported to the president as well as a powerful senator, his staff members were in a position to make any operational decision that was needed, even to the extent of assigning responsibility to different departments for reconstruction tasks. Remarkably, the informality and lack of special legal authority prescribed for the structure below the level of the commission did not lead to confusion over roles and missions. To the contrary, questions of authority never reached the executive director or the chairman. This was due in part to the fact that no part of the structure was permanent or endowed with jurisdiction-threatening legislation. After about six months, its mission was completed.

ORGANIZATIONAL INNOVATION

The federal commission was not constrained by predetermined organizational structures or procedures, leaving it free to tailor the federal recovery machinery to the unique problems of the Alaskan recovery. Anderson quickly appointed an Alaskan Construction Consultant Committee with members drawn from the Associated General Contractors of America and the International Union of Operating Engineers. Its role was to provide damage estimates with accompanying guides for emergency reconstruction planning. The Commission also accepted an April 11 offer from the American Institute of Architects and the Engineers Joint Council to provide consultancy assistance on both reconstruction plans and longer-range development programs, to be developed with input from state and local officials, University of Alaska faculty, as well as Alaskan architects, engineers, and civic leaders. They submitted their report on June 13.[11]

The Commission established nine federal interagency task forces to make special studies and prepare recommendations for early consideration by the Commission. Although they reported to the executive director, much of their work dealt with policy issues for consideration by the Commission. There was, for example, a Transportation Task Force, chaired by the undersecretary for transportation in the Commerce Department, with members from the Defense Department, the Federal Maritime Commission, the director of the Alaska Railroad in the Department of Interior, the Federal Aviation Agency, and the Office of Emergency Planning. The other task forces that were established immediately were Ports and Fishing, Natural Resource Development, Industrial Development, Financial Institutions, Economic Stabilization, Community Facilities, and a Scientific and Engineering task force that included a Scientific and Engineering Field Team temporarily located in Alaska. In varying degrees, all these task forces were concerned with both those policies needed for the immediate reconstruction period and those directed toward longer-term Alaskan economic development.

ON THE FRONT LINES OF RECOVERY

As a counterpart to the federal commission, on April 3, 1964, Governor Egan issued Executive Order No. 27, establishing the State of Alaska Reconstruction and Development Planning Commission. This state commission had limited resources to draw upon, but it worked very closely with the federal commission in coordinating programs for restoring and developing Alaska.[12]

The governor appointed a very able person with both government and business experience, Joseph FitzGerald, as coordinator of the state commission. FitzGerald participated in all executive director Alaska meetings, and accompanied every community visit. Egan also sent the attorney general of Alaska, George Hayes, to Washington as his liaison with the federal commission. Hayes's Washington office was next to that of the executive director and he attended all federal commission staff meetings. Both FitzGerald and Hayes had full access to commission documents with the exception of a few personal notes from Anderson to Johnson.

Both of these two key Eagan appointments were based on competence, not politics. They both worked well with the federal commission and a myriad of state and local stakeholders that played roles in the reconstruction effort.

ALASKA FIELD COMMITTEE

An especially important part of the reconstruction organization was the Alaska Field Committee that reported to the executive director. This was a very active group tasked with helping to coordinate and expedite operations on the ground in Alaska. Chaired by the regional coordinator of the Department of the Interior, it consisted of the senior official of each of the eighteen federal agencies having field offices in Alaska. FitzGerald, as the state coordinator, also served as an ad hoc member. In order to carry out the work of the committee effectively, some lower-grade members were quickly given much higher authority by their agencies.

Rank counted for little importance so long as their agencies permitted them to act on non-policy issues without the delays caused by having to check first with Washington. As the work progressed, several federal agencies were very surprised at the way in which their field personnel carried out heavier responsibilities so well when given the guidance and authority to act.*

---

* This Alaskan Field Committee was to serve as the model for President Nixon's later nationwide system of federal Regional Councils, an important part of his New Federalism.

POLICY BEFORE RECOVERY

Having a decentralized framework in place to undertake recovery would have meant little if broad federal policies to guide these efforts had not been quickly and clearly established. Because the commission served at cabinet level and was led by an unusually strong chair who was very close to the president, policies for the federal recovery effort were established in a remarkably short period of time—most of them within the first few weeks of its existence. Anderson demonstrated great skill in leading the commission discussions, being somewhat deferential to the status of the cabinet members in his style, yet relying on his association with the president to move the group forward to surprisingly rapid decisions. His strong personal leadership enabled speedy resolution of such issues as inadequate insurance, mortgage relief, low government assistance interest rates, tax relief, and public facilities funding.

Clearly, the "crisis" character of the recovery effort also helped move things. But new policies have rarely, if ever, been established so rapidly in other disaster recoveries. Enough early data was flowing in from Alaska to help point the way for significant new policies—thus proving the wisdom of establishing the whole recovery machinery quickly, rather than waiting until the emergency phase had been substantially completed.

The most basic policy decision had to do with the recovery timetable. Some urged a two-track approach to the Alaskan crisis. One track would focus on as much recovery during 1964 as was possible, while another, concurrent track would develop arrangements for major evacuation to the lower forty-eight (since the proponents of this option assumed rebuilding could not progress sufficiently to provide the basic needs of the affected population by the time winter stormed in—probably in mid-October).

A two-track approach would have required the government to provide temporary housing in the lower forty-eight for thousands of evacuated families, as well as funds to tide them over until the following year, when sufficient facilities could be restored to permit their return. As the practical problems involved in this option began to surface, few thought this approach would be practicable.

The "abandonment" option, as it came to be labeled, never received serious consideration in the White House. Johnson was not about "to lose a state."[13] He did not want to hear about the difficulties posed by trying to complete critical construction within a few months of the earthquake. With little regard for the negative odds, a very firm president focused everyone on the single goal of completing enough rebuilding of critical public utilities and homes during the first construction season to avoid evacuation.

At the same time, the president also recognized that several of the largest projects, such as the relocation of Valdez and the expansion of small boat harbors, would have to be extended over the next several years. Some projects would provide only temporary construction the first year, with permanent rebuilding to follow later. For example, some wooden bridges were constructed quickly during the first summer so that most traffic could be restored, but these were scheduled to be replaced by permanent bridges later. The rail bed was repaired to provide only thirty-five-mile-per-hour traffic by fall, with further rebuilding to permit regular speeds coming later should it be decided that its economic prospects warranted rebuilding.

One of the most far-reaching policies established at the first meeting of the commission was that of rebuilding Alaska in ways that would enhance the opportunity for future development of the state, rather than following the past policy of merely rebuilding what had existed before a disaster. The way for this course of action had been paved by widespread recognition, at the time statehood was granted, that Alaska would need help in planning the type of economic development required for a fiscally sound revenue base.

The decision to focus on the future paid off in important ways over the long term, but it greatly complicated the task of reconstructing sufficient public facilities and shelter during the short construction season. Enabling Alaskans to remain in the state when the severe cold weather returned was a priority that had to move ahead regardless of long-range plans. Even the relatively simple added burden of broadening a roadway or changing a road curvature to modern standards added time to tight reconstruction schedules that worried engineers. The "think for the long-term" policy had an even greater impact in places such as Seward, where the proposed doubling of the capacity of the small boat harbor would require legislation that would delay completion—even though limited dredging and repairs had to be completed quickly, so that as boats were repaired, some fishing could resume the first year.[14]

Although reconstruction was a priority, the commission also wanted to facilitate rebuilding in a prudent manner that would mitigate the damage from future disasters. There were several particularly critical areas, especially in Anchorage, where rebuilding decisions depended on the results of soil studies that were needed before difficult buttressing projects could be designed—a situation that necessarily delayed construction. With the construction period so limited, waiting for deep soil testing understandably taxed people's patience. Nevertheless, the understanding and restraint that most citizens and community leaders exercised proved remarkable. In addition, a special type of buttressing was developed, one sufficiently reliable to permit rebuilding short distances from where the earth shifted and sank during the earthquake. This engineering innovation saved many businesses and homes from abandonment.

The most controversial policy decision was that of refusing to provide federal assistance in areas determined to be especially vulnerable to future earthquake damage. The commission was disturbed that the federal government had kept providing families and business with financial help in rebuilding areas that repeatedly suffered from natural disasters, especially floods.

The federal government could not prohibit the return of people to vulnerable areas, but it was not deemed good policy for the government to continue to encourage this practice through means such as low interest mortgages and loans. Consequently, it became commission policy to redline areas deemed high risk, and to deny federal assistance to anyone returning to those areas. Determining those high-risk areas turned out to be more difficult and controversial than antic-ipated. But the process came to be generally accepted because of the professional quality of the data produced by the Scientific and Engineering task force, as well as the inability of the critics to come up with credible alternatives.[15]

Several of the more complex decisions that had to be based heavily on tech-nical assessments were left to the commission staff within guidelines established by the commission. One example that will be discussed later was the question of whether to provide assistance for the rebuilding of the town of Valdez unless it relocated. Another critical decision left to the executive director was the question of whether enough soil stabilization was possible to permit rebuilding substantial portions of Anchorage and several other towns adjacent to major earth movement that had occurred during the earthquake. This decision rested heavily on what the soil studies would produce and whether satisfactory buttressing to stabilize the ground could be designed. The commission concluded that such decisions could be made much more quickly by a professional staff working on the ground than by political leaders in distant Washington. This turned out to be correct.

THE HILL RESPONDS

Some policies required congressional action. In the first few weeks of its exis-tence, the commission developed legislative proposals with such provisions as a near doubling of the federal share of reconstruction costs in Alaska outside the National Forests; modifications of previously authorized Corps of Engineers civil works projects; authorizing the Farmers Home Administration, the Rural Electri-fication Administration, and the Housing and Home Finance Agency (HHFA) to adjust the indebtedness of certain borrowers; authorizing the HHFA to provide grants for urban renewal projects; and the purchase by the federal government of State of Alaska bonds (or the loan of a similar amount of funds).

After advance consultations with several congressional committees, these and other requests were consolidated in a proposed Alaska Omnibus Act and sent to Congress on May 27. By having a senator chair the Commission, President Johnson had paved the way for expedited legislative action that would not likely have been achieved otherwise. Because of Anderson's leadership, the president's bill was about the only legislation permitted to advance during the bitter 1964 civil rights debate and a Senate filibuster that lasted fifty-seven days. After several amendments, it was enacted into law on August 8, 1964. Knowing in advance the content of most of the final provisions, the agencies were poised to move imme-diately upon signing of the bill.

FROM RESPONSE TO RECOVERY

The role of the commission was to lead the recovery, not to replace the role of the first responders that had been providing emergency help. Indeed, it was highly unrealistic to believe that immediate operational needs could be directed effectively by a small staff in Washington. The work of OEP and the other early responders continued while the commission spent its first weeks establishing policies for the recovery and providing time for the executive director to set up task forces and interagency committees, which flew immediately to Alaska to gather scientific and economic data. Anderson, accompanied by the executive director, then headed to Alaska to explain the basic approach to federal recovery assistance planned by President Johnson and the Alaskan commission and to review initial recovery plans and actions.

Upon arriving in Anchorage on April 27, Anderson, in his eagerly awaited public pronouncement, endeavored to dissuade Alaskans from the fast-growing expectation that the federal government would write "a blank check . . . to recoup private losses." Acknowledging that some Alaskans would regard him as Scrooge, he tried to set a tone that reduced the hopes of the earthquake victims to realistic levels of federal assistance. At the same time, he firmly committed the federal government to providing enough help to "speed the recovery of your state with the objective of making Alaska a better place to live and work than it was before the tragedy of last month."[16]

RIDING THE CIRCUIT

From the outset, the commission recognized that it had to empower people in the field, not make operational decisions for them. This required constant staff engagement from the beginning. After the Anderson speech, Egan and the commission's executive director, together with state and federal staff, flew in a raging blizzard through the Chugach Mountains to visit Egan's heavily damaged hometown, Valdez. No pilot thought the flight was advisable because of the extremely hazardous weather. But it was one of the communities especially hard-hit by the earthquake, and Egan believed it important to boost the town's morale with a visit as quickly as possible.

The people of Valdez had witnessed a tidal wave, or tsunami, that towered 220 feet as it engulfed the waterfront, according to the Coast and Geodetic Survey. A piece of land, about four thousand by six hundred feet in size, had slid into the bay, taking the town's boats and fishing industry with it. It was nearly midnight before the town council could be assembled to discuss the town's future.** Meeting over the damaged fire station, a number of townspeople also packed into the room, and a reporter turned on a tape recorder. Unfortunately, the room was too small to hold many of those who wished to participate, a problem corrected in subsequent community meetings.

The council meeting began by addressing the difficult question of how vulnerable Valdez was to possible future disasters. In addition to concern about the impact of future earthquakes on the unstable soil that underlay the current location with its lowered elevation, some miles up the valley was a lake that could

---

** Immediately after the governor and executive director left the plane in Valdez, it took off in the blizzard but dove into the bay, carrying the crew and the Alaskan Adjutant General to their death, sending a new shock wave through the battered community.

flood the valley because of a natural dam consisting largely of ice that might melt at some point. At the center of the debate was the commission policy of not providing federal assistance to rebuild in hazardous areas, a huge disappointment to the Valdez citizens. The executive director assured residents that the federal government would provide help to relocate the town about four miles along the bay to an area with a rock base, should Valdez decide to do so. As dawn neared, the council, with strong support from most townspeople in attendance, decided to move. Six more meetings and inspections in other towns took place over the next week.

MANAGEMENT STRATEGIES

Although the principles of federalism—respecting the responsibilities and authorities of each level of government—remained inviolable, the normal instruments and mechanisms of intergovernmental cooperation were inadequate. Thus, in the course of this first trip to Alaska, the commission staff began developing innovative management approaches. Several proved especially critical to success.

Openness

The commission went to great lengths to plan and execute the Alaskan recovery in an open manner. Virtually all operational decisions were made during Alaskan public meetings with broad participation. The commission's first meeting in the Seward high school auditorium provided the pattern for similar sessions held in each community thereafter.

By the time of the Seward auditorium meeting, several members of the Federal Field Committee and the State Commission had been able to fly into town to participate alongside the local Seward officials. Business leaders were important attendees, and the public was also invited to participate. As had been the case in Valdez, when people realized the commission was serious about quick decisions, and that the securing of federal assistance depended on everyone assuming accountability for the work assigned to them, the general quality of most comments and suggestions was impressive. The unusual degree of openness resulted in the public being far better informed of decisions than would have been possible otherwise. Having witnessed the discussion, regardless of whether individual citizens agreed with all the decisions, they at least understood the reasoning behind them.

After the Seward meeting, key members of the Alaskan Field Committee and the State Commission accompanied commissioners and staff on all community trips. Particularly important was the active participation and cooperation of FitzGerald, the state coordinator, who was in constant touch with Governor Egan.

Intergovernmental Management

Although developing personal relationships can facilitate cooperation, that alone proved inadequate for dealing with catastrophic events like the Good Friday earthquake. Complex organizations require more substantial guidance to ensure that their efforts are integrated. Missions must be stated; roles established; the scope of responsibilities described; accountability for funding and program actions completed; and countless other management tasks accounted for. In addition, there must be a means to incorporate the efforts of the private sector, nongovernmental agencies, and the public.

Tasks, budgets, and leadership responsibilities were firmly established for each project. This decision making occurred when all stakeholders were consulted. Debate and disagreement proved unavoidable, but decisions on scheduling and expenditures were reached quickly because they were made at community meetings, rather than being filtered through multiple layers of governance in Juneau and Washington.

Scheduling

Working from schedules based on past experience, and concentrating only on how they might be realistically shortened, was often not sufficient to enable the most critical work to be completed during the short construction season. A number of projects, particularly sewer and water system restoration, had to be implemented if populations were to be able to remain in the state over the long Alaskan winter. Instead, the commission staff began by looking at what construction was so critical it had to be completed by mid-October, then working backward to develop a work plan, establishing intervening milestones to reach that goal (no matter how unrealistic these might seem at the time). Implementing these ambitious objectives, in turn, required the development of new engineering and management practices.[17]

In almost every case, the normal time of construction was slashed by impressive amounts. Managers pushed the envelope in every facet of reconstruction, and the crews responded. The long daylight Alaskan summers helped, permitting double- and triple-shift around-the-clock work. Considerable savings were also achieved through a streamlined process of scoping the contract work and awarding the contracts. For the less complicated types of construction, projects moved forward with building while design was still under way. Extreme versions of incentive fee contracts, together with stiff penalties for poor performance, were used, including those managed by the Corps of Engineers. As the summer wore on, the Corps and other groups set new peacetime construction records.[18]

Streamlined, Adaptive Process

Both Anderson and the White House staff placed saving Alaska over respecting established procedures and practices. Thanks largely to Anderson, the executive director had the tacit approval to request that any agency modify or dispense with any procedure that threatened the completion schedules of critical public facilities.

Urban renewal projects, for example, typically consumed several years just in the planning phase. The commission staff asked the House and Home Finance Agency to forego public hearings on urban renewal projects, since all of the urban renewal meetings were held in open session with public participation. Further, the recovery staffs found that the time and effort devoted to federal processes often could be greatly reduced by better management without resorting to major changes or suspension of existing procedures.

The commission quickly learned that processes had to be flexible as well as fast. The commission's Economic Stabilization task force, for example, soon learned that the Labor and Treasury Departments had no means to quickly control reconstruction-induced inflation. On the other hand, the Agriculture Experiment Station in Alaska had excellent contacts in various communities that could be utilized for a volunteer wage and price control system, which turned out to be very successful.

When complaints began to mount that the Small Business Administration (SBA) could not handle the surge in low-interest loans needed for hard-hit small businesses to survive, the commission worked out an arrangement with the SBA and several Alaskan banks in which the banks handled most of the paper processing of these applications and could approve them up to $20,000 when there was 10 percent participation by the bank, and up to $250,000 when there was 20 percent bank participation.[19]

Funding

Johnson's approach to mobilizing government-wide resources involved the simplest of financing arrangements. In 1964, departments and agencies contributed a total of only $90,200 for the operation of the commission (largely for travel costs). Of that total, $29,500 in unused funds was returned to the agencies. Agencies used their own funds and authorities for their reconstruction activities in Alaska, using their established budget, accounting, and auditing processes. Enormous monetary savings for the federal, state, and local governments resulted from the commission's success in expediting the recovery.

Oversight

As pressure on agency personnel and construction contractors to move quickly mounted, so did opportunities for waste, poor quality construction, and abuse. The commission's defense against this problem was to insist that agencies assign their most qualified people to the recovery activities and to bolster existing independent oversight mechanisms among the agencies. Several federal and state managers who were failing to control costs and manage performance were reassigned at once.

Both the federal and state commission staffs tried to make sure that the state and federal agencies had in place the capacity to monitor their work effectively, with respect to both cost and schedules. To be effective, monitoring had to link early detection of problems with quick corrective action. The commission staff had a goal of correcting every administrative delay within twenty-four hours of its detection, regardless of the agency involved.

In addition, as the agencies focused on compliance and internal auditing, the executive director asked the Comptroller General to immediately assign several personnel from the General Accounting Office (GAO) to assist in early detection of waste and abuse.

OUTCOMES

The principal goals of the recovery—preventing abandonment by a substantial portion of Alaskan residents, and averting the collapse of the state economy—were achieved. Alaska, soon aided by the development of oil, moved forward rapidly with economic development. Except for several small Indian villages, the devastated communities did rebuild, including Valdez, which relocated to a safer location. Both Valdez and Anchorage were declared All American Cities several years later.

The recovery was widely regarded as a successful demonstration of how the federal, state, and local governments can work together with business and non-profit groups and function as community teams to overcome a catastrophic disaster. Each community had special challenges, and different solutions had to be developed to meet each of them. Yet the basic management strategies fostered by President Johnson's commission provided a framework under which local solutions could be implemented at a record pace.

Five months after the earthquake, the *Anchorage Daily News*—which had initially criticized the president for not visiting Alaska and for appointing an executive director without disaster response experience—lauded the "remarkable" performance of the Commission staff:

> The staff work performed by the federal Alaska Reconstruction Commission has been a display of government at its very best. . . . In many cases the normal rules followed by federal agencies were sprung completely out of shape to fit the post-earthquake needs of Alaska. Tight time schedules established for construction work became even tighter under the staff's constant prodding and watchful eye. . . . It was a rare day when a problem was posed without being accompanied by a solution.

The article concluded: "If more government officials functioned with the same type of positive outlook and attention to needs and details, that word 'bureaucrat' would fast disappear from popular dictionaries."[20]

Governor Egan declared that the commission "accomplished more than an outstanding job" in behalf of Alaska, and that the "Federal, State and local efforts were coordinated throughout the critical phase of the Rebuild Alaska program, in a way which, I am certain, has never been previously accomplished in the history of American disasters."[21] A year later, in reference to all the public and private groups that had been involved in the recovery, the *Anchorage Daily News* wrote, "The comeback from disaster was so dramatic there hardly seemed to be a gap between destruction and reconstruction. The recovery period was almost as dramatic and breathtaking as the earthquake."[22]

PRINCIPLES OF EFFECTIVENESS

The recovery from the Good Friday earthquake demonstrated how a small but empowered and focused commission operating under the authority of the president can serve as an effective hub for interagency action, particularly when responding to a mission of limited duration that is expected to involve a wide range of interdependent activities and agencies. Under this Alaskan approach, the role of the small White House organization was to (1) establish policy, and (2) mobilize, coordinate, and expedite the existing departments and agencies of the federal government, rather than do the work itself. The departments were an integral part of this policy organization as well as the doers. They had a greater incentive to respond to demands on their own resources, since they played a principal role in determining how and where to apply them.

Notably, the commission did not diminish the need for a permanent federal agency to lead the initial emergency phase of coordinating national support in responding to a major disaster. The Office of Emergency Preparedness performed that role. It operated within the Alaskan commission framework as an independent agency and was never integrated structurally or operationally within a larger institution. OEP was free to move quickly and exercise as much initiative as it wished, and the commission role was to strengthen its ability to function, quite unlike the FEMA experience in Katrina. Indeed, for routine disasters, this emergency-focused organization may handle the principal federal coordinating role, since those recoveries will not involve the huge, complex federal effort required by catastrophic disasters or terrorist attacks.

Because the Alaskan commission existed for only a few months, and was led by the agency leaders themselves as members of the commission (with the personal support of the president), the commission was not threatening to agencies, and did not develop into another layer of the federal government. Its operations were small and inexpensive, yet capable of mobilizing resources across the federal government.

The performance of the Alaskan recovery commission does not suggest that the White House be a permanent location for an operational entity along the lines described in this study. As a permanent feature of the White House, an operational entity would lose its image as a functioning arm of the departments and agencies. Indeed, over time, a permanent office would probably weaken, rather than reinforce, the capacity of major departments to act. The result would likely be a duplication of effort, entangling the president and his top assistants in operational controversies and diverting the Executive Office of the White House from focusing on its management and policy leadership roles.

If, on the other hand, future administrations face similar circumstances, the commission concept may suit them well for addressing unanticipated, unprecedented, and pressing short-term challenges. Based on the experience of the Alaskan recovery effort, principles to guide a similar organization might include the following:

Maintain Openness

Alaska demonstrated that, contrary to conventional wisdom, a high degree of openness can at times save considerable time over the life of a major project; increase public understanding; and enhance accountability. In Alaska, it also reduced potential opposition to decisions, and developed a sense of public ownership in the recovery plans that increased their incentive to help ensure success.

Partnership of Political and Career Leaders

The Alaskan experience demonstrated the value of both (1) experienced political leadership, in this case exemplified by both Johnson and Anderson, and (2) reliance on experienced career men and women assigned to the White House and on those in the participating departments to provide operational leadership. Because career officials knew how the government was organized and how to make it work, experienced political and career public servants together proved more adept at managing risks, adapting organizations to unfamiliar roles and processes, and facilitating collaboration. Placing operations in the hands of career personnel also enhanced congressional confidence in the executive branch's professional handling of the recovery.

However, the Alaskan reliance on career leadership would not have been so successful had there not been a high level of trust between political and career leaders in both the White House and the departments. As David Abshire has reminded us, and as Bryce Harlow taught us in the Eisenhower administration, "Trust is the coin of the Realm."[23]

Unleash Innovation

One of the most rewarding developments in the recovery was the impressive degree to which the reliance on career men and women—and the freedom they were given at every level to exercise initiative—brought out the innovative characteristics which most public servants have, but normally feel constrained from using.[24] The commission contribution was not to show agency people how to invent more effective management practices, so much as to free them to seek creative solutions within the broad management strategies we outlined—and motivating them to do so.

Seek Effective Congressional Relationships

Alaska demonstrated the value of creating special relationships of limited duration between the legislative and executive branches during a crisis. For example, the assignment of professionally qualified congressional staff to the executive director proved very useful. Without the special linkages that enabled Congress to keep abreast of events at both the policy and operating levels, and without the openness that increased public confidence in the recovery plans, the legislative proposals could not have found their way through the bitter 1964 congressional civil rights debates quickly enough to move forward with critical elements of the recovery during the first several months.

Establish Interagency Management

The Alaskan experience shows that it is possible for a group operating out of the White House to quickly develop effective interagency action using innovative strategies. Special attention had to be paid to developing a strong sense of teamwork while retaining clear accountability and the capacity to act quickly. It should be noted that the Alaskan recovery would not have been organized and made operational so quickly without the institutional management staff in the Bureau of the Budget. Although the Bureau did not become involved in day-to-day operations, it facilitated the ability of the commission staff to exercise its leadership role.

Simplicity

The greater the magnitude of the disaster or attack, the greater the necessity of employing a recovery structure that can adapt quickly to unforeseen circumstances, mobilize resources throughout the government, and move into action without delay. A widely accepted approach is to develop plans which attempt to anticipate every possible situation, and maintain structures and procedures designed to deal with these countless possible scenarios. However, some believe that this concept tends to focus recovery officials too heavily on procedural and jurisdictional issues, rather than on the mission. Maintaining a predetermined, detailed machinery based on past events also runs the danger of restricting the initiative and innovation needed to tailor recoveries to the different requirements of future crises.

President Johnson and the Alaskan Commission followed an opposite approach that relied on simplicity in structure and processes, believing that this would encourage innovation and swift action. Johnson also wanted the recovery leaders to focus all their efforts on a fast recovery, without having to divert attention to the time-consuming task of also administering an agency or department. With one reporting exception, no special commission processes were established for the Alaskan recovery, but many existing ones in the participating agencies were simplified or suspended as part of the streamlining drive. No new legal authority was given to the numerous coordinating mechanisms that were utilized; instead, the recovery effort relied on the existing authority of the agencies from which the participating members were detailed. The commission's focus was on the use of highly qualified personnel, not additional structures and procedures. Following the intense commission activity for six months after the Alaskan earthquake, the longer-range recovery activities were handled very well by the participating agencies, with no need to maintain and fund a permanent recovery organization.

Innovation

It was fortunate that the commission staff was permitted to develop and install a comprehensive range of innovative management strategies for the Alaskan recovery at the very beginning. Without the unprecedented freedom to streamline agency processes through decentralization, for example; without the operating decision-making capacity given the executive director and agency career leaders; without the unusual degree of openness; without the insistence on highly qualified and experienced personnel; and without the special level of attention to monitoring and oversight, construction could not have moved rapidly enough to avoid the evacuation of many thousands of families and economic disaster.

NOTES

1. See Center of Military History files: Truman R. Strobridge, *Operation Helping Hand: The United States Army and the Alaska Earthquake, 27 March to 7 May, 1964* (Historian, U.S. Army, Alaska); *Operation Helping Hand: The Armed Forces React to Earthquake Disaster* (Headquarters, Alaskan Command, 1964), Army Medical Service Activities, Annual Rpts, U.S. Army Alaska; HQ, U.S. Army Alaska; Support Command, and Fort Richardson; 64th Field Hospital; and Bassett Army Hospital.

2. Ibid.

3. Edward A. McDermott, "The Alaska Earthquake—A Lesson for NATO," *NATO Letter* (November 1964): 8–15.

4. Office of Civil Defense, "The Alaskan Earthquake: A Preliminary Report concerning the Great Earthquake That Struck South-Central Alaska on Good Friday, March 27, 1964, and Subsequent Civil Defense Emergency Operations" (Washington, DC: 1964).

5. See, for example, Daniel Yutzy and J. Eugene Haas, "Disaster and Functional Priorities in Anchorage," Committee on the Alaska Earthquake of the National Research Council, ed., *The Great Alaska Earthquake of 1964, "Human Ecology Volume"* (Washington, DC: National Academy of Sciences, 1970), 90–95.

6. For an overview, see David R. Godschalk et al., *Natural Hazard Mitigation: Recasting Disaster Policy and Planning* (Washington, DC: Island Press, 1999), 3–20.

7. Office of Emergency Planning, Executive Office of the President, *Impact of Earthquake of March 27, 1964 upon the Economy of Alaska* (Washington, DC: Federal Reconstruction and Development Planning Commission, 1964).

8. Federal Reconstruction and Development Planning Commission for Alaska, *Response to Disaster: Alaskan Earthquake, March 27,* 1964 (Washington, DC: Government Printing Office, 1964). On April 2, 1964, President Johnson signed Executive Order 11150 establishing the Federal Reconstruction and Development Planning Commission for Alaska.

9. Anderson had recommended my appointment based on my role in the Atomic Energy Commission (AEC) that had brought me in close contact with him as chair of the Congressional Joint Committee on Atomic Energy. I had also served as the neutral "liaison" between Anderson and Lewis Strauss during the failed effort of Strauss to gain confirmation as President Dwight D. Eisenhower's nominee for secretary of commerce, arguably the bitterest cabinet confirmation battle in our nation's history. Because the AEC had developed a strong reputation of good management, the Bureau of the Budget (BOB) had also recommended my appointment. This background had earned me the trust of both Anderson and BOB, a factor that was of enormous help in the rebuilding. Even more important was the trust that Johnson placed in his close friend, Anderson. Operating under tremendous pressure, this element of trust often substituted for the more typical formal communications and clearances.

10. Dwight A. Ink, "The President as Manager," *Public Administration Review* 36, no. 5 (September–October, 1976): 508–15.

11. E. B. Eckel, "The Alaska Earthquake March 27, 1964—Lesson Learned and Conclusions," *U.S. Geological Survey Professional Paper 546* (1970).

12. Dwight Ink and Alan L. Dean, "Modernizing Federal Field Operations," in Thomas H. Stanton and Benjamin Ginsberg, *Making Government Manageable: Executive Organization and Management in the Twenty First Century* (Baltimore: Johns Hopkins University Press, 2001), 194–95.

13. Ross R. Rice, "The 1964 Elections in the West," *The Western Political Quarterly* 18, no. 2 (June 1965): 431–38.

14. Howard Kunreuther and Elissandra S Fiore, "The Alaskan Earthquake: A Case Study in the Economics of Disaster," Institute for Defense Analyses (February 1966).

15. W. R. Hansen et al., "The Alaska Earthquake, March 27, 1964—Field Investigations and Reconstruction Effort," U.S. Geological Survey Professional Paper 541.

16. University of Alaska Consortium, Special Collections, Senator Clinton Anderson Speech, April 27, 1964, Box 1, Series, tapes, April 1964, Historical Manuscripts Collection, Part 3, Tapes and Records.

17. See Lidia Selkregg and Jane Preuss, *Seismic Hazard Mitigation Planning and Policy Implementation: The Alaska Case* (Washington, DC: National Institution for Standards and Training, 1984).

18. W. A. Jacobs, *The Alaska District Corps of Engineers, 1947–1974* (Elmendorf Air Force Base, Alaska: 1976), 97–104.

19. Peter J. May, "Formulating Disaster Relief When Needs Are Unknown," *Journal of Policy Analysis and Management* 2, no. 1 (Autumn 1982): 39–54.

20. "Government at Its Best," *Anchorage Daily News*, August 10, 1964.

21. Letter to Dwight Ink, dated October 12, 1964.

22. *Anchorage Daily News*, March 27, 1965, 1.

23. David Abshire, *Saving the Reagan Presidency: Trust Is the Coin of the Realm* (College Station: Texas A&M University Press, 2005).

24. See Steven Kelman, *Unleashing Change* (Washington, DC: The Brookings Institution Press, 2005).

5
Chapter

Winning Hearts and Minds: The Vietnam Experience

Richard W. Stewart

Armies do more than fight wars. Contrary to popular belief the U.S. Army has conducted many pacification, civil support, and counterinsurgency missions, the majority of which were quite successful. During America's nineteenth-century westward expansion, the army fought on the frontier pacifying, and resettling American Indians. As U.S. influence expanded overseas, the army undertook a series of successful pacification campaigns in the Philippines. After World War II, America's army gained additional experience in guerrilla warfare and pacification from its advisory role in the Greek civil war against the Communist guerilas. Military advisors also helped the newly independent Philippine government suppress a Communist insurrection in the 1940s and 1950s.

The greatest counterinsurgency challenge that the army faced in the twentieth century was undoubtedly in South Vietnam. No trial tested the army's resolve, training, doctrine, and personnel as thoroughly as during America's longest war. Although all of the military services played a role in the conflict, the army shouldered the majority of the burden in providing the personnel and expertise for fighting the counterinsurgency war. The army also bore the major responsibility of garnering interagency support for implementing pacification and development efforts.

South Vietnam has struggled with insurgencies since its creation by the Geneva Peace Accords in July 1954. The government of President Ngo Dinh Diem and then, after his murder in 1963, a bewildering succession of generals, each developed a number of pacification schemes to "win the hearts and minds" of their citizens. Neither Diem's "Strategic Hamlet" initiatives nor the later Chien Thang, (Will to Victory) or Hop Tac (Victory) programs significantly weakened the Viet Cong hold on the countryside.[1]

The arrival of major American combat units in the summer and fall of 1965 seemingly pushed the pacification struggle into the background. The deployment of U.S. forces, however, also marked the beginning of a long ad hoc effort to build an effective support program for the South Vietnamese government. The administration of Nguyen Cao Ky and later Nguyen Van Thieu reached a degree of political stability, and began to put more of efforts into the "other war," while U.S. forces erected a defensive shield in support of these efforts.

Behind the military shield repelling both the insurgents in the south and the invading enemy armies from the north, the government began to reestablish a wide range of administration, economic development, regional security, refugee control, anti–Viet Cong infrastructure, and national police programs, as well as engage in other pacification activities. This effort proved largely successful, though it was undermined by the withdrawal of U.S. support in 1975, precipitating the collapse of resistance to a powerful North Vietnamese invasion.

AMERICA'S MISSION IN VIETNAM

In 1965, U.S. Mission offices in Saigon headed the pacification effort, while simultaneously attempting to coordinate an ever-expanding plethora of stabilization programs. The State Department, CIA, U.S. Agency for International Development (USAID), U.S. Department of Agriculture (USDA), and the U.S. Information Service (USIS) all participated in the effort. Meanwhile, Military Assistance Command Vietnam (MACV) headed the military advisory effort, focused primarily on training the Republic of Vietnam Armed Forces to enable them to provide security for their citizens.

No one entity controlled the entire pacification effort. Military assets remained outside the direct purview of the U.S. embassy. Although the MACV Commander met regularly with the ambassador, the two officials could not coordinate the military and civilian programs entirely. Even within the embassy, attempts to organize the various programs run by different agencies with different lines of authority, varying budgets, and divergent institutional cultures faltered, making integration difficult.

As the programs grew in size and complexity poor coordination got worse. By May 1967, the embassy reached the limit of its management capacity. Consequently, military and civilian authorities adopted a new organizational and management approach toward pacification—the Office of Civil Operations and Revolutionary Development Support (CORDS).

CORDS placed virtually all interagency assets involved in the pacification struggle under one civilian manager. In turn, the director of CORDS operated within the military hierarchy as the Deputy Commander of MACV. This bold move provided the pacification support effort nearly unfettered access to military resources, personnel, and logistics. An innovative attempt to build and operate a truly effective interagency headquarters, CORDS blended civilian and military agencies and personnel, focused on one mission—improving the flow of pacification support to the government of South Vietnam.

DISORGANIZING FOR COMBAT

From 1954 to 1964 the American effort to bring peace and stability to South Vietnam can be called ad hoc at best. U.S. initiatives included establishing and sustaining a wide variety of aid programs to distribute seed, tools, fertilizers, animals, and farming techniques to improve the standard of living. In addition, the United States worked with a variety of national and international programs to provide vaccinations, medical supplies, doctors, and other health services to poor villagers. American officials were also instrumental in establishing basic training programs in government and administration aimed at lasting basic reforms including fighting corruption and support for land redistribution initiatives. Either the U.S. embassy (established in 1961) or USAID organized most of these activities. USAID also operated outside of Saigon with advisors in all of the 234 districts and 44 provinces. Agency funding amounted to around $222 million per year from 1955 to 1960. USAID was by far the primary agency in South Vietnam for political and economic development prior to the military buildup in 1965.[2]

With some CIA, USIS, and military support, advisors also worked with the South Vietnamese government on a variety of initiatives to bring economic development, security, and government reform to the countryside, so as to undercut the political programs of the Viet Cong, and pacify the countryside. Because the guerrillas and their North Vietnamese supporters could be counted on to resist such efforts, the real crux of the problem was how to simultaneously provide security and promote economic development and the growth of governmental capacity.[3]

By late 1964, assistance, governance, and pacification programs were failing. Despite pressure from Washington for more dramatic actions and measurable success, it was clear that the handful of civilians on the embassy staff could not manage the growing efforts. Neither Ambassador Henry Cabot Lodge nor his successor, Maxwell Taylor, proved able to develop a workable arrangement.[4]

Taylor, who had a letter from the president giving him "full responsibility for the effort of the United States Government in South Vietnam," used that authority to create a "Mission Council" to meet weekly with senior representatives of the various programs, but it was still just a form of coordination.[5] Each major agency retained the right to appeal any decisions with their parent agency in Washington. There was no central plan, no central budget, and no central direction to force the components to work together or reallocate resources without Washington's express approval.

It took presidential power to cut the Gordian knot. Impatient with the lack of consensus and progress, President Lyndon Johnson decided to address the issue during a conference of South Vietnamese leaders in February 1966. Johnson later

stated, "I wanted to see progress, not just reports." Thus, he "ordered a reorganization of our Mission in Saigon to reflect this new emphasis on nonmilitary
programs."[6] He directed that Lodge's deputy take direct, full-time charge of the
effort in Vietnam. Johnson also established a White House special assistant for
pacification. He appointed Robert W. Komer from his National Security Council
staff to the position, and gave him the task of coordinating the Washington end of
the interagency challenge.

Little changed with the presidential appointments. The embassy remained
just a coordinator of programs, failing to transform into a hands-on, take-charge
manager. Even more critical was the inability to merge any of the military programs and civilian programs, or even to establish a mechanism to enhance unified
planning or execution of effort. The State Department "adamantly contended that
the other war ought to remain in civilian hands."[7] The U.S.-led pacification
campaign appeared to be at an impasse.

In October 1966, still unsatisfied with the embassy's approach to managing
pacification, Johnson launched a fact-finding mission. The mission's recommendations resulted in a new organization—the Office of Civil Operations (OCO).
Still housed in the embassy, the office had an explicit mandate to make dramatic
improvements across the board within 90 to 120 days or else be subsumed under
MACV. Although ostensibly giving the embassy another chance to manage the
issue, OCO was not the single-manager operation that the president believed was
the right solution.

L. Wade Lathram, the deputy director of USAID managed OCO's daily operations. All personnel supporting USAID projects, the revolutionary development
program of expanding government presence in the countryside refugee support,
the Chieu Hoi amnesty program, and public safety (police and justice) were
included in the office. Many advisors to this program were CIA personnel under
cover as USAID employees. For the first time all U.S. civilians in Saigon and the
provinces, with the exception of some sensitive CIA intelligence collection activities, reported through a single chain of command to a single manager in the
embassy. OCO still had two significant problems: (1) it did not control the
military advisors and, (2) it only had a few months to prove itself. OCO proved an
important initiative that tried, in the short time given, but failed to pull the
administrative threads together on the entire range of civilian programs working
on economic and governmental development.

OCO attempted to make a quick impact on pacification, but, from the beginning, it had faced two major problems. The office required over 175 new civilians
to staff its headquarters in Saigon as well as the positions of the senior province
representatives and regional directors. Unlike positions that were filled by military
personnel who could be, and often were, directed into positions regardless of personal preference, these positions had to be filled using a time-consuming civilian
recruitment process. The regional directorships were especially critical to the program's success, but the slow nature of the hiring process ensured that all four of
these senior management positions were not filled until February 1967. By the end

of that month, and over halfway through its projected lifespan, almost one-third of the civilian positions in OCO remained vacant.[8]

The challenges of filling civilian positions within OCO and the continuing lack of authority over the military advisors doomed the initiative. OCO was unable even to start to generate integrated civil-military pacification plans, much less establish necessary links with MACV and the Vietnamese Armed Forces personnel and programs, create goals and milestones for measuring success, and make visible progress.

A FRESH START

CORDS replaced OCO, finally combining all the elements of U.S. support. On May 9, 1967, Johnson appointed Komer to the rank of ambassador and assigned him to MACV as Deputy COMUSMACV, for CORDS. Westmoreland and Komer, despite some initial friction, very quickly recognized each other's genuine commitment to accomplishing the U.S. mission, and Westmoreland increasingly grew to trust Komer as the single component commander in charge of military and civilian support to pacification.

It is temping to view the two years of organizational effort that finally resulted in CORDS as a waste of time, but at the time the benefit of the arrangement was not as clear as it might seem in hindsight. In many other insurgency-stricken countries, somewhere the United States had substantial military aid efforts, the "country team" approach of placing various agencies and the military under the direction of the ambassador worked adequately. The ambassador was responsible for the success or failure of the assistance effort in the country. Unifying such a complex, mostly civilian, effort under the ambassador made a great deal of sense. The culture of the State Department emphasized collegiality and cooperation and shied away from operational planning and strong management or command and control systems that typified Department of Defense–led operations. This arrangement suited the various agency representatives well who had no problem serving under the ambassador's leadership as long as they were not overly supervised.

Two main factors, however, overwhelmed attempts to make the country team model work in South Vietnam:

1. The size of the American effort from 1960 to 1966 to counter the increased infiltration by the North Vietnamese made management challenges overwhelming. Assistance grew at least tenfold in just a few years. The flood of soldiers, advisers, dollars, and programs simply grew too large for a small embassy staff. Likewise, the security dangers, a combination of a wide spread insurgency and the conventional military threat of an invading army, proved too daunting to control.
2. A well-intentioned but slow effort to coordinate the actions of a host of governmental bureaucracies, all of which maintained direct links back to the interagency morass of Washington, proved dysfunctional.

CORDS IN CONTACT

As the head of CORDS, Komer had to pull together a multitude of civilian and military pacification threads; get them to jointly plan toward a set of agreed upon common goals; monitor progress; move resources; and measure those results against some as yet to be identified standard so that an objective observer could see progress. All of these objectives had to be accomplished in tandem with a barely functioning, corrupt, poorly led, and rudimentary South Vietnamese administration.

Komer's first task was to merge military and civilian personnel, with contrasting institutional cultures and competencies, into a coherent whole. He then had to energize the new organization, quickly focus it on delivering results, and subsequently set the stage for long-term cooperation between American and Vietnamese military and civilian structures. Finally, it was critical that the unity of effort exhibited at the Saigon headquarters be duplicated down the chain of command to the regions and provinces so that the "single manager" concept would run the pacification struggle at the hamlet and village levels.

The challenge of successfully mixing military and civilian personnel proved critical to CORDS's long-term success. Military personnel were to be put in charge of civilians, but civilians were also to be placed in charge of military personnel to create a truly mixed, interagency team based on skills and abilities, not agency loyalty. As proof of his commitment to a mixed headquarters, Komer choose his senior directors carefully to ensure that senior civilians received their share of the positions, dispelling the fear that the key slots would be assigned to military personnel. In addition, when a senior civilian was assigned to a key headquarters position, almost invariably he had a military assistant reporting to him and the reverse was true when a military officer was in the principal slot. This blending of military and civilian authority included the use of the power of personnel evaluation or rating authority. As Komer later wrote, "To show all concerned we intend to have a genuine civil-military team, the senior officer in each case—military or civilian—should write the efficiency reports of those next below him."[9] All in all, Komer's policies resulted in a laudable attempt to establish a careful balance between military and civilian key management.[10]

Centralized planning and centralized accountability became CORDS hallmarks. To accomplish those goals, Komer organized CORDS under a headquarters staff element with an operations office and an executive secretariat. The headquarters were comprised of four main staff elements:

1. The Research and Analysis Division (RAD) employed a variety of quantitative and qualitative measurements, including operations research and systems analysis, to assess the effectiveness of pacification efforts. The RAD collected and analyzed data from the Hamlet Evaluation System (HES), designed to measure the degree to which the population was considered under government control. The aim of the evaluation system was to collect monthly data on enemy and friendly operations and development progress in all the hamlets nationwide in order to produce an essentially subjective (yet quantified) judgment on the fluctuating

security levels over time. Evaluations yielded labels of "A," "B," "C," "D," E," or "V," with "A" equaling the highest level of government control and "V," equaling Viet Cong–controlled.[11]

2. Reports and Evaluation Division (RED) evaluated the accuracy of the regularly collected field reports by conducting continuous and independent field evaluations of all aspects of pacification, especially the degree of success of the revolutionary development cadre program.

3. The Plans and Programs Division (PPD) worked with the Vietnamese government elements responsible for pacification, especially the Ministry for Revolutionary Development and the Joint General Staff, to develop unified and coherent military and civilian pacification plans. The division coordinated the preparation of what had never previously existed: an integrated, combined, staffed, yearly plan with implementing tasks for the conduct of all pacification operations throughout the country.

4. Management Support Division assisted a variety of civil agencies and personnel involved in pacification including by managing contracts, providing telecommunications support, training CORDS personnel, hiring civilians, and supplying general administrative support.

In addition to a central headquarters, colocated with MACV, CORDS had to merge all legacy development and governance programs into its organization. The most significant of these became new divisions within CORDS: New Life Development (developmental aid to villages), Chieu Hoi (encouraging Viet Cong to defect), Revolutionary Development Cadre (good governance programs at the local level), Refugee Support (managing the movement, housing, and relocation of refugees), PSYOP (providing tactical psychological operations for the Chieu Hoi and local government programs), and Public Safety (strengthening the National Police and National Police Field Forces to attack Viet Cong infrastructure). This mix of programs included all of the key elements of U.S. government support to the developmental and local security initiatives undertaken by the South Vietnamese government.

PROJECT TAKEOFF

With the establishment of CORDS, all MACV pacification support assets fell under one headquarters, one manager. The struggle to make CORDS a fully functioning and effective headquarters, however, had just begun. CORDS had to define and implement plans and goals that would make the pieces actually work together toward common aims, while fighting off inevitable attempts by parts of the new organization to revert to its "usual" chain of command. USAID and CIA, in particular, retained contacts with their parent headquarters in Washington. Both had a penchant for playing off one headquarters against another. Equally pressing, CORDS had to ensure that the government in Saigon established a parallel pacification structure. It was, after all, South Vietnam's war to lose. Although America remained South Vietnam's "senior partner" due to its size and resources, Komer wanted to develop the Vietnamese' abilities to increasingly run their own programs.

Komer began planning for a larger headquarters using military personnel and additional funds from MACV. He also initiated a program to hire additional civilians, including third country nationals, and Vietnamese. Moving rapidly to expand his control over provincial pacification personnel, Komer nearly doubled the size of CORDS (from 4,980 to 8,327) within the first six months of its existence.[12]

To showcase successes, Komer set up eight action programs under "Project Takeoff," focusing the majority of the assets on the most imminent problems.[13] These included the following:

1. Improve Pacification Planning for 1968
2. Accelerate the Chieu Hoi Program
3. Mount an attack on the VC Infrastructure
4. Expand and Improve ARVN Support to Pacification
5. Expand and Supplement the RD Team Effort
6. Increase the Capability to Handle Refugees
7. Revamp the Police Forces
8. Press Land Reform

Komer insisted on measurable progress in every area.[14] Each initiative had to be quantifiable so that resource allocation could be justified back in Washington or shifted when programs did not deliver. Komer expected dramatic results within six months and his hard-charging and often abrasive management style began to energize Project Takeoff from day one.

ATTACKING THE INSURGENCY

Project Takeoff's first priority was to better coordinate the military and police response to the Viet Cong shadow government—the Viet Cong Infrastructure. Part of the solution lay with the revitalization of the National Police System by CORDS's Public Safety Division. The division prepared an ambitious Action Program as part of Project Takeoff including expanding the number of the police and U.S. advisors to the police; improving the resource control operations; implementing a new National Identity Card; building new police and incarceration facilities; combating corruption within the police forces (which had previously been an endemic problem); establishing better police training programs; and increasing the budgets to hire more police officers and improve their operations.[15]

The plan immediately began to show progress. By the end of 1967, police end-strength grew from 66,000 to almost 73,371. By the end of 1968, that number had grown to some 79,080. The government also was convinced to expand the National Police Field Force, a more heavily armed paramilitary structure, into sixty-seven operational companies for a total of almost 11,960 policemen by the end of 1968.[16]

Project Takeoff also attempted to improve the intelligence gathering capabilities of the National Police. A new program, known as ICEX (Intelligence Coordination and Exploitation), established a high-level U.S. committee, consisting of the deputy for CORDS (Komer), the special assistant to the U.S. ambassador (the CIA station chief), the MACV J2 (Intelligence) and J3 (Operations), and the CORDS Chief of Revolutionary Development Division. Despite the initially lukewarm response of the South Vietnamese head of the National Police, Komer pressed the Vietnamese hard to establish Provincial Intelligence Coordinating Committees and Provincial Interrogation Centers in order to create nodes of intelligence coordination.

Emphasis on finding and destroying the enemy's infrastructure led to the creation of another initiative, probably the most misunderstood and maligned of the war—Phung Hoang or the Phoenix program. Begun as a CIA operation, often with officers posing as members of USAID, Phoenix established special units in the provinces to go after the shadow government. Operating in secret deep inside enemy territory, the teams hunted down and captured or killed Communist leaders. The CIA, in conjunction with the South Vietnamese Central Intelligence Organization modeled on its American counterpart, also assisted in the creation of District Operations and Intelligence Coordinating Centers to assist in the intelligence collection and prisoner interrogation processes. CORDS integrated the CIA effort with the larger National Police and Phoenix structure and its Revolutionary Development Cadre Program. William Colby, chief of the CIA's Far East Division, became Komer's deputy. Colby brought the full range of U.S. assets, military and civilian, to the task of pacification.[17]

PLANNING FOR PACIFICATION

Komer and his staff also started planning for a pacification campaign which integrated all operational control under CORDS. He initiated a joint planning group consisting of CORDS, USAID, and psychological operations (PSYOP) planners from the Joint U.S. Public Affairs Office. On the South Vietnamese side, the central Revolutionary Development Ministry established a series of councils in each of the provinces to analyze central government plans before implementation to ensure that they accurately reflected the capabilities on the ground. In addition, the local councils, working with the newly unified U.S. province advisory network, provided a venue for coordinating and implementing the plan. In December 1968, the councils were renamed Pacification and Development Councils and expanded to include all pacification initiatives at the local level, including education and youth, economic development, public works, ethnic minorities, health and welfare programs.[18]

The CORDS planning effort resulted in Plan AB 143, the Combined Campaign Plan for 1968. For the first time, it addressed all aspects of the South Vietnamese and U.S. pacification missions. Coordination challenges persisted until the end of the American involvement in Vietnam—but at least after years of policy drift there was a published, agreed-upon road map that had the potential to achieve some measure of synergy.[19] CORDS created a new campaign plan each year. During the rest of the war, shifting pacification circumstances, such

as those which occurred during the Tet Offensive, a major uprising by the Viet
Cong in 1968, would require modifying plans, shifting focus, and reallocating
resources.

CHIEU HOI!

In its first six months, CORDS also put additional emphasis on three territorial security related elements: the Chieu Hoi enemy deserter program; ameliorat-
ing pacification support for the Vietnamese military; and upgrading the Regional
Forces/ Popular Forces (RF/PF). The Chieu Hoi program, in particular, proved
highly successful. Komer, in his initial review, declared himself a "firm believer" in
its success and urged the South Vietnamese government to give it a higher priority. It was, after all, a very cost-effective program. For a mere average of $150 per
returnee, over two hundred thousand Viet Cong defected to the government side
by the end of 1972.[20]

VC Hoi Chanh (returnees) would surrender using safe conduct passes and,
after a short period of internment to ensure that they were legitimate deserters
and not Viet Cong agents, they would be retrained in a craft or given some land
for farming and then resettled. Often they would volunteer to write letters to their
former comrades testifying to their good treatment and the government would
thereby gain additional returnees. The Chieu Hoi numbers alone, regardless of
other indicators, showed clearly that the Viet Cong were mostly a spent force by
the time of the North Vietnamese truce in January 1973 and the subsequent disestablishment of CORDS.

The growing success of Chieu Hoi led the Armed Propaganda Teams (APT)
to attempt to encourage even more Viet Cong personnel to defect. These teams
were comprised of armed units of Vietnamese soldiers that penetrated Viet
Cong-held regions with loudspeakers, leaflets, and later even small "Cultural
Drama" Teams to contact enemy soldiers and their families with information
about how to "rally." By the end of 1969, some five thousand APT members were
organized into fifty-one companies: thirty-six with three platoons each and fifteen
with two platoons each.[21]

Expanding and improving military support for pacification efforts dovetailed
with CORDS's commitment to ramp-up Chieu Hoi. While the American armed
forces took on the main opponents, Viet Cong and North Vietnamese Regulars,
the South Vietnamese military concentrated on two basic missions: building itself
into a more capable national army, navy, air force, and marines and supporting
the pacification struggle. Komer later wrote, "One key achievement was its initial
stress on generating sustained local security in the countryside as the *indispensa-
ble* [emphasis added] prerequisite to effective pacification."[22] Without adequate
security in the countryside, development and true pacification—obtaining and
retaining the loyalty of the people—was impossible.

The South Vietnamese's military support of the pacification struggle took
two forms: training support for conventional forces, especially the Vietnamese

army; and establishing mobile training teams for the provincial forces. CORDS coordinated with MACV to establish fourteen Vietnamese Revolutionary Development Mobile Training Teams. The teams, in conjunction with army units, conducted a series of two-week training sessions, including basic soldier skills and sensitizing soldiers on "how to get along with the VN populace, a skill heretofore conspicuously lacking" according to the MACV historian.[23] In essence, the Vietnamese army needed to be better trained in how not to behave so that they would not undercut pacification efforts. After a slow start, by the end of 1968, with continued pressure by CORDS and MACV on the South Vietnamese, pacification support training had markedly improved, with over 90 percent of battalions receiving the course.

REGIONAL FORCES/POPULAR FORCES

MACV retained the mission of training the conventional Vietnamese armed forces and managed all related advisory efforts, including training of advisors, overseeing training areas, distributing funds, and generating policies to support this effort. However, MACV had never been closely involved in training or providing advisors to those elements of the armed forces that were most heavily involved in supporting the Revolutionary Development programs and pacification efforts. These were the Regional Forces (RF) and Popular Forces (PF), militia-like organizations that were vital to securing hamlets and villages at the local level and served as first responders to small-scale enemy attacks in their districts.[24] Regional Forces were mobile companies capable of small unit patrolling and conducting ambushes on Viet Cong units. The Popular Forces were numerous (around three hundred thousand in 1967 by most counts), mostly static guard troops, whose men were neither well trained nor armed and who constantly lost personnel to desertion and military levies to the regular army. Increasingly, despite their shortcomings, these militia forces were seen as one of the keys to local security.[25]

MACV provided some advisors to the Popular Forces, but the militia's training had never been a priority. In 1965, MACV had only 382 officers and 353 noncommissioned officers (NCOs) assigned to this mission, though it had a plan to increase that number by 108 officers and 72 NCOs over the course of the year. Interest, however, soon leveled off as the priority shifted to strengthening the regular army forces. Poorly armed and led, the militias bore the brunt of the fight against the Viet Cong with little assistance. Despite a lack of respect from the regular military, poor pay, cast-off arms and a shortage of medical care, these units accounted for up to 40 percent of the total South Vietnamese combat casualties in 1965 and 1966. Popular Forces units were considered by some to be the "largest armed body in direct contact with the rural population" although it had not "achieved, overall, the degree of combat success of which it is capable."[26] CORDS set out to address both concerns.

Komer requested a study of the advisory support provided to the Regional and Popular Forces. The results were not promising. Komer reported to

Assistant Secretary of Defense for International Security Affairs John T. McNaughton:

> The 300,000 man regular ARVN [Army of the Republic of Vietnam]—which gets the cream of Vietnamese manpower and leadership, has the great bulk of the firepower and mobility, and receives first priority for US support—contributes relatively little to pacification. So the indispensable local security function has suffered by being assigned mostly to low quality, mostly para-military forces inadequately trained or motivated to compete with the local VC [Viet Cong].[27]

So many resources had been devoted to building a conventional army that there was insufficient time and energy to provide essential advice and assistance to the forces that were often directly engaged with the enemy on a daily basis.

CORDS requested additional advisors from MACV, with the goal of building up a mobile advisory force, including an additional 2,331 advisors for the "neglected paramilitary forces."[28] Rather than assigning advisors directly to units, CORDS organized a series of six-man teams and assigned one to every regular Vietnamese army division and one to each province. Teams traveled from unit to unit, spending about two to three weeks with each, providing training and advice on small unit tactics such as ambushes and patrols. In addition, CORDS established ten Mobile Advisory Logistics Teams to help militias account for equipment, draw supplies, and maintain gear. CORDS also moved quickly to equip the militia forces with modern M-16 rifles to replace their old M-1 and M-2 carbines, providing them with 115,000 rifles by the end of 1968 and another 114,000 by the end of the following year.[29]

FROM TAKEOFF TO RECOVERY

Project Takeoff showed some progress in its first six months. Enemy "rallier" numbers were up. More advisors were in the field with the Regional and Popular Forces. The National Police was substantially larger, with an improved intelligence structure, and the attacks on the Viet Cong infrastructure seemed to be going well. More and more hamlets and villages were rated as "relatively secure." Komer sensed that things were going well—then came Tet.

Beginning on January 30, 1968, during the Tet Lunar New Year holidays, the enemy struck some one hundred locations with waves of bombings and infantry attacks. Saigon was hit hard. Enemy sappers even briefly penetrated the U.S. embassy compound. Thirty-nine of forty-four provincial capitals were attacked from within by VC cadre. By early February CORDS had reports of thirteen thousand civilians killed, twenty-seven thousand wounded, and at least six hundred thousand new refugees. The massive and unexpected attacks appear to have shattered the pacification program as the enemy drove advisors, government officials, police, and the local militias into retreat. Nearly 10 percent of the five thousand RF/PF outposts were abandoned or overrun and many of the surviving units withdrew into larger cities. The Vietnamese government reported losing control of over 7 percent of its population in the space of a few weeks. It was a crisis situation.[30]

Tet forced CORDS to rethink its campaign. The MACV Command History reported, "As a result of the VC [Viet Cong] Tet Offensive, pacification suffered a sharp setback." At the same time, the offensive actually created an opportunity for the government to go on a counteroffensive when it was discovered, after the initial shock waned, that the attacks were "found subsequently not to have been so extensive or so damaging in detail as was first feared."[31] On February 2, President Thieu created a Central Recovery Committee to "direct and coordinate the activities of all GVN [Government of Vietnam] agencies, both civilian and military, in expediting civil recovery from the enemy's treacherous Tet campaign."[32] Similar recovery organizations were established at the Corps, Province, District, Village, and even Hamlet levels. In addition, CORDS pressured the South Vietnamese government to establish Project Recovery to ensure that ambitious recovery goals were set and met. CORDS obtained $5 million in emergency funds and made them available immediately to U.S. advisors and local officials.[33] The focus, however, was on supporting the South Vietnamese who would then run the effort. While not always entirely successful, it was considered important that the South Vietnamese appear to be in charge.

To help implement the U.S. part of Project Recovery, CORDS established an operations center at MACV headquarters to follow the crisis and coordinate the U.S. military and civilian assistance to the Vietnamese. CORDS initially tried to coordinate every action through this operations center. Since it had a small staff, however, most major actions had to be performed by the regular staffs. However, by the end of March, Ambassador Komer made some "adjustments" to this arrangement to gain greater access to all U.S. assets in Vietnam. With the approval of U.S. Ambassador Ellsworth Bunker, Komer established a Central Coordinating Staff under Major General George Forsythe which reported directly to Komer. In addition, he created six standby Interagency Task Forces, composed of a variety of interagency representatives, to respond immediately to any taskings by this Central Staff. These task forces were logistical support, engineering support, security, refugee relief and social welfare, political and psychological support, and financial support. They were empowered to cut through the bureaucratic red tape to speed the delivery of supplies and money to action agencies at the site of a problem. The benefits of creating a headquarters with sufficient logistics capability and an abundance of trained personnel soon became apparent as CORDS helped manage the Tet crisis.[34]

Project Recovery effectively focused U.S. and Vietnamese military and civilian assets on responding to the country's most critical needs. It was important to restore the equipment of the National Police, redeploy the Regional Forces/Popular Forces and Revolutionary Development Cadre into the countryside, reestablish the various District and Province Intelligence Centers, renew the attacks on VC infrastructure (critical now that the VC had come out into the open), and begin to rebuild the economic infrastructure.[35]

As a result of Project Recovery, and despite the setbacks caused by the renewed attacks of May 1968, CORDS orchestrated a remarkable outpouring of assistance. The United States provided cash relief payments to the seven hundred fifty thousand refugees generated by Tet. The cash supplement to the normal food, tents, and resettlement aid provided to the refugees, was specifically meant to demonstrate to the victims that the Viet Cong, and not the government, was the source of their problems. By mid-May, more than five hundred thousand refugees had been resettled, over thirty-three thousand metric tons of food distributed, and sixty-six thousand tons of construction materials released to aid the rebuilding process. The South Vietnamese government disbursed over $3.8 million directly to those affected by the offensive.[36]

The Viet Cong attacks during Tet dramatically illustrated the pacification problem in the countryside. The government had not had sufficient warning. The enemy had concealed their plans well. The local security forces proved an inadequate source of local security. In addition, many of the defenders were not adequately engaged in repulsing the VC attack and seemed at best neutral to the fate of their own government. The South Vietnamese leadership, with CORDS assistance, had to deal with each of these issues.

In response to Tet, the South Vietnamese government and CORDS prepared the Accelerated Pacification Campaign plan for the remainder of 1968 and into the next year. The plan focused on attacking Viet Cong infrastructure, reorganizing and expanding the Vietnamese armed forces (especially the local militias), and accelerating the pace of local development and self-development schemes. However, Thieu and his closest advisors, shocked by the collapse of so many of their efforts in the countryside, were reluctant to support this aggressive campaign, holding out for months for a strategy of slow consolidation. Komer, working with the new MACV Commander, General Creighton W. Abrams, finally got the Vietnamese government to back his plan. In November, the South Vietnamese agreed to a plan to move their troops into the countryside so as to establish government control over 80 percent of the population. By moving military units into areas virtually abandoned by the decimated Viet Cong, the government quickly asserted control over an additional thousand contested hamlets by the end of January 1969. The Viet Cong were on the run.[37]

TURNING THE CORNER

The Revolutionary Development Cadre development teams had primarily responsibility for building a sense of civic responsibility and governmental capacity in the hamlets and villages. The groups consisted of fifty-nine members, one assigned to each hamlet to lead development efforts and generate loyalty to the government. They had suffered heavily during the Tet Offensive, but with the Viet Cong on the run, the cadre reoccupied their assigned hamlets and villages. In many places they personified the central government.

The government expanded the Revolutionary Development Cadre to 971 teams for a total of 57,000 members. They worked directly with the RF/PF and the National Police. Cadre teams arranged for local police to provide ID cards to villagers and became active in identifying and helping the National Police, and later the Phung Hoang, counter-infrastructure teams to root out the remnants of the local Viet Cong shadow government.

After Tet, the government sent out even more RD teams to the countryside. The 1969 pacification plan called for the cadres along with newly formed People's Self Defense Units to work with Popular Force militia units to improve security. The teams were tasked to increase government support in a hamlet or village and then leave the locals to develop on their own while the group moved on to help other villages. However, most teams that entered villages stayed as long as the Viet Cong did not run them out and seldom were able to continue on to new villages. It was extremely hard to build a sense of trust between the government and its people. By the early 1970s, the Revolutionary Development Program had dropped the "Revolutionary" title and the teams morphed into Rural Development/Local Development teams that essentially coordinated civil works projects and sponsored Community Development mobile training teams. By 1970, the Viet Cong specifically targeted cadre because they were so effective.[38]

TET TO THE EASTER OFFENSIVE 1972

The Tet Offensive, while devastating to U.S. public opinion, represented a catastrophe for the Viet Cong and, in the mid-term, a victory for the South Vietnamese. The attacks, little short of a national uprising, served to focus the attention of the government. As Komer later commented:

> Thus in a way Tet 1968 proved a watershed for the GVN as well as for the U.S. effort in Vietnam. GVN realization that a far greater effort would be required to survive finally led to actual national manpower mobilization, extensive training programs for local officials, a major acceleration of pacification efforts, several economic reforms, and the like.[39]

Tet accelerated the pacification effort, leading to a remarkable series of successes in the years 1968 to 1972. The Accelerated Pacification Campaign of 1968, and the ambitious expansion of all pacification programs in the years 1969–71, drove what remained of the Viet Cong cadre deep underground and limited their active involvement throughout the countryside. Despite initial concerns regarding the "languid pace" of the South Vietnamese government immediately after Tet, Komer could point to dramatic pullbacks of enemy units in many areas. Statistics also showed an increase of support for the government.[40] Estimates of Viet Cong losses continued to rise over the next two years as the Phung Hoang/Phoenix counter-infrastructure campaign hit the enemy's exposed ranks. From 1968 to the middle of 1972, Phung

Hoang/Phoenix teams reported over eighty thousand enemy either captured, killed, or rallied to the side of the government.[41] By the beginning of 1972, the various CORDS-sponsored counterinsurgency and counter-infrastructure campaigns seemed to be progressing well.

Determined to reverse the slow and steady erosion of their position in South Vietnam, the North Vietnamese launched a major, conventional offensive in early 1972. The North's leaders apparently calculated that since the Americans, by early 1972, had withdrawn virtually all of their combat units, it was prime time to strike.

The North Vietnamese offensive began early on the morning of March 30, with thirteen divisions supported by tanks and massive artillery barrages. At first the Communists made "dramatic gains", but stiffening South Vietnamese army resistance and massive U.S. air power blunted the offensive. Unfortunately, the overall performance of the territorial forces was mixed, even in areas where the enemy attacks were overwhelming.[42]

The impact of the Easter Offensive, while not as dramatic as the Tet Offensive four years earlier, was substantial. The overall "relatively secure" rating of hamlets fell from 82.7 percent just before the offensive to 70.3 percent in August. Skewing the statistics, however, was the fact that one-fifth of the hamlets had been physically occupied by North Vietnamese troops. At the peak of the occupation, the North Vietnamese still managed to control only 1,164 hamlets as opposed to the more than four thousand occupied after the Tet Offensive. After the initial shock dissipated, CORDS determined that, while the pacification struggle was certainly interrupted, the situation was "much superior to that at any time during the 1968 offensive."[43]

TRANSITION: 1972–73

CORDS faced a number of problems accelerating the process of turning over control of pacification programs to the South Vietnamese government while U.S. combat forces and military advisors drew down. Increasingly fewer advisors were available to conduct refresher training for RF/PF units in the field; units had to be brought to centralized training locations.

Staff officers worked on plans, until the cease-fire in January 1973, to leave a handful of military advisors in place, teams of "high quality generalists" prepared to "function without a high level of amenities."[44] However, the cease-fire stipulated that all American military forces, including advisors, be withdrawn within forty-five days, leaving only a handful of civilians available to provide developmental advice and support. Plans to continue some military advisory effort and even a CORDS-like structure were effectively scuttled.

GRADING CORDS

Compared to its feeble state in 1965, at the onset of major U.S. involvement, the government of Vietnam was relatively stable when CORDS was dismantled in 1973. Even if the 1973 Hamlet Evaluation System figures (which showed that the government controlled some 90 percent of the countryside) cannot be fully trusted, the great majority of hamlets, villages, districts, and provinces were relatively peaceful, experiencing only the occasional ambush or guerilla attack.[45] The regional security forces were numerous and active. Members of the National Police, while never fully having lived up to their promise, were actively tracking down the remnants of the Viet Cong shadow government. The economy stabilized and rice production rose. With a reasonably stable central government in control (despite deeply flawed elections) while not peaceful, South Vietnam was, in many ways, "pacified." That dynamic only changed with the invasion by conventional North Vietnamese forces in 1975.

Establishing effective interagency coordination proved fundamental to CORDS's success. Through coordinated action and integrated planning and support, CORDS generated measurable progress, gained South Vietnamese cooperation, and established enduring programs. Despite two major conventional attacks in 1968 and 1972, the CORDS structure helped shift U.S. attention and assets to the critical "other war." The structure allowed American and South Vietnamese programs to exploit the post-Tet period.

CORDS was a true innovation—and a successful one. Komer argued the achievement resulted from:

> First, it was a field expedient tailored to particular needs as perceived at the time. Second it was a unique experiment in a unified civil/ military field advisory and support organization, quite different from World War II civil affairs or military government. Soldiers served directly under civilians, and vice versa, at all levels. They even wrote each other's efficiency reports. ... and CORDS was fully integrated into the theater military structure. ... The cutting edge was unified civil-military advisory teams in all 250 districts and 44 provinces ... [Third, CORDS took a] relatively flexible and pragmatic approach to pacification ... CORDS in effect wrote its field manual as it went along. One key achievement was its initial stress on generating sustained local security in the countryside as the indispensable prerequisite to effective pacification at that late date.[46]

CORDS succeeded because it established effective mechanisms to integrate security and development activities.

In retrospect, centralizing control over field-based pacification programs proved to be the only viable option. The U.S. government lacked an operational doctrine to guide cooperation among agencies in the field. Only centralized control could serve as a basis for unified action. On the other hand, running complex interagency activities out of Washington would have been unrealistic.

Presidential leadership proved vital in overcoming the single greatest obstacle to mission success—the reluctance of Washington officials and senior leaders in the field to relinquish control over field operations. The State Department, under two successive ambassadors (including one retired general), resisted the idea that any of its development or pacification assets should fall under a military chain of command, even one headed by a civilian. Even after several broad hints from the administration, a presidential intervention was needed to change their minds. Johnson recognized that the pacification efforts were not working. He exercised presidential power in a most effective manner—choosing to influence strategic direction rather than attempting to manage operational activities.

Creating CORDS gave Komer, Colby, Westmoreland, and Abrams the opportunity to exercise effective leadership. As Komer later wrote,

> It is significant that not until an organization was created to focus specifically on pacification as it primary mission and to integrate all relevant military and civilian agency efforts did a major sustained pacification effort begin to take shape. The bureaucratic price that had to be paid for creating this military elephant and civilian rabbit stew was to put CORDS under the military. Paradoxically, this resulted in greater U.S. civilian influence over pacification than had ever existed before; it also powerfully reinforced pacification's claim on U.S. and GVN [government of Vietnam] military resources, which constituted the great bulk of the inputs after 1966.[47]

Without CORDS, it would have been impossible to harness the potential of American power. Johnson's decision to establish CORDS had a cascading affect on the conduct of interagency operations in the theater.

THE SINGLE-MANAGER CONCEPT

The importance of integrated management for organizing the pacification effort cannot be overestimated. Unity of command and control, a central military concept, was essential to forge CORDS into a truly effective interagency headquarters. The battle to create CORDS was not won quickly or easily. Komer, even in his position as CORDS Deputy MACV and experience as a dynamic and forceful Washington-savvy power broker struggled to maintain control and had to fight numerous attempts to shrink the CORDS structure, limit its scope, or keep additional pacification-related programs from falling under its command. This effort was compounded by continued challenges in gaining political and financial backing from Washington.[48] Without the authority to direct operational activities, he would not have been able to counteract forces aiming to dilute the CORDS effort.

The size and scope of the pacification effort were too large and demanded much more manpower and resources than the small, though well-intentioned, embassy programs could deliver. While the "country team" concept might have worked sufficiently well in theaters where there was only a small or incipient insurgency, this approach could not manage a major national pacification program that also required foremost attention to territorial security.

Only the single-manager structure within the U.S. high command proved capable of combining the benefits of military personnel, resources, and planning skill with the expertise of civilian employees of USAID, DOS, and CIA. Following the beginning of the military buildup in 1965, a major reorganization of this kind was desperately needed. Unfortunately, the critical nature of the situation had to be evident for a while before the various agency interests could be forged into one structure.

PLANNING

Placing almost all pacification programs under one headquarters and investing the single manager with unprecedented access to resources granted the manager sufficient leverage to force the various agency representatives to draft, staff, publish, and implement, in conjunction with the South Vietnamese, a nationwide pacification plan. That planning process also compelled the South Vietnamese, who were key to any eventual pacification success, to create pacification councils and agencies; coordinate their activities; and merge their plans with those of the U.S military. MACV, particularly after 1968, coordinated an increasingly large share of their military operations and training efforts with the South Vietnamese, ensuring some measure of high-level military interest in pacification.

Establishing a planning process was beneficial. Keeping the planning dynamic proved even more vital. The yearly plan, modified due to changing circumstances on the ground, was an important factor in keeping the U.S. and South Vietnamese efforts focused on pacification tasks. In addition, the plan created defined measures of progress for judging program success and to shift resources in order to exploit progress and adjust to failures. Planning was no panacea, but CORDS focused its efforts and resources where they were needed and gained greater American and South Vietnamese "buy-in" to the process.

TERRITORIAL SECURITY

Komer and Colby quickly realized that pacification could not occur without security. Without this critical element, no development plans, government "pep-rallies," local elections, new irrigation ditches, or immunization schemes could ameliorate life for the South Vietnamese or make them trust in their government's legitimacy and capacity to govern. If safety concerns dictated that the Saigon-appointed hamlet or village chief had to spend the night at the provincial capital, this situation spoke volumes about the actual degree of security in those communities—more than any number of surveys or pronouncements lauding the government's ability to protect its people. Therefore, personal security had to be the first order of business.

By tying the struggle for security to CORDS, and linking CORDS to MACV, Komer was able to tap into the vast resources of a military headquarters that controlled over half a million men and had enormous financial and logistical capabilities. He obtained several thousand additional military advisors within the first few months of CORDS's existence. Their mission was to work with the essential security forces in the countryside: the much-maligned and neglected Regional

Forces and Popular Forces. Although not able to repel major attacks by main force VC or NVA regular units, the RF/PF were numerous (almost half a million at their peak) and pervasive in the countryside. The RF/PF, more so than the regular army, fought the security struggle in the hamlets and provinces, and to a lesser extent, the police. Komer was correct to place additional emphasis on their arming and training. With the proper training and supervision, a national militia force (not a private, ethnic or religious army like the Cao Dai in Vietnam or the Mahdi Army in Iraq) is the key to winning the security battle in an insurgency.

RESOURCES

Komer and Colby's other key recognition was that logistical resources were important to many aspects of pacification. By working closely with MACV, Komer and Colby were able to obtain emergency supplies during the two main crises of the Vietnam War: the Tet Offensive and the Easter Offensive. They were able to redirect emergency supplies, transportation, equipment, and money in support of South Vietnamese initiatives to alleviate the refugee crisis, move military reinforcements around the country, and provide emergency payments to the families of those killed or wounded.

Komer assured a "seat at the table" for CORDS when decisions were made and resources were handed out, something that embassy-bound officials with a welter of disconnected development and pacification initiatives could not easily obtain. Only military assets could bring sufficient resources to bear on the problems faced by the South Vietnamese pacification struggle. To further complicate matters, they would only freely provide those assets to a struggle that they identified with.

LEADERSHIP

CORDS brought another invaluable asset to the pacification fight—leadership. Interagency "coordination" and cooperation, no matter how collegial or well-intentioned, was insufficient to manage the "subsidiary corporation called pacification."[49] Leadership was important not only at the top, but at each level of the process. Komer and Colby attempted to fill leadership positions with quality military and civilian leaders. Lower-level personnel were given wide-ranging powers, were assigned various goals and targets, and were held accountable for the results. Leaders in the provinces, in the military regions, and in Saigon reported to one chain of command and worked according to one game plan.

The counterinsurgency affected the host country, not the United States. Thus, while Americans continued to commit leaders and resources to the pacification effort, their contributions alone were insufficient. The lack of depth in South Vietnamese leadership was perhaps the greatest single contributing factor to frustrating the pacification effort. Despite massive attempts to identify and train thousands of leaders at the Vietnamese National Training Center and send countless others to the United States to be trained as officers, managers, supervisors, and leaders, time and again progress reports mention failures of vision, corrupt local and national leaders, incompetence, and a sheer inability to understand the meaning of government and governance.

Vietnam's leadership shortfall was never entirely overcome by any CORDS director. On the other hand, without question, CORDS programs created a space for advancement in South Vietnamese leadership that could not have been possible otherwise. In addition, Komer's insistence on Vietnamese ownership of development programs helped encourage the advancement of national leadership.

CORDS RECONSIDERED

American pacification efforts were unified under CORDS for a mere five and a half years. During that time, a robust, well-managed, and comparatively well-funded U.S. effort to assist the South Vietnamese to defeat the insurgency was, on the whole, successful, despite the fact that the eventual fall of South Vietnam turned that success into failure. While the basic legitimacy of the South Vietnamese government and its popular support remained problematical, the indigenous Viet Cong insurgency withered after 1968. CORDS, due to its dynamic leadership and constant encouragement of the government and the military to repeatedly take the fight to the Viet Cong, deserve a good measure of the credit for the success. In large part, CORDS could galvanize the South Vietnamese because of its ability to bring significant resources to bear in support of the government.

CORDS limited, although never stopped entirely, interagency bickering. A single manager, placed under a single headquarters inside the military structure allowed CORDS's staff to access vast human and financial resources. It also established coherent and more measurable programs aimed to focus the fight at the hamlet and village level. CORDS, under both Komer and Colby, applied its resources against key nodes of the counterinsurgency struggle—security assets such as police, territorial forces, and counter-infrastructure forces. As a result, CORDS, as an interagency headquarters, helped achieve a remarkable, and measurable, degree of progress in the important pacification mission.

NOTES

1. The best analysis of the pacification struggle in Vietnam is Richard Hunt, *Pacification: The American Struggle for Vietnam's Hearts and Minds* (Boulder, CO: Westview Press, 1995).

2. Gordon M. Wells, "No More Vietnams: CORDS as a Model for Counterinsurgency Campaign Design," School of Advanced Military Studies, Fort Leavenworth, Kansas, 1991, 21.

3. Dale Andrade, "Evolution of Pacification in Vietnam," Information Paper, U.S. Army Center of Military History, February 12, 2004.

4. Thomas W. Scoville, *Reorganizing for Pacification Support* (Washington, DC: U.S. Army Center of Military History, 1982), 7; General William C. Westmoreland, *A Soldier Reports* (Garden City, NY: Doubleday and Company, 1976), 69.

5. Letter, President Johnson to Taylor, July 2, 1964, Message JGS 7217 to CINCPAC (Commander in Chief Pacific) and COMUSMACV (Commander, U.S. Military Assistance Command, Vietnam) quoted in Scoville, *Reorganizing for Pacification*, 8.

6. Lyndon B. Johnson, *The Vantage Point: Perspectives of the Presidency 1963–1969* (New York: Holt, Rinehart and Winston, 1971), 243–45; Scoville, *Reorganizing for Pacification*, 22–25.

7. Hunt, *Pacification*, 76–77.

8. Ibid., 83–85.

9. Memorandum from Robert W. Komer to General Westmoreland, Subject: Integration of OCO/RDS Activities within MACV, May 23, 1967, 2–3.

10. CORDS Files, U.S. Army Center of Military History (Hereafter referred to as CMH), File 77, Folder 16.

11. Hunt, *Pacification*, 95–96.

12. National Archives and Records Administration (hereafter cited as NARA), Records Group (RG) 472, CORDS Historical Working Group, Box 3, Personnel Strength, CORDS. Only some six hundred of these personnel were located in Saigon; the remainder was in the regional and provincial elements.

13. MACV Command History 1968 in Center of Military History (hereafter cited as CMH), I: 519.

14. CORDS Files in CMH, File Cabinet 67, Folder 94. Project Takeoff. Memo from Komer to MACV, Subject: Project Takeoff, dated July 19, 1967.

15. Memo to AC of S CORDS from Chief, Public Safety Division, Subject: Action Program FY—1968, dated June 13, 1967, in CORDS Files in CMH, File Cabinet 67, Folder 95.

16. Memorandum to Deputy COMUSMACV for Cords from AC of S CORDS, L. Wade Latham, dated January 10, 1968, Subject: Project Takeoff Year End Wrap Up 1967; Hunt, *Pacification*, 104; MACV Command History, 1968, I: 534–35.

17. Dale Andrade, *Ashes to Ashes: The Phoenix Program and the Vietnam War* (Lexington, MA: Lexington Books, 1990), 41–42.

18. NARA, RG 472, CORDS Historical Working Group, Box 3, Pacification Councils 1968. Colby to Senior Advisors in CTZs I, II, III, and IV, Subject: Establishing Pacification and Development Councils. Each of the regional organizations at Region, Province or City, and District were to be modeled on the Central Pacification and Development Council established in Saigon at the same time.

19. Ibid.

20. CORDS Historical Files, CMH, File 77, Folder 10.

21. NARA, RG 472, Box 12, Pacification Studies Group Evaluation of Armed Propaganda Teams, April 7, 1969; CORDS Historical Files in CMH, Armed Propaganda Teams 1967–68, File 77, Folder 10.

22. Robert W. Komer, *Bureaucracy at War: U.S. Performance in the Vietnam Conflict* (Boulder, CO: Westview Press, 1986), 119.

23. MACV Command History 1967, VI, 606.

24. CORDS Files in CMH, File Cabinet 71, Folder Regional Forces/Popular Forces 1966.

25. Major Paul N. Yurchak, Advisor's Handbook for Territorial Security in Vietnam, [1970], CORDS Files in CMH, File Cabinet 77, Advisor's Handbook Folder. See also NARA, RG 472, CORDS Historical Working Group, Box 20, Advisor's Handbook for Territorial Security Folder.

26. CORDS Files in CMH, File Cabinet 71, MACV Fact Sheet, March 4, 1965. See also CORDS Files in CMH, File Cabinet 71, RF/PF Advisors Fact Sheet, March 4, 1965.

27. NARA, RG 59, Entry 5045, Exec. Secretariat, Komer Washington Papers, Robert W. Komer to Secretary McNaughton, "Giving a New Thrust to Pacification: Analysis, Concept, and Management," August 7, 1966, 4.

28. Komer, *Bureaucracy at War*, 124.

29. CORDS Files in CMH, File Cabinet 77, Folder 20, MAT SOP, November 19, 1968; MACV Command Histories 1968 and 1969. Vol. I, 521, and vol. II, VIII-27.

30. Hunt, *Pacification*, 136–37.

31. MACV Command History, 1968, vol. I, 519. Hue, however, was heavily damaged and the psychological blow of that multiweek battle and the ease with which the VC were able to penetrate Saigon were serious blows.

32. Ibid., p. 536. See also Memorandum for the Record, MACJO1R, February 3, 1968, Subject: Initial US/GVN Meeting for Project RECOVERY. CORDS Files in CMH, File Cabinet 79, Post-Tet Operation Recovery, 1968. The committee was chaired by Vice President Ky and included the ministers of interior, refugees, defense, revolutionary development, health, Economy, public works, information, and the director general of the national police.

33. Hunt, *Pacification*, 145.

34. Memo for Mr. McDonald, MG Kerwin, MG Lansdale, Mr. Nickel, Mr. Lapham, Mr. Calhoun, and Mr. Cooper from Ambassador dated March 25, 1968, Subject: Refinements in U.S. Organization for Recovery. CORDS Files in CMH, File Cabinet 79, U.S. Organization for Recovery. Final approval from Ambassador Bunker was on April 13. Memo from Ambassador Komer dated April 23, 1968, Subject: U.S. Organization for Operation Recovery. Hunt, *Pacification*, 145.

35. MACCORDS Pacification Planning Division, Memo dated March 2, 1968, Subject: 1968 Pacification Planning: Project Recovery, Emergency Use of Resources, Memorandum No. 802. In CORDS Files in CMH, File Cabinet 79, Post-Tet Operation Recovery, 1968.

36. MACV Command History, 1968, I, 540, 541, 544.

37. NARA, RG 472, CORDS Historical Working Group Files, Box 27, Accelerated Pacification Campaign; Hunt, *Pacification*, 156–57.

38. NARA, RG 472, CORDS Historical Working Group, Box 44, Office of Highland Affairs, 1971; NARA, RG 472, CORDS Historical Working Group, Box 24, Revolutionary Development Cadre Report by Pacification Studies Group, October 26, 1970.

39. Komer, *Bureaucracy at War*, 30.

40. CORDS Files in CMH, File Cabinet 77, DEPCORDS Talking Paper, Meeting of Ambassador Komer with USAID Senior Staff, April 30, 1968.

41. Andrade, *Ashes to Ashes*, 287.

42. Dale Andrade, *America's Last Vietnam Battle: Halting Hanoi's 1972 Easter Offensive* (Lawrence, KS: University Press of Kansas, 1995), 25–26.

43. NARA, RG 472, CORDS Historical Working Group File, Box 70, Evaluation of Pacification Studies Group titled "The Impact of the Enemy Offensive on Pacification," October 5, 1972, 3.

44. NARA, RG 472, CORDS Historical Working Group, Box 44, 1601-10a, Advisory Teams after 1972.

45. MACV Command History 1973, Table at D-30 showing shifting Hamlet Evaluation System (HES) levels through January 1973. Although HES figures for South Vietnam in 1975 are lacking, the relative stability in the countryside reported by numerous sources through April 1975 indicates that the January 1973 security figure of 90 percent of the hamlets with "A," "B," and "C" ratings did not change much. Approximately 76 percent of the hamlets were rated "A" or "B."

46. Komer, *Bureaucracy at War*, 119.

47. Ibid., 118.

48. See in particular a memo to Mr. James Grant, assistant AID administrator for Vietnam, complaining about lack of support from Washington and about having to "fight for each dollar, sack of cement and body" with AID. CORDS Files in CMH, Komer Papers, Memo of August 24, 1967.

49. See Hunt, *Pacification*, 100.

6
Chapter

Crisis! What Crisis?: America's Response to the Energy Crisis

Ben Lieberman

Nineteen seventy-three was a fateful year. CBS sold the New York Yankees to a syndicate led by George Steinbrenner. In *Roe v. Wade*, the Supreme Court overturned state bans on abortion. The United States ended its involvement in the Vietnam War. On Yom Kippur, a coalition of Arab states attacked Israel. The brief but vicious war brought Middle East politics to a boiling point. In the "Saturday Night Massacre," President Richard M. Nixon fired the special prosecutor investigating the Watergate scandal. The president declared to a conference of Associated Press editors that, "I am not a crook." And overnight—the Organization of Petroleum Exporting Countries (OPEC) doubled the price of oil.

Among the political crises that the White House had to deal with during the turbulent year of 1973 and the tumultuous decade that followed, crafting interagency energy policies was among the most contentious, politically charged, and unsuccessful efforts. America's energy policy during the 1970s was marked by more failures than successes, especially as regards petroleum and motor fuels.

In the span of a few years, the U.S. government took a plethora of actions, implementing a proactive policy to address energy supplies, particularly oil. There were numerous pieces of new legislation, implemented by an alphabet soup of overlapping federal agencies, as well as a host of actions undertaken directly by a succession of presidents. The level of government interference with the nation's energy markets was unprecedented, and these efforts had impacts that usually ranged from ineffective to downright counterproductive.

At the same time, it was a decade when world events roiled oil markets and the U.S. economy. Burgeoning domestic demand for oil outstripped domestic supply. Consequently, oil imports grew significantly over the course of the decade. Though imports per se are not a problem, especially with a fungible good like petroleum, a significant amount came from Middle East regimes that proved to be unstable and/or unfriendly throughout the decade. Complicating matters further, these oil-producing nations were not acting individually, but had effectively organized themselves into another 1970s icon, the OPEC oil cartel.

There were two oil shocks—one sparked by the Arab oil embargo of 1973–74 following the Yom Kippur War, and the other by the Iranian Revolution of 1978–79. The so-called "energy crisis," periodic fuel shortages, gas lines, rationing, and price increases—as well as energy-related damage to the overall economy—are among the unpleasant memories from that era.

But however serious the global turmoil was at the time, it is a mistake to blame America's energy ills of the 1970s entirely on these exogenous forces. At almost every turn, Washington took an already challenging energy situation and made it worse through its own policy blunders. The federal government's newly created maze of economic and environmental regulations, and the agencies tasked with implementing them, greatly hampered domestic energy supplies and limited the ability to respond to events. In retrospect, government interagency policies contributed to the harm at least as much as any foreign entity. The errors of the 1970s should serve as a cautionary tale as America again faces similar challenges.

Many challenges faced by the interagency team may have national security implications. Energy offers a case in point. In some cases, national security instruments (such as military force and government controls) may have to be employed as part of a package of solutions. This may be particularly true during a national emergency. On the other hand, treating national challenges like energy policy as national security issues, as was done during the 1970s, can pose grave risks—encouraging overly prescriptive, bureaucratic solutions.

National issues generally require a national response—and for the most part, the most effective national responses do not come as the result of detailed, centralized direction from the national government, but from a diverse and decentralized process that allows for innovation and flexibility, relying on free markets, local governments, and individual citizens. Treating national issues as national security problems, as the 1970s energy crisis demonstrates, can generate an enormous amount of interagency activity—but may not necessarily produce the most positive outcomes.

CONSEQUENCES OF CONTROL

Energy production, distribution, and use touch virtually every aspect of American society. The availability of energy supplies has significant consequences for national security, economic development and competitiveness, and the state of the environment, as well as the needs and comforts of every individual. Few issues have such broad implications for government policy, and few require more robust and considered input from the interagency community.

Prior to 1970 America had a predominantly free-market energy policy. For the most part, the federal government did not interfere with oil industry decisions as to what to produce, how much to charge for it, and where to allocate it. To the extent that the government did influence domestic oil production, it encouraged it via favorable tax treatment of the costs associated with drilling, as well as some constraints on imports.[1]

All that changed during the Nixon administration. The Nixon administration believed that Washington could maintain energy prices below market levels without any adverse consequences. Through the Economic Stabilization Act of 1970 and subsequent measures, the administration attempted to regulate domestic markets. The White House, with the cooperation of Congress, put in place an unprecedented system of oil price controls, with the initial purpose of controlling inflation.

Over the course of the decade, the price controls grew in complexity, with the Emergency Petroleum Allocation Act of 1973, the Energy Policy and Conservation Act of 1975, the Energy Conservation and Production Act of 1976, and additional measures administered by the Federal Energy Agency (FEA) and other entities. Under this evolving scheme, the price of oil—or more accurately, the prices for various federally created categories of oil—was set by the federal government, irrespective of the realities of supply and demand.[2]

Beyond oil itself, price controls for gasoline, heating oil, and other petroleum products were also imposed, from the refinery down to the retail level.[3] The Energy Policy and Conservation Act of 1975 did contain provisions to scale back the price controls, but for the most part, they remained in place until full decontrol was achieved in 1981.

In a vicious cycle that would be repeated several times throughout the decade, price controls not only failed to solve any problems, but actually created new ones. They interfered with oil production decisions that were previously dictated by market forces, and complicated the process by which products were refined and distributed to markets around the country. In effect, the price controls discouraged production, which then led to shortages, which, in turn, led to calls for further government action to alleviate the shortages via allocation controls.

Of course, special interest politics also played a role. Politically favored categories of oil producers were allowed to charge more than others, and in some cases were granted exemptions from price controls and allowed to charge full market rates. At times the market price was three times higher than the lowest controlled price. On the consumption side, politically favored users of refined products were given priority treatment via set-asides. For example, the trucking industry and the farm lobby made certain that their needs were met. This intensified the shortages and resentments for everyone else farther back in line.

Unintended consequences became the rule rather than the exception. The most serious of these was that the controlled prices discouraged domestic production. Although this was not Washington's intention, the effect should have been easily anticipated. Subsequent efforts to eliminate this disincentive by exempting "new oil" and only controlling oil from preexisting wells also proved unsuccessful.

The disincentives to produce took many surprising forms. For example, the smallest producing "stripper wells"—usually defined as any individual well pumping less than ten barrels per day—were exempted from price controls, due to the political clout in oil patch states of thousands of such small producers. But with the market price at times two or three times the controlled one, some well owners producing more than ten barrels per day could make more money by deliberately producing less, or by using multiple wells instead of one. And with "old oil" selling for considerably less than new oil, some producers shut down producing wells simply to drill new ones to go after the same oil—disrupting production in the interim, as well as using drilling resources that would have otherwise gone into genuinely new production.

Beyond oil, price controls led to problems for refined products. For example, product-specific measures initially led to excess supplies of gasoline and a shortage of home heating oil (also made from petroleum) during the winter of 1972–73. But corrective measures caused a subsequent heating oil glut and gasoline shortage.[4] At times, the domestic energy market looked as dysfunctional as the centrally planned Soviet one, and some price control critics drew the obvious parallels.

The resultant gas lines and wintertime heating oil shortages reappeared several times throughout the decade, and greatly exacerbated consumer anger. This anger was usually directed at the oil companies, which ironically led to political pressure to expand the very government controls that created the problem in the first place. Allegations of price gouging and market manipulation, raised by Congress, brought on board yet another agency, the Federal Trade Commission, whose investigations of alleged anticompetitive conduct by the oil industry dragged on for most of the decade but ultimately failed to discover any wrongdoing.

The various prices for oil also led to problems for refiners. Large, integrated oil companies were producing much of the price-controlled oil, which they used in their own refineries. In contrast, the smaller independent refiners had no oil production of their own, and had to buy oil at the higher market price, including imports. This left them at a competitive disadvantage, which, in true 1970s form, they rectified through a modification in the law whereby they were effectively subsidized by the refiners that had access to price-controlled oil. One result of this policy was that the smallest and generally least efficient refineries were granted the most favorable treatment, further reducing output.[5]

This increasingly convoluted system—at one point there were eleven government-created categories of oil, each with its own price—had the unintended effect of increasing imports and strengthening the hand of the OPEC. "With price controls in the 1970s, which at once discouraged exploration and production and artificially stimulated demand . . . OPEC received a godsend that would pave the way for later developments," noted energy analyst Robert L. Bradley, Jr.[6] In other words, price controls served both to reduce the domestic oil supply and, by shielding the public from the full brunt of price increases, to keep demand stronger than it would have been otherwise.

THE RISING SHADOW

Worst of all was the timing, as this new energy policy was having its adverse impact just as OPEC, which had been a relatively innocuous body since its creation in 1960, was learning to flex its muscles. Created at the Baghdad Conference in September 1960, OPEC's five founding members (Iran, Iraq, Kuwait, Saudi Arabia, and Venezuela) were later joined by nine states: Qatar (1961), Indonesia (1962), Libya (1962), the United Arab Emirates (1967), Algeria (1969), Nigeria (1971), Ecuador (1973–92), Gabon (1975–94), and Angola (2007). Initially, OPEC had its headquarters in Geneva, Switzerland. In 1965, OPEC moved to Vienna, Austria.

At the time of OPEC's founding, the member countries had limited influence over global energy supplies. The international oil market was dominated by the "seven sisters," major international petroleum countries that controlled most of the production and distribution systems around the world. Over the course of the decade, however, member countries increasingly took control of their domestic oil production. As a result, states could, through OPEC, implement common pricing policies. The formation of OPEC and its interventionist policies in the 1970s did much to prompt Washington to view energy as a national security problem and formulate a national security-style response.

Viewing the rise of OPEC as a national security challenge encouraged the government to adopt a centralized, national security solution to the problem. This was a mistake. In retrospect, energy markets should have been left free. Without these economic regulations, America would have been better equipped to deal with the energy challenges caused by world events. Indeed, in one of his first acts as president in 1981, Ronald Reagan completed the process of deregulating energy markets, and the acute problems experienced in the 1970s have not returned since.

THE GREEN REVOLUTION

The first "Earth Day" celebrations in the United States took place in 1971. The popularity of the event heralded a widespread interest in environmentalism. The rise of the environmental movement in the 1970s also changed the domestic petroleum landscape. Even without new environmental regulations, it would have been virtually impossible for domestic production to keep pace with rapidly growing demand for motor fuels, due to physical limits on domestic reserves. But a maze of environmentally motivated restrictions on domestic drilling made the shortfall considerably worse. At the beginning of the decade, America was producing 9.8 million barrels per day and importing 1.4 million. By the end, it was producing 8.6 million and importing 6.3 million.[7]

The decade was preceded by the 1969 Santa Barbara oil spill, which strongly influenced the environmental movement and is still invoked as a rationale to restrict domestic production. In rapid fashion, a host of new environmental safeguards were established—the National Environmental Policy Act, Clean Water Act, Clean Air Act, Endangered Species Act, Federal Land Policy and Management Act, Resource Conservation and Recovery Act, Coastal Zone Management Act, and others. A new federal regulatory agency, the Environmental Protection Agency (EPA), was created, as well as the White House Council on Environmental Quality (CEQ), both of which continue to be involved in many decisions about domestic energy production.

The Department of the Interior had a long-standing role in oil and natural gas policy, because much of the energy-rich lands in the rural west and Alaska are federally owned and thus under its control. In addition to these public lands, the federal government controls much of the offshore area as well, pursuant to the 1953 Outer Continental Shelf Lands Act.[8] The department's Bureau of Land Management handles onshore energy leasing, while the Minerals Management Service handles offshore leasing. Prior to 1970, the Department of the Interior's focus was on ensuring a fair rate of return on these leases while complying with a relatively short list of environmental requirements. Afterward, it was responsible for ensuring that all energy leasing complies with the greatly expanded regulatory gauntlet, and preventing energy production that does not.

A recent study conducted by the Departments of the Interior, Agriculture, and Energy estimates that only 3 percent of onshore federal oil is accessible under standard lease terms, with 51 percent restricted outright and the rest subject to one or more limitations.[9] Substantial offshore areas are also off-limits or restricted.[10]

Even where drilling is not prohibited outright, these requirements add greatly to the costs of oil production and introduce procedural delays that routinely last for many years. In effect, ramping up production in response to a discrete event is all but impossible. These statutes also provide opportunities for lawsuits from environmental groups, which quickly became a routine part of the energy production business in the 1970s.

Complicating matters further, the Department of the Interior must work with the other agencies that also have authority over one or more aspects of the oil production process.[11] For example, the process of drilling offshore and sending the oil to a refinery will, at various stages, involve not only various branches within Interior, but also the Environmental Protection Agency, the Department of Energy, the Federal Energy Regulatory Commission, the National Oceanic and Atmospheric Administration, and state authorities.

At the same time that oil companies were contending with these regulatory costs, they were also subject to price controls. Thus, the cost of drilling was rising just as the ability to recoup those costs was being constrained by law. Both the price controls and these environmental requirements—which are far more stringent than in any other oil-producing nation—gave a comparative advantage to foreign producers, and had the effect of reducing the supply and raising the cost of domestic oil production relative to imports.

Environmental regulations hurt oil markets in other ways as well. For example, though petroleum is mostly used for transportation, it was also used as a means of generating some electricity. The rising price of oil during the 1970s provided the incentive to replace it with other sources of electric generation, chiefly coal. However, the Clean Air Act greatly raised the cost of building and expanding coal-fired power plants, thus slowing the transition away from oil to coal.

Most of these environmental statutes apply regardless of economic considerations. In fact, several of these provisions explicitly prohibit the consideration of costs, and only some allow waivers during fuel emergencies. Thus, the federal government created a system with considerably less flexibility to deal with unforeseen circumstances.

THE 1973 ARAB OIL EMBARGO

The price control system was already in place, and tougher measures were already under debate, when the Yom Kippur War (also called the Ramadan War and the October War) broke out on October 6, 1973, coinciding with the Jewish holiday of Yom Kippur.

In the Six-Day War of 1967, Arab states had lost control of significant portions of their territory to Israel. In 1973, Egypt and Syria made a bid to regain these territories. The surprise attacks led by the Egyptians and Syrians simultaneously against the Golan Heights and the Sinai Peninsula met with initial success, but where overwhelmed by Israeli counterattacks, resulting in a crushing military and diplomatic defeat as well as sparking widespread domestic turmoil among the Arab states. During the conflict, the Soviets provided extensive logistical and technical support to the Arab states. In turn, the United States extended strong backing to Israel.[12]

As a consequence of America's support for Israel during the conflict, Saudi Arabia and other Arab oil producers declared an oil embargo on the United States, forbidding direct sales. OPEC also cut overall production by about 20 percent.

Though the embargo against the United States received considerable attention, it was of relatively minor consequence. Oil is a fungible commodity, and OPEC has no control over secondary sales. Thus, the embargo could not stop non-U.S. recipients of OPEC oil from diverting sales to the American market. As a result of this fungibility, the price of oil in the United States (and the Netherlands, the other country singled out by OPEC) was little different from that in countries not subject to the embargo—or, for that matter, the price in nations like Britain, whose oil was almost all produced domestically.

In contrast to OPEC's inability to single out nations, its cutback in overall production did have an impact, raising the global price of oil for the six-month duration of the embargo and beyond.

The regulatory scheme in place not only complicated any response to the embargo, but it in fact made things worse. Granted, the embargo and production cutback were bad enough, and an ominous signal of OPEC's newfound power. However, it was the coincidence of America's domestic policy backfiring around the time of the oil embargo that gave the impression that the embargo had been far more effective than it actually was. The real problems were already in place before the embargo—sporadic gasoline shortages were popping up in the month before the outbreak of the Yom Kippur War—and persisted after it had been lifted. American consumers suffered shortages and gas lines to a greater extent and for a longer duration than any other country, including those like Japan that are completely dependent on imports.

Overall, there was little American markets did in response to lower oil supplies and higher prices. Even after the price rise, domestic producers still had little incentive to ramp up production, because their prices were fixed by Washington. Indeed, domestic production continued its gradual decline even after the price of imports quadrupled from 1973 to early 1974.[13] Consumers, who were partially shielded from the rise in prices because of price controls, had less incentive to temporarily cut back on unnecessary driving.

Other problems seen by the public as caused by the embargo were actually unrelated to it. For example, the product-specific shortages—gasoline, then heating oil, then vice versa—as well as localized shortages, had to do with federal micromanagement of energy markets, not reduced oil supplies.

The problems had a way of feeding on themselves. By this time, lack of public confidence in federal energy policy encouraged gas hoarding. At the first sign of trouble, consumers would top off their gas tanks and fill their gas cans, fearful of what tomorrow would bring—thereby worsening existing problems, or creating ones where none existed.

Without the web of economic and environmental measures, the price rise caused by OPEC's production cutback would have encouraged increased domestic production and the efficient utilization of inventories. It would have also encouraged the public to temporarily reduce consumption. But America's energy policy effectively negated any market-based corrective measures, dragging out what would have otherwise been short-term and minor problems into lengthy and serious ones.

ENERGY INDEPENDENCE

Growing concerns about rising petroleum imports from nations that had demonstrated their hostility toward the United States led to a strong desire for greater energy independence. This again reflected the penchant to view energy policy through a national security lens. Unlike other aspects of American policy, other interests trumped administration efforts to curb foreign imports or dramatically increase domestic production.

In the 1970s, energy independence primarily meant reducing oil imports. But with the notable exception of Congress's 1972 approval of the Trans-Alaska Pipeline carrying oil from the north slope of Alaska, this concern did not translate into efforts to increase domestic production of conventional oil, which was still shackled by economic and environmental regulation.

The main push was for domestically produced alternative fuels, as well as energy conservation. Neither idea had gained much traction prior to the Arab oil embargo, but both became a significant part of the post-embargo energy debate. In addition, both goals were justified by another popular 1970s fear—that the world was simply running out of oil, and that we had to quickly develop alternatives to power our cars and trucks while rationing what little oil was left.

Petroleum-based gasoline and diesel fuel had remained the predominant transportation fuel source since the early twentieth century, and many in post-embargo Washington were growing frustrated that nothing new appeared to be in the works. This technological stagnation was widely seen as a failure on the part of the private sector, and led to calls for large-scale federal programs to develop alternatives.

From Nixon's Project Independence to President Jimmy Carter's National Energy Plan, massive efforts were undertaken by the federal government, either acting alone or in partnership with the private sector, to develop alternatives. President Gerald Ford, who inherited Project Independence when he assumed the presidency after Nixon's resignation over Watergate, promoted energy independence and alternative energy sources. Ford established the Energy Research and Development Administration with primary responsibility for promoting the development of new energy technologies. Carter's plan included approximately l00 proposals ranging from administrative actions to new laws and regulations. The plan placed heavy emphasis on reducing energy consumption, implementing conservation, and developing alternative energy technologies. Though Carter eventually abandoned hopes for energy independence, throughout his tenure he remained a strong advocate for developing alternative fuels.[14]

The largest effort was the revival of synthetic fuels (synfuels) programs during the Carter administration. One aim of synfuels was to commercialize the vast reserves of shale oil in Colorado and neighboring states. Another goal was to find a way to transform coal, the only fossil fuel America has in great abundance, into a transportation fuel.

In addition to synfuels, the federal government launched a major effort to find energy answers in America's thriving and abundant agricultural sector. Favorable tax treatment was given to ethanol, mostly derived from corn, and research efforts were undertaken into other means for growing our way toward energy independence.

Beyond fuels, the federal government also backed the development of electric vehicles. By using electricity, nearly all of which is generated from domestic sources (coal, nuclear, natural gas, and hydroelectric), it was thought that America could greatly enhance its energy independence by moving away from the need for liquid fuels.

Naturally, every alternative had its constituency in support and in opposition, and the jockeying between these special interests for favor in Washington had at least as much to do with their prospects for obtaining federal assistance as with their actual merits. For example, ethanol garnered strong support from politically well-connected Midwestern corn farmers, to an extent likely out of proportion to its potential.

Many arguments were advanced to justify federal involvement in alternative energy research and development. Some claimed that the major oil companies lacked the imagination to come up with new technologies. Others darkly hinted that "big oil" was deliberately sabotaging any potential alternatives to petroleum and that the major automakers were similarly hostile to the electric car. Some argued that the payoff for alternative fuels or vehicles was too far off for short-sighted businessman to see past the initial costs and risks. Still others made the point that the geopolitical benefits of reduced imports were not captured by the market price of substitutes. These putative market failures were used to justify heavy government involvement.

A few critics of these programs argued that there was no market failure at work. This minority view held that these alternatives had problems of their own—especially high prices, but also technological shortcomings. They also questioned the ability of the federal government to do a better job at energy research and development than a private sector free of government meddling.[15]

These critics proved to be right. The billions of dollars spent by the government yielded virtually no worthwhile advances, and there was very little change in the percentage of transportation fuels reliant on petroleum. Rather than pick winners, the agencies and federal laboratories amassed a remarkable record of backing losers. And joint public/private efforts only seemed to drag the private sector down to the level of government inefficiency. For all the talk of market failures, government failures proved at least as bad, if not worse. And by diverting resources toward projects like synfuels that proved fruitless, the federal government may have diverted resources away from more useful avenues of research and development.

One retrospective of this effort came to the conclusion that "the experience of the 1970s and 1980s taught us that if a technology is commercially viable, then government support is not needed; and if a technology is not commercially viable, no amount of government support will make it so."[16] It took more than a decade for that lesson to be learned, and many have yet to grasp it.

Complicating matters further, at the same time that the federal government was encouraging the development and use of alternatives, many of its other efforts were discouraging them. For example, the price controls on oil and petroleum products made it harder for costlier substitutes to compete. And several alternative energy projects were made more difficult by the new environmental statutes. Indeed, the oil shale leasing program was one of the first things to be tripped up by the exhaustive requirements under the National Environmental Policy Act.[17]

In addition to the search for petroleum alternatives, the other major effort toward energy independence involved efforts to reduce energy and especially, gasoline usage. Petroleum consumption had been rising sharply, as more Americans owned vehicles and drove them more miles. However, any efforts to interfere with free choice by imposing fuel economy standards or other conservation measures on the American driving public were seen as too unpopular for Congress to touch.

As with the push for alternatives, the Arab oil embargo expanded the possibilities for federal intervention, and conservation measures thought politically impossible just a few years earlier were enacted. The Energy Policy and Conservation Act of 1975 authorized the first-ever corporate average fuel economy (CAFE) standards for passenger cars and trucks. The Emergency Highway Energy Conservation Act of 1974 created the fifty-five-mile-per-hour speed limit, enacted as an energy-saving measure.

These measures had some impact on petroleum use—which was in decline by the end of the decade—but it is unclear how much can be attributed to CAFE or federal speed limits. Some argue that the rise in prices at the end of the 1970s did more to reduce consumption than government measures.[18] And there were costs associated with conservation. For example, CAFE standards have added to the highway death toll by forcing vehicles to be smaller, and therefore less safe.[19] In any event, there were limits to how much the American people were willing to accept in terms of conservation measures, especially given the growth in the population and economy.

CREATING THE DEPARTMENT OF ENERGY

As the 1970s progressed, it became clear that efforts to develop a coherent national policy were quickly turning into an interagency Tower of Babel. Many agencies had competing and often contradictory agendas. For a number of reasons, the National Security Council (NSC) had proved a poor venue for vetting interagency policy. Henry Kissinger, first as national security advisor and later as secretary of state, played a dominant role in national security affairs. Traditional foreign policy issues, including relations with the Soviet Union and the crisis in the Middle East, dominated his interest and attention. In addition, the NSC lacked the staff, expertise, and tools to evaluate the many economic, political, and social consequences of energy policy and coordinate with the plethora of government, domestic, and foreign stakeholders that wished to influence the debate. National security decision-making processes were ill-equipped to deal with the challenges of formulating an interagency energy policy.

The president had other interagency bodies at his disposal, but they were equally ill-suited to dealing with the complexities of interagency policies. For example, the Council of Economic Advisors had been established by the Employment Act of 1946 to provide the president with objective economic analysis and advice on the development and implementation of a wide range of domestic and international economic policy issues. The council, however, while well suited to address competitiveness issues, lacked the expertise to deal with other aspects of energy policy. Likewise, the White House had established a Domestic Policy Council under the presidency of Lyndon Johnson to coordinate the domestic policy-making process of the Executive Office. This council, however, also lacked jurisdiction and expertise over all the aspects of energy policy.

It is also worth noting that during these tumultuous years presidential leadership was arguably at its nadir. Nixon had to contend with the scandal of Watergate, which eventually forced his resignation. Gerald Ford, who replaced him, was an unelected president with a weak political mandate. His successor, Carter, inherited an economy wracked by "stagflation," a combination of skyrocketing inflation, high unemployment, and slow economic growth; a polity still rent by divisions over the war in Vietnam; and an aggressive Soviet Union supporting insurgencies abroad. The Iranian Revolution, the Soviet invasion of Afghanistan, and political upheavals in South Korea added to his woes. It was a difficult time for asserting presidential leadership over an issue as divisive as energy policy.

In the maelstrom of managing the White House, successive presidents wrestled with the challenge of overseeing energy policy. That there were too many federal agencies with a hand in energy policy—not to mention state and sometimes local agencies with overlapping jurisdictions and functions—was an indisputable fact. As one oil industry executive complained in 1972, "The present dispersion of effort among 61 different government agencies creates delays and confusion and will inevitably tend to accentuate whatever energy shortages may lie ahead."[20] This, of course, proved to be correct.

Discussions over forming a single cabinet-level agency for energy dragged on for several years. After all, the Constitution had been crafted to allow for government to shift and change over time. At its origins, the core competencies of government had consisted of little more than defense and foreign policy. Over the decades that followed, as American society grew and became more complex, Washington had to adapt. The notion that in an advanced economy, energy had risen to the point where a coherent national policy was only possible with consistent government leadership made sense on the surface. As often occurs, only in the wake of crisis was Washington moved to act. After years of debate following the 1973 energy crisis, legislation worked its way through Congress. A bill creating the Department of Energy passed the Senate on May 18 and the House on June 3, 1977. Carter signed the bill into law on August 4. The next day, the president named James Schlesinger as the first secretary of energy. The department was officially activated on October 1, 1977.

Schlesinger had to assemble his department from the hodgepodge of inherited component agencies and their various supporting offices and functions, including about forty regional and field offices, research centers, university programs, and laboratories. In total, they would comprise a new, unified Department of Energy with about twenty thousand employees and an annual budget of $10.4 billion.[21]

The agency was given a number of duties, including cleanup for federal nuclear sites and research and development of conventional energy and energy alternatives, as well as managing a network of national laboratories and nuclear production facilities. The Department of Energy could have been beneficial if the existing regulatory authority was consolidated within it. But this was not done, and the Department of Energy simply existed alongside Interior, the EPA, and the others. Instead of cutting the red tape, the Energy Department added to it.

One of the challenges of major reform within the executive branch is that innovation requires the consent and support of Congress. Establishing new core competencies is particularly difficult, since oversight of the various federal agencies is distributed among various congressional committees in the House and Senate. Thus, establishing new centers of authority within the federal government also requires redistributing power and authorities within the congressional committee structure. Such restructuring can be highly contentious. Debates can range from frivolous to significant. While some committees may merely be concerned about seeing their jurisdiction diminished or enhanced, others may raise responsible objections—that they retain the core expertise necessary to provide sufficient oversight, for example, or that combining various functions in one agency may create conflicts of interest within the organization. As a result, congressionally driven organizational reform often reflects political compromise as much as rational planning. This certainly appeared to be the case in the establishment of the Department of Energy. The agency lacked adequate authority and sufficiently expansive roles and missions to drive national energy policy. In the end, the Department of Energy became merely another player vying for influence over the national policy-making process.

Within a few short years of its creation, many in Congress and the administration had already soured on the agency. In fact, by 1979 the Carter administration was contemplating yet another new federal body, this time an Energy Mobilization Board that would have authority to override the regulatory barriers to energy projects created by all the other agencies.[22] This agency never came into being, largely because of resistance from environmental activists and other special interests that did not want to be bypassed in setting energy policy.

SHOCK FROM THE AYATOLLAH

Little was learned from the first oil shock; in fact, the regulatory shackles on the domestic oil markets were even more severe toward the end of the decade, when Iran began to destabilize. America was as ill-prepared for this crisis as it had been for the 1973–74 embargo.

In 1979, the long-serving Shah of Iran and staunch ally of the United States, Mohammad Reza Pahlavi, fled the country amid a storm of domestic protest. Exiled religious leader Ayatollah Ruhollah Khomeini returned to Iran proclaiming an "Islamic Revolution" and quickly gained control, establishing a religious theocracy. In the chaotic transition period, the country's oil production operations were significantly disrupted. More than two million barrels per day of production disappeared from the global supply chain. Iranian oil exports eventually resumed, though supplies were inconsistent and much lower than the prerevolution levels. The global loss of production was about 4 percent. OPEC producers tried to make up for part of this shortfall by increasing production. Nevertheless, oil markets panicked and prices skyrocketed.

The nature of the crisis was exacerbated by the antipathy of the Iranian government toward the United States. During the revolution, on November 4, 1979, Iranian militants stormed the United States embassy in Tehran. They sacked the facilities and took sixty-six Americans captive. The "hostage crisis," which lasted over a year, proved a prolonged and intractable challenge for the Carter presidency, as well as a political and media disaster. Arguably, the crisis—and a spectacularly failed military covert operation to rescue the hostages—diminished the president's prospects for reelection.[23]

Despite the humiliation of the hostage crisis, U.S. oil supplies were not significantly endangered by the confrontation with Iran. Nevertheless, hamstrung by a number of obstacles, domestic production could do little to immediately offset the higher prices driven by panic buying. At this point the environmental restrictions on drilling were having an effect. With the exception of the Trans-Alaska Pipeline, the domestic oil industry had continued its slow decline in production throughout the decade. Once again, it was not feasible to ramp up production.

But even more than the environmental constraints, it was the impact of price and allocation controls that did the most damage. The public may have blamed the Iranian revolutionaries whose hostage-taking exploits dominated the news, but the truth was that the gas lines and rationing were unique to the United States and largely attributable to Washington, not Tehran. Even those countries that were far more dependent on Iranian oil than the United States did not have similar problems.

Revelations that U.S. policy made things worse rather than better are not simply the product of hindsight. They were acknowledged by experts at the time. In September 1979, Massachusetts Institute of Technology Professor Murray Adelman summed it up to Congress:

> There is a widely felt need for energy action, because of the gasoline lines of last Spring. But we did this to ourselves. The gasoline shortage was very small, perhaps 3 percent. Absent price control, there would have been a price increase, less than what actually occurred. But given price control, there had to be allocation: product by product, week by week, place by place. There was pressure on refiners to turn out more heating oil, then more gasoline, then more heating oil again. Set-asides of 5 percent to States guaranteed a 5 percent shortage, aggravated by set-asides to favored groups like farmers or truckers. Scattered shortages led to hoarding and panic buying and worse shortages yet—and those gasoline lines. No other consuming country cooked up this kind of purgatory for itself. The cure is simple: decontrol of oil product prices.[24]

Yet interagency policy, despite the creation of the Department of Energy to formulate a more coherent approach to energy initiatives, took the government in the opposite direction.

THE CRISIS THAT WASN'T

Evidence that federal price and allocation controls greatly exacerbated the Middle East oil shocks of the 1970s came in the 1980s, in the form of the next Middle East conflagration—the Iran-Iraq war. The war began on September 22, 1980. Following a long history of border disputes, and with the government in Tehran weakened by the Iranian Revolution, Iraq conducted a surprise invasion. An Iranian counterattack quickly reversed early Iraqi gains, and the war devolved into a static conflict reminiscent of World War I trench warfare. During the eight years of war, significant disruptions of oil supplies occurred. The most notable was an Iranian effort to interdict oil flows through the Straits of Hormuz. The United States became directly involved in this conflict when it assumed primary responsibility for ensuring freedom of navigation through the straits.[25]

The Iran-Iraq War, a major conflict between two large oil exporters, lasted from 1980 to 1988, and at times had a comparable or greater impact on Middle Eastern oil supplies than the events of the 1970s. Yet, after domestic oil markets were decontrolled in 1981, the conflict, and the resultant cutbacks in Iranian and Iraqi oil production, had far less impact on the price and availability of gasoline in the United States. In fact, there were virtually no shortages or gas lines in the United States, and by 1983 prices had actually begun to decline.[26] America's energy "crisis that wasn't" (at least as far as consumers and the economy were concerned) in the 1980s demonstrated the extent to which U.S. difficulties during the 1970s were self-inflicted.

CAUTIONARY TALE

Policy-making stands on the highest rung of the interagency process. Without clear, suitable, feasible, and acceptable policies, it is difficult to implement long-range interagency solutions to any national challenge. Washington's response to the energy crisis offers a case in point.

In the 1970s the nation did not have a federal energy policy, so much as it had an anti-energy policy. A plethora of laws, regulations, and agencies implementing them constrained both the domestic production of oil and the efficient operation of energy markets. This left America less able to deal with the exogenous threats posed by growing reliance on Middle Eastern imports, and exacerbated the impact of the decade's two oil shocks. The mistakes of the 1970s should not be repeated now that America is again facing similar energy challenges.

The response to the dual energy crises of the 1970s also bears remembrance when considering any effort to institute broad interagency reform. Washington is not structured to manage an enterprise-wide core competency of government. Even presidents, with their myriad of duties and responsibilities, could not do so if they wished. Certainly, a small staff could not exercise effective management and oversight of interagency policy over a prolonged period of time. Roles and missions that rise to the level of core competency should be consolidated in a federal agency. While it is largely impossible to consolidate every aspect of any federal mission entirely in one federal entity, it is nonetheless possible to place the preponderance of functions into a single organization. Such consolidation, however, must be the product of rational reform rather than political compromise — to do less may create more of a crisis than the crisis.

NOTES

1. Congressional Research Service, "Energy Tax Policy," May 25, 2006, 2; Richard H. K. Vietor, *Energy Policy in America since 1945* (Cambridge: Cambridge University Press), 119–44.

2. Jerry Taylor and Peter Van Doren, "Economic Amnesia: The Case Against Oil Price Controls and Windfall Profit Taxes," Cato Institute, January 12, 2006, 9–11.

3. James Ramsey, *The Oil Muddle: Control vs. Competition* (Washington, DC: The Ethics and Public Policy Center, 1981), 71–88.

4. Ibid., 71–72.

5. Ibid., 80.

6. Robert L. Bradley, Jr., *Oil, Gas & Government: The U.S. Experience* (Lanham, MD: Rowman & Littlefield, 1996), 484.

7. Ibid., 522–26.

8. U.S. Department of Energy, Energy Information Administration, "Overview of U.S. Legislation and Regulations Affecting Offshore Natural Gas and Oil Activity," September 2005.

9. U.S. Departments of the Interior, Agriculture, and Energy, *Scientific Inventory of Onshore Federal Lands' Oil and Gas Resources and the Extent and Nature of Restrictions or Impediments to Their Development,* 2006, xxvi, at http://www.blm.gov/epca/phase2/text/Executive_Summary.pdf.

10. U.S. Department of the Interior, Minerals Management Service, *Report to Congress: Comprehensive Inventory of U.S. OCS Oil and Natural Gas Resources,* February 2006, at http://www.mms.gov/revaldiv/PDFs/FinalInvRptToCongress050106.pdf.

11. Energy Information Administration, "Overview of U.S. Legislation and Regulations Affecting Offshore Natural Gas and Oil Activity," 9, at http://www.eia.doe.gov/pub/oil_gas/natural_gas/feature_articles/2005/offshore/offshore.pdf.

12. For details, see *The Yom Kippur War: The Epic Encounter That Transformed the Middle East* (New York: Schoken, 2004).

13. Robert L. Bradley, Jr., *Oil, Gas & Government,* 523–24.

14. Terrence R. Fehner and Jack M. Holl, "The United States Department of Energy, 1977–1994," (accessed September 6, 2007), at http://portal.grsu.by/portal/LIBRARY/CD1/politics/cabinet/doehist.htm.

15. Thomas H. Lee, Ben C. Ball, Jr., and Richard D. Tabors, *Energy Aftermath* (Boston: Harvard Business School Press), 159–67.

16. Ibid., 167.

17. Vietor, *Energy Policy in America,* 328.

18. Robert W. Crandall et al., *Regulating the Automobile* (Washington, DC: Brookings Press, 1986), 117–40.

19. Robert W. Crandall and John D. Graham, "The Effect of Fuel Economy Standards on Automobile Safety," *Journal of Law and Economics,* XXXII (April 1989): 97–118.

20. John G. McLean, chairman, Continental Oil, cited in Vietor, *Energy Policy in America,* 320.

21. Fehner and Holl, "The United States Department of Energy."

22. Vietor, *Energy Policy in America*, 320.

23. See Mark Bowden, *Guests of the Ayatollah: The First Battle in America's War with Militant Islam* (New York: Atlantic Monthly Press, 2006).

24. M. A. Adelman, testimony before the Subcommittee on Energy Regulation, Committee on Energy and Natural Resources, September 18, 1979, 95.

25. David B. Crist, "Joint Special Operations in Support of Ernest Will," *Joint Force Quarterly* (Autumn–Winter 2001–2): 15–22.

26. Robert L. Bradley, Jr., *The Mirage of Oil Protection* (Lanham, MD: University Press of America, 1988), 137.

7
Chapter

Breaking Ranks— Breaking Rules: The Iran-Contra Scandal

Alex Douville

Ronald Reagan believed in the transforming power of the presidency. His administration took as axiomatic the executive branch's authority as principal executor of American foreign policy, and with that power, the mission to remake the global agenda. Historically, the development of foreign policy had been entrusted to the secretary of state, and after the establishment of the National Security Council (NSC) in 1947, with the assistance of the council staff and the national security advisor—all serving the president. The Reagan White House, however, was not satisfied that the traditional means of conducting foreign policy were adequate for galvanizing government to meet the most pressing challenges of the day.

While Reagan consistently pushed to pursue an activist agenda in foreign affairs, internal personality and policy conflicts fractured administration teamwork, even though the senior White House staff consisted mainly of extremely competent and intelligent people (many of whom were personal friends of the president). That was a problem. Reagan's leadership style depended on a functioning cabinet-style of government. He felt comfortable delegating.

Corporate leadership also served Reagan well because it moderated the president's tendency to act on intuition. Reagan often viewed the policy world in simplistic terms—black and white, good and bad, right and wrong—basing many of his decisions on gut reaction, personal experience, and instinct rather than on quantitative analysis or historical precedent. Having little expertise in international issues or foreign policy development, the president left the details of policy implementation to others. Moreover, the president frequently relied on subordinates, seldom micromanaging the implementation of his policies.

As debates within the administration over the course of foreign policy raged, Reagan became increasingly frustrated. Instead of operating within the existing national security system to construct a clear, unambiguous national policy, he and his national security advisors (Robert McFarlane and later John Poindexter) resorted to decision making behind closed doors which excluded the statutory members of the NSC. Consequently, developing and executing policy shifted from traditional authorities, the heads of the Departments of State and Defense, to the national security advisor and selected members of the NSC staff.

Efforts by Congress to limit funding and restrict covert operations only cemented the power shift within the national security apparatus. Reagan felt forced to rely increasingly on trusted agents within the Executive Office of the President to conduct the most sensitive foreign policy initiatives. They failed him. Taken alone, any of the shortfalls of White House operations might not have fractured the national security process, but taken together, compounding circumstances led to the Iran-Contra affair, a certified failure in interagency innovation.

NATIONAL SECURITY COUNCIL

The outbreak of the Cold War on the heels of America's post–World War II preeminence as a global power found the president and his personal staff unable to keep up with their expanding administrative responsibilities. The president regularly required assistance in dealing with a myriad of overwhelming defense and international policy issues. These problems also appeared increasingly multidimensional exhibiting economic, diplomatic, political, and military aspects that could not be dealt with independently. National policies needed to be coordinated with a number of federal agencies. The National Security Act of 1947 created the NSC to serve as a sounding board for the president on foreign policy decision making. Originally, the NSC consisted of the president, the vice president, and the Secretaries of State and Defense, although the president had the power to appoint other members as he saw fit. Thus, NSC meetings allowed the president's closest national security and foreign policy advisors to vet ideas and debate issues in a collaborative, structured environment. Once decisions had been debated, ideally the president would have sufficient information to guide sound policy making.[1]

Although not conceived in the authorizing legislation to be a substantial presence in the NSC, by the 1970s the post of national security advisor emerged as an extremely powerful agent in foreign policy decision making. The advisor is the only NSC member who is not elected or confirmed by the Senate. McGeorge Bundy, who was appointed by President John F. Kennedy in 1961, is considered the first modern national security advisor. However, it was Henry Kissinger, serving under President Richard M. Nixon, who propelled the advisor to a preeminent position of power, virtually usurping Secretary of State William Rogers's authority as the primary foreign policy force in the administration.

As the power of the national security advisor grew, so too did that of his staff, which Henry Kissinger relocated from the White House basement and expanded to over two hundred people. As David Rothkopf notes:

> Over time—and this is much of the story of the NSC—this group has inexorably gained power. Today it is a formidable government force, with more personnel than some cabinet-level agencies, and vastly more powerful than any of the vastly larger major bureaucracies.[2]

By the time Reagan became president in 1981, the national security advisor had a formidable reputation as a center of power within the White House. Reagan's team, however, was suspicious of the advisor's traditional relationship with the president. The president's closest advisors attempted to restrict the power of the national security advisor. Reagan did not want to have to contend with another Henry Kissinger. Unfortunately, Reagan's cabinet was beset by personal and ideological conflicts—principally between Secretary of State George Shultz and Secretary of Defense Caspar Weinberger, but also between Director of Central Intelligence William Casey and the two advisors, McFarlane and Poindexter. Surrounded by controversy, gradually Reagan turned to his national security advisor to streamline a usually discordant policy-making process and implement foreign policies initiatives unilaterally.

AN AFFAIR TO REMEMBER

The Iran-Contra affair erupted into one of the most explosive government scandals in American history. Investigations ultimately exposed secretive arms sales to Iran and the diversion of profits from the sales to the Contras, an insurgent group fighting against the Nicaraguan leftist government. Responsibility for the scandal fell squarely on the White House and the NSC.

Iran-Contra had it roots in a congressional initiative that intended to restrict the administration's initiatives to combat Communist expansion in Latin America. In late 1982 the Democratic-controlled Congress enacted legislation, known as the Boland Amendments, prohibiting the Defense Department, the Central Intelligence Agency, or any other government agency from providing military aid to the Contras for fiscal years 1984 and 1985. The Reagan administration circumvented this law by using NSC staff, which was not explicitly covered by the legislation, to oversee covert military aid to the Contras. Under the tenure of National Security Advisors McFarlane (1983–85) and Poindexter (1985–86), the NSC staff raised both private and foreign government funds for the Contras. NSC staffer, Lieutenant Colonel Oliver "Ollie" North, directed these operations.

Separately, McFarlane and North also developed a plan to secretly ship arms to Iran, despite a U.S. trade and arms embargo, to secure the release of American hostages taken in Lebanon. Beginning in 1985, Hezbollah, an Iranian sponsored Lebanese terrorist organization, kidnapped thirty Westerners, six of whom were Americans. Hezbollah hoped that the kidnappings would force the

U.S. government to pressure Kuwait to release a number of Iraqi militants it had imprisoned for their role in a series of terrorist bombings. However, some in the administration believed that if the United States sold arms directly to Iran—at that time locked in a desperate war with Iraq—Iran might persuade Hezbollah to release their American hostages. Regardless of the mechanism or agents employed, these arms deals violated Reagan's pledge not to sell arms to nations that sponsored terrorism. Three Presidential Findings—classified presidential orders authorizing covert operations required by Congress—written and signed by the president between December 1985 and January 1986 provided justification for the arms deals.

In early November 1986, the scandal broke when reports in Lebanese newspapers forced the administration to disclose the Iranian arms deals. A month before, the Contra operation began to unravel after a pilot, Eugene Hasenfus, failed to destroy documents linking him to the CIA when he was shot down during a resupply mission over Nicaragua. Researching the extent of the arms-for-hostages deals, Attorney General Edwin Meese stumbled upon a "smoking-gun" memo written by North that suggested profits from these arms deals were diverted to the Contras. In short order, North was fired from the NSC staff and Poindexter was forced to resign. Congress held joint hearings, and appointed special prosecutor Lawrence E. Walsh to investigate the affair.

The extent of the president's involvement in the diversion of profits from the arms deals to the Contras remains unclear. North testified that Reagan knew the details of the diversion. On the other hand, Poindexter refused to implicate the president, even though he stated he had briefed Reagan about the diversion and obtained approval. Throughout the investigation, Reagan stated that he had been left out of the details of the operations.

Today, what is clear from the historical record is that Reagan approved the two operations that made up the Iran-Contra affair, although he may not have been privy to all the details of the diversion. Although not linked to any crime, the special prosecutor's report, released in 1994, held the president at least partially culpable for the cover-up. In addition, the investigation of a presidential-appointed commission detailed the failures of the NSC staff. There was little question that the operation had been marred by deception and mismanagement. The president's reputation suffered a significant blow.

DECONSTRUCTING THE SCANDAL

No single explanation provides an adequate understanding of the Iran-Contra affair. Certainly, the poor choices made by the individuals managing the effort had a significant impact. Of equal consequence, however, was the inability of the administration's national security policy making team to forge effective responses to sensitive and pressing issues. This led the president to turn to ad hoc solutions for roles and missions traditionally performed by various federal agencies. The president's initiative, however, placed inordinate power in the hands of an organization that lacked the resources, accountability, and oversight to implement effective operations. The result was a national scandal.

The impact of individuals who exercised operational control over Iran-Contra affairs, their personalities, and how they exercised the extraordinary authority they had been given are vital to understanding what occurred. The following played a major role.

Robert "Bud" McFarlane, National Security Advisor

The national security advisor's power derives from regular access to the Oval Office, allowing him or her to shape issues and debates and couch the manner in which the president addresses vital foreign policy issues. In the Reagan White House, Bud McFarlane played an even more prominent role because his authority was not balanced by other cabinet members. "In theory," writes Rothkopf, "the Secretary of State, Secretary of Defense, Director of the CIA, and National Security Advisor were expected to cooperate and coordinate. In practice, the national security adviser was put in the most strategic position to serve the policies and interests of the president."[3] Thus, the manner in which advisors chose to exercise their responsibility had a significant impact on how things got done. McFarlane was not shy about using his authority. "What an organization needs," McFarlane concluded, "is somebody to lead it, to command it, to manage it. And that's the role that I've tried to fill."[4] With open warfare all but declared among Reagan's cabinet members, McFarlane played the role of peacemaker and, increasingly, referee. "I managed the staff," McFarlane declared. "My primary responsibility was to keep the staff organized and productive and keep them [the other Cabinet members] from killing each other."[5] McFarlane spent the majority of his time as national security advisor attempting to manage these competing entities and assemble coherent policy options. As the process increasingly failed to produce consensus policies that pleased the president, McFarlane and the NSC staff sought to fill the void.

McFarlane took responsibility for overseeing operations in Nicaragua and Iran. In addition, he had to continue to coordinate U.S. foreign policy, including a deteriorating and confrontational relationship with the Soviet Union. In fact, the Soviet threat demanded the majority of McFarlane's time. During the summer and autumn of 1985, McFarlane was preoccupied with preparation for the November superpower summit in Geneva, Switzerland. To clear his plate, McFarlane delegated much responsibility for other projects to subordinates—including North, an up-and-coming star on the NSC staff who could seemingly accomplish any task given to him.[6]

Sometime during 1984, Reagan informed McFarlane that the Contras must be kept together, "body and soul." McFarlane understood that comment to reflect Reagan's desire to support the resistance movement, notwithstanding congressional oversight or the prohibitions established by the Boland Amendments. This responsibility he charged to North, who took control of the project from the CIA.

Following up on another NSC initiative, in November 1985, North and McFarlane traveled to Iran to secure the release of the remaining Hezbollah hostages in Lebanon with one arms deal. This mission was a complete failure. Both parties had been misinformed of the others' intentions by Iranian middle-man Manucher Ghorbanifar, and no prisoners were released.

After the Lebanon failure, McFarlane soured on any future arms-for-hostages deals. He believed Ghorbanifar could not be trusted. Before he unexpectedly resigned for personal reasons on December 5, 1985, McFarlane informed Reagan that future arms shipments to Iran should be curtailed. In this recommendation, he concurred with Caspar Weinberger, George Shultz, and Chief of Staff Don Regan. McFarlane assumed that the secret deals would end when he left. However, on January 17, 1986, Reagan signed a Presidential Finding approving direct arms sales to Iran. This finding, written by Poindexter, was never seen by other NSC members.

McFarlane resigned before the scandal came to light but he contributed to the breakdown of the interagency process by subverting the departments of State and Defense in his initial arms-for-hostages deals with Iran. This set the tone for deeper involvement by the national security advisor and elements of the NSC staff, namely North and his associates.

Admiral John Poindexter, National Security Advisor

Serving as Assistant National Security Advisor under Bud McFarlane, Poindexter assumed the advisor post when McFarlane resigned. Poindexter grad-uated top of his 1958 Annapolis class and had a distinguished naval career. He was a doer, not a policy maker. In contrast to many senior personnel on the NSC staff, his long experience in military service made him comfortable in taking on the operational challenges of managing a covert program.

The national security advisor presumed to know what the president wanted and did not deem it necessary to inform him about the details of every operation conducted in Reagan's name. This policy preserved "plausible deniability" in case an operation failed or was uncovered. At one point Poindexter even tried to keep Casey out of the loop because the CIA chief had to testify before Congress.[7]

Poindexter felt that he was doing the president's bidding, and wanted to pro-tect him from the outcomes of these operations. According to Poindexter:

> Now, because the cost of failure is very high, the bureaucracy is not willing to recommend, often recommend, or certainly endorse high-risk operations, because [of] the fear of failure and the resulting harangue that comes about because of failing. Therefore, they don't make those kind of decisions to the President, and because the bureaucracy is often not willing to push them once a decision is made, push them vigorously. I feel that in the very real world that we live in, the NSC staff has got to be a catalyst that keeps the process moving

forward, keeps the President's decisions moving along, and helps to make sure that they are implemented, and that often involves an operational role for the NSC staff. Their only loyalty is to the President.[8]

Poindexter also attempted to control access to information. For instance, when Casey told Poindexter that the White House counsel needed to be involved, the national security advisor declined this advice because he did not know whether he could trust the White House counsel.[9]

Poindexter also believed that he should take the commander in chief at his word: if the president said that he wanted to pursue policies to support the Contras and free the hostages through arms deals with Iran then those policies should be adopted, despite the consequences. At the same time, Poindexter saw his job to shelter the president as much as possible from the implications of these decisions, even to keep him unaware of operational details. As biographer Robert Timberg writes:

> Poindexter had an almost childlike belief that the system worked. . . . The incongruity of Poindexter's high-handedness is that he, alone among the President's most senior aides, managed to ignore the evidence of his own eyes and cling to the notion that Reagan was a man to be taken seriously, not manipulated for his own good.[10]

Poindexter took responsibility for both getting the job done and shielding the president from the consequences. News of the scandal garnered front page news and congressional inquiries surged. Poindexter took responsibility for Iran-Contra operations. He continually denied that the president had any knowledge of the diversion of profits from the Iranian arms deals to the Contras. Poindexter did not present Reagan with options for policy decisions because he wanted to preserve plausible deniability. He often made decisions by himself because he felt that he understood the president's thinking and that if he had taken it to him it would have been approved.[11] Throughout the televised congressional hearings on the Iran-Contra affair, Poindexter stated that the buck stopped with him.

Lieutenant Colonel Oliver North, Deputy Director of Political-Military Affairs, NSC Staff

North, a 1968 graduate of the United States Naval Academy, served as an infantry officer in Vietnam where he won numerous medals and decorations, including a Silver Star and two Purple Hearts. By the time he joined the NSC staff in 1981, North had a reputation as a workaholic, prodigious self-promoter, and fierce bureaucratic infighter who had no qualms about challenging others.[12] According to Timberg, McFarlane "also noticed that sometimes North would send him memos that undermined his colleagues and exaggerated his own efforts. In response, McFarlane tried to get him to coordinate more with other members of the staff," but these attempts failed, as North "liked to operate on his own and take credit on his own."[13] North's immediate superiors, McFarlane and then Poindexter, knew about the colonel's idiosyncrasies, but did little about it as North proved he could handle the workload successfully.

During his tenure, McFarlane attempted to use his deputy, Don Fortier, to manage North. After Poindexter replaced McFarlane, Fortier left the NSC to undergo cancer treatment. Partly to keep up Fortier's hopes of recovery, Poindexter did not fill his position until many months later. Jonathan Miller, an NSC staffer during this period, writes "Bud kept Ollie on a chain. Don Fortier was another chain. He was Mr. Caution—it drove Ollie nuts. Poindexter let go of that chain. Ollie went from being a good staffer to being almost a megalomaniac."[14] Furthermore, Poindexter's many responsibilities precluded him from closely monitoring North's activities. Thus, North undertook major responsibilities with virtually no oversight.

North, however, was far from being a rogue operator who worked outside the interagency process. Indeed, he kept Poindexter meticulously informed, inundating him with memos at every step of the process. (This later exposed the cover-up because a large paper trail existed that could not be deleted, burned, or shredded). In his defense, North believed that everything that he passed to the national security advisor (McFarlane or Poindexter) was ultimately reviewed and approved by the president. This was an unfortunate assumption.[15]

Moreover, given his military background, North possessed the ability and commitment to manage a covert operation. As Theodore Draper concludes:

> The NSC staff had no experience or structure for such extended covert operations. It took over the work of the CIA without the CIA's resources. The next-best thing was to call on the services of a Marine who was most available and willing to take on whatever he was called on to do. North happened to be a marine who flung himself into unfamiliar political territory as if he were engaged in a military operation or crusade. The "can do" marine could never admit that he was not capable of doing anything and everything. Meanwhile, the rest of the NSC staff went on doing what it had always done, such as collecting information and writing papers for higher-ups, sealed off from North's little band.[16]

North, in fact, managed to circumvent the normal interagency process and enact unilaterally what he thought were the president's policies.

William J. Casey, Director of the Central Intelligence Agency

An investment banker by trade and a shrewd businessman, Casey had worked with General Billy Donovan, the founder of the Office of Strategic Services, a forerunner to the CIA, during the Second World War. When Casey took control of the CIA in 1981, he resolved to restore the agency's authority over covert operations.

The CIA, Casey believed, had been crippled in the 1970s by the Church Committee, a congressional investigation prompted by Watergate, the Vietnam War, and a perceived lack of congressional oversight over covert operations. Casey increased the budget for covert operations and began to search for geographic regions where the CIA could reassert influence over foreign policy.

Casey shared Reagan's abhorrence of Communism and considered it the greatest challenge facing the United States. Everywhere Casey looked he saw the shadow of the Soviet Union—in the removal of the Shah of Iran which led to the rise of Ayatollah Khomeini and the Iranian embassy hostage debacle, the collapse of the Somoza dictatorship in Nicaragua and the rise of the leftist Sandinista National Liberation Front, and the Soviet invasion of Afghanistan. Casey believed in fighting back.

The CIA director saw Latin America, specifically, Nicaragua, as the best place to counterattack. If the United States could not stop the march of Communism in America's backyard, the administration would lose credibility with the rest of the free world.[17] Initially, the NSC tasked the Defense Department with taking the lead in Nicaragua but Weinberger refused—therefore, the operation fell to Casey and the CIA, who readily snatched it.[18] In taking the offensive, Reagan's unstructured Cabinet government gave Casey the leeway to pursue policies that circumvented the Departments of State and Defense. The CIA director pursued policies based solely on private meetings with the president.

Before Congress passed the Boland Amendments, which shut off all funding for covert or overt military operations in Nicaragua, the CIA directed covert operations in the region. Initially, Casey circumvented the Boland Amendments through private contributions and personal fundraising, assisted by North. When money ran out, Casey and North faced the prospect of either giving up support for the Contras or evading congressional oversight. Casey shifted control of the Contra operations to McFarlane. Because the NSC staff had very limited resources to conduct covert operations, unsurprisingly, North continued to use CIA assets and staff to conduct the Contra operations with Casey's knowledge and approval.[19] As the reporter Bob Woodward describes:

> More and more Lt. Col. North found himself making that short trek from his own office to Casey's. Casey was not a boss but a soul mate. The DCI had evolved into a father figure, an intimate and adviser. He had become a guiding hand, almost a case officer for North. When the Colonel had arranged the secret supply operation for the Contras in 1984, it was Casey who had almost drawn up the plan, instructing North to set up a private entity to be headed by a civilian outside the government. It was to be nonofficial cover for a covert operation that was as far removed from the CIA as possible. Casey had recommended General [Richard] Secord for the task, and had explained to North how he could set up an "operational account" to be run out of the NSC for petty cash, travel and special anti-Sandinista activities inside Managua.[20]

Casey also knew and approved of the arms-for-hostages negotiations with Iran, His support for the operation rested on his belief that the Middle East was also a crucial front in the Cold War.[21] North and McFarlane (then Poindexter) ran this operation out of the White House, and it, too, could not have progressed without Casey's approval and CIA assistance.

Richard Secord, Albert Hakim, Michael Ledeen, the Agents

With limited resources and the necessity of secrecy, the NSC turned to recruiting its own staff. Both the Nicaraguan and Iranian arms-for-hostages operations involved the role of "semicovert" agents. These included former military officers, businessmen with connections to the regions involved, or fringe bureaucrats. These "nongovernment" officials were approached by Casey, North and McFarlane to help run their operations and funnel funds—mostly private donations—to the Contras or to act as intermediaries for arms shipments to Iran and to set up meetings between the principals.

Richard Secord, a retired air force major general, Albert Hakim, an Iranian businessman and naturalized U.S citizen, and Michael Ledeen, a part-time consultant to Bud McFarlane were three crucial personnel. Secord and Hakim partnered to create a company to filter arms shipments to Iran and supply the Contras in Nicaragua, while Ledeen used his contacts with Israeli Prime Minister Shimon Peres to arrange meetings with high-ranking Iranian officials, the CIA, and Ghorbanifar, the principle Iranian intermediary involved in the arms-for-hostages deals. Profits from these sales went to Swiss bank accounts controlled by Secord and Hakim's subsidiary businesses. For a fee, these businesses filtered money for both covert operations. Profits from one operation were used to subsidize the other.

The actions of these operatives perpetuated the illusion that the U.S. government was not officially involved. As with all aspects of the Iran-Contra affair, every action was aimed to supply the administration with "plausible deniability". That some of those employed gained a significant profit through these actions seemed an unavoidable consequence of the operations.

A CURE WORSE THAN DISEASE

Interagency failure birthed the Iran-Contra affair. The inability of the Reagan administration to forge a common policy to respond to Soviet aggression in the wake of the Vietnam War frustrated the president. Reagan opted for an ad hoc solution that used the NSC to manage operational initiatives. While those who ran the program made a number of inappropriate and illegal decisions, the failures of Iran-Contra are deeper. Personal culpability alone does not fully explain the nature of the problem. The NSC lacked the staff, resources, and authorities to manage the operation. Senior leaders, distracted by the NSC staff's principal role in coordinating the development of interagency national security policy, provided poor oversight of the program. Congressional oversight was also completely lacking. The result was a solution to an interagency failure that proved as disastrous as the problem it was intended to solve.

When Attorney General Edwin Meese announced at a press conference on November 25, 1986, the existence of a program to divert profits from an arms-for-hostages deal with Iran to the Contra in Nicaragua, he framed the scope of the debate of what became known as the Iran-Contra affair. Meese emphasized that the president did not know about the diversion; therefore, he was cleared of any criminal offense, even if others in his administration were culpable. Resolving the question of the diversion, however, distracted attention from the larger issue of the origin and management of two separate, convoluted covert operations. "Nevertheless, once the diversion was discovered, it swept everything else aside," Draper notes, "Whatever else was wrong with Reagan's policy no longer mattered."[22] Still, there was no question as both a congressional investigation and commission chartered by the president revealed, the president could not avoid personal responsibility and criticism for the NSC's conduct. Thus, the scandal demonstrated one of the significant shortfalls of managing operational activities out of the White House. The problem arises because such actions become inextricably linked to the president, and when operations go awry, they represent more than an operational failure—they directly threaten presidential policies, and sometimes—the presidency.

Because management of the Iran-Contra program emanated from the White House, Reagan could not avoid culpability for the overall direction of the operations. As Draper notes:

> The main question is whether President Reagan made the critical decisions, not whether he approved of every detail. Of his responsibility for the critical decisions, there can be no doubt. The most fateful one was the Finding of January 17, 1986; from it the entire sequence of events for the rest of the year flowed. At that time, he did not make the decision to go ahead with the Iran initiative hastily or absentmindedly. He made it after weeks of indecision and against the opposition of his two senior cabinet secretaries.[23]

The president's decision to abandon the established process of achieving interagency coordination was without question the first step toward disaster.

SUBSTANCE AND STYLE

Opting to run an operational mission in ad hoc manner out of the White House was completely contrary to the president's normal method of management. Reagan's leadership style favored consensus building. Unfortunately, decision making could stagnate when agreement could not be achieved.

In addition, Reagan rarely made decisions directly. In fact, it was not unusual for participants to leave a meeting with contradictory interpretations of what the president had actually wanted.[24] The president's emphasis on consensus building would have been less troubled if the dynamics of the cabinet had not been marred by continuous infighting among his foreign policy advisors.

Disagreements between the chief military and diplomacy advisors made crafting national security policy problematic. After having served as governor of California, Reagan was very comfortable with domestic issues. Foreign policy was another matter. While he had clear principles and vision, Reagan was not a master of details on international relations. He had to rely upon his advisors and cabinet members. Already uncomfortable with his lack of knowledge, Reagan did not have the confidence to mediate between his two feuding Cabinet secretaries, Secretary of Defense Weinberger and Secretary of State Shultz.

Disagreements between Weinberger and Shultz were exacerbated by the fact that Reagan attempted to continue to rely on cabinet government, where the major agency and department heads met to discuss and decide policy, even after it became clear that there were major substantive disagreements preventing collaboration among the president's principal national security agencies. Constant bickering between Shultz and Weinberger only accelerated the shift from open policy discussions to closed-door meetings.[25] According to David C. Martin and John Walcott:

> Although he projected the image of a strong leader, Ronald Reagan frequently relied on ambiguity to resolve—or bury—the conflicts within his administration. Never one to master the intricacies of a problem, he was dependent upon his advisors to tell him not only the facts but also what they meant. When his advisors gave him conflicting opinions, when the time came for him to make a complex and truly difficult decision that only the President could make, he frequently failed. The President's involvement in foreign affairs was episodic, anecdotal, impulsive, and rarely decisive. It was no wonder that the staff of the National Security Council later concluded that the best way to serve Reagan was to do the job for him.[26]

In time, President Reagan dealt with his feuding secretaries, Shultz and Weinberger, by removing them and their agencies from the decision-making process.

The collapse of cooperation between Defense and State left a policy-making gap in the White House. In previous administrations, cabinet infighting had been handled by strong national security advisors such as Henry Kissinger and Zbigniew Brzezinksi. The chief advisors in the incoming Reagan administration—including Meese, James Baker, and Michael Deaver—advised against establishing a powerful national security advisor to serve as a broker for policy making in the cabinet.[27] While the national security advisor was not a central figure in the White House leadership, Reagan's advisors, MacFarlane and later Poindexter, found a prominent role attempting to fill a void by pushing forward the president's foreign policy initiatives.

ADVICE AND DISSENT

The failure of the interagency during this period cannot solely be laid at the doorstep of the White House. Shultz and Weinberger both articulated their displeasure with the decision to pursue the arms-for-hostages policy with Iran; once they were overridden by the president, however, they turned their backs on the program and did little to monitor operational initiatives in the NSC, which were arguably impinging on the statutory roles and missions of both departments. According to the Tower Board Report:

> Secretary Shultz and Secretary Weinberger in particular distanced themselves from the march of events. Secretary Shultz specifically requested to be informed only as necessary to do his job. Secretary Weinberger had access through intelligence to details about the operation. Their obligation was to give the President full support or, if they could not in conscience do that, to so inform the President. Instead, they simply distanced themselves from the program. They protected the record as to their own positions on the issue. They were not energetic in attempting to protect the President from the consequences of his personal commitment to freeing the hostages.[28]

Additionally, the constant bickering of Shultz and Weinberger in many ways led to the fracture of Reagan's cabinet government and the rise of the national security advisor and the NSC staff as implementers of foreign policy.

Indeed, McFarlane felt compelled to act. Speaking to the *Washington Post*, McFarlane described the disintegration of Reagan's cabinet government:

> You have two very, very fundamentally opposed individuals—Cap and George—both men of good will—each believing that they are expressing what the President wants. Now this cannot be—[and] leads basically to paralysis for as long as the decision-making model is a cabinet government. . . . When it became a matter of each of those opinions going laterally to the president in a very chaotic fashion, that's dysfunctional.[29]

McFarlane's desire to fix a broken system only further distanced the departments from the White House. Both secretaries believed that the Iranian operation was counterproductive to American interests. As time went by they became increasingly suspicious of the NSC staff, which they believed, correctly, had gone behind their backs to implement policy.

The loss of Shultz's steady, measured leadership proved particularly injurious to the conduct of foreign policy. As the president funneled more and more foreign policy proposals toward the NSC staff, Shultz and the State Department found increasingly they were not even consulted on new initiatives. Poindexter, for example, did not want the secretary to know about the secret mission to Iran in May 1986 or the details of Saudi and Taiwanese private funding of the Contras.[30]

Though the national security advisor and the NSC lacked the prestige and power of the cabinet agencies and were not part of Reagan's inner circle, their proximity to the Oval Office allowed them to wield extraordinary power. Poindexter, in particular, became a de facto primary foreign policy figure in the White House due to his presidential access. He could meet with the president every day. In contrast, Shultz saw Reagan infrequently. Poindexter's capacity to confer with Reagan often led many to assume that he was both acting in accordance with the president's wishes and keeping him fully informed.

Likewise, North accomplished much because he utilized the "White House mystique,"—getting things done by acting in the president's name. Assistant Secretary of Defense Richard Armitage spoke about this tendency, "I think it's become painfully clear to most of your bosses and painfully clear, embarrassingly clear to the rest of us, that [when] the National Security Council [calls], when a staff officer asks, whether it's Ollie [North] or anybody, generally you respond."[31] Deferring to the NSC staff reflected a deeper problem, the usurpation of the departments' statutory roles and missions with little effective opposition.

SIDESTEPPING CONGRESS

Congressional investigations into CIA operations in the 1970s led to additional oversight of the agency and the conduct of covert operations. Intelligence oversight committees could summon the Director of Central Intelligence at any time to testify. Congress could also shut off funding for covert operations in specific countries, as it did with the Boland Amendments for Nicaragua. However, the investigatory power of the committees was limited. As Draper points out, circumventing their authority proved not an insurmountable challenge:

> By ostensibly staying out of Iran and Contra operations, the CIA avoided giving any information to the committees for almost two years. In this way the secret shift of the operations to the NSC staff created a dilemma for committees. The president considered the NSC staff to be his personal staff and thereby, according to the doctrine of the separation of powers, exempt from Congressional oversight. As a result, the committees were charged with overseeing covert activities but were prevented from overseeing the very staff that was carrying them out.[32]

In addition, legal loopholes in the Boland Amendments allowed Casey, Poindexter, McFarlane, and North the necessary leeway to carry out the president's instructions—or at least their interpretation of them—with a semblance of legitimacy.

One such loophole was with the language of the Boland Amendment. The law did not specifically prohibit the NSC staff from acting on behalf of the president. Because the national security advisor and NSC staff fell under the Executive Office of the President, they were arguably not subject to the law.

Poindexter did not see congressional prohibitions as a sufficiently good reason to stop the operation. He argued:

> When people write about it today, invariably they say that we were doing something illegal or that we violated the Boland Amendment, which is not true. . . . In fact, the intelligence oversight board had ruled sometime in 1984 . . . that there wasn't anything in the Boland Amendment that prohibited the NSC staff from being involved in supplying arms to the Contras, since NSC staff was not part of the intelligence community.[33]

By proactively seeking to set up operational activities outside the purview of Congress, Poindexter removed another of the mechanisms of governance meant to ensure appropriate interagency operations.

UNRAVELING

In the fall of 1986, two events began to bring the existence of the White House-run covert operations to light. On October 6, Hasenfus, a CIA agent and pilot, was captured after his plane was shot down by Sandinista forces while resupplying Contras in Nicaragua. The second incident occurred on November 3 with the publication of an article in *Al-Shiraa*, a weekly Lebanese newspaper that detailed the secret negotiations and arms deals between American officials and Iran.

In subsequent months, more details of the Iran-Contra operations became public. Key members of the administration began to realize how estranged they had become from decision making on some of the most sensitive foreign policy issues. Disparaged cabinet members, Weinberger and Shultz, expressed their opposition to the initiatives in public — highlighting the extent of their anger at being sidelined from the national security process and further undermined confidence in the administration's capacity to develop coherent, comprehensive policies.

In early November Casey told North to "clean things up," prompting a concerted effort to eliminate evidence relating to the diversion of funds.[34] Before long, however, the Department of Justice began looking into allegations over the arms-for-hostages deals that had been reported in the press. Two of Meese's assistants, while examining North's files, uncovered a memo outlining the diversion of funds from the Iranian arms deals to the Nicaraguan Contras, through a Swiss bank account, run by North, Hakim, and Secord. It was the proverbial smoking gun.

The Iran-Contra affair was largely exposed from within. Initial press reports and congressional critics raised concerns. Officials from the agencies bypassed by the effort of a small, seemingly autonomous team in the NSC to manage national security missions, however, proved to be some of the most vociferous advocates for uncovering details about the operations. In particular, both Shultz and Weinberger used the opportunity provided by the press reports.

Shultz confronted the president on November 19 with allegations that Casey and Poindexter had been misleading Reagan about the arms-for-hostages deals and making statements that would not hold up to scrutiny. Weinberger leaked his opinion that the arms deals were "absurd."[35] In the end, pressure from the cabinet and the investigations by the Justice Department rooted out what reporters and congressional critics could not.

The investigations, while necessary, also served to further poison the government's capacity to conduct effective interagency activities. According to testimony by Robert Earl, an aide to North:

> It [the State Department] was being disloyal, that it was leaking information, that it was just not supporting the President in coming to grips with this problem, . . . the sharks were out for Admiral Poindexter and the entire NSC structure, not just at Colonel North, but it was payback time for getting at the NSC as an organization from the various bureaucracies.[36]

Because the Iran-Contra operations were neither transparent nor accountable, they became particularly vulnerable to criticism once their existence became public knowledge. Opponents of independent NSC action had little difficulty undermining the credibility of the programs and questioning the actions of those charged with implementing them.

When the extent of CIA involvement in the NSC-directed operations became known, the validity of the White House effort came under further scrutiny. Deputy CIA Director Robert Gates examined the agency's involvement in Iran-Contra. The fact that only Poindexter had a copy of the January 17 Presidential Finding, which was the sole incontrovertible evidence that Reagan had approved of the arms-for-hostages deals, deeply troubled Gates. Without access to the document and knowledge of its contents, he felt hard pressed to justify CIA involvement in the operation. The apparent lack of accountability appalled Gates. He pressured Casey to clarify his role—and that of the agency.[37]

While Meese pressed the Department of Justice investigations, the infighting within the administration increased. Officials directly and indirectly involved struggled to explain their dealings with Casey, McFarlane, Poindexter, and North. North bristled at a memo written by the CIA that implicated the NSC staff as being largely responsible for the Iran operation. The memo went on to allege that the CIA was left largely in the dark on the details of the operation.[38] North felt that he and his small staff, who, he reiterated, only acted under orders, were being framed to protect the president from political fallout.[39] Investigations and allegations sowed distrust throughout the administration, further diminishing the trust and confidence between agency staffs required for effective interagency action.

In the end Iran-Contra damaged more than just the president's reputation. NSC management of the operations revealed another negative unintended consequence: not only did they fail to improve operational coordination, but the mismanaged activities worsened the already poor capacity of the agencies to forge coherent policies on critical, sensitive and divisive national security issues. Even before the exhaustive congressional hearings that followed in the wake of the Justice Department investigation, it was apparent that the interagency policy-making process had been severely damaged.

AFTERMATH

In November 1986 Reagan announced the creation of a Special Review Board set up specifically to address and investigate NSC actions during the affair. The president appointed former senator John Tower, former secretary of state Edmund Muskie, and former national security advisor Brent Scowcroft to serve as members. With Tower as chairman, the board became known as the Tower Commission, the first presidential commission constructed to assess and evaluate the NSC. The board was specifically asked to examine the NSC staff's proper role in operational activities, especially in extremely sensitive diplomatic, military, and intelligence missions. Board members also were asked to review NSC implementation of the president's foreign policies.

The Tower Commission held the administration's most senior leaders only marginally accountable. Indeed, the commission reprimanded and criticized the president only for not properly supervising his subordinates and for not being adequately aware of their actions. The commission also criticized the actions of Oliver North, John Poindexter, Defense Secretary Caspar Weinberger and others. However, it did not conclude that the president had personal knowledge of the extent of the program.

Another report, commissioned by the Congress and released on November 18, 1987, attacked the president more pointedly. It concluded: "If the President did not know what his National Security Advisors were doing, he should have." This congressional report stated that the president bore "ultimate responsibility" for wrongdoing by his aides and that his administration exhibited "secrecy, deception and disdain for the law."

Both major investigations into the scandal highlighted weaknesses within Reagan's entire national security interagency system. The attempt of the Reagan White House to keep decision making in the hands of a few close advisors allowed individuals to have influence over events disproportionate to their actual positions and authority. Indeed, these individuals thrived within the culture of the administration precisely because of the president's amorphous leadership style.

On March 4, 1987, Reagan spoke to the nation about the Iran-Contra affair, during which he accepted "full responsibility" for his own actions and those of his administration.[40] The president described his efforts to restore public trust in the presidency and outlined a plan to restore the national security process, mainly by adopting the recommendations of the Tower Commission. The report did not recommend wholesale changes to the national security system, but did recognize that "[t]he NSC system will not work unless the president makes it work."[41] Reagan acknowledged that the commissioners were correct.

NOTES

1. For the development of the evolution of the National Security Council, see Amy Zegart, *Flawed by Design: The Evolution of the CIA, JCS, and NSC* (Palo Alto, CA: Stanford University Press, 1999).

2. David J. Rothkopf, *Running the World: The Inside Story of the National Security Council and the Architects of American Power* (New York: Public Affairs, 2005), 7.

3. Ibid., 74.

4. Quoted in Theodore Draper, *A Very Thin Line: The Iran-Contra Affairs* (New York: Hill and Wang, 1991), 371.

5. Quoted in ibid., 371.

6. Robert Timberg, *The Nightingale's Song* (New York: Simon and Schuster, 1996), 423.

7. Draper, *A Very Thin Line*, 559.

8. Quoted in Draper, *A Very Thin Line*, 219.

9. Ibid., 442.

10. Timberg, *The Nightingale's Song*, 447.

11. Draper, *A Very Thin Line*, 276.

12. Timberg, *The Nightingale's Song*, 353.

13. Ibid, 356.

14. Quoted in ibid., 381.

15. Bob Woodward, *Veil: The Secret Wars of the CIA, 1981–1987* (New York: Simon & Schuster, 1987), 465.

16. Draper, *A Very Thin Line*, 565.

17. Rothkopf, *Running the World*, 231.

18. Woodward, *Veil*, 239.

19. Draper, *A Very Thin Line*, 380.

20. Woodward, *Veil*, 466.

21. Ibid., 433.

22. Draper, *A Very Thin Line*, 524.

23. Ibid, 571.

24. Timberg, *The Nightingale's Song*, 339.

25. Ibid., 289, 292.

26. Quoted in Timberg, *The Nightingale's Song*, 339–40.

27. Rothkopf, *Running the World*, 217.

28. Quoted in Timberg, *The Nightingale's Song*, 444.

29. Quoted in Rothkopf, *Running the World*, 230.

30. Quoted in Draper, *A Very Thin Line*, 462.

31. Ibid., 576–77.

32. Ibid., 392

33. Quoted in Rothkopf, *Running the World*, 249.

34. Woodward, *Veil*, 483.

35. Ibid., 485.

36. Quoted in Draper, *A Very Thin Line*, 471.

37. Woodward, *Veil*, 482.

38. Draper, *A Very Thin Line*, 487.

39. Ibid., 524.

40. "Address to the Nation on the Iran Arms and Contra Aid Controversy," The Ronald Reagan Presidential Library at http://www.reagan.utexas.edu/archives/speeches/1987/030487h.htm.

41. "Excerpts from the Tower Commission's Report," The American Presidency Project at http://www.presidency.ucsb.edu/PS157/assignment%20files%20public/TOWER%20EXCERPTS.htm.

8 Chapter

Interagency Paralysis: Armed Intervention in Bosnia and Kosovo

Vicki J. Rast

The new world order was not orderly.

President George Bush described his vision for the emerging post–Cold War era as an opportunity for a "new world order" in which a coalition of free, democratic nations ensured global peace and security. Instead the decade of the 1990s experienced a flood of geopolitical turmoil that made the nearly half-century of Cold War standoff between the superpowers seem an age of relatively tranquil stability.

On the heels of the former Soviet Union's implosion, Iraqi dictator Saddam Hussein invaded Kuwait. A year later Europe found war breaking out within its borders as spiraling rounds of violence accompanied the breakup of Yugoslavia. Less than two years after the West liberated Kuwait, the nations formerly known as Yugoslavia engaged in a form of warfare that reached a level of savagery not seen since World War I.

America became involved in resolving the two most bitter conflicts resulting from the breakup of Yugoslavia, the wars in Bosnia and Kosovo. The U.S. response in both cases was flawed from the start. In particular, federal agencies demonstrated they had not adjusted quickly or well to the need to respond cooperatively to the ambiguous challenges presented by the new world disorder.

THE CENTER WILL NOT HOLD

Established as a state in 1918, Yugoslavia reemerged as a nation after World War II under the rule of Communist strongman Josip Broz Tito. After Tito's death in 1980, tensions between the various ethnic groups within the country grew. By 1991, the disintegration of Yugoslavia appeared inevitable. With the international community's silent approval, Slovenia successfully seceded from the federation. Croatia quickly followed suit. In October 1991, fearing a complete rupture, Serb nationalists established the Assembly of the Serb People of Bosnia and Herzegovina. The assembly established the Republika Srpska in 1992. The official purpose of the assembly was to sustain Tito's federation.

Although the war in Bosnia and Herzegovina officially began in March 1992, it did not draw the world's attention until three years later. Before the North Atlantic Treaty Organization (NATO) intervened, over a hundred thousand deaths occurred and millions were displaced within the Balkans.[1] For much of the conflict the United States, the world's lone remaining superpower, watched from the sidelines, along with those most capable of intervening—the United Kingdom, Germany, Italy, Spain, and France.

What slowed the response of nations most was the torturous and protracted decision to intervene. Each government employed complex decision-making processes that weighted both national interests and domestic political concerns far above the humanitarian impulse to end the violence. Within the United States, an interagency process comprised of key diplomatic and military professional staff and elected officials endeavored to generate suitable, acceptable, and feasible options—ones they could sell to Congress, the American public, and international partners. This proved no easy task.

THE LEGACY OF SOMALIA

During 1991 an estimated three hundred thousand Somalis starved. The United Nations (UN) decided in mid-August 1992 to intervene on humanitarian grounds, launching Operation Provide Relief (UNISOM I). As security conditions began inhibiting food distribution, at the UN's request Bush provided U.S. military force support for an American-led UN Task Force (UNITAF) in Somalia—Operation Restore Hope.[2] In January 1993, as President William J. Clinton took office, conditions appeared to stabilize, ultimately leading to a cease-fire by all parties in late March. Seeing this as progress, the United States prepared to return lead agency status to the UN. With American concurrence, the UN transformed its mission into Somali disarmament and nation building (UNISOM II). Simultaneously, U.S. forces began drawing down. By June, a mere 1,200 American troops remained.

Ill-equipped and undersized, UNISOM II peacekeeping forces began searching local towns and villages for weapons caches. When the search turned violent within an area controlled by warlord Mohammed Farah Aidid, Army Rangers engaged an unanticipated, yet determined armed force. According to one report:

> On October 3, 1993, elite units of the U.S. Army's Rangers and Delta Force were ambushed by Somali men, women, and children armed with automatic weapons and rocket-propelled grenades. The Rangers were pinned down in the most dangerous part of Mogadishu, Somalia, and taking casualties. What had started out as an operation

to capture warlord Mohammed Farah Aidid—turned into a tragic firefight that lasted seventeen hours, left eighteen Americans dead, eighty four wounded and continues to haunt the U.S. military and American foreign policy.[3]

Known as the "Somalia Syndrome," this political-military failure would become an overarching consideration in American foreign policy making throughout the remainder of the 1990s. It is against this backdrop that policy makers confronted the decisions to intervene in Bosnia and Kosovo.

THE ESSENCE OF DECISIONS

Interagency policy making can be a complex ordeal. This analysis focuses upon the interrelationships among the government's primary policy-making agencies—the president, the Departments of State and Defense, and the National Security Council (NSC). While other actors within the NSC policy-making process can play a crucial role in policy determination, in the decision to use force the White House, the Pentagon, the State Department, and the NSC staff are preeminent. The manner in which the president and chief policy makers work together can be anything but hierarchical. Contrary to public expectations, the government determines policy via a negotiating process that oftentimes proves unable to make "rational choices."[4] The confluence of all actors compels decision makers (at all levels) to create a consensus position around which each executive department can rally. Such practice tends to create suboptimal outcomes for individual agencies and for the government as a whole.

Understanding the government's approach regarding intervention for armed crises begins with examining the confluence of six interrelated variables. They are (1) leadership style, (2) the nature of crisis analysis, (3) executive administration policy making, (4) interagency behaviors, (5) the NSC role in policy making, and (6) the ways in which strategic vision and planning processes affect decisions. Drawing heavily upon interviews conducted by the author with 135 government officials, this analysis examines the six variables and the processes they affected in deciding how to respond to armed crises in Bosnia and Kosovo.[5]

LEADERSHIP STYLE

Clinton's 1992 electoral platform included a commitment to help end the violence in Bosnia.[6] The Somalia experience, however, reframed the administration's approach to Bosnian intervention. Having accrued one foreign policy "loss," he recognized that his ability to enact his party's domestic agenda—not to mention his personal reelection prospects—remained predicated upon his capacity to succeed abroad. Consequently, the probability of accumulating "loss number two," especially in consecutive years, dominated his decision calculus and made the Clinton administration acutely risk averse.

According to one NSC official, Brent Scowcroft and Lawrence Eagleburger, who both had considerable experience with Yugoslav issues, played a decisive role in the interagency analysis of the crisis.[7] As a result of their influence, agencies continued to frame the crisis in Bosnia as a "case of a relatively artificial country breaking apart: We had little interest outside humanitarian." Secretary of State James Baker characterized the situation by saying the United States "[didn't] have a dog in this fight."[8] Although presidential leadership changed in January 1993, career bureaucrats and military officials who shared the Scowcroft–Eagleburger image of "Bosnia imploding" still filled the halls of the Pentagon and the State Department buildings at Foggy Bottom.[9]

Domestic political considerations influence decision making as well. A Defense official noted, "On Bosnia, the [Clinton] administration is committed to maintaining the situation, not solving it—this administration is risk averse . . . the mandate is 'don't solve it, keep it off the front page [media] and out of the front office.'" Such risk aversion was magnified when coupled with an overwhelming desire to build consensus within the interagency process.

In contrast to the first Bush administration's centralized national security policy-making process (when the national security advisor explicitly acted on the president's behalf), Clinton's principals pursued foreign policy consensus as a goal almost in and of itself. The national security advisor was only one of several players in the policy-making process.[10] At the time, a State Department Deputies Committee participant stated, "people do not want to ask the tough questions— How long will this take? Ten years, no way—8 months. . . . Part of it is we do not have a strong/focused foreign policy president." Another echoed this official's experience, offering that the Clinton administration chose

> consensus over process—it is the way the president wants it. He is not eager to have his principals delivering [problems] at his door. He is not comfortable with reports of dissent and dissatisfaction from his cabinet and is particularly sensitive to dissent from the Pentagon, and the opposing party—Cohen. It means he is trying to manage his own principals while waiting for consensus to emerge.

The drive for consensus decisions increased the likelihood that the policy process would not only be slow, but was unlikely to produce anything other than cautious choices that differed little from the status quo.

Relations with the military high command proved particularly contentious. While Clinton wrestled with Bosnia, he was also working steadily to repair his credibility with the military's highest-ranking officers because of the 1993 "Don't Ask, Don't Tell" policy. The president had sought to impose a policy that would have allowed for military personnel to serve regardless of sexual orientation. The opposition of the uniformed military leadership and Congress resulted in an uneasy compromise. Homosexuality remained grounds for barring service or dismissal from the military, but the armed forces would not actively seek information on the sexual orientation of service members. The bitter nature of the policy debate that achieved the compromise undermined trust and confidence between Pentagon and White House leadership.

Clinton believed in the wake of the "Don't Ask, Don't Tell" controversy that he could ill-afford to push Pentagon leaders into a Bosnian ground war absent significant public support. The president felt he could not force the military to act until the military service chiefs believed the prospects for success were high. This did not occur until after the warring parties accepted the Dayton Accords (a general agreement on a framework for peace adopted in late 1995). Richard Holbrooke, the administration's principal negotiator, recalls Clinton remarking:

> My sense . . . is that the diplomatic breakthrough in Dayton has given us a chance to prevail in Congress and in the nation. . . . But we can't get congressional support without Defense and the military fully behind this. . . . I know there has been ambivalence among some of your people—not you, Shali [General John Shalikashvili, Chairman of the Joint Chiefs of Staff], but some of your people—about Bosnia . . . but that is all in the past. I want everyone here to get behind the agreement.[11]

Holbrooke believes this interaction between the president and the military chiefs turned the tide.

Clinton also enjoyed the advantage of a widely supported UN mandate to stop the bloodshed in Bosnia-Herzegovina. Added to this, a few years later Croatia's success relative to Serbian military forces enabled the White House to advocate military action, first in the form of an air operation to enhance the Croat army's success in regaining their own territory; later, in putting military boots on Balkan soil to guarantee outcomes produced via the Dayton Accords. It was not until the president had accrued this critical mass of domestic and international support, however, that he felt able to lead.

In the decision to intervene in Kosovo, the president believed he was equally constrained. According to analysts Ivo Daalder and Michael O'Hanlon, Clinton found himself marginalized when he most needed to direct the national security process. They conclude "when hostilities began, President Bill Clinton had just survived his impeachment ordeal. He faced a Congress that was not just politically hostile but also increasingly wary of U.S. military action designed to serve humanitarian goals, including in the Balkans."[12] A lame duck president in spring 1998 because of personal improprieties—not his status as a second-term president—Clinton could not mobilize senior officials toward military action in Kosovo. At the same time, NATO members reported that they were ill-prepared to employ military force. As a result, the United States and its NATO partners adopted a "wait-and-see" approach to the escalating violence.[13] Almost a year after Serbian leader Slobodan Milosevic began purging Kosovo of ethnic Albanians, the massacre in Racak on January 15, 1999, compelled the United States and NATO to reassess its ambivalence to events within the Balkans.

The fatal flaw in a consensus approach is that it fails to provide strategic leadership when needed most. As the Bosnia and Kosovo examples demonstrate, such a void creates both the motive and the opportunity for competing analyses to paralyze the interagency process.

MANAGING ARMED CRISIS

Policy analysis provides a foundational perspective upon which policy makers frame their options for responding to an armed crisis. The absence of strong leadership from the president empowers interagency members to develop perspectives on crises that remain bound by disparate worldviews—perspectives framed in part by an analyst's institutional expertise.

Worldviews have a significant impact on how organizations make policy. Individuals within an institution recognize that their parent organizations reward those who perpetuate organizational paradigms, particularly relative to those of competing agencies.[14] Therefore, as the crisis unfolds their tendency is to push hard to adopt the solutions most favored by their own agency. These are usually reflected in the position taken by the "principals," the heads of the department or agency or the "deputies," the senior representatives of a federal entity that represents their organization at the NSC.

Agencies rethought their worldviews as the geopolitical context changed. Initially, at the end of the Cold War, the Pentagon and Foggy Bottom saw as unaffected their core competencies and how they should be exercised. The Department of State managed foreign affairs and framed policy. The Defense Department "broke things and killed people" in pursuit of national security objectives. The NSC refereed the interagency process to generate national security policies designed to integrate national-level instruments of power.

As the new world order became disorderly, perspectives began to be reformed. In the wake of the Somali debacle, the Pentagon appeared to assume a larger role in determining, not just how force would be applied, but whether the use of force was appropriate at all. This shift in perspective further complicated the already fractious process of generating consensus in the Clinton White House.

The State Department viewed crises as part of the continually evolving international landscape. Accordingly, the department's analysis tended to be process-oriented, focusing on managing relationships. Defense, on the other hand, saw crises as situations with beginning and ending points. Pentagon views tended to be more substance-oriented, looking for concrete tasks and measurable objectives. The military also had a penchant for fractionating crises into distinct phases, in which milestones would be identified and achieved before proceeding to the next phase. The Pentagon believed that responding to a crisis was a linear project with clear turning points. These divergent worldviews shaped the debate, driving the course of decision making more strongly than the formal processes intended to produce policies in the NSC.

Disparate institutional views also affected how agencies viewed America's adversaries. Decision makers generally fail to recognize the extent to which their worldviews affect how they analyze problems. In responding to a crisis, leaders are particularly liable to adopt "good guy/bad guy" stereotypes regarding adversaries, mirror-imaging their own concepts of what constitutes acceptable and contrary policies. In a crisis, decision makers are also less adept at examining more rigorously the underlying causes and conditions of conflict. This is precisely the dynamic that framed the American intervention relative to Bosnia. "I would say," concluded a State Department representative who served on the Principals Committee at the NSC,

> during 1993 to 1995, people in Washington didn't have a clue as to what to do: They reacted to the crisis of the day. . . . in late 1993, we ended the Croat-Moslem war by negotiating with the Croats and the Moslems. Washington said the Croats were bad actors. I argued that both were bad actors and sanctions offered no exit situation. If the Croats were willing to end the war against the Serbs (Tudjman excepted in 1994), then the Croats benefit us. Washington was so paralyzed and bewildered on what to do about the situation—they were closed to almost any course of action.

When confronted with an armed crisis where clear friends and enemies were difficult to discern, the interagency process nearly ground to a halt.

Eventually, under the impetus of Secretary of State Warren Christopher and National Security Advisor Anthony Lake, Clinton began considering policy options that would employ military force to stem escalation of the conflict.[15] Clinton hoped the preemptive use of force would prevent open warfare and another humanitarian tragedy akin to the Somalia debacle.

Still, the Defense Department proved reluctant to endorse intervention. The armed services were still reconstituting combat forces in the wake of Operation Desert Storm, the military campaign that ended the Iraqi occupation of Kuwait. At the same time, the Pentagon was still grappling with completing the downsizing of the military after the war. The Pentagon had a full agenda and not recognizing a vital U.S. national interest at stake in the Balkans, the Joint Chiefs of Staff had little appetite for employing force to stem the spiraling violence.

Describing the Principals Committee's approach to Bosnia, an NSC Principal conveyed the nature of the divergent interagency perspectives:

> Late in the Bush administration and early in the Clinton administration, Bosnia was considered a "European problem." [Richard] Holbrooke's book [To End a War] is pretty accurate. In the spring/summer of '96, the Europeans felt more of their blood was being shed and ours was not . . . and if we did not help them with this, they were going to get out and we had an obligation to help them get out. Basically, [this was a] test for

NATO—we would be in Bosnia. There were also individuals who thought we should be involved: Tony Lake (sensitive moral compass), Holbrooke, [James] Pardew (the arms embargo was a horrendous mistake), [William] Perry (he encouraged "lift and strike" long before it got done), and JCS [Joint Chiefs of Staff] ([Colin] Powell and [John] Shalikashvili opposed—"quagmire potential"—not in our interests, high costs, they have been fighting for 1,000 years, and lack of public support). Some said sanctions [could] work, but they take time. I do not know [whether] the Weinberger-Powell Doctrine has been discredited— the military [was] still attached to it.[16]

There was literally no consensus—and without consensus there was no decision.

A WORLD OF CONSEQUENCES

The worldviews held by various institutions mattered more than discerning accurately the nature of the crisis on the ground. A Defense Principal engaged in the Bosnia interagency dynamic characterized this problem by saying:

> There are immense amounts of ignorance being shared because informa- tion is not shared. You go to the PC or the DC meetings: the deputy secretary [or] undersecretary (PC)—these folks do not have all the infor- mation in their heads because they are the top folks. It is terrible how ignorant the process is because it is top-down in these committees/groups and they do not have time to get, or to know, all the facts and the right peo- ple are not there with the information.

As a consequence of having limited information, Clinton policy makers drew upon prior analyses conducted by the Bush administration. A senior Bush official reported:

> We applied the process we had to Bosnia (same as Iraq), but came to a different conclusion than the Clinton administration. Starting with U.S. national interest, other than humanitarian, we found interest to be mar- ginal unless it spread to Kosovo and Macedonia. We looked at the con- flict in Bosnia and whether the application of U.S./NATO force was an appropriate way to try to deal with conflict. We determined it could not be done at a cost which the American people would be willing to pay and at a cost commensurate with the benefits.

Once elements of the national security team had taken the Bush conclusions as truisms it became almost impossible to move the debate in the NSC.

The dominant view held that Bosnia was a case of a relatively artificial coun- try breaking apart. In light of the traditional American position regarding support for democratic nationalist movements, it seemed natural that peoples formerly held hostage by what Paul Seabury and Angelo Codevilla termed the "peace of the prison" would seek opportunities to determine their own future.[17] By most official accounts, the violence occurring in Bosnia reflected the natural social dynamic attendant to any nationalistic self-determination movement. In essence, one Defense official argued, "the Yugoslav family of nations was asking to return back to what they were before [WWII]."

Subsequent to the Srebrenica massacre and marketplace bombing, conventional Washington wisdom started to change, but only after officials began questioning the stakes beyond the humanitarian crisis; as perceived risks for U.S. military personnel diminished; and as the prospects of repairing NATO's damaged credibility for its failure to act decisively in response to the Balkan crisis improved. Further, broad support did emerge in the NSC for what appeared to be a winning diplomatic strategy formulated during the peace talks in Dayton, Ohio. One State official concluded:

> The reason we did Dayton was (1) humanitarian disaster and (2) NATO's credibility—in light of the humanitarian disaster. What good is NATO if Bosnia goes down? . . . see light bulbs going on all over town. Now, it's no longer a European civil war, it was our institution, NATO, at stake; and (3) the situation was ripe—UNPROFOR [UN Protection Force] was there before that. They landed their troops in the midst of an ongoing civil war whose purpose was ethnic cleansing on all sides. By the time we got to Dayton, new lines had been drawn. Everybody had won except the Bosniacs. So, for those reasons the conditions were recognized as ready and [we needed to] do it.

In short, the NSC process managed to put off making tough choices until the toughest choices were no longer required.

In hindsight, both American officials and the international community realized they had waited far too long to act to prevent a widespread humanitarian disaster. In the run up to the decision to intervene, Washington had failed to achieve analytic objectivity. The absence of strategic leadership allowed the interagency process to drive decision making and the process served to promote institutional equities and favor the perspectives of individual organizations rather than reflect rational, cost-benefit based analysis. When framed by dissimilar conceptions of national interest, policy making rarely emerges as a rational process. Bosnia was a case in point. Remorseful due to its ambivalence regarding Bosnia, the White House would apply a different lens to analyzing the Kosovo crisis.

SALIENCE OF INTERESTS

Ironically, in the case of Kosovo there was far less international pressure compelling the United States to intervene, yet more of a concerted effort on the part of the president to act. Indeed, in contrast to the Bosnian crisis, international opinion in the Kosovo case was more of a hindrance than an asset. The UN did not promulgate Security Council resolutions supporting intervention. Led by Secretary General Kofi Annan, many within the international community viewed U.S. action as a violation of Serbia's national sovereignty and a threat to international stability.[18] After all, the international community acknowledged Kosovo not as an independent state, but a province of Serbia. Milosevic argued that the Kosovo Liberation Army's activities were terrorist acts and a threat to Yugoslavia's existence. In an interview with United Press International CEO, Arnaud de Borchgrave, Milosevic explained, "in Yugoslavia, we have 26 different ethnic groups. Any one of them could cause trouble if agitated from the outside."[19] Throughout 1998 and into the following year, international opinion argued against armed action.

Nevertheless, Kosovo presented what many in Washington deemed a more clear-cut violation of human rights—a much more concrete black-and-white problem.[20] Kosovo had an aspect of "marketability" that Bosnia had not.

Having a "hook" is one means to compel the interagency process to act decisively. For most crises, that hook is the identification of a vital national interest at stake. The framing of national interests can be problematic, particularly when they are filtered through institutional equities during the crisis analysis process. As the United States (and Western world) has continued to achieve new levels of prosperity, Bosnia presented a conundrum. Absent an apparent vital national security interest, the White House realized it could not mobilize the American populace to support armed intervention.

Throughout interagency discussions, those considering options for Bosnia recognized the deteriorating security situation on the ground. Admittedly, the "Somalia Syndrome" weighed heavily upon their minds. Although Lake recognized the potential for the situation to become intractable, a Defense Deputies Committee member reported that Powell voiced the most poignant opposition by referencing his Vietnam experience:

> In Bosnia, the Weinberger Doctrine [prevailed]. Oddly, it's a murkier situation, but the Weinberger Doctrine played a more significant role because in GEN Powell's mind the down-side of not seeing a clearly determined exit strategy, end state, etc., [was] not worth the costs of intervention. [This] cost [was in terms of] dollars, with risk and feasibility being criteria. There was no effective way to go about it. The Weinberger criteria [were] discussed formally and informally on the Joint Staff. The story that [became] a tone-setter early-on was that someone brought GEN Powell a map [and he remarked], "Looks like Dien Bien Phu."

With the nation's ranking military official drawing a parallel between modern-day Bosnia and the U.S. military's "only defeat" (Vietnam), decision makers naturally became more guarded in terms of their cost-benefit calculi.

The symbology of Dien Bien Phu resonated with everyone in the interagency community. Powell achieved his objective of delaying ground troop involvement.

Susan Woodward contends that the absence of policy ensured reactive decision making:

> The reluctance to use military force therefore remained a cover for major disagreements among the major powers about their objectives in the Balkan peninsula and their continuing absence of policy toward the conflict itself. This has been transparently clear when decisions *were* made to use military force, such as air power to defend safe areas, because the use was reactive, crisis-driven, motivated almost by pique at Bosnian Serb defiance.[21]

Thus, from 1992 to 1995, absent clarity regarding national interests and any confidence in managing risks if America put "boots on the ground," policy makers adopted the course of action generally considered the "throw away" option—do nothing.

On the other hand, when the Clinton administration faced its second major challenge from Milosevic in the Balkans, it proved more adept at prompting the system to act. Although initially opting to "give peace a chance," by early 1999 horrific acts of violence—transmitted worldwide by the international media—compelled the United States and NATO to do something.

In Kosovo, like Bosnia, the U.S. government had no compelling national security concern. Consequently, a State Deputies Committee participant remarked, "it did not make sense to be more aggressive in Kosovo to further national security interests." Still, the administration saw good reasons to respond: NATO's credibility was *again* in doubt. Some in Washington believed the international military response in Bosnia had been an abject failure—too little too late. "The UN has not recovered from its failure in Bosnia," one U.S. official concluded, "Wherever the UN was [prior to now], it will stay; but, it will not act in Europe ever again." Kosovo offered an opportunity to reestablish that NATO and the international community could intervene effectively when circumstances warranted. In addition, with the onset of winter conditions that would exacerbate operational requirements, force could be justified based upon an escalating humanitarian crisis and fears that violence might spillover into Albania and Macedonia.

The combination of humanitarian crisis and the imperative of restoring the credibility of NATO became the Clinton administration's hook. The United States framed the bloodshed in Kosovo as a test of NATO's resolve and ability to control rogue actors within Europe. In turn, Washington would demonstrate its willingness to act based upon the NATO charter (ignoring the UN position regarding Serbia).

THE LIMITS OF ENTHUSIASM

Having watched from the sidelines for long enough, analyst Benjamin Lambeth writes, "on March 24, 1999, NATO embarked on a seventy-eight-day air war aimed at compelling the government of Yugoslavia and its elected president,

Slobodan Milosevic, to halt and reverse the human rights abuses that were being committed by armed Serbs against the ethnic Albanian majority living in Yugoslavia's Serbian province of Kosovo."[22] Galvanized by a president with a cause to champion, the interagency community formulated an intervention action—the air war, bombing Serbian military targets and units would force Milosevic to end his campaign of ethnic cleansing.

While the hook prompted Washington to intervene, it proved less useful in forging a long-term strategic vision for how to resolve the status of Kosovo after armed intervention solved the immediate crisis. According to a State Department principal, contrary to its support for Slovenian secession the U.S. government did not favor Kosovo's independence: "It ends up as a landlocked Albanian country and strips away critical mass from Montenegro. It opens the door for other irredentist issues." Defining an alternative to independence, however, proved far more perplexing than mounting an air operation to halt ethnic cleansing. In December 1998 a State Deputies Committee participant characterized the problem in this manner:

> What I have seen here with respect to Kosovo is an abomination. There are broad-brush strokes on the end state and talks of exit strategy. But my heartburn is with the fact that no one talks about what to do with Milosevic, the Balkans writ large, how our Albania policy fits. I have been told that the pol-mil [political-military] plan is good for only our philosophy (100 pages long)—it is to be put on the shelf and used as a doctrine. Some have told me that it will only sit on the shelf. It is so loose, vague, and disconnected that it will serve no purpose.

With armed intervention well underway, the NSC still lacked any consensus at all on what to do after the bombing stopped.

Washington's continued inability to define its interests toward promulgating sound policy was not lost on Milosevic. A little over a month into the bombing campaign, Milosevic declared, "the U.S. Congress is beginning to understand that bombing a country into compliance is not a viable policy or strategy."[23] In fact, such actions served the leader's overarching goal of forcing ethnic Albanians to leave Kosovo. Reports indicate that during the NATO air campaign, "approximately 863,000 civilians sought or were forced into refuge outside of Kosovo. An estimated additional 590,000 were internally displaced. Together, these figures imply that over 90 percent of the Kosovar Albanian population [was] displaced from their homes."[24] Indeed, the use of armed force seemed to further undermine, rather than reinforce, the purpose of the intervention—to restore confidence in NATO's capacity to maintain order in Europe.

In the end, Milosevic saved NATO. With ethnic cleansing virtually complete, and NATO having turned its firepower upon Serbia's "military-industrial infrastructure, media, and other targets,"[25] on June 10 Milosevic agreed to talk. Analysts believe that pressure applied to Serbia's economic base (through the bombings) convinced Milosevic's cronies to withdraw support for prolonged military engagement. According to NATO reports, "70% of the electricity production capacity and 80% of the oil refinery capacity was knocked out."[26] Timing could not have served NATO better: Although political cohesion persisted throughout the air war, planners had exhausted NATO's list of viable targets. The United States and its NATO allies had "won" despite their inability to design an intervention policy to achieve their desired outcomes. They had been very lucky.

INTERAGENCY BEHAVIOR AND MISBEHAVIOR

During a crisis, senior policy makers expect principals to interact cooperatively as they work, according to each agency's roles and responsibilities, to formulate rational and realistic national policy. For the most part, policy development in Washington reflects this practice. Sometimes, however, relations between agencies prove far from collegial. As the challenge of armed intervention in the Balkans demonstrated personal concerns can override the mandate to cooperate and collaborate. One State Department official concludes:

> The closer you get to an institution's core interests, the more competitive a department gets. State's core interests tend to be process oriented and institutional: the reputation of the Foreign Service, the role of the ambassador. They conduct American foreign policy through traditional diplomacy—a non-isolationist perspective of the world. . . . [O]n substantive issues, State tends to be weak because we don't have the resources or clout.

A contributing factor in diminished influence was that, increasingly, State Department officials were identified as being in the "president's camp." Rather than being seen as public servants and impartial participants in the policy-making process, the "people who come into the government are increasingly younger, have less political stability, and their future prospects are tied directly to the perceptions of loyalty (firstly) to the president," a State Department Deputies Committee member observed, "as opposed to having individual personal standing. Most of the people in this administration [Clinton's] are tied directly to the president." The closer Foggy Bottom seemed to the White House, the less Defense and other agencies trusted the State Department's judgment.

The reputation of being a political instrument of the White House increased after Madeleine Albright became secretary of state. Early in her tenure, Albright expressed the view that the post–Cold War world presented vastly different challenges, but also opportunities. She envisaged the use of military force in the Clausewitzian sense—as an extension of policy, a tool to "shape" the geopolitical environment, but also in a Wilsonian sense—an instrument for imposing international order. Albright's assessment reinforced preconceptions in the Pentagon that the State Department could not be trusted in discussions regarding when and how to use armed force. After Somalia and Haiti, a Defense official remarked, "The perception of this building is that State runs around with their hand in our [DoD's] pocket. State's view is that if Defense has all the toys, why don't they use them." Powell, and later, General John Shalikashvili, successive chairmen of the Joint Chiefs of Staff, held similar views. They insisted on sound policy to guide force employment. One Defense Principals Committee member complained that the administration did not understand the appropriate use of military force:

> We have a de facto policy—see [Harry] Summers' [defense commenta-tor] editorial where he talked about the U.S. being the big bully. We do not take on Russia for the Chechnya situation; we pick on Kosovo and Hussein. Our current policy on the use of force is not to fight and win the nation's wars. Someone has to ask the question—what do you do with the military? You go bomb something to move to policy objectives, but war is different than a three-day—[it is not] TLAM [Tomahawk Land Attack Missile—cruise missile] diplomacy. I think this adminis-tration has developed a policy about the de facto role for the military's use: fighting, launching, and committing lives in a place like Kosovo that you know you cannot bring these people to peace.

As a result of entrenched institutional views like this, during the Kosovo cri-sis interagency representatives engaged in fiercely competitive behaviors. State and Defense held steadfastly to their positions.

As the intensity of the war grew so did the intensity of the debate. An NSC Principal recalls, "State pushing for the credible use of force and Defense saying, 'let's think this thing through.'" Interagency actors aligned, according to this official only:

> when it became apparent that only a credible threat/use of force would affect Milosevic. The turning points were: (1) Milosevic's security forces continued to flatten village after village and (2) when it became clear that the president was willing to use force [based upon] advice from the APNSA [Assistant to the President for National Security Affairs], discussions with [British Prime Minister] Tony Blair, and our own gut instinct.

Once the decision to use military force had been made, the interagency process became less contentious. The NSC shifted to the less divisive issue of how to implement policy. The shift, however, only masked deeper troubles. A Defense Principals Committee member explained:

> Here is what happens. We get hung up with the tactical and cannot make progress in the interagency forum. We spend 2 hours [talking] and start over at the same point the next day. The leadership is afraid to

develop/define policy—at its best, it is containment. How does our policy then relate to Kosovo? You cannot define the policy—that is a real problem, we just work tactically.

Although the NSC was as busy as ever, it was not doing best the task for which it had been created. As a manager of the nation's interagency process, the NSC staff was designed to integrate agency views to build consensus across the government. Competing priorities, however, overwhelmed the NSC staff during the crises, impeding its ability to mediate differences and integrate options for the White House.

THE LIFE CYCLE OF CONFLICT

Within the American government, the president is responsible for national security policy. Consequently, NSC members tend to echo the White House's desires. Simultaneously, the president charges the NSC staff with managing the interagency policy-making process, acting as arbiter between agencies and a synthesizer for their often competing views. This process works poorly in responding to an unanticipated armed crisis. "There is a tendency to be reactive," one Defense official concluded. "The NSC cannot manage all foreign policy problems out there. We [NSC staff] deal with the problem du jour—the immediate crisis. We have looked in advance on prevention in Montenegro, some in Bosnia, but Kosovo was reactive." This reactive posture extends from the NSC staff's tendency to mobilize actors within the interagency process at different stages of a conflict's life cycle.

During routine policy making, the NSC staff relies upon the State Department to assess "ground truth" and inform the White House of regional changes that may require security policy decisions. Meanwhile, Defense continues to "train and equip" based on national security policy promulgated by the executive branch (e.g., *The National Security Strategy*). Aside from information gathered by the intelligence community (e.g., the CIA), the Pentagon too relies upon State to monitor international affairs and inform the military staffs of the significance of ongoing events.

The engagement and influence of agencies on the NSC policy-making process, however, do not remain constant throughout all phases of a crisis. All too often, the tyranny of the urgent consumes the NSC staff and they rely upon State and Defense to augment them in analyzing crises and authoring policy papers to inform NSC Principals regarding viable options. Such practices create turning points/handoffs relative to agency influence.

As a situation moves from prehostilities to hostilities, the relative influence of Defense and State becomes inverted. State effectively takes a "backseat" to Defense during the armed violence phase of conflict. As parties move toward cease-fire—State resumes its dominant position as lead agent for posthostilities diplomacy. This approach creates serious disruptions as Defense engages seriously only when the crisis is at hand, often absent a comprehensive understanding of the international situation. In addition, once hostilities begin State must rethink its initial analysis. As history demonstrates, when wars start, ground truth changes, at times altering the objectives of the parties in conflict. Nevertheless, after the bullets begin to fly the Pentagon tends to ignore the State Department's update of the situation until victory is in hand. Once the violence ends, Defense cedes control to State and attempts to disengage rapidly from the politics of international affairs.

PAPERS, POLICY, AND CONGRESS

The dynamic of the interaction between State and Defense is manifested in two important NSC institutional activities: (1) the process of preparing policy papers and (2) relations with Congress. Both offer significant insight into the framework for crisis analysis and interagency discussion.

Policy papers compel agency representatives to exchange ideas regarding a particular issue. In addition to arbitrating policy, the staffing process for "white papers" requires coordinating departments to present their views officially to the White House. Designed to generate support, identify options/alternative courses of action, and/or expose flaws in logic/capabilities, white papers reflect issues holistically, usually including recommended actions for the decision taker (often the president).

According to one Defense official with experience during the Bosnia effort:

> in theory, papers are produced for the interagency working group (IWG), and then refined for the DC [Deputies Committee] and PC [Principals Committee]. This was followed much more so in the Bush administration. For the major issues today, the tendency is to make decisions without a vision for what we are doing. We are concerned about spin and play in the press, not what's the real end state. Policy positions are an afterthought.

A high-ranking State official offered similarly critical assessment of the policy paper process:

> At the PC [Principals Committee] meeting no one in the room is an expert. I worked Bosnia at the senior level for one year—some of us had been to Bosnia. Papers are supposed to be good and we're supposed to read them. What's the possibility one of them will be constructively creative? Not! Intellectually, some of us know this—the real experts are not in the meetings. When you look at the top level, Leon Sigal's "macho factor," "don't call me weak" . . . that thing around a table with PCs [Principals Committees] is incredibly powerful for why we said what we said. If the press smells weakness where military force is an issue, it is disastrous.

As the danger of armed crisis swelled, the intensity of the debate over the content of policy papers increased. On the other hand, the significance of their role in driving the interagency policy-making process appeared to decline.

Likewise, as crisis looms consultation with Congress becomes more vital, yet agencies seek more and more to shield their institutional views from the Hill. Government organizations make a serious effort to make their deliberations less transparent. One Principals Committee participant with Bosnia experience noted that "as the importance of the issue increases, the importance of avoiding leaks increases. The more important the issue, the more likely the experts will be excluded. This isn't good government and is a real danger . . . the press is more important!" One reason why agencies work so vociferously to shield policy debates from the media is that they do not want to allow Congress to observe policy debates within the administration prematurely.

On the other hand, when agencies need support from Congress to press their institutional opinions they are not above taking a risk to leak information to congressional supporters both directly and through the media. Organizations are also not above citing views from members to bolster institutional positions during interagency debates. In the end, information sharing between the executive branch and Congress represents much more than just sharing information. The strange dynamic of both masking differences and sharing concerns serves to shape, rather than merely elucidate, the congressional response to international affairs.

The executive branch devotes considerable resources to congressional liaison functions. White House officials and virtually every federal agency maintain an office to manage legislative affairs. The military services staff congressional liaison offices on the Hill; NSC staffers also keep their fingers on the legislative pulse. With regard to military actions for Kosovo an NSC official conveyed, "The attitude on the Hill set boundaries on Kosovo policy—there is no support for ground troops on the Hill. We adopted a humanitarian focus and related air strikes to [it]." The NSC staff used congressional preferences to help frame policy options.

LACK OF LOOKING FORWARD

In part the post–Cold War interagency process struggled to respond to the ambiguities of the new world disorder, in part because the NSC lacked an integrated analytic mechanism to filter the input from State, Defense, and the other agencies participating in policy making. No one agency controls or "owns" an entire crisis response effort. As a result, the dearth of cross-fertilization of ideas and influence among the agencies that played a prominent lead during various points in the crisis life cycle resulted in many misconceptions and missteps.

During the normal process of staffing interagency policy, the absence of an integrated system for assessing risks and weighing options was not an insurmountable challenge to formulating coherent policies. In those situations, adequate time was available to sift through agency opinions and data. The Balkans was different. "In Bosnia," a Defense principal concluded, "we did nothing essentially until the crisis was already there. When Croatia [and Slovenia] declared independence in 1991 . . . at that point we [DoD] began to look at it, but with no interagency mechanism to look at it—[we have] no mechanism to look at those things." An NSC principal asserted that Bosnia was:

> a very complicated country and very dysfunctional. You can make some assumptions about interest on the ground but it's impossible to control the outcome. You need to do as much planning as possible, but have no faith that your plan will come out as planned. It's hard for someone not steeped in these issues to understand their complexity. It's not just the internal situation in Bosnia, but it's also the external—dealing with a multinational context. Dealing with Europeans and the Congress—so, to try to figure out, to make a multinational, complex civil emergency operation work is a hell of a puzzle, but no one understands the whole puzzle and everyone comes at it from a different perspective.

The NSC lacked a "systems approach" to capitalize upon the core competencies each agency brings to bear upon the crisis.

Because no interagency mechanism existed to conduct long-term forecasting, agencies independently engaged in crisis analysis and then came together to battle out a decision. One State principal with experience during the Persian Gulf War reflected:

> So much depends on individuals that it isn't the process at fault—it's the failure to utilize the process in decision-making, a failure to look in advance at what are likely to be future challenges. All too often, we wait for a crisis to erupt before developing a policy: You never know how it might erupt.

Lower-level analysts and decision makers push their independent perspectives upward to the highest levels where the principals attempt to synthesize fragmented images of the "puzzle." This approach fails because the principals remain reluctant to get involved with the details of the planning process (e.g., identifying contingency operation funding sources). Such inaction pushes problems back down the interagency hierarchy where lower-level decision makers dogmatically protect their respective equities.

BUDGET BLUES

Budgetary realities also drive institutional planning processes. Presidents are significantly constrained by plans for federal expenditures established long before they took office. Although the Congress appropriates a new federal budget each year, several factors tend to make the process reflect more continuity than change. The share of the budget allocated for each federal agency remains fairly consistent from year-to-year. Federal outlays are also limited, in part, to expectations on revenue projections and the amount of tax dollars that need to be set aside for mandatory spending programs, such as Medicare and Medicaid. Proposals to change spending or tax plans must navigate a difficult course of congressional committees and a host of public and private stakeholders and lobbyists. Shifting spending priorities can require the investment of significant political capital. Adjusting spending to respond to a crisis can be even more difficult.

Though supplemental appropriations are usually required for major military operations overseas, the resources required for preparing and sustaining the force and the support required to mount military campaigns are funded and forecasted long before the battle. For Operation Desert Storm, for example, the Joint Chiefs of Staff began with an established operation plan (OPLAN) to deal with Iraqi aggression: The intelligence community (J-2) predicted Saddam Hussein's invasion of Kuwait—component commanders (i.e., army, navy, air force, and marines) had "trained and equipped" their forces for years to respond to such action. Though the final campaign differed significantly from the initial planning concept, the armed forces were prepared for the "sticker shock" of mounting a land war in the Middle East.

The same cannot be said for Yugoslavia's disintegration. Vague plans existed, but the complexity of the challenges underwritten by competing analyses hindered effective interagency discussion and fragmented its focus. More importantly, the White House had not allocated resources to take action in Bosnia, further impeding planning and policy consideration. According to one principal, "Nothing happens in Washington unless you're prepared to assign resources against it. Until you're sure you will assign resources, nothing happens until the crisis is upon you." In the case of Bosnia, once the crisis loomed the Pentagon quickly grasped the potential budgetary risks connected with intervention. That contributed, in part, to its reluctance to endorse armed intervention. An NSC principal noted, "The cost . . . and getting the force back out again. You are right about military reluctance to get involved."

In addition, the Pentagon does not like supplemental appropriations. The military service chiefs recognize that additional funding from Congress is essential for mounting contingency operations. Military operations, however, are launched on their own timeline. Frequently, the services must shift funds from ongoing programs, such as training and maintenance, to pay for contingency operations and then reimburse these accounts once Congress provides supplemental appropriations. Shifting funds can be disruptive. Likewise, if Congress passes the supplemental appropriation late in the fiscal year, the money does the military little good. There may not be sufficient time to conduct training or other activities that had to be deferred to pay for ongoing operations. Thus, contingency spending typically has a negative impact on military readiness.

Armed intervention in Bosnia seemed particularly troubling since the commitment appeared open ended. As one Defense official recalled:

> State assumed Milosevic would go away. We saw him as the linchpin—
> State thought student protests would be effective and also thought we'd
> take on a broader role with war criminals and we'd remove Milosevic

and Mladic. We left them in place. Our vision of the end state was to come up with the right lines on the map and balance the power through the "Train and Equip" plan written here without much input from the State Department. It was trotted out and State saw it and said, "Holy cow, we thought you were going to put the Bosniacs in power and pull Milosevic out." They (State) did all the negotiation with Bosnia and we did all the negotiation with the other side. We ended up with State seeing Milosevic as a threat—their vision was so different from ours and they didn't see it. We had a balance of power whereas State thought we'd come to the aid of those abused. We now have a situation where you have two entities instead of one. We were dealing with Milosevic—he's got the guns. So we balanced the power out and State assumed there would be an imbalance of power they could come in and negotiate. I think Holbrooke's view was to end the fighting—we do a lot of those simplistic things. Holbrooke's view was "How do I stop this war?" The State Department was more Pollyannaish—[their] focus was on future trade, etc. State takes a very simplistic view—"Everyone will see the situation through our lenses. Because the U.S. is there, everyone will work cooperatively with one another." I don't think State recognized that they are political entities, not ethnic entities. Holbrooke was a realist—[he] balanced the power. State's view was Bosnia would be part of "engagement and enlargement" and then we'll move out.

The Defense Department, whose budget would bear the lion's share of managing the Bosnian crisis, proved less willing than State to gamble on a positive outcome.[27]

Pentagon officials had little confidence in the ability of the State Department to design strategic vision for the operation, much less a plan to fulfill it. Many in the State Department agreed. An insider to State's planning function conveyed, "DOS/SP [Department of State, Strategic Planning office] gets into much of the day-to-day stuff more than the long-term vision; it's not a J-5 [JCS Strategic Planning office]. The successful SPs don't do long-term stuff—they put out fires (i.e., crises) for the secretary. SP is marginalized if focused on the long term." Defense officials had no confidence in their counterpart's ability to mitigate risks to the military's budget.

Budgetary concerns initially played a prominent role in Kosovo intervention discussions. In January 1999 a State principal complained that the Pentagon put budgeting ahead of strategy:

Every time now—food, northern Iraq, concise bombing in Bosnia—all are missions the military culture deems inappropriate. Their dissent is growing stronger and stronger. It is still the way the Pentagon is organized . . . still no budget for contingencies, only readiness and training. It [funding] needs to be taken out of the budget as a whole. The building is still resisting the notion that these are appropriate military functions. The disconnect is greater now than during the Cold War! Look at Kosovo: The answer is "we are not designed to do it, not funded for it."

According to Daalder and O'Hanlon, lack of White House leadership exacerbated the problem. "The president failed to prepare the country for the possibility that NATO's initial bombing raids might be the opening salvo of a drawn-out war," they write, "nor were he and his top advisers really prepared for the possibility themselves."[28] They certainly did not press the military to rethink long-term budget issues.

CAUSE FOR CONCERN

The American response to Bosnia and Kosovo demonstrated the shortfall of the interagency policy-making process in responding to an armed crisis. The main problem, as a State Department Deputies Committee member conveyed, was that "elements of policy have dominated decision making that have nothing to do with the context of the crisis." The NSC proved ill-prepared to shift effectively from long-term policy making to crisis action planning. Instead of an integrated effort led by the NSC, planning tended to reflect the negotiations of prominent agencies whose own analysis was dictated by their institutional perspectives and agency interests.

Establishing corporate practices that create a better framework for crafting policies during a crisis could revolutionize interagency practices. Developing more timely and informative crisis analysis; fostering interagency collaboration; creating a systems approach that compels integrated planning and sound strategic vision; managing congressional relations; and addressing contingency funding for crisis operations must all be addressed.

With the end of the new world disorder nowhere in sight, future administrations will have to address the shortcomings endemic to the interagency crisis action process. Otherwise, in the future every ambiguous, ill-defined international conundrum will present a crisis for interagency policy development.

NOTES

1. Ivo H. Daalder and Michael E. O'Hanlon, *Winning Ugly: NATO's War to Save Kosovo* (Washington: Brookings Institution Press, 2000), 1.

2. Public Broadcasting Service, "Chronology: The US/UN in Somalia, 1995–2007," *Frontline: Ambush in Mogadishu*, April 22, 2007, at http://www.pbs.org/wgbh/pages/frontline/shows/ambush/etc/cron.html.

3. Public Broadcasting Service, "Synopsis," *Frontline: Ambush in Mogadishu*, September 28, 1998, at http://www.pbs.org/wgbh/pages/frontline/shows/ambush/etc/synopsis.html.

4. Vicki J. Rast, *Interagency Fratricide: Policy Failures in the Persian Gulf and Bosnia* (Maxwell Air Force Base, AL: Air University Press, 2004).

5. Unless noted otherwise quotes from government officials are from interviews with the author. See Rast, *Interagency Fratricide*, Appendix A, for the complete list of 135 research participants and their credentials relevant to this work; signed participant

letters are on file. To ensure speaker anonymity, quotations/ideas are identified only by an individual's executive department and level within the interagency process.

6. See Richard C. Holbrooke, *To End a War* (New York: Random House, 1998).

7. Rast, *Interagency Fratricide*, 303. David Gompert, a senior NSC member during the Bush administration, characterized the Bush administration as being "divided and stumped" in its approach to Bosnia. See David C. Gompert, "The United States and Yugoslavia's Wars," in R. H. Ullman, ed., *The World and Yugoslavia's Wars* (New York: Council on Foreign Relations, 1996). However, interview data analyzed in Rast, *Interagency Fratricide*, indicate that Scowcroft's and Eagleburger's perspectives ensured a status quo policy approach.

8. James A. Baker III, *The Politics of Diplomacy: Revolution, War, and Peace, 1989–1992* (New York: G. P. Putnam's Sons, 1995). See also Warren Zimmerman, *Origins of a Catastrophe* (New York: Times Books, 1996); Warren Christopher, *In the Stream of History: Shaping Foreign Policy for a New Era* (Stanford, CA: Stanford University Press, 1998); and Susan L. Woodward, *Balkan Tragedy: Chaos and Disintegration after the Cold War* (Washington: The Brookings Institution, 1995).

9. Rast, *Interagency Fratricide*, 272.

10. A former State Department Deputies Committee official informed the author that "the interagency ran differently for two administrations (Bush and Clinton). The interagency during the Persian Gulf War was 'textbook'—as well as I have ever seen it since the early 1970s. It ran the best because (1) the president wanted it to run and (2) the president set up the heart of the system as Scowcroft, Baker, and Cheney—people who shared aims and were intensely loyal both to the president and the process, and were capable of being totally cold (i.e., not shrinking from the more unpleasant sides of policy implications) with their analyses."

11. Holbrooke, *To End a War*, 316.

12. Daalder and O'Hanlon, *Winning Ugly*, 2.

13. Ibid., 2–3.

14. Thomas S. Kuhn, *The Structure of Scientific Revolutions* (Illinois: University of Chicago Press, 1962).

15. After touring Bosnia, Christopher "was describing Bosnia as 'an intractable "problem from hell"' that no one can be expected to solve. . . . less as a moral tragedy . . . and more as a tribal feud that no outsider could hope to settle." Quoted in Susan L. Woodward's *Balkan Tragedy: Chaos and Disintegration after the Cold War* (Washington: The Brookings Institution, 1995), 307.

16. For a discussion of the Weinberger-Powell Doctrine, see Earl E. Abonadi, "Weinberger-Powell and Transformation: Perceptions of American Power from the Fall of Saigon to the Fall of Baghdad" (master's thesis, Naval Postgraduate School, 2006).

17. Paul Seabury and Angelo Codevilla, *War: Ends and Means* (New York: Basic Books, 1989).

18. Kofi Annan, "The Effectiveness of the International Rule of Law in Maintaining International Peace and Security," in William Joseph Buckley, ed., *Kosovo: Contending Voices on Balkan Intervention* (Michigan: Wm. B. Eerdmans Publishing Company, 2000), 221–23.

19. Arnaud de Borchgrave, "We Are Neither Angels nor Devils: An Interview with Slobodan Milosevic," in Buckley, *Kosovo*, 273–81.

20. Even in the face of verifiable humanitarian atrocities, writers such as Edward Luttwak argued that the United States and European nations should remain indifferent and avoid the impulse to intervene into others' wars. See Edward N. Luttwak, "Give War a Chance," in Buckley, *Kosovo*, 349–55.

21. Woodward, *Balkan Tragedy*, 377.

22. Benjamin S. Lambeth, *NATO's Air War for Kosovo: A Strategic and Operational Assessment* (California: RAND, 2001), v.

23. Borchgrave, "We Are Neither Angels nor Devils," 275.

24. The Independent International Commission on Kosovo, *The Kosovo Report: Conflict, International Response, Lessons Learned* (New York: Oxford University Press, 2000), 90.

25. Ibid., 93.

26. Ibid.

27. For a comprehensive account of daily events surrounding interagency decision making for Bosnia, see Holbrooke, *To End a War*.

28. Daalder and O'Hanlon, *Winning Ugly*, 2.

Fighting in Financial Foxholes: America and the Asian Financial Crisis

9

Chapter

Rozlyn C. Engel

In July 1997, the Thai baht crashed. The central bank, after months of defending the currency, could no longer maintain the baht's official value. The ensuing turmoil sparked an international financial crisis. Within weeks, deeply shaken financial markets throughout Southeast Asia wavered. Within months, the crisis had severely weakened national economies and threatened the viability of ruling governments. The Asian Financial Crisis, a set of interconnected devaluations and widespread bankruptcies, was well under way.

In time, the crisis went global. Within the next few years, Russia, Brazil, and Argentina all experienced currency troubles of their own, which many observers believe had origins in the Asian Financial Crisis. The economic dislocation caused by the crisis and the international financial community's response spawned a vast and impassioned literature on the risks of globalization.[1]

Not unlike physical catastrophes, the forces of an international financial crisis inflict real damage on societies, contributing to uncertainty, instability, and economic disruption. In October 1998, Thailand's Deputy Foreign Minister, Sukhumbhand Paribatra, warned of social chaos in places where "millions are unemployed, where the weak and poor are provided with little or no protection in times of trouble and where racial and religious differences already exist."[2] The UN Economic and Social Commission for Asia and the Pacific (2003) estimated that roughly 13 million people across Asia sank into poverty between July 1997 and the end of 1998. Unemployment rates across the region hit double digits. Thailand alone lost of 7.9 percent of GDP (gross domestic product—a measure of all the goods and services produced by a country) in 1997, 12.3 percent in 1998, and 7 percent of GDP in the first half of 1999. The U.S. government estimated that the costs of resolving the banking crisis in Indonesia to be 45 to 80 percent of GDP; 15 to 40 percent of GDP in Korea; and 35 to 45 percent of GDP in Thailand. Economic contraction put pressure on the financial systems:

nearly all of Indonesia's banks became insolvent during the crisis; about half of Korea's merchant and commercial banks were insolvent or could not meet capital adequacy standards by December 1997.[3] Large economic losses across Asia became irrefutable.

Unlike more traditional conflicts, however, when Asian currencies tumbled there was no "enemy," no one state or nonstate group to blame for the misery. Nations did not face a classic national security problem—and traditional national security solutions would not suffice. Literally billions of individual decisions propelled societies along the path to crisis, and so billions of individuals had to be persuaded to make different decisions to stop the downward spiral.

Ending the crisis required coordinated international action. The effort of the American interagency team to lead the response to the crisis highlighted the failures of international financial policy and have implications for U.S. national security. Responses to the crisis also offered insights into the roles and missions of the agencies involved and the framework required for developing and executing interagency strategy, policies, and competencies to meet similar challenges in the future. In *Mapping the Global Future*, the National Intelligence Council (which authors authoritative assessments for the American intelligence community) identified the management and containment of financial crises as a key uncertainty for the future.[4] Developing interagency capacity to respond to an international economic crisis is imperative.

UNFOLDING CRISIS

Although financial markets are considered among the world's most efficient, they nevertheless remain prone to instability and sharp correction.[5] When a speculative bubble bursts or "hot money" reverses direction, investors with less liquid positions (such as real estate, fixed business investment, and foreign direct investment) can become exposed to significant exchange rate and interest rate risk.[6] A dollar-denominated liability, for example, can increase sharply when a dollar-linked currency devalues. In this manner, a set of short-run events in global money markets can trigger a domestic economic crisis, with a sharp downturn in lending and economic activity. In some cases, the political fallout is considerable. In a few cases, the fallout poses risks for regional security and stability. In the Asian Financial Crisis both occurred.

The volatility of the world's financial markets in the 1970s proved unprecedented. World foreign exchange and global capital markets changed profoundly in 1973, when the United States exited the Bretton Woods system of fixed exchange rates. The international monetary system was developed at a 1944 conference in Bretton Woods, New Hampshire, and implemented after the close of the Second World War. Under the Bretton Woods arrangement, central banks of countries other than the United States were given the task of maintaining fixed exchange rates between their currencies and the dollar. Arbitrage and speculation in foreign exchange were practically nonexistent. International financial flows were largely limited to those necessary for the conduct of international trade and commerce. After 1973, a mixed system of fixed and floating rates emerged that vastly widened the scope for international financial investments, including profitable short-term positions in foreign currencies.

In the post-1973 world, international investing acquired a sophisticated calculus that took into account both the expected return on the underlying asset and the expected return on the currency in which the asset was denominated (whether dollars, pounds, or francs). Economies with strong growth potential, stable (or appreciating) currencies, and good macroeconomic fundamentals became favorite destinations for the world's financial capital. The free-exchange era of the 1970s birthed an age of emerging markets.

Investment flows into emerging markets followed predictable patterns. In the early half of the 1990s, interest rates across the major developed economies were relatively low. Real growth rates in Asia, particularly the Asian "Tigers" of Thailand, South Korea, Malaysia, and Indonesia, were high, which translated into high-performing assets from equities to real estate. During this period, the exchange rates of many Asian countries were fixed relative to the U.S. dollar, making the valuation of the assets straightforward in the short run. For the small, open economies of East and Southeast Asia, the "dollar peg" facilitated trade by reducing the volatility of the prices of exports. Similar price stability was gained for all dollar-denominated imports. The fixed exchange rate also insulated these economies from external shocks resulting from short-run movements in their exchange rates relative to a major trading partner, the United States. Because of high growth rates and perceptions of a stable currency, the assets of these countries attracted the attention of international investors, who poured $80 billion of foreign capital inflows (net) into the region in 1996 alone. In Thailand, net capital inflows for 1996 totaled $19.5 billion. (The country did not see positive net inflows again until 2005.[7])

Ultimately, international markets could view the Thai baht as overvalued at its official rate. When this happened, speculative pressure mounted. Depending on domestic economic conditions and the size of the country's foreign exchange reserves, the costs of defending the official exchange rate became overwhelming, forcing devaluation. The European currency crisis of 1992–93 and the Mexican peso crisis of 1994–95 had highlighted such risks vividly.

Throughout 1996, the warning lights for the Asian "Tiger" economies were starting to flicker. In the case of Thailand—they burned steady. (One powerful warning sign was the collapse of the Bangkok Bank of Commerce in May 1996.) After a long period of expansion, domestic prices were rising, leaving Thai exports less competitive. China's emergence as a highly competitive regional exporter put additional pressure on the country's competitiveness. Rising interest rates in the major world economies and the recovery of U.S. equity markets meant that international investors were primed to rebalance their portfolios. Ominously, currency speculators had begun taking substantial short positions in the Thai baht. Official attempts at defending the value of the baht entailed higher interest rates, which in turn reinforced the recessionary pressures on the Thai economy. The central bank was also running dangerously low of foreign reserves.

On July 2, 1997, Thailand announced a devaluation of the baht, and the bubble burst. The currency depreciated from twenty-four baht to the U.S. dollar on July 1 to twenty-nine baht on July 2. In the days that followed, the baht began a steady depreciation, ending the year at forty-six baht to the U.S. dollar. It hit its nadir of fifty-six baht to the dollar in mid-January of 1998.

Investors quickly realized that Thailand's domestic banking system was dangerously exposed. Bank loans denominated in baht (such as those to local Thai enterprises) lost value in dollar terms. Yet, many Thai banks had borrowed heavily in dollars, debts that had suddenly become much more costly to repay. The effect on the balance sheets of Thai banks was obvious and devastating. Observing these developments, capital flight became a huge issue, the currency fell still further, and new bank lending dried up almost completely. Within weeks, the country's currency crisis had morphed into a systemic banking catastrophe.

Soon investors became suspicious of any Asian economy that resembled Thailand. In short order, the speculative pressure mounted on Indonesia, Malaysia, and the Philippines. The contagion then ebbed until October, when Taiwan devalued its currency, which then put pressure on Hong Kong and Korea. By late 1997, the economies of Southeast Asia had fallen into deep recessions. In 1998, real per capita GDP fell by 9.4 percent in Thailand, by 9.1 percent in Indonesia, and by 9.0 percent in South Korea. Foreign banks sharply curtailed new lending throughout the region.[8]

Growing economic insecurity put governments under tremendous pressure to find solutions and provide relief. The prospects of social unrest and political instability escalated—everywhere. Admiral Joseph W. Prueher, commander in chief of Pacific Command (the U.S. military command responsible for the region), warned Congress, "we are watchful for early signs of instability . . . and some increases in anti-American rhetoric. . . . U.S. Pacific Command is taking steps to maintain the visibility of American military presence."[9] Stanley Roth, the U.S. assistant secretary of state for East Asian and Pacific affairs, stated, "As the economic crisis forces millions back below the poverty line and threatens to eradicate much of Asia's nascent middle class, progress made on the security front can no longer be taken for granted. As 1930s Europe so dramatically demonstrated, debilitating economic pressures can destroy cooperative instincts and convert constructive competition into controversy and conflict."[10] Washington began to worry.

A REGION AT RISK

Although the Asian Financial Crisis never posed a direct and imminent threat to U.S. national security, the spiraling Asian economies certainly had national security implications. National security instruments might well have been called upon to help address the problem. Without question, the interagency community would have to understand the implications of the crisis for security and stability in Asia. The problems faced were daunting. Virtually every country touched by the crisis was deeply troubled.

Thailand revised its constitution in November 1997, culminating a process started in 1996. Prime Minister Chavalit Youngchaiyudh was forced to resign in November 1997, and a five-party coalition led by Chuan Leepai took control of the government. Charges of corruption plagued the new government, however, and it could not make progress against the economic recession. A new prime minister, Thaksin Shinawatra, took control in August 2001 after months of political uncertainty. He held power until a military coup in the autumn of 2006. Since 2003, Islamic militant activity has become an increasing concern.

Malaysia entered a period of unrest starting with political scandals involving government officials accused of misconduct and corruption. By the fall of 1999 the parliament was dissolved. In the subsequent elections, the opposition doubled its number of seats, though the government maintained its dominant majority. Later persecution and imprisonment of political opponents were deemed unjust by international observers. Throughout the crisis, Prime Minister Mahathir continued to hold power. He retired in 2002.

In South Korea, presidential elections were held at the close of 1997. Kim Dae-jung's victory was the first true victory of an opposition party in a Korean presidential election. It occurred at the height of the country's economic crisis. The opposition party had a clear mandate to pursue significant structural economic reform. By 2000 a virtual two-party system had emerged with the resurgence of the previous ruling party, renamed the Grand National Party. Numerous scandals, usually involving charges of corruption, have roiled the successive governments of South Korea.

By early 1998, riots erupted in Indonesia. Amid popular disillusionment with corruption and economic instability, Suharto was forced to resign on May 21, 1998. Vice President B. J. Habibie took power. In June 1999, Indonesia held elections for its national, provincial, and subprovincial parliaments, with nearly fifty political parties competing for seats. Although a step toward greater democratization, the elections created another round of political unrest and fed the ongoing economic instability. In the summer of 1999, the armed forces were used to quell the political upheaval.

Indonesia is of particular strategic importance. The country controls the Strait of Malacca, a major oil-shipping lane, and has the largest (Sunni) Muslim population in the world, about 200 million. The financial shocks experienced by Indonesia during the financial crisis stimulated Koran study and Islamic school attendance and not other social activities nor secular school attendance. Daniel Chen attributes the Islamic resurgence to the lack of government-provided social insurance after the crisis. For example, when public support is more widely available, so that basic needs of the population can be met, fewer people turn to radical religious organizations for that help.[11]

In one sense, the economic crisis across the region made the calls for needed political reform and greater accountability more credible. Throughout the region, opposition parties gained strength, and more competitive elections occurred. But the process was fraught with risk. Stanley Roth's warning in 1998 is still worth noting: "Political transition under economic duress can be difficult and even dangerous, and a democratic outcome is in no way assured."[12]

KEEPING WASHINGTON UP AT NIGHT

In responding to any international financial crisis the immediate U.S. goals were

1. restoring stability to international financial markets;
2. protecting U.S. commercial interests at home and abroad;
3. promoting U.S. strategic interests globally.

These three goals enjoy widespread acceptance. Other commonly recited goals for U.S. policy that enjoy somewhat less consensus were

4. promoting the economic stability and growth of lower-income countries;
5. defending the gains from liberalizing international trade and financial markets.

No one federal agency had the mission or capacity to meet all of these objectives. Dealing with the Asian Financial Crisis would have to be a team effort.

As is usual the Treasury Department served as the lead agency during the international financial crisis. Secretary Robert Rubin, former chief of Goldman Sachs, and Deputy Secretary Lawrence Summers, a Harvard professor and former chief economist at the World Bank, directed the activities. They were aided by Undersecretary of International Affairs David Lipton and Assistant Secretary for International Affairs Timothy Geithner. Although Treasury took a leadership role, it never moved far from the shadow of the White House. The secretary of the treasury had regular contact with the Oval Office. Rubin's relationship with President William J. Clinton was close. Rubin had served as the first director of the National Economic Council and was deeply involved in the resolution of the Mexican crisis that began in 1994. He moved to Treasury in 1995. The White House was reassured by the department's traditionally close ties with the financial sector. Rubin's professional credibility and personal networks on Wall Street were generally viewed as added strengths.

Other U.S. agencies played largely supporting roles during the Asian Financial Crisis. The U.S. Federal Reserve, the "Fed," has the mission to provide the nation with a safe, flexible, and stable monetary and financial system. Its international scope has been generally limited to tracking and interpreting international market events as they pertain to U.S. economic fundamentals. It is rare for the Fed to intervene in currency markets for the purpose of stabilizing either the U.S. dollar or other major currency, much less the Thai baht. It can, however, play an important role in providing independent research and analytical support to the department and act as the U.S. Treasury's fiduciary agent in the markets.

The State and Defense Departments also had to be involved. The roles and missions of both departments touched on the tasks required to promote security and stability in Asia. The crisis threatened to make their jobs much more difficult.

Neither department, however, had the deep technical expertise to grasp the nature of the crisis and think strategically about their role in the policy response.

Congress played a predictably complex part in supporting and guiding the federal effort. Members of Congress were assigned to various committees that had the authority to draft legislation within their jurisdictions. The power to write and submit legislation gave the committees and the members who controlled them significant political clout. Within the House of Representatives, the Subcommittee on Domestic and International Monetary Policy (Committee on Banking and Financial Services) and the Joint Economic Committee followed the crisis. Of particular interest, the proposed quota increase for the International Monetary Fund in early 1998 triggered a contentious debate within Congress, largely managed by the Joint Economic Committee under Chairman Jim Saxton. The politics in the Senate were equally contentious. The many aspects of a regional crisis did not fit neatly into the jurisdictions of the committees organized to dovetail with providing appropriations and oversight to various federal agencies. When one committee began to investigate, hold hearings, or legislate on activities that touched on the jurisdictions of another committee, sparks normally flew.

In responding to the crisis the U.S. government could not act unilaterally. Regional powers would want to have their say—in particular, China and Japan. These Asian powers, because of their importance in Asian markets and their influence as regional economic policy, would demand special consideration. A number of the governments, such as the Australia and the Philippines, had long-standing ties with the United States as staunch anti-Communist allies in the Cold War.

Dealing with the various governments in the region required a nuanced approach. Each Asian government brought a common (and limited) set of policy tools for managing the crisis: fiscal policy (exercised by the central government) and monetary policy (exercised by the central bank). Except for the most advanced economies in the region, like Japan, the quality of institutions within Asia was markedly lower than what is typically found in developed economies.

The final set of public institutions involved in managing trans-national crises was the international and multinational organizations, particularly the International Monetary Fund (IMF), the World Bank, and the Association of Southeast Asian Nations (ASEAN). In the Asian Financial Crisis, the IMF proved by far to be the most prominent and influential international agency in promulgating policy. With a mission of promoting international monetary cooperation and stability, as well as fostering economic growth and sound macroeconomic policies, the IMF saw responding to incidents like the Asian crisis as central to its purpose. The managing director, Michel Camdessus, and the chief IMF strategist and first deputy managing director, Stanley Fischer, were both expected to play a leadership role.

Nominally, the highest decision-making body at the IMF is its Board of Governors, which comprises a single "governor" from each of its member-countries and meets once a year. In practice, the smaller Executive Board wields more significant power and formulates day-to-day policy responses, especially during crises. The Executive Board comprises twenty-four directors, five of whom hold permanent seats (the United States, Japan, Germany, France, and the United Kingdom). Voting power within the Executive Board (and the Board of Governors) is apportioned by size of a country's quota. The United States holds 17 percent of the total votes at the IMF. Japan and China together hold about 10 percent.

The IMF's sister institution was the World Bank. Chartered to help reduce poverty and improve living standards, the bank was led by President James Wolfensohn and Chief Economist Joseph Stiglitz, both Americans, during the Asian Financial Crisis. With a governance structure similar to the IMF, the bank differs in that voting powers are assigned on a one country-one vote system. Although the World Bank remained largely on the sidelines during the initial phases of the crisis, it became involved as poverty alleviation and sectoral reforms (two areas of core expertise) emerged as pressing needs. While coordination between the World Bank and the IMF was fairly regular across many levels, there was significant disagreement. Stiglitz, in fact, became a leading critic of the IMF.

Finally, responding to the crisis would also require accounting for the role of a plethora of financial firms—collectively called the global capital market. These agents served their own private interests, not the public good. They could and did swiftly shift investment positions without regard to the economic and social consequences in the region. At the same time, however, international investors, by seeking the highest possible returns from a given asset, had been credited with deepening capital markets throughout the 1990s and improving access to credit for many enterprises throughout Asia. No policy response can ignore the likely market reactions.

FIGHTING THE LAST WAR

A common military adage holds that generals prepare for the last battle. The same could be said of the international financial community. A balance-of-payments crisis is an episode during which imbalances in a country's external flows (goods and services on one side; financial payments on the other) become unsustainable. Until the Asian Financial Crisis, the "classic" balance-of-payments crisis tended to involve heavy public sector borrowing, large current account deficits, a fixed and overvalued exchange rate, and growing national debts. Mexico's "tequila" crisis of 1994–95 was a case in point. Unsustainable deficit spending, recessionary pressures, and a sudden rise in the default risk associated with the government's debt forced a painful devaluation of the peso. Indeed, Mexico was on the minds of many at the outset of Thailand's troubles.

Asia, however, proved a different case. The depth and severity of the Asian Financial Crisis genuinely surprised many experts because, with the notable exception of Thailand, the standard macroeconomic indicators remained relatively benign through the first half of 1997. Consumer prices were stable. Public sector borrowing was moderate. GDP growth had been impressive for many years.

Unemployment remained low. Personal income had been rising. No Asian economy had suffered a major recession in more than a decade.

At the time of the Asian Financial Crisis, much of the research into the dynamics of international financial crisis focused on the domestic mismanagement of fiscal policy as a leading culprit. Fiscal policy becomes especially important under a fixed exchange rate system because it is the primary policy instrument for influencing the domestic internal balance. As such, fiscal discipline is crucial. Public sector deficits and cumulative government debt must remain low and manageable during periods of growth because the country must retain the capacity to increase spending during recessions. Keeping public debt low and sustainable also protects the country's exchange rate from excessive speculative pressure when additional borrowing is required. These lessons were learned the hard way by Latin American countries in the 1980s and 1990s.

They turned out to be less important in resolving the Asian crisis, but they do explain some of the early policy responses.

THE WORLD HAD CHANGED

The 1980s and 1990s saw a profound shift toward more open markets as a spur to economic growth. Together with the calls to reduce trade barriers came calls to reduce the barriers to international capital flows. Full capital account convertibility—meaning unrestricted flows of funds into and out of a country—became a goal of the IMF by the mid-1990s with strong support from the United States, especially the U.S. Treasury. Financial markets began to liberalize across the emerging markets of Asia, substantially reducing the costs of capital for local banks and enterprises.

The foreign funds that flowed into Asia were a mix of long-term capital flowing into enterprises (sometimes termed foreign direct investment) as well as short-term capital flowing mainly into local financial institutions (really loans). The composition of these flows varied substantially across countries. In Thailand, only 16 percent of net capital inflows were classified as long-term foreign direct investment; nearly all the rest were portfolio equity (11 percent) and private credit (67 percent). By contrast, Malaysia had nearly equal amounts of foreign direct investment and portfolio equity. In China, 73 percent of all net capital inflows were long-term foreign direct investment.[13] Short-term investments were of particular concern because, like a highly volatile jet stream, they could shift quickly. Lawrence Summers once referred to these investors as guided by "casino instincts."[14]

The large flows of private credit ultimately entered local Asian banks, which had historically played the role of quasi-public lender to enterprises deemed of key economic importance for the country's long-term growth and development. Ironically, such state-directed lending had been credited with channeling these countries' substantial savings into investments that fueled subsequent development; however, they were not well designed to manage short-term foreign capital flows. In hindsight, the close ties between banks and enterprises led to excessively risky lending, often for longer-term projects like real estate, using inherently unstable short-term loans from abroad. Weak banking supervision proved incapable of tightening the standards for credit analysis, corporate accounting, and lending criteria. Asia's crisis centered on the international exposure of private borrowing rather than the public borrowing of earlier financial crises.

DEVELOPING THE RESPONSE

In the autumn of 1997, as the Asian Financial Crisis rippled across the region, the relevant federal agencies began earnest discussions of policy and strategy options. The frameworks for these discussions varied across the agencies in question.

The first public statements by Treasury occurred in early August, brief statements of support for IMF negotiations with the Thai government. Treasury initially viewed the crisis as limited—a garden-variety balance-of-payments problem. Blame was laid at the feet of the Thai government's fiscal mismanagement, and in the early months the United States refused to contribute to the IMF support package for Thailand. Indeed, the U.S. government continued to push for financial market liberalization through the fall of 1997, suggesting that Treasury did not fully appreciate the linkages among Asian economies, the potential for a systemic banking crisis, and the role played by short-term capital flows.

As Treasury formulated its response, the perspective of the national security community did not figure prominently. Treasury is not well equipped to track the impact of an economic crisis on the political stability of the country or the region. Except at the highest levels, the National Security Council, the broader discussions taking place at the State and Defense Department were largely divorced from the economic prescriptions being developed by Treasury and the IMF.

With the spread of the crisis to Korea and Hong Kong in the autumn of 1997, the United States and global financial institutions entered a second stage of policy formulation, with the IMF taking the most visible leadership role in containing the crisis; however, Treasury maintained influence through its voting power on the IMF Executive Board. The United States, David Hale writes, "used the IMF since the Cold War as a proxy agency for American foreign policy."[15] In the end, because the bulk of foreign institutions lending in the region involved European and Japanese banks, Treasury was relatively unconcerned about the direct impacts on U.S. financial firms and assumed a muted national response masked by IMF initiatives.

Within the IMF, the area departments charged with monitoring the macroeconomic health and stability of the individual countries in that region took the analytical lead. Under normal conditions, the IMF departments conduct regular country consultations (and additional meetings when a country is deemed at risk). Each country is assigned a desk economist (or groups of economists for major countries) who tracks and analyzes the macroeconomic data from that country. In situations where policy reforms are indicated, staff from the functional departments (such as monetary or fiscal affairs) may become involved. In the case of the Asian Financial Crisis, the five major countries involved fell under the purview of the Southeast and East Asia Department.

In the year leading up to Thailand's devaluation, the IMF was aware of the growing risks but was unable to move the Thai government to action. In 1998, Stanley Fischer wrote: "In the 18 months leading up to the floating of the Thai baht in July 1997, neither the IMF in its continuous dialogue with the Thai authorities nor increasing market pressure could overcome the government's reluctance to take action." Interestingly, throughout this crucial period, the IMF kept its concerns to itself, unwilling to risk triggering the crisis that it felt was possible.[16]

A long history of rescuing countries, often due to macroeconomic mismanagement, has shaped how the IMF tackled the policy-making process. Like other central banks, the IMF was also conservative by nature. Its experience and culture led the IMF to favor predictable rules-based policy frameworks for countries, believing that they lend local institutions—especially weak ones—greater credibility and efficacy. As a result, the IMF response to the Asian Financial Crisis was wedded to traditional remedies—strict monetary and fiscal discipline.[17] Statements from the U.S. Treasury indicate general support for the use of multilateral loans from the IMF that were conditional upon local country policies that raised interest rates, reduced government spending, and reformed the financial sector.

While the IMF reacted, Japan and China also began to marshal a response. Both Japan and China managed their exchange rates relative to the dollar, and the devaluation of currencies across the region posed significant risks for the competitiveness of their exports. Japan also faced the prospect of a banking crisis at home, given the dangerous exposure of Japanese commercial banks throughout the region. China faced the pressure of a sudden reversal in capital flows, though its restrictions on short-term flows proved helpful in this regard. Neither country stood to gain from widespread economic and political chaos in the region.

In 1997, Japan proposed an Asian Monetary Fund, an initiative strongly opposed by the IMF and Treasury. In October 1998, Japan allocated funds to a $30 billion two-year credit plan. The next year, after overcoming resistance by the United States and the IMF, Japan started an effort to create a standby fund to prevent a recurrence of the financial crisis. By the autumn of 1999, five nations had drawn a total of nearly $21 billion in loans and currency support from the Miyazawa Fund.[18]

TAKING ACTION

The Federal Reserve, via its New York branch, disbursed U.S. bilateral aid during the Asian Financial Crisis. In the case of humanitarian aid the New York Fed, at the request of Treasury, electronically transferred funds from Treasury's account at the Federal Reserve, to each country's fiscal agent.

IMF distribution of loans generally occurs in a similar manner. Once a final decision was reached and policy conditions met, the IMF credited the account of the relevant member-country. A country's central bank could count those credits as part of their central bank reserves and lend against them to the domestic banking system if necessary.

In return, the countries receiving IMF loans undertook significant reforms in their macroeconomic policy and their financial sectors as part of their loan packages. In 1997 and 1998, for example, the Thai government agreed to sharp budget cuts and high interest rates. Only after a deep recession was the fiscal austerity relaxed, with a $3.5 billion fiscal spending program announced in spring 1999. The country also made significant moves to liberalize domestic and foreign investment and increase rate of privatization.

Regarding the financial sector, Asian governments established ad hoc agencies to relieve failing banks of nonperforming assets, close or merge insolvent banks, and then sell the assets. In October 1997, Thailand set up a state commercial bank to manage the assets of bankrupt financial firms. Several auctions of bad assets took place from June 1998 to August 1999. By August 1999, the Bank of Thailand had closed one private bank and fifty-seven finance companies. In Indonesia, the Indonesian Bank Restructuring Agency was established in January 1998. Bank runs in Indonesia led to additional liquidity support from the Bank of Indonesia in 1997 and 1998. By July 1999, sixty-six banks had been closed. In 1998, Korea established the Korea Asset Management Corporation. The corporation acquired $17 billion in nonperforming loans, using government-guaranteed bonds; it then sold these assets in the next several years. By January 1999, eighty-six financial institutions had been closed or temporarily shut down.

The IMF has significant funds at its disposal but not enough to stem a major regional financial crisis. IMF lending is intended to act as a catalyst for additional private sector investment by stabilizing the economy, enhancing the credibility of macroeconomic policy, and restoring confidence in the markets. In the case of the Asian Financial Crisis, however, these private flows did not return quickly. A strong equity market in the United States and the deep recessions induced by the crisis, likely aggravated by IMF policies themselves, meant that Asia saw net capital outflows through 1999.

In addition to the IMF funds, the Miyazawa Plan, as mentioned earlier, disbursed $30 billion from Japan to Asian countries hit by the crisis. As for China, it maintained the value of its currency, the renminbi (RMB), throughout the crisis despite its outward claims of allowing the currency to float. In this case, the stability of the RMB earned China the praise of the international policy community. The central government's ability to regulate financial markets was notable as well.

FLAWED RESPONSE

Today, debate continues about the relative importance of various factors in causing the Asian Financial Crisis and the overall effect of policy on the short- and medium-term outcomes. With the benefit of hindsight, three "global" policy failures by the American interagency policy team are apparent: (1) an initial underestimation of the systemic risks posed by the global capital market's unexpectedly strong reaction to Thailand's devaluation; (2) a weak understanding of the impact of financial linkages across emerging markets; and (3) a lack of flexibility in IMF policy and a poor representation of Asian interests in the institution.

Baht devaluation was not unexpected. The Thai government's unwillingness to rein in a large and growing current-account deficit contributed to the loss of investor confidence throughout 1997. While the government did raise interest rates in 1997, it refused to develop a clear and effective strategy for devaluing the baht—it lacked a legitimate exit strategy. The government also did not address the fundamental issues raised about the fragility of its banking sector in the wake of the Bangkok Bank of Commerce collapse. Both the United States and the IMF proved reluctant to impress upon the Thais and the global financial markets the scope of the risks they faced, nor did either prepare a contingency plan for a potential regional crisis.

The failure to contain the Thai "financial contagion" was closely linked with the second policy failure—misunderstanding the impact of market liberalization on the financial sectors in emerging economies. It was not until November 1997, when the Asia Pacific Economic Cooperation (APEC) forum met, that the notion that private capital flows were playing a key role in the crisis gained public traction. At that meeting, Clinton agreed to hold a series of high-level meetings to address the crisis. Those meetings began in February 1998 and became known as the Willard Group (or Group of 22).

By late 1997 the failure to anticipate the regional linkages and to contain the crisis seriously undermined the credibility of the IMF.[19] As the trouble spread, the IMF appeared to do little more than react to each new event. Within six months, the currencies of the most seriously affected countries (excluding Thailand) had lost about three-fourths of their value relative to the U.S. dollar. In the case of Asia, net capital inflows of $80 billion in 1996 became net capital outflows of roughly $20 billion in 1998.[20] Of course, blaming the IMF for turmoil did have a certain political convenience: Asian governments were certainly to blame for institutional weaknesses. The Suharto family, for one, engaged in large-scale capital flight at the same time the IMF was attempting to stabilize the economy.

Yet failures in local governance do not exonerate the IMF, which simply did not appear to have anticipated the risks of a systemic crisis nor be able to stem it once it had started. IMF policy during the period reflected its inflexibility in the face of emerging information about the nature of the crisis. Foremost, the IMF insistence on monetary contraction, which aimed at restoring credibility to the exchange rate and stemming the capital outflows, contributed to the regional banking crises. High interest rates forced more bankruptcies, deeper recessions, and social unrest, all of which undermined—rather than restored—overall confidence in these markets.

In the end, the Treasury and many private sector officials viewed the IMF loans as ineffective and (perhaps ironically) excessive. Yet, the United States sent mixed messages throughout the crisis. Congress held up contributions to the IMF until American farming interests made a case that the financial instability was damaging U.S. exports. Treasury publicly endorsed the IMF austerity plans despite some internal dissent and concern about their efficacy. The department also showed reluctance in backing off its push for greater openness in Asian financial markets, a policy that benefited large, competitive financial firms in the United States and left it open to charges of pandering to special interests at the expense of important Asian allies.[21] It also blocked efforts by Japan to strengthen regional monetary cooperation and failed to address the balance of voting power within the IMF.

MAKING CHANGES

The IMF faced withering criticism during and after the crisis. In response, it has reformed its capacity to predict and resolve crises. The IMF developed its Vulnerability Assessment Framework, which comprises a somewhat wider range of predictive tools: the World Economic Outlook, country expert perspectives, country external financing requirements, market information, an Early Warning System model, and financial sector vulnerability measures.

The IMF has also instituted a set of initiatives to enhance long-term reforms and prevent crisis. They include the Financial Sector Assessment Program and Reports on the Observance of Standards and Codes. Finally, the IMF developed new means for the resolution of financial crises—the Sovereign Debt Restructuring Mechanism, Collective Action Clauses, and the strengthening of lending policies.[22] For its part, Treasury supported most of the IMF reforms, with the exception of the Sovereign Debt Restructuring Mechanism, which provided an international legal framework to expedite the restructuring of private sector loans to a sovereign government. These misgivings reflected uncertainly about the implications for U.S. financial firms.

Apart from encouraging incremental change at the IMF, the prospect of organizational learning within Treasury—and across all the agencies—appears to have been overtaken by a change in presidential administrations, the terrorist attacks of September 11, 2001, and the Global War on Terrorism. Although the prospect of a catastrophic terrorist attack is real and demands national attention, the fallout from an untamed and mismanaged financial crisis can be deeply threatening to national interests as well. Indeed, the United States is so integrated into the global economy that virtually every regional financial crisis will be an issue of American concern. In the year following the devaluation of the Thai baht, the United States saw the economies of every major trading partner enter recession. The Asian Financial Crisis contributed to Russia's near implosion in 1998, to Brazil's devaluation in 1999, and then to Argentina's default and devaluation in 2001.

U.S. leaders need to be particularly attentive to conditions in the developing world. Emerging markets are a growing destination for global funds. They also provide significant funds for equity finance. The U.S. government estimates that 13 percent of global market capitalization came from emerging markets. But they also pose systemic risks.[23] Resolution costs of banking crises in all developing and transition economies since 1980 have approached $250 billion. The crisis has also been linked to the rise of economic populism to Latin America, to the rise of antiglobalization forces, to increased momentum for Asian-centered and Asian-led institutions, and to the radicalization of vulnerable Muslim populations.[24]

BUILDING BETTER RESPONSES

The urgency for reforming the capacity of federal agencies to respond to international financial crisis has been dulled by the subsequent recoveries across Asia, the relative political stability in the region, and the fixation with the Global War on Terrorism. Future crises will occur—and they could well dwarf the Asian Financial Crisis, which while deep and widespread did not touch any global economic power. None of the affected states were nuclear powers. None controlled a vital natural resource like energy supply. None abandoned free markets or democracy. Next time, the United States might not be so fortunate.

Effective collaborative action by the U.S. government in a future crisis will be vital. The economies of developed states, which depend on diffuse market forces for generating dynamic growth and national wealth, are not easily harnessed to accomplish national foreign policy goals. Yet such goals have important long-run impacts, and the capacity to conduct coordinated intergovernmental policy is essential. No one country can dictate economic terms in the long term, and punitive economic policies frequently hurt the country using them. Effective intergovernmental policy requires effective interagency coordination, as U.S. policy makers strive to integrate the elements of nation power for exercising U.S. leadership. Much can be done to improve America's capability to respond to a financial crisis.

Better National Security Strategy

Strategy is the lifeline of a guiding idea. The articulation of ends, ways, and means toward achieving a national goal drives the interagency process by establishing a foundation for formulating policies, programs, and processes to implement the strategy. With respect to Asian markets, U.S. strategy was flawed. The economies of the affected countries liberalized their financial markets before undertaking fundamental reform of their banking sectors. With weak oversight, unreliable corporate accounting standards, and close ties between banks and state-owned enterprises, large short-term capital inflows created the potential for a banking crisis. The fact that several large international investors—mainly based in Japan and Europe—were exposed in several countries made matters worse. The U.S. integration of these lessons into current national security strategy has been incomplete at best. The National Security Strategy of 2006 argues that international financial stability is best served by encouraging adoption of flexible exchange rates and open markets for financial services. Both are long-term goals but require careful implementation in the short and medium runs. It elaborates, "In particular, we will continue to urge China to meet its own commitment to a market-based, flexible exchange rate regime. We will also promote more open financial service markets, which encourage stable and sound financial practices."[25] This objective seems motivated at prodding China into a "fairer" exchange rate policy; however, it does not seem to have duly weighed the risks for a country with a fragile banking sector. Liberalization of capital accounts should be complemented by broader market and institutional reforms.[26] Full convertibility of the capital account is not sufficient for financial stability and efficient credit markets. Full convertibility should probably be the long-term goal. Policy makers, however, should not underestimate the risks nor overestimate the benefits of pushing for this ultimate objective. U.S. strategy should better reflect this reality.

Sound Policies Facilitate Effective Action

Even with a sound strategy, the interagency team cannot effectively conduct operations if the policies guiding their efforts are unsound. Several need to be rethought.

1. The United States should continue to encourage countries to move away from hard currency pegs. In general, floating exchange rates reduce the risk of balance-of-payments crisis and increase the range of domestic policy options for managing the domestic economy. Asia, in particular, with its history of high saving and low inflation, seems well positioned to manage the risks associated with a floating rate. Its reluctance to do so stems from a desire for stability in its trade with the United States, which has served as a reliable engine of growth for two decades. Yet that is not enough. Like full convertibility of the capital account, moving to a floating exchange rate is not a sufficient condition for greater financial stability. Only a commitment to deeper institutional reform will achieve that.[27] The management of economic policy under a floating exchange rate is affected by the quality of the domestic policy institutions, by the degree of international capital mobility, by the size and composition of the country's international reserves as well as the pattern of its trade, and by its political environment and history. The United States should devote resources to working closely with central banks on developing their capacities to manage macroeconomic performance with open trade and capital flows.[28]

2. Fiscal and monetary austerity is not always the right policy. In the case of the Asian Financial Crisis, the mix of high interest rates and budget cuts deepened the troubles and undermined the goal of restoring confidence. "The Fund recognized that the underlying problems in East Asia were weak financial institutions and overleveraged firms," Joseph Stiglitz writes, "yet it pushed high interest rate policies that actually exacerbated those problems."[29] The strict adherence to fiscal consolidation requires a critical rethinking in light of the Asian Financial Crisis. In the absence of any social safety nets, these policies deepened the social crisis emerging within these societies.[30] U.S. policies should foster a more holistic approach that balances fiscal reforms, civic responsibility, and social services.

3. U.S. policies that back away from the promotion of free trade are counterproductive. Despite the criticisms of antiglobalization parties, economic growth remains the single best avenue to alleviating poverty and raising living standards in the long run. As a consequence of the region's strong economic

performance, standards of living rose significantly, with some economists estimating that tens of millions of people in Southeast Asia left poverty between 1985 and 1995.[31] The fundamental causes of the Asian expansion are still debated, but most agree that high savings and investment rates, an emphasis on human capital accumulation, high levels of social cohesion and cooperation, and openness to international trade all mattered for the successful transition from traditional agrarian societies to middle-income countries with more diversified manufacturing bases and service sectors.

Mechanisms for Effective Action

In order to deal with an international financial crisis, the government will need better instruments for implementing policies. These should include the following:

1. Reconsider the U.S. funding process for international financial rescue. During the Asian Financial Crisis, a mixture of domestic political interests and antiglobalization activism successfully hindered the U.S. response. The IMF funding was blocked in Congress. Treasury had difficulty providing leadership on the need for urgent assistance. Developing mechanisms to enable the Treasury and related agencies to act during a crisis should be a priority.
2. Refocus current institutions. In recent years, the IMF has reached beyond its traditional missions by introducing structural reform elements and poverty alleviation schemes. These moves blur the lines between the IMF and World Bank, create redundancy and waste, increase the unconstructive turf wars between the two organizations, and send mixed signals to member-countries. Since the United States plays a lead role in both institutions, it must pioneer reforms.

Also in regard to this point, the IMF's governance structure, which came under scrutiny during the Asian Financial Crisis, needs reform. Currently, only Japan is a permanent member of the Executive Board. The other four are North Atlantic allies: the United States, Germany, France, and the United Kingdom. Of the remaining nineteen rotating members, only four represent the remainder of South Asia, East Asia, Southeast Asia, and the Pacific Islands. Europe has nine seats total. If current projections of Asian growth are realized, Asian grievances will only grow and gain greater legitimacy. "Such post–World War II creations as the United Nations and the international financial institutions risk sliding into obsolescence unless they adjust to the profound changes taking place in the global system," concludes the National Intelligence Council, "including the rise of new powers."[32] The United States must address this long-term issue and temper the strong temptation to use current unilateral power to preserve the status quo. In addition, the need for the professional staff of the IMF to increase its permanent presence in its member-countries seems self-evident. Perhaps a system of regional districts, resembling the Federal Reserve System, would better suit the policy-making needs of a global monetary authority.

3. Produce more reliable analyses of exchange rate risk in the global financial system. During the Asian Financial Crisis, the IMF and Treasury were increasingly aware that the heavy reliance on debt financing, combined with exchange rate exposure,

generated serious risk for a financial crisis. Their models and the methods of analysis, however, did not reflect the growing informal awareness of trouble. Both require better analytical tools and more effective means for communicating risks to governments, financial institutions, and the public.

4. Make progress toward "unified statecraft." The Department of Defense *Quadrennial Defense Review* (2006) defines unified statecraft as "the ability of the U.S. Government to bring to bear all elements of national power at home and to work in close cooperation with allied and partners abroad."[33] It continues by noting that unconventional trans-national threats require "military diplomacy" and "complex interagency coalition operations." During the Asian Financial Crisis, the State and Defense Departments did little other than talk. For example, Secretary of Defense William Cohen made three high-profile visits to Asia in 1998 and spoke directly to the region's insecurity. The U.S. Congress was even more difficult to persuade and tended to undermine U.S. efforts at a coordinated policy, especially as it related to U.S. goals within the IMF. The United States will not develop the capacity to undertake unified craft unless Congress insists that agencies develop the requisite expertise, doctrines, and mechanisms to undertake joint operations—and provides the authorities for interagency teams to act.

5. Improve capacity to conduct joint security and economic missions. In the aftermath of the invasion of Iraq, the difficulties of postconflict economic stabilization are apparent to U.S. policy makers. Similar challenges would complicate the need to stabilize a China, India, or major Middle East country spiraling out of economic and political control during a major financial crisis. According to the National Intelligence Council, "the problem of state failure—which is a source or incubator for a number of transnational threats—argues for better coordination between institutions, including the international financial ones and regional security bodies." Indeed, the council identified two primary roles for the United States in the coming decade—providing global security and stabilizing the world's financial system.

WARNING SIGNS

Despite the successful resolution of the Asian Financial Crisis, there is little cause for complacency. As the National Intelligence Council concludes, "it is unclear whether current international financial mechanisms would be in a position to forestall wider economic disruption [in the event of another major international financial crisis]."[34] Current U.S. strategy and policies are not prepared for a major financial crisis. The interagency team lacks the analytical tools, expertise, and funding mechanisms for effective action. At the same time, the United States must demonstrate more decisive leadership in international organizations like the IMF and the World Bank.

NOTES

1. For the controversies surrounding globalization, see Jagdish Bhagwati, *In Defense of Globalization* (New York: Oxford University Press, 2004); William Easterly, *The Elusive Quest for Growth: Economists' Adventures and Misadventures in the Tropics* (Cambridge, MA: The MIT Press, 2001); Joseph Stiglitz, *Globalization and Its Discontents* (New York: W.W. Norton, 2002).

2. Michael Richardson, "'A Potential for Chaos' Haunts the Region: Asian Turmoil Raises Fears of Civil Violence," *International Herald Tribune*, October 16, 1998, at http://www.iht.com/articles/1998/10/16/pacif.t_0.php.

3. General Accounting Office, "International Finance: Actions Taken to Reform Financial Sectors in Asian Emerging Markets," GAO-99-157 (June 1999), 5, at http://www.gao.gov/archive/1999/gg99157.pdf.

4. National Intelligence Council, "Mapping the Global Future" (December 2004) at http://www.dni.gov/nic/NIC_globaltrend2020.html.

5. Charles Kindleberger, *Manias, Panics, and Crashes: A History of Financial Crises* (New York: Wiley, 2000).

6. "Hot money" is the hundreds of billions of dollars that flow into short-term positions globally each day. It is also referred to as "portfolio investment."

7. Anoma Sukkasem, "Post-crisis Recovery: Foreign Investment Tide Surges Back," *The Nation* (March 2, 2006).

8. Penn World Tables, "Penn World Tables: PWT 6.2" (Philadelphia: Center for International Comparisons, University of Pennsylvania, 2007).

9. Joseph W. Prueher, testimony before the House Armed Services Committee, (March 4, 1998), at http://www.shaps.hawaii.edu/security/98-3-4prueher.html.

10. Richardson, "A Potential for Chaos."

11. Daniel L. Chen, "Club Goods and Group Identity: Evidence from Islamic Resurgence during the Indonesian Financial Crisis," National Bureau of Economic Research Working Paper (September 2004): 1–51, at http://www.religionomics.com/erel/S2-Archives/REC04/Chen%20-%20Club%20Goods%20and%20Group%20Identity.pdf.

12. Richardson, "A Potential for Chaos."

13. Xiao-Ming Li, "China's Macroeconomic Stabilization Policies Following the Asian Financial Crisis: Success or Failure?" *Asian Survey* 40, no. 6 (November–December 2000): 941.

14. See, for example, J. Bradford De Long, Andrei Shleifer, Lawrence H. Summers, and Robert J. Waldmann, "The Size and Incidence of the Losses from Noise Trading," *The Journal of Finance*, 44, no. 33 (July 1989): 681–96.

15. David D. Hale, "The IMF, Now More than Ever: The Case for Financial Peacekeeping," *Foreign Affairs* 77, no. 6 (1998): 12.

16. Stanley Fischer, "In Defense of the IMF: Specialized Tools for a Specialized Task," International Monetary Fund (1998) at http://www.imf.org/external/np/vc/1998/073098.htm.

17. General Accounting Office, "International Finance."

18. Michael Richardson, "Japan Endorses Standby Fund to Stabilize Southeast Asia," *International Herald Tribune*, November 27, 1999, at http://www.iht.com/articles/1999/11/27/a1_30.php.

19. See, for example, Stiglitz, *Globalization*.

20. See Guillermon A. Calvo and Frederic S. Mishkin, "The Mirage of Exchange Rate Regimes for Emerging Market Countries," *Journal of Economic Perspectives* 17, no. 4 (2003): 99–118.

21. Alan S. Blinder, "Eight Steps to a New Financial Order," *Foreign Affairs*, 78, no. 5 (1999): 50–63.

22. General Accountability Office, "International Financial Crises: Challenges Remain in IMF's Ability to Anticipate, Prevent, and Resolve Financial Crises," GAO-03-734 (June 2003), at http://www.gao.gov/new.items/d03734.pdf.

23. General Accounting Office, "International Finance."

24. Patrick Honohan, "Banking System Failures in Developing Countries: Diagnosis and Prediction," Working Paper No. 39, Bank for International Settlements (1997).

25. The Office of the White House, *The National Security Strategy of the United States* (Washington, DC: Government Printing Office, 2006), 30, at http://www.whitehouse.gov/nsc/nss/2006/nss2006.pdf.

26. Ronald I. McKinnon, *Money and Capital in Economic Development* (Washington, DC: The Brookings Institution, 1973).

27. Calvo and Mishkin, "The Mirage of Exchange Rate Regimes."

28. Ibid.

29. Stiglitz, *Globalization*, 110.

30. Daniel L. Chen, "Islamic Resurgence and Social Violence during the Indonesian Financial Crisis," National Bureau of Economic Research Working Paper (2004).

31. See Xavier Sala-i-Martin, "The World Distribution of Income: Falling Poverty and . . . Convergence, Period," *Quarterly Journal of Economics* 121, no. 2 (2006): 351–97.

32. National Intelligence Council, "Mapping the Global Future," 13–14.

33. The Department of Defense, *Quadrennial Defense Review* (2006), at http://www.globalsecurity.org/military/library/policy/dod/qdr-2006-report.htm.

34. National Intelligence Council, "Mapping the Global Future," 32.

10
Chapter

"Interagency Overseas": Responding to the 2004 Indian Ocean Tsunami

Gary W. Anderson

It was Christmas week. Washington was on holiday. And that is when *it* happened.

It struck with the power of 23,000 Hiroshima atomic bombs. On December 26, 2004, two massive tectonic plates that comprise a major portion of the earth's crust moved. The shock waves from this massive displacement created a *tsunami*: a series of massive waves that swept across Southeast Asia, killing about 230,000 — the worst disaster of its kind in modern history.

The United States was among the nations that mobilized humanitarian aid for the victims. Indonesia, Thailand, Sri Lanka, and the Maldives were the primary recipients of assistance. In addition, the United States Agency for International Development (USAID) provided funding to India for to increase its preparedness to respond to similar disasters in the future.

Ultimately, harnessing the interagency community to provide aid to millions of people over thousands of miles of land and ocean was less a matter of crafting policies in Washington than an issue of organizing and managing activities in the field — mastering the operational aspects of disaster response.

U.S. humanitarian assistance in response to the tsunami vividly illustrates well the obstacles faced in coordinating the efforts of multiple federal agencies with a plethora of international organizations and foreign governments. In many respects the response demonstrates that, despite many difficulties, the United States manages international humanitarian relief operations in a responsive and effective manner.

THE DAY THE EARTH SHOOK

In the early morning hours on December 26, 2004, an earthquake off the coast of Sumatra spawned a tsunami (tidal wave) that had worldwide repercussions. The wave traveled through the open ocean virtually unnoticed. As massive as these disturbances are, they only manifest themselves as overwhelming walls of waves when they reach shallow waters. Then they make landfall. Scores of fishermen at sea in the fourteen countries never knew what passed beneath them until they returned to their ports to find their homes and families gone.

In addition to the hundreds of thousands missing, some 1.7 million were rendered homeless. In a few moments, schools, businesses, and whole communities were plowed under by a wall of water. The tsunami literally destroyed inhabited areas in many coastal regions. In some areas the damage extended miles inland. Tens of thousands found themselves in makeshift refugee camps without medical supplies, shelter, or food and water.

Responding to a catastrophe that stretched throughout South Asia to the coast of Africa required the largest humanitarian relief and recovery operation the world has ever seen in the wake of a natural disaster. It was arguably the most extensive relief effort ever undertaken by the international community. The breadth of the response was as remarkable as its scale. Government agencies from many countries participated. Militaries from the United States, the United Kingdom, Japan, Australia, Singapore, and the Philippines sent troops, ships, aircraft, and landing craft. International organizations (such as the United Nations Children's Fund—UNICEF) and nongovernmental organizations (like the Red Cross) contributed assistance, as did the private sector and many individuals. The immediate disaster relief operation lasted approximately until the end of January 2005. The total assistance provided is estimated at $13.6 billion.[1]

For the United States, a successful response effort quickly became a foreign policy and public diplomacy imperative. American policy makers had a deep desire to improve the U.S. image in that part of the world. Washington was interested in building a strategic relationship with India. In addition, the United States sought greater cooperation from countries in the region in combating transnational terrorism. At the time, however, America's public diplomacy efforts were under siege as U.S. combat operations in Iraq and the U.S.-led global war on terrorism became increasingly controversial. In addition, the initial press reports criticized the White House for being slow to recognize the scope of the disaster and offer timely and generous assistance. Recovering from the initial bad press became a presidential priority.

UNDERSTANDING INTERNATIONAL DISASTER RESPONSE

Disaster relief experts generally define humanitarian operations as responding to natural or technological (i.e., man-made) disasters in which there are no human attempts to interfere with the response effort. Operation Sea Angel, the 1991 relief effort in the wake of a tropical cyclone (hurricane/typhoon), is an example of this.[2]

In contrast, complex humanitarian operations face some human opposition to the relief effort. During these operations, responders have to be concerned with providing security for victims and relief agencies as well as offering humanitarian assistance. One example is the 1992–93 relief effort in Somalia. In this case, a drought-induced famine was exacerbated by the looting of relief supplies by militias in a failed state. Meanwhile, the militias harassed aid workers and attacked UN security forces.[3]

Before the 2004 tsunami, two of the affected nations (Indonesia and Sri Lanka) faced concerns about insurgencies and civil war. Conducting relief missions in these countries demanded complex contingency responses. Providing assistance to other nations ravaged by the tidal waves represented more conventional humanitarian disaster relief and recovery operations.

When the tsunami hit, the United States lacked a clear doctrine and standardized processes for dealing with either kind of international disaster response. The military, USAID, and the State Department, as well as other federal agencies, all had their own methods and procedures for dealing with disasters. Although they had some experience in working together, each response was unique.

Following the end of the Cold War, when an international disaster required a robust American response, the U.S. military was frequently the first responder on the scene. To enhance joint military-civilian cooperation, the military tried to create a standing concept for responding to disasters. After Somalia, Lieutenant General Anthony Zinni, who had been involved in the initial relief effort in 1992–93 and the subsequent evacuation of U.S. forces, hosted a series of conferences, dubbed "Emerald Express," to improve interagency response between U.S. government agencies, particularly the military, and nongovernmental organizations (NGOs). Interagency committees worked to improve information-sharing and standardizing assessments. Unfortunately, after Zinni left the First Marine Expeditionary Force, the effort flagged.

In May 1997, President William J. Clinton issued Presidential Decision Directive (PDD) 56, which established an interagency planning and coordination process for responding to humanitarian disasters overseas. PDD 56 identified responsibilities, specified planning and coordination tasks, and required issuing strategic guidance to responding agencies. But as the directive was based on a military-planning model, many in the interagency community were unfamiliar with its requirements, lacked the expertise to participate, and proved reluctant to join in a process that appeared to mimic military organizations and roles and missions.[4] President George W. Bush rescinded the directive. As a result, when the 2004 tsunami occurred, the United States lacked a comprehensive formal process that had incorporated the lessons learned from Somalia and other complex contingencies. Many of these lessons were relearned in 2004.

On the positive side, while agencies found PDD 56 too Washington-centric, the procedures developed, exercised, and implemented in the Pacific theater by regional staffs and experts proved more effective at meeting the operational needs of the crisis than plans drafted, negotiated, and supervised from back in the United States. Long before the tsunami, the Pacific Command (PACOM) routinely dealt with disasters large and small. Working with federal agencies, host nations, and the international community, PACOM had processes and procedures in place that served as the rough equivalent of an interagency doctrine for handling contingency operations.

IN THE WAKE OF THE STORM

The initial U.S. military response involved U.S. Pacific Command headquarters in Hawaii, which designated a Marine Corps–led task force. Unlike typical military missions, it was not dubbed a Joint Task Force, but was given the less military-sounding title of Combined Support Force (CSF) 536. As with Operation Sea Angel in Bangladesh, the military effort was built around the command element of the III Marine Expeditionary Force from Okinawa. The Pacific Command's Deployable Joint Task Force Cell provided a "joint" presence, representing the other armed services including the navy, air force, army, and coast guard. The force had to support civilian efforts in multiple countries where the U.S ambassador acted as the overall American coordinator.

To support the JTF, PACOM put its Joint Operations Center (JOC) in a fully staffed, full-time mode under the leadership of the Director of Operations (J3). In addition, PACOM set up two organizational initiatives designed to foster interagency cooperation in the operation. The first decision was to create a tsunami HA specific JIACG (Joint Interagency Coordination Group). The second was to integrate a two-man team from OFDA into the JOC, to function as the primary liaison between PACOM and OFDA headquarters in Washington and the OFDA DART teams deployed into the region.

The JIACG experiment was not very successful for a number of reasons, the most important of which was probably that the emergency operational phase of the tsunami relief operation was over before the pickup JIACG could get itself organized and into effective operation.

The utilization of the OFDA team, on the other hand, was extremely successful. Fully integrated into the JOC and provided the full range of PACOM resources, especially communications, the OFDA representative was assigned by the J3 the task of leading off the twice daily command briefings (upon JOC floor shift changes). The free flow of information up and down the chain—from the deployed military units and the DART teams to and through PACOM to Washington—fostered a high degree of mutual confidence between the various USG participants (military and civilian), and therefore encouraged extensive interagency cooperation and coordination.

The Marine-led CSF itself was forward-based in Utapao, Thailand, but had elements in most of the countries most severely impacted. Among the first major U.S. units on the scene were the *Abraham Lincoln* battle group, centered on the aircraft carrier USS *Abraham Lincoln* in Indonesian waters, and the Expeditionary Strike Group, centered on the helicopter carrier USS *Bonhomme Richard* and the Fifteenth Marine Expeditionary Unit. Other nations, including Australia and Singapore, quickly sent forces as well. The CSF never exercised operational control over coalition units, but military relief centered on the CSF due to the considerable command, control, and communications capabilities that the Americans brought to bear.

American relief involvement was most intense in Indonesia, Thailand, the Maldives, and Sri Lanka. In India, USAID funding is credited with playing a major role in increasing that nation's readiness, even though U.S. efforts on the ground were not required or requested. The response of the American military and other governmental agencies had to be tailored to each nation. This made the undertaking even more complicated.

Indonesia was the first and worst hit by the disaster. Because the disaster occurred in the rebellious Aech Province, the Indonesian relief effort was complicated—as was the relationship between the Indonesian military and the U.S. government, which is just now beginning to improve after the United States cut off aid during the Suharto dictatorship. The diffuse nature of command over the Indonesian military vastly complicated relief efforts; often, UN, U.S. military, and NGO officials had to go to each military service separately to get cooperation.[5]

The Indonesian military was also constrained in that it had service members and families in Banda Aech enforcing martial law in the rebellious province, many of whom were lost when the waves hit. This was exacerbated by mutual distrust between the military and the NGOs.

In Thailand, the government quickly invoked their Civil Defense Act, which helped focus Thai government coordination and facilitated cooperation with international relief efforts.[6] Many observers credited the annual Cobra Gold military exercises held with the United States and other regional allies with sharpening the Thai response.[7] The Thai government formed a task force to coordinate internal relief, and another under the Minister of Foreign Affairs to coordinate foreign relief.[8]

By gross national product, the Maldives was the worst hit of the affected nations, and had no real experience in disaster management. However, the government acted quickly to respond by forming a Ministerial Task Force and setting up a National Disaster Management Centre.[9]

In Sri Lanka, the nation's military responded first, but the response was ultimately placed under civilian control, unlike Indonesia where the army remained prominent throughout. The presidential secretariat initially coordinated relief, and was later augmented by a Centre for National Operations.[10] However, in both Sri Lanka and Indonesia, security in the face of insurgent threats gave the situation the character of a complex humanitarian emergency, whereas the other nations discussed here treated the disaster as a simple humanitarian emergency. The American response had to take these differences into account.

As one Indian diplomat told the author, "we wanted to show the world that we are capable of helping ourselves." The Indians did not require or request large-scale military assistance, but they did accept monetary aid working primarily through four agencies: the Asian Development Bank, the United Nations Development Program, the International Fund for Agricultural Development, and the World Bank. The majority of the $17.9 million in U.S. government aid seems to have come through these sources.[11] The real contribution from the United States came prior to the disaster, in the form of USAID funding for disaster relief preparedness.[12]

LEARNING FROM DISASTERS

While the United States had to respond to the unique situation presented by the conditions on the ground in each country, examining the operations in total provides some common lessons for dealing with interagency teams leading large-scale international disaster response.

The Importance of Assessment

Disaster relief should be what the military calls a "reconnaissance pull operation." In theory, the assessment of the situation should drive the operation. In reality, most disasters become largely supply driven operations. This is usually due to two factors. First, assessments tend to be inadequate and overlapping among agencies. Second, uncoordinated relief efforts by many NGOs and other well-meaning foreign agencies tend to clog ports and airfields in the underdeveloped countries most vulnerable to these disasters with unneeded and unwanted relief supplies.[13] Unfortunately, the tsunami relief effort was ultimately plagued by both of these problems.

The Myth of Medical Emergency

There is a popular misperception that the most pressing need for immediate relief in natural disasters is medical. The harsh reality is that in most floods, major storms, earthquakes, and tsunamis, trauma casualties tend to sort themselves out quickly. Those killed by blunt trauma or drowning in the initial disaster die almost immediately, and those that survive usually get first aid rather quickly from local sources. The real medical problems tend to show up in the guise of disease several weeks after the disaster. This can largely be prevented by making the restoration of clean drinking water an immediate priority. The disposal of human and animal remains is an immediate problem, but several of the most competent NGOs are very good about funding local citizens to conduct this work, which can help prevent well-meaning foreigners from disposing of bodies in seemingly efficient but culturally inappropriate ways.[14]

The Importance of Transportation and Communications

The urgent requirement in most disasters is transportation and distribution of aid, as these disasters tend to disrupt road systems and destroy boats needed to distribute supplies coming in at major ports and airports. They also tend to disrupt local communications. This is why the helicopters, landing craft, and communications provided by foreign militaries are so important in the immediate aftermath of ongoing disasters—the operative word being *immediate*. Foreign militaries need to recognize when the roads have dried out and the civilian transportation infrastructure has recovered to the point where they (the foreign militaries) are no longer necessary, lest they overshadow the host nation's government. Working oneself out of a job should be the main objective of any military relief effort.[15] Foreign militaries seemed to have recognized that in this particular disaster, and made the transition smoothly.

Transition from Relief to Reconstruction

Transition can be more difficult for other assisting foreign agencies and NGOs, many of which get donor support based on their continued and visible presence in the host nation. This largely depends upon the competence of the NGO involved. International organizations such as CARE, OXFAM, and Doctors Without Borders regularly have missions in developing countries for long-term development purposes. They seem to transition fairly seamlessly from disaster relief to long-term development in a crisis. Other, less experienced and less competent NGOs have a more difficult time. This is often exacerbated by the varying attitudes of host nation governments toward NGOs, which can often be viewed as subversive to government goals. The welcome of such organizations is likely to wear out quickly.[16] This happened in some cases in this operation.

On-Site Coordination Mechanisms

The interagency coordination methods involved in humanitarian operations in failed states such as Somalia, or areas where governance is not in place, such as Northern Iraq (Kurdistan) in 1991, differ from those required in friendly host nations. In Kurdistan and Somalia, where the U.S. and coalition governments had no effective governments to deal with, the military-developed Civil-Military Operations Centers, which were military-led, and in many cases had to handle government duties such as security and law enforcement. They served the necessary function of coordinating the efforts of the military, other federal agencies, UN international organizations, and NGOs. This is not appropriate in situations where the host nation is functioning and where we are supporting the host nation government. The CSF had to work with the U.S. embassies in Thailand, Indonesia, the Maldives, and Sri Lanka to adapt to the unique coordination mechanisms of each country.[17]

The Importance of Cultural Awareness

Every humanitarian crisis is unique, and an understanding of the local culture and the type of disaster is fundamental to effective relief efforts. For example, during one cyclone-generated disaster in Bangladesh, a French NGO set up water purification units. They had signs printed in Bangla that read "sterilized water." The local religious leaders misinterpreted this as meaning that people who drank the water could no longer have children. This is very critical in a country where having many children to take care of parents in their old age is virtually the only form of social security.[18] This kind of cultural misunderstanding is common in many of these operations, and the 2004 tsunami relief effort suffered its share. However, the U.S. interagency community seems to have gone to great lengths to avoid such problems when it could.

ALL DISASTERS ARE LOCAL

The response to the 2004 tsunami illustrates that major international disasters often have recurring characteristics which the interagency community will be forced to address. Disasters, however, are also unique, and are shaped by many factors, from geography to local politics. In responding to each contingency operation, interagency activities must be sufficiently flexible and agile to adjust to conditions on the ground. Providing assistance to a number of countries across the breadth of the Indian Ocean encountered a number of exceptional challenges.

Surveying the Destruction

Most operations suffer from poor or overlapping assessments, but in this operation, stretching as it did over fourteen countries, with over 150 relief organizations involved, the problem was staggering. In some cases, whole areas were over-assessed. Two particular problems cited in several studies were UN financial procedures that hinder rapid deployment of assessment teams, and the sheer volume of agencies doing assessments for their own specialized needs.[19] It has been noted in post-operation conferences that a standardized format is needed, but one has never been universally adopted even by the major participants, although the U.S. military and other agencies have had some success at adopting the USAID Assessment Handbook.[20]

To facilitate interagency operations, assessments should be improved and standardized. The need for a central information open source database has also long been recognized. This will help responders ascertain what the country looked like before the disaster occurred, so assessors can understand what is really wrong. Disaster expert Jonathan Dworken often asks, "Better that what?" Unfortunately, to Western eyes, a good day in some of these countries looks like a disaster in Europe or the United States.

Competencies and Competition

Sometimes, aid delivered is simply inappropriate for the situation. Some of this can be written off to poor assessment, but too often it is a result of overeager or incompetent NGOs dumping ill-thought-out supplies on already overcrowded tarmacs at airports in underdeveloped countries.[21] In the aftermath of a tsunami, this problem becomes particularly acute, especially in regions where airports and seaports only have one runway and limited ramp space, or when the port or airfield has been damaged by the course of the disaster. When this happens, or when an unwanted infusion of supplies such as winter clothes is delivered to a tropical country, it can be counterproductive. When the convergence of unnecessary aid prevents the delivery of lifesaving supplies, the problem can turn deadly.

Convergence on a disaster is, in part, a reflection of the natural impulse to provide assistance after witnessing horrific visions of a disaster on television. Humanitarian impulses are on occasion exploited by one-time shipments from unscrupulous NGOs, who rent a plane, make a one-time delivery of supplies, and then head out of the country after a fundraising photo opportunity. Without some form of professional certification that would allow nations to identify "fly by night relief" operations and deny them country clearance, such problems will persist.

Even among legitimate relief agencies (including governmental entities), however, organizational motivations can skew short-range relief efforts. CARE, OXFAM, and other major development NGOs have long-term development goals and also do disaster relief in extremis. They know that the high profile work done in an emergency under the glare of international media will focus donors on their efforts in the nation. They do superb work in both capacities, and usually the two efforts complement each other—but not always.

For NGOs and the UN "alphabet" agencies performing diverse missions—including refugee relief, short-term disaster relief, medical assistance, protecting human rights, and long-term development projects—there is no standardized means to judge competencies, foster cooperation rather than competition, and ensure that assistance is distributed in an efficient and effective manner. In the case of the tsunami response, the scale of the effort made the challenge of convergence and deconflicting the competing goals of responders very significant. When UN agencies, for example, clashed with the secretary-general's representative, there was no clear way beyond compromise to resolve the issue.[22] The NGOs are even more problematic as they compete for donors, often fiercely.

U.S. government agencies, including the State Department, USAID, and the Defense Department, are not immune from the challenges of reconciling competencies and competition. For these agencies, although they may have contrasting long term objectives, an interagency mechanism for resolving them exists at the country level, at the embassy. But when operations require regional programs (where operations are spread over several nations), coordinating actions and priorities is more difficult and, as was the case in the tsunami response, mostly an ad hoc effort.

Transition from Relief to Recovery

The U.S. military generally makes this transition well, as it is usually anxious to return its focus to defense priorities. Similarly, the U.S. State Department and its foreign counterparts have little appetite for involvement in long-term recovery missions. NGOs are more problematic.[23] Some observers blame this on a lack of long-term planning capacity.[24] Part of it may also be the desire to see other governmental organizations, which they often see as competitors, leave quickly. Sometimes, poor relations with the host nation government may dictate the course of transition. Again, the scale of the Indian Ocean disaster made the difficulty of managing transitions even more acute. Different countries, and even different regions within countries, operated different transition schedules.

Host Nation Support

The ability of the different countries to accept and manage assistance varied considerably. After-action reports indicate that the Indonesian military coordination effort should get the lowest marks. The Thais were undoubtedly the best. The Maldives did surprisingly well in responding to their first major disaster. Sri Lanka and India both faired tolerably.

Clearly, some countries did better than others. Factors that made a difference include the quality of the legal regime and local governance for responding to disasters, and the level of planning and exercises conducted. Thailand appeared to have the best coordination mechanisms, based upon an existing law for dealing with emergencies. In addition, the Thai military's experience participating in the annual Cobra Gold field exercises gave them valuable expertise in coordinating with the U.S. military and other international partners. The creation of a national coordination mechanism in the Maldives appears to have been very useful in facilitating cooperation with other nations and NGOs. In the case of India, years of USAID preparation prior to the disaster appears to have greatly improved the ability of local authorities to respond appropriately to the disaster. At the national level, India seems to have done the best job of planning for the transition to long-term recovery by coordinating with the four agencies previously mentioned.

In fairness to Sri Lanka and Indonesia, both were involved in internal civil conflicts which significantly complicated organizing response operations.

Lack of a Tsunami Warning System

This is one area where the international community moved in very quickly and effectively to address a problem. In an August 17, 2005, press release, USAID announced a $16.5 million, two-year effort to install an Indian Ocean Warning System (IOWS), similar to the one in the North Pacific that provides warning for the U.S. West Coast, Alaska, Hawaii, Japan, Korea, and other regional neighbors. A year-and-a-half later, when a tsunami-producing earthquake struck near the Solomon Islands, those portions of the system that had been completed gave warning to many of the nations affected in 2004. In addition, an increased public information campaign was credited with helping many in the Solomons to escape to high ground, although that area is not yet fully integrated into the IOWS.

UN Operations

The UN got decidedly mixed reviews in this operation and in its coordination with NGOs. It moved swiftly to take control of the coordination of the overall international relief effort from the ad hoc, American-led effort that began within hours of the tsunami. However, it has been faulted in the execution. Jan Egeland, the UN undersecretary for humanitarian affairs, made an unfortunate statement within days of the operation's commencement, to the effect that the United States was being stingy with aid.[25] This pronouncement was made before most initial assessments were complete and anyone knew what the money would be spent on, much less how much the effort would cost. Egeland's misstep undercut his credibility and the international community's trust and confidence in the UN relief operations.

Other problems surfaced soon after. One independent report cited six major problem areas: (1) the UN lacked authority over the NGOs and international organizations, including the UN's own agencies; (2) support and funding for coordination activities were inadequate; (3) the lack of skills and experience among some senior UN coordinators; (4) inadequate coordination between the UN Resident Coordinator and the Humanitarian Coordinator; (5) UN officials often failed to take a firm line with purveyors of inappropriate aid and local customs officials who became aid "bottlenecks"; and (6) UN officials did not appoint liaison officers to the large number of agencies that they should have been sharing information with.[26] In addition to these general complaints, most officials found the United Nations Disaster Assessment and Coordination Team to be very weak in the field.[27]

EVALUATING AMERICA

Despite the number of general response challenges which confronted aid workers in the aftermath of the tsunami, as well as the specific issues related to the unique conditions encountered in the Indian Ocean region, the United States performed overseas, in extremis humanitarian assistance fairly well. For example, a Google search of "problems in U.S. interagency operations in the Indian Ocean tsunami" revealed no hits. A similar search for domestic disaster response efforts after Hurricane Katrina six months later revealed 103,000 hits. The Congressional Research Service report on the tsunami made no major findings on the immediate relief effort, although it did have observations on long-term reconstruction.[28]

The U.S. government reacted quickly to the disaster. As usual, USAID and OFDA's ability to quickly dispatch qualified personnel to provide an initial professional assessment was crucial. Assessment teams from both the State and Defense Departments followed almost immediately on their heels, as did liaison officers who knew the language and the culture. Seventeen ships and over 170 aircraft eventually responded. At the height of the operation, over seventeen thousand U.S. military personnel and seventeen warships personnel took part. Disaster Assistance Response Teams (DARTs), embassy staffs, and other agency personnel likely swelled the total U.S. personnel contribution to over twenty-five thousand.

Ambassadors in the stricken nations quickly formed teams to deal with coordination issues. In most of these countries, the State Department had some kind of disaster contingency plan in place. The one in Indonesia appeared to be less mature. Even though Indonesia and the United States have mended a number of fences, aid to the security services is still pending the resolution of potential war crimes and human rights issues.

The U.S. military, particularly in the PACOM (the regional U.S. military command responsible for Asia) area, has a great deal of institutional experience in the area of humanitarian relief. Many of its annual bilateral exercises, such as Cobra Gold, have humanitarian relief components. PACOM's forces reacted quickly. The *Abraham Lincoln* battle group was assigned to the Indonesian area, and the Expeditionary Strike Group, centered on the helicopter carrier *Bonhomme Richard*, sailed for Sri Lanka. The hospital ship *Mercy* sailed quickly for the Pacific from the United States and arrived in time to relieve the *Lincoln* group, which was no longer needed several weeks into the operation.

During the course of the operation, the CSF commander, Marine Corps Lieutenant General Blackman, realized that he could not exercise detailed operations in each nation. Consequently, he formed Combined Support Groups for each of the countries where significant U.S. forces would operate. At that point, the operation began to resemble a smaller version of the decentralized Pacific-Asian sub-theaters of World War II, with the CSGs waging separate campaigns, and the CSF playing the "Admiral Nimitz" role of coordinating and arbitrating the allotted resources.[29]

Combined Support Groups provided a model of flexibility, adapting to the unique conditions and needs in each country. Each group supported the ambassador and the on-site country team. The CSF, through the support groups, contributed assessments, emergency transportation, and distribution of relief supplies, as well as search and rescue. On occasion, to facilitate communications and coordination, NGOs and international organizations stayed aboard ship.

Each country presented unique challenges, but the military appeared to adapt well. The government of Indonesia, for example, limited the length of time that the battle group could stay in Indonesian waters, fixing March 28 as the deadline for their departure. American forces concluded operations considerably before that.

State Department operations also adapted to the challenge of the tsunami response. When the disaster occurred, each embassy began to self-organize and coordinate with the host nation, other national diplomatic missions, international organizations, and NGO representatives. The State Department formed teams and developed coordination mechanisms. These teams dovetailed with the military support provided through the CSF.

In Washington, the State Department formed a cooperative arrangement with USAID and PACOM to coordinate aid at the policy level, while embassies worked on local issues such as establishing Status of Forces agreements, smoothing the flow of relief supplies from customs, and working with the host nations and other agencies to establish a smooth flow of information. Indonesia provided

the greatest challenge, while preexisting mechanisms in Thailand made things easier there. The degree of difficulty varied from nation to nation.

USAID quickly dispatched the Office of Foreign Disaster Assessment's
DARTs to impacted countries, and sent culturally proficient experts to act as
liaisons (as mentioned previously). These teams can be the most effective way for
USAID, State, and the military to determine what is wrong and what relief is really
needed. Due to the overwhelming magnitude of this disaster, U.S. military teams
provided a great deal of assistance. Special Operations Forces and Marine Corps
Expeditionary Units, such as the Fifteenth Marine Expeditionary Unit aboard the
Bonhomme Richard task force, received some training in disaster assistance and
relief. They were not a substitute for DARTs, but could augment the teams, particularly when they used the Office of Foreign Disaster Assessment's field guide
and its reporting formats.

Anecdotal evidence indicates that other federal agencies provided effective
support as well. This was particularly true of the Departments of Agriculture and
Justice and the Federal Aviation Administration.

As was the case with host nations and the UN, the Americans found that the
astounding number of people and agencies who wanted to help was sometimes
overwhelming. Managing information flow, coordinating with American NGOs,
and maintaining necessary day-to-day operations in host nations was a distinct
challenge in the hours and days immediately following the disaster.

For U.S. efforts in particular, the efforts of NGOs proved a mixed blessing.
They could provide funding for things that the American military and other agencies could not or should not have done. They also provided one of the transition
bridges to long-term recovery. On the other hand, they also occasionally impeded
the operation by bringing inappropriate aid or upsetting established processes.
The most frustrating obstacle was that there was no way of certifying useful NGOs
while screening out the bad ones.

Perhaps the most onerous problems came from human rights NGOs. Most of
them are not geared for relief efforts. They watch others work and report if anyone's human rights have been violated. Traditionally, this has been the official
mission of the International Committee of the Red Cross (ICRC), but in the past
few decades they have repeatedly outsourced some of their activities to other
human rights NGOs. Many military, USAID, and NGO personnel complained
that these people took up valuable boat and airplane space that could have been
better used to transport relief supplies and expert personnel.

The proper mechanism for solving this problem would be for the NGO community to develop standards of certification and professional conduct and make
a list of certified NGOs available to potential host nations. Then, if the nation
chooses to ignore the list and let and uncertified NGO join the operation, it would
do so at its own risk.

As in many previous humanitarian operations, establishing effective NGO-
military relations proved a perplexing challenge, though over the years both communities have made efforts to improve coordination. Some of the larger and more

reputable NGOs have hired retired military officers to act both as security advisors and as liaisons to the military, as well as to educate employees and volunteers regarding relationships with the military. Most professional military educational institutions have some instruction on NGO and international organization functions. Nevertheless, as NGOs have proliferated, problems have persisted.

During tsunami relief operations there were many complaints, particularly from U.S. Navy officers regarding the conduct of NGOs aboard the USS *Abraham Lincoln*. Some of this can be written off as a clash of cultures. The navy is perhaps the most traditional of the U.S. services, and etiquette aboard navy ships at sea is very important to them.[30] Having a group of young people more inclined to join the Peace Corps than the Marine Corps, and with no military grounding, would undoubtedly be disruptive to shipboard routine. The conduct of most NGO personnel, however—particularly those from older, more established organizations—was exemplary.

In contrast to the tension of working with NGOs, the military managed its relationships with the host countries very well. Internal security often determined how host nations cooperated with U.S. forces. In particular, security dictated how much access was allowed to foreign NGOs, and sometimes to military units in Indonesia and Sri Lanka. The U.S. government relied on SOFA and Memorandums of Understanding (temporary cooperative agreements) to address issues related to basing forces and legal issues associated with military individuals and property. To the extent that standing agreements for humanitarian operations can be worked out in advance, they facilitate host nation cooperation. In the case of tsunami relief, SOFA agreements in nations like Thailand proved invaluable.

Rapidly gaining permission to fly non–Defense Department personnel aboard DOD aircraft was sometimes problematic, creating a significant impediment to interagency cooperation in the field. Procedures should be pro forma, but in practice, gaining clearances has been a problem in every fast-breaking humanitarian operation, including the 2004 tsunami response.

The United States had difficulty addressing customs delays among host nations in importing relief supplies. This became a problem in several countries. In large part, difficulties appeared in countries where the customs functions of governments were not made a part of the disaster mechanism from the beginning. In most instances during the tsunami relief, situations were addressed once they became a crisis. Standing procedures for obtaining clearances would be very helpful. The Department of Homeland Security could play a lead role in addressing this and similar issues regarding customs functions in international disaster response.

Another operational issue that requires resolution is the challenge of gaining permission to overfly nations with restrictive airspace policies. This became a particular problem with nations such as Burma, which does not have good relations with the United States. During Operation Sea Angel, because of the urgency of the situation, the military Joint Task Force commander had to authorize the aircraft to overfly the tip of Burma when the Burmese ignored overflight requests.

LOOKING FORWARD

British World War II General Viscount William Slim once remarked that a lesson learned is not a lesson learned unless you learn it. Since the end of the Cold War, the United States and the international community have become more adept at dealing with humanitarian emergencies. Much, however, remains to be done.

Certification of NGOs

The United States should press the NGO community to better professionalize itself and identify the "weak sisters" among its ranks. Responsible NGOs such as CARE, OXFAM, the Red Cross, the Red Crescent, and Doctors Without Borders must cooperate to ensure that fly-by-night NGOs do not undermine the credibility of legitimate organizations. The United Nations Office of Coordination for Humanitarian Affairs is the most obvious organization to do certification. NGOs should help them establish standards of professionalism, conduct, and training for their workers. Publishing a list of certified NGOs by a recognized body would greatly help nations in need decide who to let in to help. If this is not done in some form, responders will continue to have chaos on the landing strips and ports in every place where a humanitarian disaster occurs.

The United States can and should support such efforts. Americans should also require transparency from the ICRC regarding which human rights NGOs the ICRC subsidizes. Anyone may have a right to set up an NGO, but the American public should not be obligated to pay for incompetence or outright hostile political bias.

Assessments

The handmaiden of establishing professional standards for NGOs should be to standardize procedures for damage and needs assessments and reporting. The current system is a Tower of Babel in which overlapping and often contradictory assessments are given equal credibility. The rest of the relief community should not be required to accept the DART standard, but some standard should be established, as should assessment procedures.

Coordination Mechanisms and Exercises

The U.S. interagency community should use military exercises and tabletop war games as a way of increasing the readiness of host nations to respond to such situations. Nations that do not normally want to participate in bellicose military exercises are much more likely to take part in humanitarian coordination mechanisms, particularly if the carrot is U.S. military funding. These mechanisms can be used to encourage the participation of international organizations and NGOs, as they do not have overtly war-fighting connotations. Moreover, the kinds of cooperation and interoperability that these mechanisms develop can be useful in dealing with other types of crises.

Tsunami Warning System

This was a gross deficiency in a region primarily made up of poor and developing countries. It is also being addressed more rapidly than any other deficiency identified in the disaster. A long-term assessment will be needed to address how successful the implantation of the warning system will become. But in a region nicknamed the "Ring of Fire," this may be one of the most positive developments to come out of the tragedy. As one officer attending an after-action review somewhat cynically put it on condition of anonymity, "Earthquakes and tsunamis are on the training schedule out here, all we can do is be prepared."

Continued Improvement in the Rapid Deployment and Response Capabilities of UN Relief Organizations

The United States should continue to encourage and fund the development of competent, rapid-deployment UN humanitarian mechanisms that are at least as competent as USAID teams, and the more responsible NGOS. One of the most disturbing elements of the response was that UN personnel were often bypassed because they were not up to the task. Most nations want to look to the UN for leadership. However, when that leadership is not forthcoming, they will look elsewhere.

Coordination with NGOs

U.S. federal agencies need to be global leaders. Since 1991, when U.S. military assistance bungled into Kurdistan and Bangladesh without knowing what the acronym "NGO" stood for, the armed forces and federal agencies have vastly improved their capacity to work with the NGO community. More, however, needs to be done. The NGOs simply do not have the resources or time to lead the outreach effort. The State and Defense Departments, as well as USAID, must have proactive NGO engagement strategies. These would be easier to develop if efforts to increase the professionalism and certification of NGOs (as recommended above) were implemented.

Assisting Host Nation Governments in Preparing for Disaster Relief

Perhaps the two best-prepared nations examined in this study were India and Thailand. In each case, U.S. assistance was tailored to suit our relations with the host nation. In Thailand, the military largely led the way via the Cobra Gold exercise series. In India, USAID had the lead role in providing funding to encourage preparedness. One size does not fit all, but in each case, U.S. interests were served. The reaction to the tsunami was not a cynical one, but it did serve to bolster U.S. prestige, albeit temporarily, during a time when the American image in the developing world was on the wane. Small investments in money and exercises can pay large dividends in the long run.

All combatant commands should be encouraged to increase the number of exercises that include humanitarian relief scenarios. Moreover, the humanitarian portion of these exercises should be unclassified so that NGOs and international organizations can participate, along with other U.S. agencies—notably the State Department and USAID.

Eliminate Potentially Harmful Interagency Problems in Advance

Here, the problem of quickly gaining permission for non-DOD civilians to fly aboard Defense Department aircraft is a case in point. Interagency operational obstacles should be resolved long before the call to act. Operational contingency planning, a structured exercise program that tests the adequacy of plans, doctrines, and policies that facilitate collaborative action would help minimize the friction experienced in interagency operations in the field.

Overflight Issues in Humanitarian Operations

An international framework for quick approval of overflight rights to respond to humanitarian disasters must be established. This should be taken up with the International Civil Aviation Organization (ICAO). ICAO members should be required to provide overflight rights for legitimate missions during declared humanitarian emergencies certified by ICAO, and a system of disseminating such information should be developed.

FINAL THOUGHTS

It has been said that evil exists when good men do nothing. In this case, whatever mistakes were made, good men (and women) did something. In the wake of this disaster, humanity won the day. The United States should be proud of its capacity to muster the interagency community in support of disaster relief. It is worth building on that competency: it reflects the capacity of the United States to act around the world in its own and others' interests, and it demonstrates America's willingness and intent on doing good in the world. Thus, these operations are of great import for advancing U.S. security interests, public diplomacy, and foreign economic development, as well as humanitarian causes.

Finally, the U.S. international disaster response capabilities offer a blueprint for the requirements of effective interagency operations. They also stress the importance of enabling the capacity of the interagency team to operate effectively at the operational level.

NOTES

1. Center of Excellence in Disaster Management and Humanitarian Assistance, "Indian Ocean Earthquake & Tsunami Emergency Update" (December 22, 2005) at http://coe-dmha.org/Tsunami/Tsu122205.htm.

2. See Charles R. Smith, *Angels from the Sea: Relief Operations in Bangladesh, 1991* (Pittsburgh: Superintendent of Documents, 1995).

3. Kenneth Allard, *Somalia Operations: Lessons Learned* (Washington, DC: National Defense University Press, 1995).

4. Melinda Hostetter, "Battling Storms: Interagency Response to Hurricane Mitch," *Joint Force Quarterly* (Autumn 2000): 76–77.

5. J. J. Telford and R. Cosgrove, *Joint Evaluation of the International Response to the Indian Ocean Tsunami* (London: Tsunami Evaluation Coalition, 2006), 45, at http://www. tsunami-evaluation.org/NR/rdonlyres/2E8A3262-0320-4656-BC81-EE0B46B54CAA/0/ SynthRep.pdf.

6. Telford and Cosgrave, *Joint Evaluation*, 45.

7. Senior U.S. military officers who attended several after-action conferences in Hawaii credited the Cobra Gold exercises with honing skills, as most have a significant humanitarian relief component. Author's notes.

8. Telford and Cosgrave, *Joint Evaluation*, 45.

9. Ibid.

10. Ibid.

11. Figures extracted from the Asian Development Bank at http://www.adb.org.

12. Center of Excellence in Disaster Management and Humanitarian Assistance, "Indian Ocean Earthquake & Tsunami Emergency Update."

13. USMC Warfighting Lab Experimental, "Humanitarian and Disaster Relief," X-File (1998) at http://www.mcwl.usmc.mil/x-files.cfm#AAR.

14. Ibid.

15. Ibid.

16. Subject of concern in the 1995 Emerald Express conference on relief operations. Author's notes.

17. Noted in a 2005 after-action conference hosted by Marine Corps Forces Pacific. Author's notes.

18. Statement of CARE worker during Operation Sea Angel in Bangladesh. Author's notes.

19. Telford and Cosgrove, *Joint Evaluation*, 100.

20. U.S. Agency for International Development, *Field Operations Guide for Disaster Assessment and Response, Version 4.0* (November 2005) at http://usaid.gov/our_work/ humanitarian_assistance/disaster_assistance/resources/pdf/fog_v4.pdf.

21. Telford and Cosgrove, *Joint Evaluation*, 51.

22. Author's experience while serving as the military advisor to the U.S. Liaison Office to UNOSOM II in Somalia.

23. Telford and Cosgrove, *Joint Evaluation*, 101.

24. Subject of a presentation at the 1995 Emerald Express Conference at Camp Pendleton, California. Author's notes.

25. See Brett D. Schaefer, "American Generosity Is Underappreciated," The Heritage Foundation (December 30, 2004), at http://www.heritage.org/Research/Tradeand ForeignAid/wm630.cfm.

26. Telford and Cosgrove, Joint Evaluation, 62–63.

27. Ibid., 58

28. Rhoda Margesson, "Indian Ocean Earthquake and Tsunami Relief Operations," Congressional Research Service, RL 32715 (February 10, 2005), at http://www.fas.org/ sgp/crs/row/RL32715.pdf.

29. Presentation at Enhancing Cooperation in Disaster Relief Operations, Conference March 15–17, 2005, The Asia-Pacific Center, Honolulu, Hawaii. Author's notes.

30. Comments by several Navy officers at a PACOM-sponsored after-action conference in 2005.

11
Chapter

In the Wake of the Storm: The National Response to Hurricane Katrina

John R. Brinkerhoff

President George W. Bush called the response to Hurricane Katrina "unacceptable." Most Americans agreed.

Press accounts characterized the Federal Emergency Management Agency (FEMA), responsible for organizing the federal response and coordinating with state and local authorities as incompetent, unprepared, and unable to deal with the hurricanes and floods that struck New Orleans and the Gulf Coast. Media coverage, however, told only a small part of the story—and, for the most part, focused only on the worst part. In fact, the FEMA response was proactive, well organized, and adequate in Alabama, Florida, Mississippi, Texas, and much of Louisiana. The most severe response shortfalls occurred mostly in New Orleans. Even there, difficulties centered on the Superdome and the Convention Center, where many of those trapped in the city during the storm had unexpectedly congregated in large numbers for an unanticipated prolonged period.

Although much has been written about Katrina, it is hard to find reliable data separating fact from fiction. The sources vary greatly in quality and objectivity. Most press and online "blog" accounts are of little use. Books rushed to print are anecdotal and consist mostly of complaints. Conclusions of official investigations are fairly reliable but reflect a defensive attitude—many lessons-learned reports dwell on details and emphasize faults. An objective history has yet to be written.

What is known for certain is that hurricane Katrina made landfall in the Gulf Coast on August 29, 2005. The response to the storm involved numerous federal agencies, the state governments of Florida, Alabama, Mississippi, Louisiana, and Texas, numerous local communities, including the city of New Orleans, other cities, parishes, and counties, as well as nongovernmental organizations, the private sector, and many individual citizens.

Together, the consequences of hurricanes Katrina and Rita, and the failure of the levees protecting New Orleans constituted the worst natural disaster in U.S.

history. Katrina was particularly devastating, affecting an area over ninety thousand square miles, disrupting the lives of millions and destroying or degrading most of the region's infrastructure. The response phase, the immediate effort to mitigate the loss of life, treat or evacuate individuals at risk, and restore basic services, lasted twelve days from August 26 to September 6. Evaluating the emergency response to this disaster is instructive to understanding the ability of the interagency community to lead a national effort in the immediate aftermath of a catastrophic emergency.

The results are unquestionably mixed. The Katrina response was not, however, a case study in abject failure. While challenges abounded, when viewed from a five state perspective, the national response proved to be a remarkable effort. More than a million people were successfully evacuated, tens of thousands of others were rescued from disaster zones, and hundreds of thousands more received emergency shelter and relief. Nevertheless it is difficult, given the events' recency and a dearth of objective analytical studies, to quantify the successes and breakdowns of the interagency response.

Many lessons can be learned from Katrina. The response demonstrated both the strengths and shortfalls of the FEMA-led interagency effort. Katrina highlights the value of doctrine for effective decentralized execution of large-scale operations, which was lacking in the federal response despite the existence of the National Response Plan (NRP). Improving the NRP, which guides the federal response, is the first step to ensuring preparedness in the face of a future disaster.

THE ROAD TO KATRINA

Recognizing the need to mount a national response to a natural disaster is not new. Authorities have attempted to formulate and implement a single response plan covering the full range of emergencies since FEMA's establishment in 1979. The organization's founding goal has been to establish a national "all hazards" system, one capable of responding to both natural and man-made disasters. FEMA was created by consolidating five different organizations each of which addressed a particular aspect of emergency management. The Defense Civil Preparedness Agency (DOD), Federal Disaster Assistance Administration (HUD), U.S. Fire Administration (DOC), Federal Preparedness Agency (GSA), and the National Flood Insurance Administration (HUD) were transferred to a new independent agency reporting directly to the president.[1]

Developed during FEMA's first twelve years of operation, the classical formulation of emergency management posited four phases: response, recovery, mitigation, and preparedness. Concerns regarding terrorism prompted the addition of a fifth phase, prevention. Phases of the emergency management cycle occur both sequentially and simultaneously. They include (1) prevention—a set of actions (including deterrence, protection, and defense) taken to avert an emergency; (2) mitigation—steps taken to reduce the adverse consequences of an emergency; (3) preparation—actions that get people, equipment, and supplies ready for response and recovery operations and mitigation programs; (4) response—efforts during

and after the incident to save lives and minimize disruption; (5) recovery—
actions taken to restore normal conditions after an emergency has occurred.

Of the phases, response invariably draws the most attention because lives and
property are most gravely at risk. Response is concerned with immediate actions
to save people and provide essential care and assistance to those affected by an
emergency. Response is a short duration operation that must be able to accomplish
a few things very well and very quickly. The following capabilities are needed to
mount an effective response; management; situational awareness (knowledge of
requirements, assets, and risks); situational control; lifesaving techniques; life support capacity; as well as administrative and logistical support. Law enforcement,
firefighting, or emergency medical professionals are usually the first to notice or
be notified of the onset or existence of an emergency. Local and state governments
capably manage most emergencies, but catastrophic contingencies require
immediate and proactive intervention by the federal government.

From its creation, within FEMA there was tension between those working on
national security emergency preparedness (civil defense, national mobilization,
national stockpile, and counterterrorism) and those involved in national disaster
response, recovery, mitigation, and preparedness. The stress between these missions was never fully resolved. After the end of the Cold War, FEMA's national security emergency preparedness directorate was largely dismantled, and management
of natural disasters became the agency's predominant responsibility. During the
Clinton administration, FEMA's management of natural disasters, particularly
hurricanes, was widely regarded as competent. The Bush administration followed
similar policies and FEMA continued to successfully respond to natural disasters.[2]

The attacks of September 11, 2001, and the formation of the Department of
Homeland Security (DHS), which incorporated FEMA into its structure, placed a
renewed emphasis on national security issues, particularly terrorism. The tension
returned. In this transformation, FEMA lost funds and senior personnel, many of
whom found employment elsewhere in the emergency management community.
The preparedness function and responsibility for allocating homeland security
grants was assigned to a domestic preparedness directorate outside of FEMA.
Nevertheless, the agency continued to operate largely as before, responding to
routine disasters. Indeed, dozens of FEMA-directed operations, in the years prior
to hurricane Katrina, garnered only a modicum of criticism.[3]

Creating the Department of Homeland Security shifted the operational and
organizational approaches to federal disaster response by building on FEMA's
expertise in the area. Before FEMA's creation, federal support of local emergency
response was entirely reactive. When a disaster struck, ad hoc coordination
addressed the special requirements of each emergency. FEMA created a top-level
coordination committee. Each department and agency appointed an emergency
coordinator.

In addition to coordinating national emergency response policy, FEMA also
had limited operational and training responsibilities. The agency established a
national emergency operations center. The organization also instituted programs

to hire temporary workers and purchase emergency supplies. Its National Emergency Training Center taught courses and conducted exercises on emergency response operation management.

FEMA's operational concept relied on voluntary collaboration to organize federal agencies, most of which willingly cooperated. FEMA's operations adhered to the principle of federalism when interacting with state and local government officials. Embodied in the U.S. Constitution, the principles of limited government and federalism give citizens and local communities the greatest role in shaping their destinies. The Tenth Amendment states that "powers not delegated to the United States by the Constitution, nor prohibited by it to the States, are reserved to the States respectively, or to the people." In community matters, local jurisdictions have the preponderance of authority and autonomy. Thus, states and local governments shoulder primary responsibility for responding to disasters. The federal government provides assistance at the request of state and local officials, after they had exceeded their own emergency response capacity. Federal support and funding is to be provided incrementally in response to states' requests for assistance.[4]

In 1992 hurricane Andrew devastated Florida. Although FEMA's response was substantial, it was judged insufficient to meet the public's needs and expectations. FEMA received scathing criticism, which damaged the reelection hopes of President George H. W. Bush.[5] FEMA's first formal emergency response plan—the Federal Response Plan (FRP)—had just been approved. Over the years, FEMA continued to refine the plan. The FRP remained in effect until it was superseded by DHS's NRP, finalized and approved in December 2004, eight months before Katrina struck. The NRP was intended to guide how FEMA, and DHS, would coordinate federal, state, and local efforts in the event of a national emergency.

PREPARING FOR NATIONAL RESPONSE

On February 23, 2003, President Bush issued Homeland Security Presidential Directive-5 (HSPD-5) that required the secretary of homeland security to "develop, submit for review to the Homeland Security Council, and administer a National Response Plan (NRP) . . . This plan shall integrate Federal Government domestic prevention, preparedness, response, and recovery plans into one all-discipline, all-hazards plan."[6] Presidential Directives are executive orders issued by the White House that set strategy or direct policy implementation by federal agencies. HSPDs are drafted by the Homeland Security Council in consultation with federal departments.

The initial version of the NRP was sent out for coordination in May 2003.[7] It differed considerably from the approved version that was issued in December 2004 and remains in effect. The original plan called for DHS to cover all homeland security functions in a single plan, as directed by HSPD-5.[8] The preliminary version asserted the right of the secretary of homeland security to designate the duties and direct the activities of the other departments and agencies involved in homeland defense, as opposed to solely disaster response. After receiving comments and criticisms from other federal agencies, state, and local governments, and a plethora of nongovernmental organizations, the revised and approved document focused almost exclusively on disaster response.

The NRP is an impressive 465-page volume that includes a Base Plan, seven appendices, fifteen emergency support annexes, nine support annexes, seven incident annexes, and a twenty-seven-page quick reference guide, in addition to a 160-page catastrophic incident supplement marked "For Official Use Only" published separately.[9] Appendices include definitions of 141 key terms, identify 153 acronyms, and cite seventy authorities and references.

The NRP is inextricably intertwined with another document, the National Incident Management System (NIMS).[10] Both must be considered to understand the national framework for disaster response. HSPD-5 specifies that the secretary shall "develop, submit for review to the Homeland Security Council, and administer a National Incident Management System (NIMS). This system will provide a consistent nationwide approach for Federal, State, and local governments to work effectively and efficiently together to prepare for, respond to, and recover from domestic incidents, regardless of cause, size, or complexity."[11] Also created by DHS, NIMS is based on the Incident Command System (ICS), originally developed by the National Park Service and later used by local governments to clarify chain-of-command issues intrinsic to emergency situations. NIMS certification is required for emergency managers and is taught by the National Emergency Training Center as well as numerous academic institutions.

The NIMS bottom-up command structure is based on the ICS principle that the senior fire captain on the scene remains in charge of suppression operations regardless of how many bells the fire triggers. The NRP imposes a top-down command structure that consists of a wide variety of Washington-based committees and regional committees to manage the operation collaboratively along with the appointment of numerous senior officials to be in charge of response operations in the field, plus a similar hierarchy of committees and officials for each of the numerous participating agencies. Frequently, although not always, the two systems manage to interface smoothly. Discontinuity was duly noted in the White House lessons-learned report, and it was proposed that the NRP be amended in order to better fit with NIMS.[12]

EMERGENCY SUPPORT FUNCTIONS

NIMS and NRP were to provide the structure for funneling federal support to state and local entities. The available support was organized under fifteen Emergency Support Functions—ESFs. The FRP was comprised of twelve ESFs. Three additional ESFs were added during the preparation of the NRP, and several changes were made in content and emphasis in some of the other functions. The NRP designates primary coordinators and support agencies for each ESF. An ESF coordinator is responsible for preincident planning, maintaining contact with support agencies in the ESF, holding periodic meeting and conferences, and coordinating ESF activities for catastrophic incident planning and critical infrastructure protection. When an ESF is activated for an operation, the primary agency becomes a "Federal Executive Agent" reporting to the Federal Coordinating Officer, usually a Homeland Security official, to accomplish the ESF mission.

The ESFs were created to delineate the relationships and interdependencies among the agencies in emergency situations. Every ESF requires the coordination of multiple federal agencies. Even small functions, such as regulation and oversight of radioactive waste movement and disposal, depend on close collaboration among a dozen or so components of various agencies. Simply designating a department responsible for some function would not take into account that the operating elements of that department would need to organize a cluster of bureaus, offices, and regions from other departments to get the whole thing done. The ESFs are tasked with identifying each agency that has to be involved and designating a coordinator to assure that the implementers of a particular function are familiar with their role in a potential disaster.

FEMA serves as a hub for identifying response requirements, matching them to an ESF and coordinating the delivery of assistance. In addition to these duties, FEMA, which was originally envisioned solely as a coordinating agency, was also tasked with operational responsibilities, primarily in the recovery phase (such as direct economic assistance). For example, during Katrina, the National Disaster Medical System and the Urban Search and Rescue teams functioned under FEMA.

The National Disaster Medical System is a federally coordinated effort to augment medical service providers in the aftermath of a disaster.[13] Urban Search and Rescue Task Forces are employed to recover victims in cases of structural failure such as those caused by earthquakes, explosions and fires. FEMA coordinates with twenty-eight fire departments to create, fund, and equip teams and deploy them in domestic and foreign emergencies. Although FEMA could oversee the operations of these response elements during Katrina, at the time, the agency did not have directive authority over ESF activities.

Although the NRP and NIMS had been implemented before Katrina, they remained works in progress. Before the summer of 2005, there had been scant opportunities to conduct plan-based training exercises and educate senior leaders and emergency professionals at the federal, state, and local level. The NRP catastrophic incident supplement was completed after the 2005 hurricane season was well underway.

UNDER A DARKENING SKY

Hurricane Katrina began as a tropical depression on August 24 and became a tropical storm as it moved over the Bahamas. On August 25 Katrina was upgraded to a category one hurricane as it crossed Florida, killing nine people and causing significant damage. Early on Friday, August 26, Katrina grew into a category two hurricane as it moved out into the Gulf of Mexico and triggered warnings along the Gulf Coast. The hurricane made landfall along the Gulf Coast on August 29, as a category four hurricane. Levees around New Orleans started failing on that same day.[14]

Hurricane Rita made landfall on September 24 as a category three hurricane and resulted in extensive damage along the coast of Texas and Louisiana west of New Orleans. About a million people were evacuated, and 120 individual people died as a result of the storm or the effects of the evacuation. Damage was extensive and caused additional problems in Louisiana and New Orleans. The storm dissipated on September 26. Although recovery from Rita is considered part of the overall Katrina emergency, the response operation was separate. Due in great part to the presence of emergency management personnel, military troops, and volunteers already assembled for Katrina in the Gulf Coast, Rita's response operation was successful. Hurricane Rita literature does not include many of the complaints and criticisms of FEMA that were prevalent during Katrina itself.

Katrina's Gulf Coast response phase lasted twelve days, during which victims were evacuated, rescued, fed, sheltered, and given medical care. The response phase began at 9:00 a.m. on August 26, when the White House declared an impending disaster and deployed federal resources. The federal emergency response began three full days before the hurricane landed. The response phase ended on the night of September 6, when only ten thousand people remained in New Orleans and the emphasis shifted to recovery. Federal accomplishments in the Katrina response included rescuing over sixty thousand people and evacuating over two hundred thousand, as well as coordinating shelter and supplying food for millions.[15] Approximately one thousand three hundred persons lost their lives as a direct result of Katrina. This is about 0.1 percent of the approximately 1.25 million persons evacuated. Despite this very low fatality rate and the impressive federal accomplishments, the conventional wisdom is that the government's response was a failure.

MANAGING MAYHEM

The NRP outlines an elaborate set of instructions for the top level management of the response operation. A Principal Federal Official (PFO), according to the NRP,

> is personally designated by the Secretary of Homeland Security to facilitate Federal support to the established ICS Unified Command structure and to coordinate overall Federal incident management and assistance activities across the spectrum of prevention, preparedness, response, and recovery. The PFO ensures that incident management efforts are maximized through effective and efficient coordination. The PFO provides a primary point of contact and situational awareness locally for the Secretary of Homeland Security. . . . The PFO does not direct or replace the incident command structure established at the incident, nor does the PFO have directive authority over the SFLEO (Senior Federal Law Enforcement Official), FCO, or other Federal and State officials.[16]

The PFO was a new position established by the NRP. Because the president and the secretary were responsible for supervising the entire homeland security enterprise, the PFO would serve as their representative in overseeing the operational response. On scene coordination, however; remained the responsibility of the FCO. According to the NRP, the FCO,

> manages and coordinates Federal resource support activities related to Stafford Act disasters and emergencies. The FCO assists the Unified Command and/or the Area Command. The FCO works closely with the PFO, SFLEO, and other SFOs [Senior Federal Officials]. In Stafford Act situations where a PFO has not been assigned, the FCO provides over-all coordination for the Federal components of the JFO [Joint Field Office] and works in partnership with the SCO [State Coordinating Officer] to determine and satisfy State and local assistance require-ments.[17]

FCOs are appointed for every presidential-declared disaster. In fact, this had been standard practice before Katrina. The FCO is, in effect, the "field boss" for FEMA operations.

The basic authorities for emergency management are the Stafford Act and the Homeland Security Act of 2002. The Robert T. Stafford Disaster Relief Act of 1984 (as amended in 1988), often referred to as the Stafford Act after its legislative author, is the authority under which the federal government provides disaster assistance. The act requires a state, usually through its governor, to request a pres-idential declaration of a state of emergency following a natural disaster. Once a state of emergency has been declared, federal assistance is provided under FEMA's auspicies.[18] The Homeland Security Act establishes DHS's authority to oversee all aspects of disaster preparedness and response. The Stafford Act requires that an FCO be designated for every declared disaster. A PFO is required by the Homeland Security Act and HSPD-5. There is no statutory link between the PFO and an FCO. The NRP does not clarify the ambiguous relationship between the two officials.

On August 29, when Katrina made landfall along the Gulf Coast, FEMA had thirteen FCOs and fifteen Joint Field Offices dedicated to declared disasters in Alaska, California, Utah, Montana, North Dakota, Oklahoma, Maine, New York, Florida, Alabama, Mississippi, and Louisiana. Each of these FCOs was specially trained and certified as a federal coordinating officer. For the Katrina operation, there were six disasters with a Joint Field Office for each.[19]

This arrangement linked each state to a FEMA representative and a JFO for coordinating with FEMA. However, coordinating rescue efforts and allocating resources among the disaster-stricken states was hindered by an uncertain relationship between the PFO and the FCOs.

DHS Secretary Michael Chertoff appointed Michael Brown, the undersecre-tary for emergency preparedness and response and FEMA director, as PFO of the Katrina response. Brown arrived in Baton Rouge, Louisiana, on August 29. Removing Brown from his executive position in Washington, where he was responsible for running FEMA and leading a number of executive coordinating councils, diminished his role as an effective policy maker and strategic manager. At the same time, trying to command the disaster response from a field office, where he had neither the staff, resources, nor arguably the skill, to direct an unprecedented massive, multistate operation, proved unsatisfactory as well. Thus, not only was he unable to serve as an effective bridge between policy and operations, but both suffered.

The critical press reports and unremitting partisan attacks that followed in the immediate aftermath of the floods further undermined confidence in Brown's capacity to manage the response. Portrayed as indifferent and incompetent, he was recalled to Washington and resigned as FEMA director on September 12, 2005.

Chertoff appointed U.S. Coast Guard vice admiral Thad Allen as the new PFO. Unlike Brown, Allen did not have to serve as both an agency director and an operational commander. He also had significant field operational experience. Allen was also granted the authority to issue orders to other FCOs. Coordination improved, though by the time Allen arrived on the scene on September 8, the immediate response phase had ended. In addition, problems remained. Allen complained that some agencies persisted to call their Washington headquarters for direction, bypassing the PFO.[20]

The trials of effectively organizing national leadership reflected more than the competencies and actions of individuals. The doctrine that they were attempting to implement was far from proven. Specifically, the PFO concept had not been tested. Katrina demonstrated the chasm between how the position was understood and the manner in which it was implemented. As troubling as this realization was, what is perhaps even more notable and remarkable was the decentralized style in which many operations continued, despite the absence of high-level integrated leadership.

OPERATING FROM THE CENTER

The challenges of implementing a new leadership framework for the NRP are exacerbated by the flaws in structure; leaders have to manage information, gain situational awareness, and make and disseminate decisions. The NRP establishes three interagency groups to manage disaster response operations: the Interagency Incident Management Group, the Homeland Security Operations Center, and the National Response Coordination Center. Coordination centers are the conventional means of achieving interagency collaboration in operational activities. They assemble representatives from each department or agency involved at the same place. The typical layout is a large room with workstations reserved for agency representatives and wall displays to convey and share information. Each workstation has computers, telephones, and additional communications devices. There are usually backup rooms where staff personnel can congregate and separate rooms for senior executives to meet privately.

Prior to 1979, the Catastrophic Disaster Response Group was the senior-level interagency group responsible for FEMA emergency response and recovery operations.[21] The group was a forum for senior-level representatives of all the departments and agencies involved in the FRP to meet and make disaster response policy.

After FEMA merged with DHS, the Catastrophic Disaster Response Group was renamed the Interagency Incident Management Group, and the emphasis shifted from "disasters" to "incidents." The latter denote a broader set of tasks that include everything from managing events of national significance (such as the Super Bowl or a presidential inauguration) to counterterrorism efforts. According to the NRP, the group "coordinates with and provides incident information to the White House including, but not limited to situational awareness and operational prevention, protection, preparedness, response, and recovery activities, as well as policy course of action recommendations."[22] In short, the Interagency Incident Management Group is charged with relaying communications between the department's operations and the headquarters of the federal agencies supporting response efforts.

The Interagency Incident Management Group was assembled at the direction of the homeland security secretary. It was tasked with (1) providing a focal point for federal strategic incident management planning and coordination; (2) maintaining situational awareness of threat assessments and incident-related operational activities; (3) offering decision-making support for incident-related efforts; (4) synthesizing information, framing issues, and making recommendations to the secretary of homeland security; (5) providing strategic coordination and recommendations for application of federal resources; (6) assessing national impacts of the incidents and of actual or proposed response actions; (7) anticipating evolving federal response and operational requirements; (8) continually coordinating with the PFO and JFO Coordination Group; (9) liaising with the FBI on terrorism-related issues; (10) facilitating interagency operational coordination and coordination with other public and private entities; and (11) developing strategies for implementing existing policies and provides incident information to the Department of Homeland Security and the White House to facilitate policy making.[23]

According to the NRP, the Homeland Security Operations Center (HSOC) is "the primary national hub for domestic incident management, operational coordination and situational awareness . . . [and] a standing 24/7 interagency organization fusing law enforcement, national intelligence, emergency response, and private sector reporting."[24] Though collocated, the difference between the Interagency Incident Management Group and the HSOC is that the former includes senior officials who can speak for their respective departments and agencies, while the HSOC is staffed by mid-level desk officers who can receive and transmit information but do not have decision-making authority.

The roles and responsibilities of the HSOC include the following: (1) establishing and maintaining real-time communications links to other government emergency operations centers; (2) maintaining communications with private sector critical infrastructure and resource entities and federal incident management officials; (3) coordinating resources for domestic incident management and prevention of terrorist attacks; (4) collaborating with other government entities for terrorism related threat analysis and incident response; (5) providing domestic situational awareness, common operational picture and support to and from department leadership and the Interagency Incident Management Group; and (6) acting as the primary conduit for the White House Situation Room and the Interagency Incident Management Group.

The National Response Coordination Center (NRCC) is separate from the HSOC though the NRP describes it as a functional component of the Department's operations center. Managed by FEMA, the NRCC: (1) monitors the preparedness of national-level emergency response teams and resources; (2) coordinates with FEMA's Regional Response Coordination Centers (RRCCs) to initiate mission assignments or reimbursable agreements to activate other federal departments and agencies; (3) activates and deploys national-level entities, such as the National Disaster Medical System capabilities, Urban Search and Rescue Task Forces, Mobile Emergency Response Support, and Emergency Response Teams; (4) coordinates the federal response to incidents of national significance, including coordinating the use of federal remote sensing/disaster assessment support; (5) provides management of field facilities, supplies, and equipment; (6) coordinates operational response and resource allocation planning with the federal agencies; (7) tracks and manages federal resource allocations; and, (8) collects, evaluates, and disseminates information regarding the incident response and status of resources; and, (9) drafts and distributes operational warnings and orders in coordination with other elements of the HSOC.

NRCC composition varies depending on the emergency, and FEMA provides management and support staff for functions not filled by ESF personnel. The NRCC relies on the HSOC, which has observers on duty 24/7, to alert FEMA and notify departments and agencies of potential or actual activations of ESFs. When operational, the NRCC operates out of FEMA headquarters. With minor exceptions, the same departments and agencies are represented in each entity.

To support the NRCC, FEMA has an extensive network of subordinate operations centers designed to manage multiple simultaneous emergencies nationwide. These include the following:

1. The FEMA Operations Center, located in Mount Weather, Virginia, which is a 24/7 operations center that "provides a centralized point of management for collecting, analyzing, and disseminating time-critical information to emergency management decision-makers."[25] It is also a backup for the NRCC.
2. The Regional Response Coordination Centers exist at each of FEMA's ten regional offices. They are maintained on standby and are activated when necessary. Predesignated representatives of regional offices of other federal agencies work there to augment FEMA staff.
3. Mobile Emergency Response Support teams provide communications support to the Regional Response Coordination Centers, Joint Operations Centers, and other operational elements in disaster-stricken areas.

4. The National Logistics Center is a FEMA entity that is activated in order to plan for and manage the distribution of supplies in an emergency.

In addition to these operations centers, there are numerous additional operations centers involved in a crisis response. The NRP mentions also the FBI Strategic Information and Operations Center and the National Counterterrorism Center. Each of the subordinate elements of DHS also has an operations center. Each of the departments and agencies has a headquarters operations center, and many of their subordinate elements also have operations centers. There is a substantial network of operations centers organized hierarchically to obtain guidance from above and report circumstances from below. Most of these are organized within a single department, but many of them, particularly those within FEMA, are multifunctional and multiagency in their membership.

During the Katrina response, FEMA operations centers were deployed and performed as prescribed by the NRP. As a result, a network of operations centers with communications and support was in place and operational before landfall on August 29. The Interagency Incident Management Group met three times during the response phase. Meetings occurred on August 26 to discuss how to best manage Katrina's approach, three days later to consider the effects of landfall, and again on August 30 to reflect on the consequences of the unanticipated flooding.

The NRCC at FEMA headquarters was on partial activation status on August 26, having been alerted earlier to manage Katrina as it passed over Florida. The next morning, the NRCC was taken to RED TEAM Level 1 staffing. All ESFs were activated. FEMA headquarters was on full alert.

The two FEMA regions directly involved in supporting the response operation were activated early and managed the deployment of teams to the affected states. On August 26, the center for Region VI, Atlanta, was already at Level 2 alert with twelve ESFs activated to deal with Katrina's impact on Florida. On August 27, the Region VI center was fully activated and began to deploy FEMA assets to Alabama and Mississippi. That same day, the RRCC for Region IV, Denton, Texas, was fully activated and started to deploy assets to Louisiana. A Region VI Mobile Emergency Response Support team was sent to Jackson, Mississippi, and two Mobile Emergency Response Support teams were dispatched to Baton Rouge and Camp Beauregard in Louisiana. On August 28, a Region IV Mobile Emergency Response Support team was sent to Barksdale AFB, Louisiana, and a team from Region VIII, Denver, was sent to Denton, Texas, to provide backup. These preparations were made in order to provide communications and support for the operations center being set up in Baton Rouge and in each of the three states affected by the storm. The FCOs for each of these states and for the overall operation were in place and operational before the storm made landfall. Although there were a few instances of misunderstanding and miscommunication, the FEMA field organization appeared to work well.

The fact that FEMA's national network had been activated so quickly and efficiently should have come as no surprise. In the years and months preceding

Katrina, and even after the formation of the Department of Homeland Security, FEMA managed numerous disasters and emergencies from this facility. Most, if not all, of the other agencies integrated into DHS also had an operations center.

With the NRP still new and never tested in a catastrophic emergency, the relationships between the operations centers and the reporting protocols were not sufficiently clarified. This became apparent shortly after Katrina made landfall. The HSOC was overwhelmed with monitoring the consequences of a catastrophic natural disaster. During the initial stages of the emergency, duplication of effort and uncertainty about procedures between FEMA, NRCC, and the HSOC caused some delays in alerting the White House and issuing instructions to field teams. When it became apparent that Katrina was going to be a large-scale emergency, the NRCC dutifully relayed its alert messages to the president through the HSOC. The HSOC, however, allowed some messages to languish overnight before notifying Chertoff so that he could forward them to the White House. This may have caused the president to be late in addressing the nation and visiting the area, for which he was criticized. There is no evidence, however, that the error delayed the issuance of presidential emergency and disaster declarations needed to commit federal funds and assets to the response operation.

Effective interagency collaboration is hampered by confusing and overly complex command arrangements. It is sufficiently difficult to persuade officials from different agencies to work together harmoniously without instituting a complicated set of committees and councils at the top of the hierarchy. In the case of Katrina, the organizational structure established in conformance with the Stafford Act was in place and appears to have worked well enough considering the extraordinary extent of the emergency. There is no question that more clearly established protocols, better operational practices, and more joint exercises could have improved information management between key operations. Nevertheless, the fundamental structure of information-sharing appears sound enough.

SEARCH AND RESCUE OPERATIONS
While overall leadership and management of federal disaster response operations remained troubled, each of the ESFs also experienced a number of unique challenges. Among these, search and rescue operations and mass care deserve particular scrutiny as they proved to be the most essential in addressing the gravest dangers of the response phase.

Search and rescue proved especially challenging. Hurricanes are short duration incidents that do not usually require a lot of waterborne or airborne rescues. A storm hits an area and then moves on leaving structural destruction that often requires special skills and equipment to extricate victims. With the exception of flash floods in arid climates, major floods usually occur slowly and with ample warning, so there is time to mobilize boats as well as local and state resources to rescue people stranded by floodwaters. Katrina, however, was different. In this case, the flood occurred almost instantaneously and several thousand people needed to be rescued immediately. While emergency managers were controlling the effects of the hurricane, the levee breach created an unanticipated demand for airborne and waterborne rescue of thousands of people in New Orleans. That challenge was unprecedented.

Arguably, search and rescue proved the most demanding and vital component of the national response effort—and, without question, the most successful. Improvisation and extraordinary efforts on the part of several federal agencies involved in the response made the difference. The Coast Guard, which had anticipated the need, established a base at a relatively safe distance from New Orleans but also in sufficiently close proximity to direct its search and rescue operations.[26] The Coast Guard alone rescued over thirty thousand people, often under very hazardous conditions. When National Guard units arrived on the scene, they applied their helicopters to the task as well. All together, over sixty thousand individuals were saved by federal assets.

Despite the numbers rescued, the official White House assessment of the response faulted the coordination of search and rescue operations.[27] Indeed, there were a number of shortfalls of note. The Department of Interior (DOI), for example, had rescue boats that would have been valuable to the effort, but making arrangements to use them proved protracted and significantly delayed their use. FEMA claims that Interior did not know how to contact the FCO and instead reached out to FEMA headquarters. Interior officials countered that they made a concerted effort, but were ignored by FEMA.

A number of issues on the ground complicated search and rescue, such as airspace coordination over the disaster area and lack of operable communications at the operational level. However, problems (such as the failure to coordinate with the DOI) could be attributed to the structure of ESF-9. ESF-9 covers Urban Search and Rescue and did not adequately prepare for performing search and rescue in a flood. FEMA is the coordinator and primary agency for ESF-9, and the group's main objective was to deploy Urban Search and Rescue assets. Although these teams have saved many lives in the past, particularly in earthquakes and similar incidents where structural damage presented a significant challenge, they turned out not to be entirely appropriate for search and rescue operations after Katrina where floods and hurricane surges were the main obstacles. The NRP, however, scarcely addressed waterborne rescue. According to an official FEMA lessons-learned report, the Coast Guard is mentioned only as being able to assist in "water rescue in areas of inundation" with aircraft and boat teams. The Department of the Interior, which has "valuable expertise in operating watercraft and conducting civil search and rescue missions . . . [was] not formally considered a part of ESF-9, [and] DOI's offer to deploy shallow-water rescue boats during the response apparently never reached the operational level."[28] As a result, ESF-9 proved inadequate for facilitating interagency coordination and the majority of rescue efforts had to be improvised.

During Katrina FEMA ESF-9 leaders formed an informal search and rescue organization to coordinate the efforts of the many agencies involved in the relief operation, including; Jefferson Parish Public Safety Agencies, National Guard, Department of Defense, Louisiana Department of Wildlife and Fisheries, Louisiana State Police, New Orleans Fire and Police Departments, federal law enforcement agencies, the Department of the Interior, the Los Angeles Police Department, Vancouver, Canada, USAR TF-1, and assets from other jurisdictions sent in accordance with the Emergency Management Assistance Compact (which allows disaster-stricken communities to obtain emergency response assets from other states).

In spite of the difficulties, the search and rescue operation was successful. Despite some duplication of effort a large number of people were rescued and brought to safety, and there is no evidence of deaths because people were not rescued in time. This feat was accomplished due to the initiative and hard work of the numerous agencies that participated in the search and rescue portion of the response operation. The Coast Guard benefited from anticipating the need and preparing for it well in advance of landfall. The National Guard and local police and fire departments all used their capabilities to good effect. Military helicopters were particularly valuable. Despite not being trained or equipped for waterborne missions, FEMA Urban Search and Rescue Task Forces contributed significantly to the effort.

In responding to Katrina, the NRP was too narrowly focused on a specific kind of search and rescue mission and did not take an all-hazards approach. ESF-9 was written to assure that the Urban Search and Rescue Task Forces would be able to perform their important, but limited work, and broader applications of search and rescue were not considered. Clearly, the doctrine was flawed. The NRP and the ESFs need to address the full range of possible emergencies and make provisions for all contingencies.

MANAGING MASS CARE

Similarly, during the hurricane response ESF-6 suffered from a lack of imagination.[29] In the FRP, ESF-6 was responsible only for mass care. The American Red Cross served as the primary agency. The NRP also added two additional functions to ESF-6—housing and human services—and FEMA was designated as the coordinating agency, with the Red Cross as the primary organization responsible for mass care and FEMA as primary agency for housing and human services. This resulted in FEMA ESF-6 personnel being drawn from the Recovery Division rather than the Response Division. This move put Red Cross people with experience in provision of mass care for immediate response with FEMA people experienced in long-term recovery. As it turned out, this did not work well because the objectives of the two cultures were at odds.

The dispute was related to procedures for approval of requests for mass care. "Each organization had a different understanding of certain ESF-6 operating procedures, according a Government Accountability Office report, "This disagreement was primarily about the role of the ESF-6 coordinator, a FEMA official tasked with providing strategic vision and leading efforts to coordinate mass care, housing, and human services."[30] FEMA officials wanted the Red Cross to direct all requests for mass care through the ESF-6 coordinator. Red Cross personnel argued that these requests should be sent directly to the FEMA Operations Section Chief. "Tensions resulting from this disagreement negatively affected the working relationship between FEMA and the Red Cross. Because of the lack of clarity about roles and responsibilities, the agencies spent time during the response effort trying to establish protocols and procedures, rather than focusing solely on coordinating services."[31] The argument descended to the level of who would be allowed to speak at meetings, with the ESF-6 Coordinator insisting that she, and not the Red Cross representative, should speak. The two sides never did reconcile, and Red Cross employees became frustrated by what they regarded as mismanagement and went outside of the official channels to distribute emergency supplies.

On the surface, this issue is merely one of turf and prestige. However, the dispute also attempted to discern the proper balance between centralized control and decentralized operations, as well as the difference between response and recovery.

The operational tempo of response differs from that of recovery. Response is a short-term operation intended to save lives and provide only temporary basic life sustaining goods and services. Recovery seeks to repair the damage done and restore the status quo ante or better. The purpose of mass care, as understood by Red Cross officials, was to provide only minimal support. Sheltering is part of mass care and seeks to keep evacuees out of the elements by packing people into large common spaces with little concern for privacy or space. On the contrary, housing, a part of the recovery phase which has a long-term outlook, places people into private homes that afford sufficient living space. Sheltering is provided in schools, auditoriums, sports areas, and convention centers. Housing is provided in trailer homes, rental money, and funds to rebuild houses destroyed by the emergency. Response is rapid and chaotic; recovery is deliberate and orderly.

The proper balance between centralized control and decentralized operations is also affected by whether response or recovery is being addressed. Response must be decentralized with push logistics, even if that means losing some accountability for supplies. Recovery has to be more careful about keeping track of goods and money because critics are predisposed to find waste no matter what is done. The Katrina experience implies that it may not be a good idea to combine response efforts with recovery, suggesting another area where doctrine requires refinement.

THE SUPERDOME

The most significant mass care incident occurred in New Orleans. Although over 1 million people self-evacuated safely, and another two hundred thirty thousand were evacuated from New Orleans and other areas, the drama at the New Orleans Superdome, and to a lesser extent, at the Convention Center, became a focal point for media attention and criticism. The Superdome was designated an emergency shelter by New Orleans city planners, but the city had made no efforts to prepare it as a long-term shelter. FEMA was aware of the Superdome, paid attention to it from the outset, and took action to provide resources for the people there.

FEMA responded quickly to requests for assistance during Katrina and provided substantial resources. Some of FEMA's actions were unprecedented and unanticipated. For example, it was New Orleans' responsibility to provide the buses used to evacuate hurricane victims to the Superdome. However, because local buses were not repositioned before the storm and were lost in the floods, ESF-1 had to quickly provide transportation for a use outside of its normal purview. Therefore, widespread criticism of FEMA and ESF-1 for failing to provide busses is unfounded. Security at the Superdome was another local responsibility that failed to materialize. A perceived lack of security also hampered response operations.

In this instance, the NRP worked as intended despite communication problems and conditions that made it more arduous to deliver commodities. Once the NRCC was made aware of the situation, FEMA marshaled enough transportation assets to evacuate all of the people at the Superdome in seven days, in addition to supporting the evacuation of over two hundred thousand people from other parts of New Orleans, other areas of Louisiana, as well as Alabama and Mississippi. Six people died at the Superdome, one committed suicide. These deaths were not resultant from failure to coordinate mass evacuation or provide basic food and shelter at the site.

The collapse of the New Orleans emergency response agencies, and the withdrawal of the mayor from a leadership role during the crisis, left the Superdome without anyone with the authority and the means to see that it operated properly. There was no dedicated "shelter manager," and there was no official responsible for submitting assistance requests or reporting on conditions. First responders often left soon after arrival due to the chaotic security situation at the Superdome. A permanent law enforcement or military presence that could have controlled the violence and enabled the delivery of relief supplies never deployed to the area. Critics have taken FEMA and ESF-1 to task for failing to provide buses more quickly, even though that was a local responsibility.

THE NEW ORLEANS CONVENTION CENTER

Another controversial episode of the response operation occurred at the New Orleans Convention Center, a large facility located on high ground near the Mississippi River. The Convention Center was not a designated shelter; therefore, food, water, and medicine were not stored there. It was, however, a designated rally point for evacuees waiting to be transported out of the city. For five days, the Convention Center served as an impromptu shelter and spawned some of the exaggerated stories that emerged from Katrina as well as one event that led many Americans to believe that the federal government and FEMA were completely incompetent.

On the evening of August 29, rescue teams started dropping evacuees off at the Convention Center, and other people heard about the Convention Center and made their way there on foot. By the time more people arrived over the next three days, the place was overcrowded, food and water were scarce, and security was poor. The total number of evacuees sheltered there is estimated to have been about twenty thousand. When the initial evacuees arrived, two National Guard Engineer battalions were stationed at the Convention Center, but the units did not take the initiative to get things organized and left on September 1. These units were tasked with establishing a base from which to deal with debris removal and other engineering issues. After securing their area, they took no action to intervene in the havoc caused by the arrival of thousands of evacuees. At one point, the troops took up loaded weapons to defend themselves and left promptly the next day.[32] On September 2, a National Guard Brigade arrived from Arkansas, established order, and provided supplies. The next day, buses moved the evacuees, and by the following day, all of the victims had been transported inland to safe locations. The entire episode lasted seven days.

The Convention Center was a major media attraction, which broadcast and published numerous reports of murder and rioting that were later shown to have been exaggerated. Most of the reporting was emotional and anecdotal. Typical of the accounts is one by CNN that was published on September 1, headlined "Katrina: People Dying at New Orleans Convention Center."[33] The article goes on to relate that "people are dying. . . . CNN's Chris Lawrence describes 'many, many' bodies inside and outside the Convention Center and there are multiple people dying at the Convention Center." While it is difficult to obtain official casualty estimates, a later account reported that ten people died at the Convention Center.[34] Although regrettable, this was not the mass casualty event suggested by media accounts. There are reports that some of the dead were victims of violence, and it appears that there was lawlessness and conflict among the evacuees stranded at the Convention Center without food or water. This is just one example of false reporting during Katrina that remains "the truth" to many Americans despite later having been proven false.

A storm of media criticism arose after Chertoff and Brown stated that they had not heard of the problems at the Convention Center until the afternoon of September 1. Their lack of knowledge astounded media reporters, who equated this gap in situational awareness to incompetence on the part of FEMA. Subsequent to this admission, Brown was fiercely attacked by the media.

Notwithstanding the exaggerated media reports, at least three major errors were made in responding to the situation at the Convention Center:

1. Not ordering the National Guard units already at the Convention Center to take charge upon the evacuees' arrival. These units could have provided security, radioed for help, and served as points of contact for additional responders. Unfortunately, neither FEMA nor the federal government had any knowledge of the decision or control over this action.
2. The failure of local authorities to provide a modicum of supplies and security for the Convention Center as soon as it became apparent that a large number of

evacuees had begun gathering there. Once it was clear that the city of New
Orleans was not going to provide buses for the evacuation of the victims, local
authorities should have informed the Louisiana Emergency Operations Center as
well as the FEMA JOC of a potentially unforeseen problem.

3. The revelation that two of the senior people in charge of the federal response
effort did not have complete situational awareness. While Chertoff and Brown
cannot be held directly responsible—as they are entirely dependent on subordinates to keep them well informed—their ignorance points to a staffing and
communications failure among the various elements involved in the response
operation. Following exposure to the media criticism about such alleged lapses as
the Superdome, operations officers in the field and at the JOC should have realized the importance of making top officials aware of any situation akin to that
which had developed at the Superdome. The fact that emergency managers were
already overburdened trying to address pressing issues in their own areas of
responsibility would probably not have made them amenable to suggestions of
extra work. Thus, a problem involving relatively few people, no longer in danger
of drowning, might not have caught their attention. Still, a field officer should
have noticed the negative publicity as soon as it started and passed the information up the chain of command. Once the situation at the Convention Center was
made known to Chertoff and Brown, action was taken. Critics could have inter-
preted this action as a good example of rapid response to resolve an urgent situation, but instead they used it to reinforce their preexisting views that FEMA had
failed.

AFTER THE STORM

The NRP was found guilty in the court of public opinion. The White
House lessons-learned document made 125 recommendations, many of them
changes to the NRP, a set of which was duly compiled and issued. However,
many of the problems cited with the plan and some of the implemented
changes dwell on image, turf, and circumstances that are likely to be unique to
any emergency response operation occurring in New Orleans. Indeed, a sober
assessment of preliminary observations suggests that the NRP not only served
well but also had proved essential for marshaling effective interagency
operations in the field.

Although it is called the National Response Plan, there is some difference of
opinion on whether the NRP really is a plan. It is certainly not a strategy with
broad general platitudes akin to many other high-level federal documents issued
in the wake of the 9/11 attacks. It is not a system like the NIMS. But it is also not
a plan as that kind of document is normally regarded.

The military planning process, designed to produce a plan, is comprised of
five elements: (1) a statement of the mission; (2) description of the situation (conditions on the ground such as terrain and weather and resources available);
(3) tasks for subordinate elements; (4) logistics and administration; and (5) and
command and signal. Based on that model, the NRP is indeed not a plan, nor
could it be considered one because the mission and situation are not provided and

the specific actions to be taken and the circumstances under which are to be taken cannot be identified in advance.

Considering the manner in which it was developed, the NRP could be called a treaty among sovereign departments and agencies. This has both positive and negative implications. The negative aspect of this term is that documents negotiated to obtain consensus usually sink to the level of the lowest common denominator. The positive connotation of this label is that such a document takes into account the differing viewpoints of the various federal agencies and provides a way to achieve coordinated action. The NRP was approved and signed by all of the cabinet secretaries and agency heads, indicating agreement upon its premises and policies.

The NRP assigns responsibilities to federal departments and agencies and provides a general concept of how they are to operate jointly in the event of an emergency requiring federal action. The NRP provides a framework in which to develop an initial operational plan, to either an actual or a potential emergency, and adjust that plan according to novel situational developments. In that sense, the NRP is a doctrinal statement that governs how emergency management officials are expected to behave under a wide variety of circumstances. As doctrine, the NRP allows participants to do the "right thing" even if they are not issued orders to perform specific tasks. Doctrine is a valuable resource during emergencies when there is no time to create it from scratch. That being the case, it is essential that all parties to the NRP familiarize themselves with its provisions and learn how they would be implemented in an actual emergency. This learning process should be enhanced by rehearsals that apply the doctrine to a range of assumed emergencies. The NRP is not the plan. It is something more important—the doctrinal basis for emergency response planning.

Despite some flaws, the NRP aided in the response to Katrina. Emergency response personnel expended much more effort than in any previous emergency, including the 9/11 attacks, and the results were likewise better. While an objective analysis of the overall results has not yet been conducted, the initial data suggest that the federal portion of the response was very good. Using the NRP as a guide, FEMA (1) responded promptly when Katrina was forming and took steps to lessen its effect; (2) managed the response to Katrina's landfall in Florida; (3) deployed teams and established a field command structure with FCOs in each of the affected states a day before Katrina made landfall in the Gulf Coast; (4) satisfactorily performed rescue operations in Alabama, in Mississippi, and in Louisiana outside of New Orleans; (5) coordinated the work of the ESFs without many problems; (6) provided large amounts of commodities and services to hurricane victims; and (7) compensated for New Orleans' inability to perform its assigned work.

There were problems with the NRP. Some of them resulted from the way in which the NRP was written. None of these problems was a major factor in coordinating the overall national response. None resulted in an increase in deaths or destruction during the response phase. The NRP served as a useful doctrinal basis for planning and implementing the emergency response operation.

FEMA DID NOT FAIL

Almost all media, academic, and government reports that address the federal response to Katrina reinforce the public view that FEMA failed "dismally" in its mandate. This perception does not make the distinction between response and recovery, but even allowing for the problems implicit in the ongoing recovery, FEMA has been characterized as a failure. Why is this? There is no single answer, but some of the contributing factors are described below.[35]

Media Performance

Media coverage focused on New Orleans, the Superdome, and the Convention Center, effectively concentrating on the worst episodes of the entire response operation, while failing to mention the good news from other parts of the affected area. This may be merely a reflection of a natural tendency to report negative stories that are exceptions and ignore the good stories that are the rule. Many reporters may have been shaken by being in the disaster area and experiencing firsthand the death and destruction caused by the hurricanes and floods. It is now clear that many media reports exaggerated the number of dead, the violence, and the confusion. These initial pictures are hard to erase once they are lodged in people's minds.

Partisan Party Politics

A big factor fueling the blame game during and after the response is the bitter partisan warfare waged between the Republican administration and the Democratic Party on a wide variety of topics—notably Operation Iraqi Freedom. This inability to agree flavors the assessment of the response. Congress's natural tendency to find fault with the Executive Branch was exacerbated by media reports, and all members were zealous in determining what went wrong. It is instructive to note that, up to this point, with the exception of an appendix in the federal lessons-learned document, there has been no compilation of the results of the performance. The normal tendency of the party out of power to criticize the one in power was reinforced by some Congress members' personal animosity toward President Bush—a sentiment that was not eased by his apparent disinterest in the emergency during its first few days. This problem was exacerbated by the failure of New Orleans and Louisiana to do their part in the disaster-relief effort.

The Race Card

Some observers chose to characterize the response operation as racist by alleging that white victims were given priority assistance and African Americans were deliberately left to die by the authorities. The data do not support this hypothesis.

Antigovernment Attitudes

Although Americans like government checks, many of them do not like the government. The government is portrayed in the media, movies, and television as evil at worst and bumbling at best. This attitude is prevalent among people of all kinds and beliefs. When the government has to take charge, as in the response to Katrina, the good it does is taken for granted but the errors are magnified and a cause for recrimination.

Perfectionism

It appears that the American people expect perfection from their government and will not tolerate even the slightest margin of error due to human frailty or extenuating circumstances. This is a curious attitude, for the public is forgiving of blatant cases of human error by celebrities, criminals, and even ordinary people. In the case of hurricanes Katrina and Rita and the New Orleans flood, intolerance for imperfection has reached a level of intensity that defies reality and precludes appreciation for what was a very successful response.

ASSESSING THE INTERAGENCY PROCESS

Despite unanticipated problems, and with some notable exceptions, federal departments and agencies worked well enough as a team to deal with the consequences of Katrina. Without the work, discussion, rehearsals, and arguments that went into the writing and approval of the NRP, the situation would have been much worse.

The successful federal response to Katrina was made possible by the NRP, which, as doctrine, provided a common understanding for emergency managers at all levels and established a general framework for organizing and conducting the response operation. In that sense, the NRP can be regarded as the product of a successful interagency process.

NOTES

1. Executive Order #12127, Federal Emergency Management Agency, March 31, 1979, at http://www.presidency.ucsb.edu/ws/print.php?pid=32127, and Executive Order #12148, Federal Emergency Management, July 20, 1979, at http://www.fas.org/irp/offdocs/EO12148.htm.

2. James Jay Carafano and Matt A. Mayer, "FEMA and Federalism: Washington Is Moving in the Wrong Direction," Heritage Backgrounder #2032, May 8, 2007, at http://www.heritage.org/Research/HomelandDefense/bg2032.cfm

3. Ibid.

4. James Jay Carafano and Richard D. Weitz, "Learning from Disaster: The Role of Federalism and the Importance of Grassroots Response," Heritage Backgrounder #1923, March 21, 2006, at http://www.heritage.org/Research/HomelandSecurity/bg1923.cfm.

5. Carafano and Mayer, "FEMA and Federalism."

6. The White House, "Homeland Security Presidential Directive, Management of Domestic Incidents (HSPD-5)," February 28, 2003, at http://www.whitehouse.gov/news/releases/2003/02/20030228-9.html.

7. Department of Homeland Security, "National Response Plan, Initial Plan," Draft, May 2000, at http://www.nemaweb.org/docs/national_response_plan.pdf.

8. Government Accountability Office, "Observations on the National Strategies Related to Terrorism," GAO-04-1075T, September 22, 2004, at http://www.gao.gov/new.items/d041075t.pdf.

9. Department of Homeland Security, National Response Plan, December 2004, at http://www.dhs.gov/xprepresp/committees/editorial_0566.shtm.

10. Department of Homeland Security, "National Incident Management System," March 1, 2004, at http://www.fema.gov/pdf/emergency/nims/nims_doc_full.pdf.

11. The White House, "HSPD-5."

12. The White House, "The Federal Response to Hurricane Katrina: Lessons Learned," February 2006, at http://www.whitehouse.gov/reports/katrina-lessons-learned.

13. Responsibility for managing the National Disaster Medical System has been reassigned to the Department of Health and Human Services.

14. The principal sources for the timeline are The Brookings Institution, "Hurricane Katrina Timeline," undated, at http://www.brook.edu/fp/projects/homeland/katrina timeline.pdf; Federal Emergency Management Agency, "Hurricanes Katrina, Rita, and Ophelia Timeline, as of 28 March 2006" at http://www.fema.gov.

15. Michael W. Lowder briefing to Disaster Response Operation and Cross Border Events for Trilateral Conference on Preparing for and Responding to Disaster in North America, November 7, 2006, at http://www.google.com/search?hl=en&ned=us&q=Michael+W.+Lowder%2C+Deputy+Director%2C+Response+Division%2C+Disaster+Response+Operation+and+Cross+Border+Events+for+Trilateral+Conference+on+Preparing+for+and+Responding+to+Disaster+in+North+America%2C+November+7%2C+2006&btnmeta%3Dsearch%3Dsearch=Search+the+Web.

16. Department of Homeland Security, "National Response Plan," 33.

17. Ibid., 34.

18. Thomas R. Lujan, "Legal Aspects of Domestic Employment of the Army," *Parameters* (Autumn 1997): 82–97. http://www.carlisle.army.mil/usawc/Parameters/97autumn/lujan.htm.

19. Federal Emergency Management Agency, "National Situation Report: as of 5:30am Wednesday, August 31, 2005," at http://www.fema.gov.

20. John R. Harrald, testimony for the Senate Homeland Security and Government Affairs Committee, March 8, 2006.

21. Department of Homeland Security, "National Response Plan," 22.

22. Ibid., 23.

23. In the aftermath of Katrina, the Interagency Incident Management Group was converted to the Interagency Advisory Council. Department of Homeland Security, "Notice of Change to the National Response Plan, Version 5.0," May 25, 2006.

24. Department of Homeland Security, "National Response Plan," 24.

25. Lowder Briefing, Slide 7.

26. Douglas Brinkley, *The Great Deluge* (New York: William Morrow, 2006), 327.

27. The White House, "The Federal Response to Hurricane Katrina," 57.

28. Ibid., 38.

29. Government Accountability Office, "Hurricanes Katrina and Rita: Coordination between FEMA and the Red Cross Should Be Improved for the 2006 Hurricane System," GAO-06-712, June 2006, at http://www.gao.gov/new.items/d06712.pdf.

30. Ibid., 12–13.

31. Ibid.

32. Wil Haygood and Ann Scott Tyson, "It Was as If All of Us are Already Pronounced Dead, Conventional Center Left a Five-day Legacy of Chaos and Violence," *Washington Post*, September 15, 2005, at http://www.washingtonpost.com/wp-dyn/content/article/2005/09/14/AR2005091402655.html.

33. James Joyner, "Katrina: People Dying at New Orleans Convention Center, Outside the Beltway," September 1, 2005, at http://www.outsidethebeltway.com.

34. Haygood and Tyson, "It Was as If."

35. For a detailed discussion of these issues, see Marvin Olasky, *The Politics of Disaster: Katrina, Big Government, and a New Strategy for Future Crises* (Nashville, TN: Thomas Nelson, 2006).

Interagency Problems and Proposals: A Research Review

Richard Weitz

The study of the history of the U.S. interagency process has a history all its own. Although the attacks of September 11, 2001, catapulted the issue of U.S. interagency performance in foreign policy to a new level of prominence, scholars, policy makers, and others have long debated the optimal U.S. national security establishment. After the passage of the National Security Act of 1947, the literature on the U.S. interagency process centered on the function and operations of the newly established National Security Council (NSC). In the decades after the Vietnam War, this literature became increasingly critical as commentators reacted to foreign policy setbacks and new challenges to the national security system. From the 1980s onward, intelligence issues, the threat of terrorism, and the challenges of interagency emergency response became common topics for discussion. The September 2001 terrorist attacks intensified these concerns and resulted in a major overhaul in how the United States manages homeland security threats.

In identifying flaws in interagency performance in the realms of national security and foreign policy, policy makers and pundits continually cite failings in interagency coordination as a particularly critical problem. There is a diverse body of literature that attempts to illuminate the reasons behind these problems while recommending specific solutions—as well as more general advice—for strengthening interagency performance in support of foreign policy.[1]

THE COLD WAR ERA

Within the executive branch, the NSC is responsible for advising the president with respect to the integration of domestic, foreign, and military policies related to national security. Yet, many analysts argue that the NSC lacks sufficient authority to successfully mandate interdepartmental coordination.[2]

Created by the National Security Act of 1947, the NSC was intended to provide the president the collective as well as the individual advise of the various department heads responsible for U.S. defense, intelligence, and foreign policy. Although the NSC does not have the authority to make policy as an independent body, as a cabinet-level group it can exercise considerable influence within the executive branch. After the National Security Act laid the foundations for the current national security system, much of the early literature on the NSC concentrated on assessing the council's proper structure, role, and authority.

Presidents have organized and used the NSC in diverse ways, thereby underscoring the malleable nature of the institution. I. M. Destler's article "National Security Advice to U.S. Presidents: Some Lessons from Thirty Years," observes that presidents tend to design the NSC to coordinate foreign policy on the basis of their personal objectives rather than to provide objective analysis of the national security situation. Destler also charts the evolution of the NSC from a transparent interdepartmental advisory group to an established, formal national security structure. Foreshadowing future analysts' recommendations regarding homeland security, this article stresses the need to combine domestic and foreign policy perspectives in order to create a complete national security posture.[3]

Alfred Sander notes that President Truman emphasized the advisory nature of the council, and only began to make a significant use of the body after the start of the Korean War.[4] Paul Hammond remarks that under the Eisenhower administration, the NSC was viewed as a talking group where top officials could discuss national security matters and make recommendations for the government as a whole, not just with regard to their particular department or agency.[5]

According to Edward Kolodziej, Destler, and other commentators, the Kennedy and Johnson administrations adopted an ad hoc approach toward the NSC that resulted in more informal membership and procedures for the Council.[6] During a 1970 congressional subcommittee hearing on national security and international operations, Henry Kissinger said the approach "of the 1960s often ran the risk that relevant points of view were not heard, that systematic treatment of issues did not take place at the highest level, or that the bureaucracies were not fully informed as to what had been decided or why."[7]

Former national security advisor Zbigniew Brzezinski writes that the Eisenhower administration also tried to institutionalize, through procedures and secondary bodies, the council's role as a decision-making and policy-making body. More generally, Brzezinski delineates two systems of foreign policy: the presidential system, where the president is intimately involved in the execution of foreign affairs, and the secretarial system, where the president allows a cabinet secretary to steer foreign policy. Brzezinski discusses the problems of "over-personalization" that he believes diminished the council's strategic coherence during the Johnson and Kennedy administrations, but he also details the pitfalls of "over-institutionalization" that undermined NSC innovation during the Eisenhower administration. Ultimately, Brzezinski favors a presidential system of foreign policy characterized by orderly procedures as well as a clearly defined relationship with the president. Brzezinski also concludes that the NSC should be engaged in policy planning, coordination, and implementation, even advocating the establishment of new NSC machinery to monitor implementation activity.[8] While serving as the national security advisor to President Jimmy Carter, Brzezinski accordingly established a smaller NSC that emphasized effective policy oversight.[9]

Arthur Schlesinger, however, criticizes the traditional, top-down administrative structures of the Eisenhower presidency, and endorses the "increasingly horizontal arrangements" that reflect "the way that presidents like FDR and JFK operated instinctively," since these structures better correspond to the present threat environment.[10]

In the 1970s the Nixon administration established a particularly strong NSC led by an authoritative national security advisor. The administration believed that a council responsible for policy making and implementation of all major issues within clearly defined NSC structures and procedures would most effectively promote creative, systematic, and effective policy.

Charles Yost criticizes the expansion of NSC authority that occurred during the Nixon-Kissinger period. He maintains that the council had detrimentally usurped the traditional role of the State Department. While finding fault with the over-politicization of both the State Department and the NSC, Yost recommends that the State Department have sole responsibility for foreign policy decision making, with the NSC confined to the role of a small deliberative body for major strategic issues involving both military and foreign affairs.[11] In contrast, in his 1972 monograph, *Presidents, Bureaucrats and Foreign Policy: The Politics of Organization*, Destler argues that both the Kennedy and Nixon systems of foreign policy possessed strengths and weaknesses. In general, Destler concludes that an ideal NSC structure entails a high degree of presidential involvement combined with an effective system of delegation.[12]

In the 1970s and 1980s the national security system faced heightened challenges and suffered numerous setbacks. Unsurprisingly, commentary on the NSC in the 1980s and 1990s became increasingly critical. Brzezinski labels the first six years of the Reagan administration as a period of NSC "degradation" characterized by malfeasance in Iran-Contra, a ballooning bureaucracy, and a loss of purpose. In writing about his own tenure as national security advisor (NSA), Brzezinski also describes the problem of interagency rivalry at the NSC. In particular, he illustrates how the State and Defense Departments impeded interagency harmonization by continually resisting NSC coordination.[13] Flora Lewis's 1981 article for the *New York Times* critiques the NSC's effectiveness under President Reagan. She points to persistent and increasingly harsh turf battles as well as a lack of coordination and proper policy consideration as fundamental to this administration's NSC difficulties.[14]

When discussing the interagency coordination role of the NSC, many authors over the past half-century are quick to point out the council's status as a presidential tool with no independent authority of its own. Brzezinski remarks that the

NSC can be very influential, but only when the president decides to take the lead in foreign affairs. The body's authority wanes if a department secretary is given the primary responsibility for managing international issues.[15]

The position of the NSA is similarly malleable depending on the person filling the position and the attitude of the president. According to David Hoffman, President George H. W. Bush wanted his NSA to follow an "honest-broker" model by generally adopting a low public profile and being able to provide comprehensive advice when called upon.[16] Brzezinski describes the more active role that he adopted as President Carter's advisor, which included taking on some oversight responsibilities such as clearing State Department cables.[17] John Burke, writing in *Presidential Studies Quarterly*, argues that after 9/11, Condoleeza Rice's role as an honest broker declined, partially because of changing expectations on the part of the president about the NSA's appropriate role.[18] Thus, under the current government organization, the functions of both the advisor and the NSC itself can change according to very different interpretations of their roles by top policy makers.

Many recommendations on improving the NSC's ability to coordinate the interagency process have focused on expanding its authority or scope. In *Keeping the Edge: Managing Defense for the Future*, John Deutch, Arnold Kanter, and Brent Scowcroft recommend increasing the planning and coordination authority of the NSC while limiting its power to implement interagency operations.[19] They also advocate integrating domestic agencies into the NSC and establishing a much closer relationship between the NSC and the Office of Management and Budget (OMB) in order to guarantee the feasibility of interagency operations. Gregory Martin, writing for the Army War College after 9/11, recommends creating a director of national security operations within the NSC, who would be responsible for monitoring the implementation of national security strategy.[20]

Successive commentators describe the problem of integrating the NSC processes with the departmental structure of the U.S. cabinet. As early as 1949, Sidney W. Souers's examination of the first two years of the NSC concluded that interdepartmental unity of purpose was critical for an effective national security structure.[21] In his 1960 analysis for the *American Political Science Review,* Paul Hammond argues that NSC policy making is impeded by the "cabinet level problem" where departmental self-interest leads cabinet members to issue overly vague policy recommendations.[22]

OUTSIDE THE NSC

In assessing the U.S. national security structure, scholars have also offered critiques of other major institutions, besides the National Security Council, that help determine American foreign policy. In a 1985 article, Destler, Leslie H. Gelb, and Anthony Lake offer a sweeping critique of U.S. foreign-policy making. They identify organizational disarray, a widening disconnect between the president and the bureaucracy, a credibility gap, over-politicization, and other perennial problems impeding effective policy making.[23] Similarly, James Kitfield's 1995 book *Prodigal Soldiers: How the Generation of Officers Born of Vietnam Revolutionized the American Style of War* discusses micromanagement, demoralizing doctrine and policy conflicts, and a failure of leadership as critical national security flaws of the Vietnam War era.[24]

The failures attributed to U.S. policy formation and execution during the Vietnam War, along with other perceived military problems, led to a major effort during the 1980s and 1990s to reform the U.S. Department of Defense, which aimed, among other goals, to improve its ability to cooperate with non-DOD agencies. The Goldwater-Nichols Act of 1986, the 1995 Commission on Roles and Missions, the National Defense Panel of 1997, the Hart-Rudman Phase III Report of the U.S. Commission on National Security, and the final report of the National Commission on Terrorist Attacks Upon the United States (the 9/11 Commission) each represent an important effort to redesign government capacities to deal with new security challenges.

An initial focus of these assessments was improving the manner in which the individual military services operate together in joint missions. A pioneering 1985 Staff Report to the Committee on Armed Services criticizes the organization, decision-making procedures, and interagency performance of the Department of Defense. The authors fault the Department of Defense for failures including limited mission integration at the policy-making level, an imbalance between service and joint interests, redundancy, inadequate joint advice, and a lack of clarity regarding strategic goals.[25] The critique provided a foundation for the major reforms the Defense Department adopted after the 1986 Goldwater-Nichols Defense Reorganization Act. The perceived success of these reforms in turn encouraged subsequent efforts to improve U.S. interagency coordination across the U.S. national security establishment.

A DECADE OF TRANSITION

The end of the Cold War prompted a resurgence of interest in interagency operations. The 1996 Commission on Roles and Missions of the Armed Forces proposes measures that seek to build on the Goldwater-Nichols reforms and address the Defense Department's "unclear future" in the face of rapid change and evolving national security policies. The commission urges improved efficiency, responsiveness, management, and "jointness."[26] Writing for *Parameters*, John E. Lange focuses on the need for the government and, more specifically, the Defense Department, to address interagency challenges like those posed by the Rwanda refugee humanitarian relief crisis in 1994. Though skeptical about his recommendation's chances for success, Lange hopes the military would become more open to executing missions other than war-fighting.[27]

In a 1998 monograph, *Getting Agencies to Work Together*, Eugene Bardach concludes that bureaucratic cultures often deter collaborative activities.[28] In 2000, the Government Accountability Office illustrates the existence of substantial mission fragmentation and overlap as a result of poor interagency coordination.[29] In a 2001 study, Richard Best highlights coordination problems between intelligence and law enforcement agencies in spite of NSC oversight coordinative mechanisms.[30]

In calling for government reform to meet the challenges of the post–Cold War world, a number of analysts and policy makers focused on U.S. deficiencies in combating the terrorist threat even before the events of 9/11. As far back as the early 1980s, Robert Taylor recommends that the U.S. national security structure reorient itself to combat terrorism more effectively. In particular, Taylor urges the government to address shortcomings such as inconsistent policy making, ineffective organizational coordination and communication, and a lack of assets capable of dealing with terrorist events.[31]

The fact that Dan Carney and Chuck McCutcheon, in a piece published in 1998, identify problems in interagency coordination of U.S. counterterrorism efforts similar to those discussed by Robert Taylor suggests that many of these issues were not effectively addressed in the interim between the two reports.[32] In 2000, the Government Accountability Office criticizes the synchronization of government efforts against terrorism. The report also faults the federal government for failing to establish a national terrorism response strategy with clearly defined procedures.[33] In his 2001 analysis, Kevin C. Coyler characterizes U.S. efforts to prepare against terrorism as disjointed and inefficient. He urges the government to adopt an improved organizational structure.[34]

COMPLEX CONTINGENCY OPERATIONS

The issue of how the United States could best respond to the series of international conflicts that arose after the end of the Cold War became an object of considerable attention in the national security literature of the 1990s. These "complex contingency operations" include the major U.S. military interventions in Haiti, Somalia, and the former Yugoslavia. The Bosnia and Kosovo operations, as well as the intervention in East Timor, also raised additional issues related to conducting military operations in coalitions with foreign allies.

Complex contingency operations are uniquely taxing on the American security architecture because they typically demand a much greater degree of interagency cooperation and coordination than standard military operations. They regularly require the active participation of multiple branches of the U.S. armed services, many civilian agencies such as the United States Agency for International Development (USAID), nongovernmental and international organizations like the World Bank Group (WB), the International Monetary Fund (IMF), and the World Health Organization (WHO), as well as supranational bodies (e.g., the United Nations, the European Union) and other sovereign nations. Neyla Arnas, Charles Barry, and Robert Oakley postulate that the ad hoc nature of these operations has contributed to the difficulty the interagency process has encountered in responding to them.[35]

Students of these interventions see unhelpful policy discontinuities, especially between presidential administrations, in how the U.S. government responds to these complex emergencies. Even within individual administrations, the substantial amount of staff rotation mandated by protocol impedes the creation of a coherent doctrine of cooperation. Douglas Stuart adds that "there is a high turnover and the injection of new talent, at times inexperienced and equipped with new predispositions about national security, at the top echelons of American government every time the part that controls the White House changes."[36]

Another concern manifested especially in the U.S. interventions during the 1990s has been a lack of coordination between the U.S. military and U.S. civilian agencies. For instance, observers see the Haiti intervention as evincing a lack of cooperation between USAID and DOD. To take just one example, USAID officials were unable to transport equipment because they could not effectively communicate with DOD officials. In the postconflict phase, U.S. military planners were surprised that their civilian counterparts were not immediately prepared to institute the nation-building phase. Development planners were upset that the military refused to accept responsibility for civic action and nation-building efforts at the outset, although that policy had been determined at the presidential level. Observers also believe the U.S. military failed to appreciate the potential value of nongovernmental organizations in assisting with the intervention and recovery.[37]

In contrast, Donald Dreschler argues that, during U.S. involvement in the Kosovo crisis in 1999, the State Department effectively subordinated the Department of Defense to its lead.[38] According to his interpretation, this unexpected role reversal yielded surprising results—rapid military and postconflict operational success. He speculates that the State Department's leadership abilities, combined with its capacity to make concessions to its military counterparts, helped make military and postconflict success a possibility. Kosovo can therefore be viewed as a paradigm of functional and effective State-Defense cooperation.

A more common view is that the Department of State (DOS) lacks sufficient financial, personnel, and other resources to lead the U.S. response to complex contingencies.[39] According to Douglas Stuart, "The Department of State, which has a responsibility to conduct foreign affairs, is a veritable pauper."[40] This "paucity of operational capability in the State Department," also referred to as a lack of civilian "surge capacity," is emblematic of the resource disparity between the military and civilian sectors.[41] The Center for Strategic International Studies' Beyond Goldwater-Nichols project concludes that this phenomenon is by no means limited to the State Department. According to its analysis, "Most civilian agencies do not focus on the conduct of operations and therefore lack an operational culture. Consequently, even though these agencies may be tasked with performing critical tasks in a particular operation, they generally lack personnel who are trained and ready for these missions as well as the authorities and resources to rapidly deploy them and to quickly establish programs in the field."

The effects of these limitations were disastrous for the U.S. stabilization mission in Haiti in the early 1990s. Insufficient communication on tactical, strategic, and operational levels made coordination between the military and political components of the operation impossible, and the resulting lack of dialogue between agencies doomed the mission.[42]

Many authors believe that establishing regular and frequent contact between federal agencies is vital to building a rapport and trust between personnel. Part of the challenge for developing a routine, meaningful dialogue in the interagency space is that many executive agencies do not speak with a single voice. Morton Halperin, the former director of the Policy Planning staff at the State Department (1998–2001), recalls that multiple representatives from a single agency were often sent to interagency meetings with varying (and often discordant) agendas and talking points.[43] Intra-agency dialogue is, in many ways, fundamental to the task of promoting interagency unity. Once a dialogue commences, cultivating relationships among various agencies helps ensure future operational and strategic success.

The related problem of insufficient regional collaboration is also cited by multiple authors as an impediment to strategic cooperation between constituent elements of executive agencies.[44] While bureaucratic cooperation at the highest levels of agency command in Washington is integral to strategic interagency cooperation, coordination among the various regional bureaus of the executive agencies situated in geographic areas around the world is also required.[45] A panel report from the Center for the Study of the Presidency, chaired by General Edward C. Meyer and former U.S. ambassador to the UN, Thomas R. Pickering, underscores the importance of "creating relationships in Washington and in the field that strengthen the ability of military and State Department leaders to operate regionally in a more coherent fashion."[46]

SEPTEMBER 11—BEFORE AND AFTER

The pre-9/11 interagency literature, like much of the literature after 9/11, has faulted disparate cultures, interdepartmental friction, inadequate information sharing, and departmental self-interest for contributing to ineffective interagency coordination.

Scholars propose a number of solutions to deal with these underlying issues. In their 2000 piece, Deutch, Kanter, and Scowcroft, while identifying defects in the U.S. national security structure and U.S. interagency processes, nevertheless caution against a "wholesale overhaul" of the system. They instead recommend delineating clear lines of responsibility in the interagency process, giving the NSC greater authority for coordination of interagency programs, and more efficiently aligning policy instruments to primary national security threats and objectives.[47]

To lessen the influence of independent agency cultures, Thomas Gibbings, Donald Hurley, and Scott Moore, recommend establishing a permanent interagency operations center for each of the U.S. military's geographic commands.[48]

To improve information sharing, Sharon S. Dawes's 1996 article "Interagency Information Sharing: Expected Benefits, Manageable Risks," advocates addressing the issues of interoperability among information systems, the standardization of departmental terms and reference systems, and the sharp definition of boundaries between agencies' responsibilities, among other issues.[49]

Carnes Lord's "NSC Reform for the Post-Cold War Era" calls for improving government effectiveness through reformed interagency procedures, budgeting practices, information management, and personnel policies.[50] Anthony Zinni's *A Military for the 21st Century: Lessons from the Recent Past*, echoes the commissions of the 1990s in calling for military transformation and a reevaluation of the national security decision-making structure in order to manage U.S. foreign and security policy more effectively in the face of uncertain threats.[51]

A recurring recommendation to improve interagency coordination has been to better educate civil servants on interagency processes and allow for routine short-term rotations of service among U.S. government agencies. In 1980, Philip Odeen argued that interagency cooperation would be facilitated by encouraging members of departmental staffs to work outside their home departments.[52] In *Interagency Operations: Coordination through Education*, Robert Smith advocates establishing an interagency professional education system and introducing inter-agency curriculum at the National Defense University to improve interagency coordination.[53] Mark Walsh also proposes enhanced interagency training as a partial solution to inadequacies in interagency emergency response policies and capabilities.[54] Douglas Stuart likewise calls for "a systematic effort to develop civilian and military cadres that are experts in interagency policy coordination, integration, and operations."[55]

A recurring recommendation by analysts for addressing the problem of differing bureaucratic cultures is for the United States to adopt a standardized doctrine to define how U.S. government agencies respond to complex emergencies. Michelle Flournoy and Shawn Brimley complain that, some fifteen years after the conclusion of the Cold War, the U.S. government has yet to adopt a strategic planning mechanism for foreign or domestic policy.[56] A report by the Beyond Goldwater-Nichols Project similarly observes that "unlike the military, which has a doctrine and a standard approach to planning operations, the U.S. government as a whole lacks established procedures for developing integrated strategies and plans."[57] The report also warns that the lack of an agreed doctrine also hampers multinational coalition interventions in complex emergencies.

National Defense University workshop panels echo the sentiments of the Beyond Goldwater-Nichols Project, with participants recommending that policy makers "develop both doctrine and procedures for civil-military planning for emergencies like disaster assistance, humanitarian assistance, and peacekeeping operations in which civilian and military are likely to be co-equal and co-terminus participants."[58] According to Albert Zaccor, improving the interagency process does not require a major reorganization, only the development of a common conceptual framework "with the associated policies, procedures, and organization to implement that doctrine." Zaccor recommends the publication of a presidential directive on security cooperation and the subsequent development of an interagency planning process based on the directive.[59]

Desai argues that a coherent doctrine and planning culture can be inculcated in the interagency process following the pattern set by Goldwater-Nichols, which solidified standard operating procedures by establishing a strong doctrine for the Department of Defense. Since then, a joint culture among the branches of the armed forces has emerged, enabling all military personnel to cooperate in the spirit of the American mission. This could easily happen for the interagency process, Desai believes, if momentum for reform grows within and beyond current interagency circles.[60]

The Clinton administration's 1997 Presidential Decision Directive (PDD) 56 aimed to improve interagency response to emergencies by establishing standard procedures to govern the U.S. response, but many authors conclude that problems continued. In "Complex Emergencies: Under New Management," Mark R. Walsh characterizes U.S. emergency response as ad hoc despite PDD-56, although he argues that the directive possessed great potential. Walsh proposes creating an interagency team to develop policy for responding to emergencies and to help ensure that PDD-56 receives the strong interagency and NSC support it needed to succeed.[61] In contrast, Tonya Langford identifies flaws in PDD-56. She is particularly concerned that the directive fails to integrate regional and international efforts.[62]

Other observers have sought to address perceived flaws in the national security establishment and improve government capacity to manage post–Cold War challenges through a reorganization of the U.S. national security system rather than a simple change in doctrine. The 1993 National Partnership for Reinventing Government (formerly the National Performance Review) labels many government processes as ineffective and advocates a number of measures to improve interagency performance, though the Commission largely failed to implement these recommendations.

Several other pre-9/11 government commissions advanced organizational recommendations for improving interagency coordination. The 1997 "National Security in the 21st Century Report" of the National Defense Panel calls for broad government transformations to address long-term issues facing the U.S. defense and national security communities. It recommends establishing a fully integrated national crisis center, streamlining the transfer of funds within and among agencies, aligning civilian agencies' geographic bureaus with the U.S. military's unified commands, and institutionalizing an interagency long-range strategic planning process. The National Defense Panel also advocates reviewing the entire national security structure to anticipate and shape changes in the international environment and making improvements to interagency effectiveness through the establishment of a cadre of interagency professionals.

The Hart-Rudman Commission in many ways logically builds on and refines the National Defense Panel review. The common theme of both reports is the need to provide greater operational flexibility in a stove-piped U.S. government bureaucracy, in part to anticipate the unconventional security challenges of the future. Most importantly, the commission advocates creating an independent National Homeland Security Agency with a single person of cabinet rank responsible for planning, coordinating, and integrating various U.S. government activities involved in homeland security. The Hart-Rudman report calls for appointing an assistant secretary for homeland security to oversee Defense activities in this area and promote the provision of necessary resources. The commission also endorses making homeland security a primary mission of the National Guard.

Furthermore, the commission recommends that the president personally guide a top-down strategic planning process linked to resource allocation decisions throughout the government. In this capacity, the president would prepare an overall national security budget, supplementing the budget submissions of the individual national security departments and agencies, which would focus on the country's most critical strategic goals. The members urge that the NSC advisor and NSC staff return to their traditional role of coordinating national security activities as honest brokers, and resist becoming policy makers or high-profile operators. Overall, the Hart-Rudman commission calls for the relevant departments and agencies involved in foreign operations to cooperate more comprehensively in regional planning and in anticipating unconventional security challenges.[63]

Like many analysts, Gabriel Marcella highlights coordination problems between the State and Defense departments. The author identifies differing agency cultures, resources, and goals as general causes of interagency friction. Marcella concludes that the lack of a singular authority in interagency efforts constitutes the greatest challenge to successful interagency collaboration. To improve coordination, he proposes the creation of a new national security structure in which the functions of the State and Defense departments would be more closely synthesized.[64]

Other pre-9/11 analyses emphasize improving leadership and technology for enhancing national security structures. James Kitfield and Arthur Schlesinger underscore the necessity of strong management, with Kitfield calling for leadership at several levels and Schlesinger more specifically urging the president to maintain active direction of foreign policy.[65] The 1997 National Defense Panel urges greater efforts toward integrating technologies, transforming the U.S. industrial base and infrastructure, and developing a unified multimedia communications system to improve the effectiveness of U.S. foreign and security policies. By emphasizing the importance of developing American scientific and technological expertise, the 2001 Commission on National Security/21st Century also underscores the importance of technology for the U.S. national security system.[66]

Some commentators refrain from offering specific recommendations, preferring instead to provide general guidelines for reform. Destler offers several suggestions for understanding how bureaucracies work and how individuals work within them.[67] In "Leading Change: Why Transformation Efforts Fail," John P. Kotter investigates why reorganizations fail and proposes eight necessary stages toward the successful transformation of any organization.[68] In 2000, David Tucker maintains that "the interagency process may not be as incompetent as the military believes." He advises that before attempting reform, one must understand the interagency process and realize that the process is, in fact, "a network disguised as a hierarchy," which, in his view, has its advantages. Tucker recommends general procedural and technological solutions to interagency flaws, arguing against a massive structural reorganization of the national security apparatus.[69]

A few analysts believe that the existing NSC structure has performed fairly effectively at promoting interagency coordination. For example, a publication by the Henry L. Stimson Center values the NSC for forging common institutional policies out of the viewpoints of disparate agencies. The report recommends applying the NSC model down to lower levels of government in order to increase the effectiveness of U.S. foreign affairs initiatives.[70]

Many authors, however, suggest formalizing the NSC structure and expanding its authority to make national security policy. According to Odeen's "Organizing for National Security," which appeared in the summer 1980 issue of *International Security*, the NSC should coordinate the foreign policy decision-making process and advise the president. In this role, the NSC would identify critical national security issues, force decisions, push interagency policy implementation cooperation, and ensure that clear alternatives to policies put forward by different departments are seriously weighed and researched. In addition, Odeen urges the NSC to ensure that departmental decision making on issues that clearly belong to one department but affect other departments incorporate the concerns of those other agencies. More generally, Odeen argues that past administrations have suffered from national security problems when they failed to rely adequately on the Council.[71]

Brzezinski believes that these reforms would make the body more capable of integrating U.S. diplomatic, military, and financial efforts to achieve national security goals.[72] Matthew Bogdanos, writing in the *Marine Corps Gazette*, cites the NSC's inability to formulate a credible interagency plan for Operation Iraqi Freedom as one of the key reasons why other agencies had to "volunteer" to participate in the war effort rather than be assigned specific areas of responsibility.[73]

The arguments against an expansion of the NSC's powers have been largely based on the lack of constitutional authority for such a body. In his 1956 *Foreign Affairs* article, "The Development of the National Security Council," Robert Cutler worries that the NSC might disrupt the proper constitutional relationship between the president and his cabinet.[74] Paul Hammond argues that, since the NSC originated as a small advisory panel, it lacks the membership and legitimacy to make policy in a democracy. In his assessment, only the president and Congress have such authority.[75]

Hammond raises an alternative explanation for the NSC's often limited effectiveness in promoting interagency coordination: the possibility of factionalization within the council itself. He fears that relying on cabinet-level officials to make

NSC recommendations leads to vague statements based on the lowest common denominator of agreement because secretaries prove naturally reluctant to discuss the failures of their departments with the broader council. Instead, department secretaries take their concerns directly to the president, which undermines the effectiveness of the NSC as an interagency coordinating body or discussion group.[76]

Fred Greenstein and Richard H. Immerman argue that the NSC requires more coherence and organization. In "Effective National Security Advising: Recovering the Eisenhower Legacy," they maintain that an ideal NSC system would include a separate organ for policy implementation and would be led by an NSA who serves as a process manager rather than a policy advocate. They also point to the Eisenhower-era Operations Coordinating Board as an effective body for turning NSC recommendations into concrete policy.[77]

Gregory Martin recommends establishing a new senior position on the NSC staff: the Director of National Security Operations. The director would be supported by a small interagency staff and would monitor the implementation of national security strategy as well as close the gap between operational planning and execution.[78]

Some authors believe that the NSC's close relationship with the presidency taints its ability to be an effective, impartial integrator. John Lucynski argues that while the NSC was originally intended to inspire unity among the various elements of the national security apparatus, it now appears to be used as a means of bringing other agencies in line with an agenda dictated exclusively by the president.[79] Sunil Desai argues that the National Security Act of 1947 fails to give the NSC the necessary authority to develop a coherent interagency doctrine. Without it, he claims, the effectiveness of the NSC organizational structure has degraded over time as each new generation of employees became weaker due to inadequate standardized training.[80]

In *Public Administration Review*, W. Henry Lambright proposes that the government use the Committee on Environment and Natural Resources (CENR) as a model for future interagency cooperation at the committee level. According to Lambright, following the CENR example would lessen interagency rivalry through the selection of a high-level bureaucrat from a small agency to lead interagency committees and instill a common goal among committee members. Moreover, the CENR model would facilitate the fulfillment of four prerequisites for effective collaboration: common interests, presidential and congressional support, group leadership, and group authority.[81]

The terrorist attacks of September 11, 2001, brought to light major problems in the U.S. government's organizational planning and response capabilities as they applied to acute domestic emergencies. Many analysts anticipated these potential problems well in advance, but their warnings failed to generate successful efforts to rectify them.

Warnings about the need for the United States to prepare for a possible terrorist attack on U.S. soil came as early as the middle of the 1980s. For example,

Robert Taylor produced a report decrying the limited American capability to respond to domestic terrorism. He assessed the interagency policy mechanisms in this area as chaotic.[82] More than a decade later, Dan Carney and Chuck McCutcheon again emphasized the grave nature of the situation when they published a report asserting that, despite the obvious threat of a terrorist attack (there had already been multiple attacks on U.S. targets overseas, in addition to the first attacks on the World Trade Center in 1993 and the 1995 destruction of the Alfred P. Murrah Federal Building in Oklahoma City), the United States continued to lack a coordinated plan for adequately responding to a terrorist attack.[83]

In 2000 John Deutch, Arnold Kanter, and Brent Scowcroft advocated creating a Homeland Security department—with jurisdiction over all domestic security functions that involve foreign threats—to improve U.S. policy making in this area. Given the pre-9/11 climate in which they were writing, however, they did not believe Congress would prove willing to create an agency along these lines. Even after the events of 9/11, the legislative and executive branches declined to create the expansive homeland security organization the authors envisaged.[84]

Similarly, a 2000 assessment by the Hart-Rudman Commission also recommends that the government create a new agency tasked specifically with overseeing domestic security issues. This "National Homeland Security Agency" would be responsible for planning, coordinating, and integrating the activities of the various government agencies that address domestic security issues. Additionally, the commission argues that the National Guard should be re-equipped and re-tasked to make homeland defense a primary mission.

After the attacks on New York and Washington, the president authorized the creation of the Office of Homeland Security. Although this new interagency body possessed a clear mission, it lacked clear authority or a developed organizational structure. Ashton Carter considers the office's development less as a catalyst for interagency cooperation than an impediment. He maintains that the creation of an additional agency further complicates the already complex bureaucracy and interagency relations that many fault for impeding the government's ability to prevent the 9/11 attacks.[85] In assessing the creation of the office as well as that of the subsequent Department of Homeland Security (DHS), Richard Clarke caustically observes that it is "easier to waste time on reorganization than it is to accomplish anything concrete."[86]

Some authors believe that the creation of the Office of Homeland Security and the Homeland Security Council (HSC) by President George W. Bush in the wake of September 11 further handicaps the NSC's ability to serve as an effective consensus-building and integrative organization.[87] They worry that the HSC, comprised of representatives of twenty-two federal agencies, simply adds yet another layer of bureaucracy to the already bewildering interagency landscape in the area of national security. According to the authors, the decision-making and enforcement processes for the NSC and HSC are different, personnel for the organizations receive dramatically different training, and there exists no formal bridge between the two organizations. The result is that two interagency bodies, holding similar if not redundant objectives, now compete for interagency space.

Several authors complain that these various bodies are ineffective actors in their own right.[88] Lynn Davis believes that the Office of Homeland Security cannot "translate its various coordinating responsibilities into practice."[89] Besides complaining that the HSC competes with the NSC and duplicates existing homeland protection efforts, William Newmann sees the HSC as problematic because it "has no representation from the state or local level, nor from organizations that represent the functionally based institutions that are operating at those levels—police, firefighters, emergency medical technicians, and hospitals." In short, its vertical coordination is weak despite the essential role that local emergency personnel play in disaster response.[90]

In September 2002, just as Bush announced his intention to turn the OHS into the Department of Homeland Security, *Public Administration Review* presented a symposium of articles discussing the potential department.[91] In his contribution, William Newmann stresses any effort to manage homeland security must bring cohesion to agencies traditionally separated by domestic law and national security functions. For this reason, he believes it would be more difficult to impose unity through a large department, which would need to take over both domestic and international roles to cover all functions related to homeland security, than to develop a process of interagency cooperation. At about this time, Ivo Daalder and Destler authored an article likewise contending that it is neither desirable nor possible to bring all the major homeland security functions under a single umbrella.[92] Instead, they focus on the need for leadership, cross-governmental coordination, and mobilization of the relevant agencies and their leaders.

Stephen Brummond expresses reservations regarding the need to create a new department dedicated to homeland security because doing so, he argues, would merely consist of "moving colored boxes around on an organizational chart." Four years earlier, John Schall recommended using the NSC model for building interagency coordination at the strategic level, writing that "the model should not only be maintained, it should be replicated."[94] J. R. Barnes cites the history of DOD in arguing for the need to grant considerable authority to the heads of homeland security agencies.[95]

Almost as soon as the new Department of Homeland Security was established, policy analysts began to recommend ways to enhance its effectiveness. For example, Katherine Peters called on DHS to oversee policy coordination and information sharing between existing government agencies.[96] In order to facilitate the gathering and sharing of information related directly to terrorism, a December 2002 Joint Inquiry Staff Proposal recommends that DHS should establish and house a counterterrorist intelligence fusion center.[97] William Waigh and Richard Sylves express concerns that a new agency that focuses on weapons of mass destruction and terrorism would divert attention away from preparing for more "routine" emergencies such as natural disasters.

Other analysts caution that DHS should not define its mission as controlling the emergency response to domestic disasters. Even after Hurricane Katrina, authors warn that it would be antithetical to the U.S. system of governance and its philosophical underpinnings for local responsibilities and response to be "federalized" too early. For similar reasons, they argued against giving the Department of Defense excessive responsibility for homeland security. Besides philosophical concerns about respecting the principle of federalism, they also raised practical considerations, such as the superior knowledge of local conditions that emergency responders living and working in stricken regions would likely possess.[98]

Some analysts have sought to address homeland security activities within a regional framework in order to enhance knowledge of local conditions within a national planning system. John Marsh, Frank Cilluffo, and other scholars have recommended that regional interagency offices, based on the regional offices of the Federal Emergency Management Agency (FEMA), be established to better coordinate federal responses to disaster areas.[99] Employing a different focus, Lynn Davis advocates giving the National Guard a greater role in conducting homeland security activities. In her assessment, this restructuring would allow Guard units to collaborate more closely with FEMA and other civilian organizations in the event of a domestic emergency.

The role of other elements of the Defense Department in homeland security also concerns experts. James Kitfield cites an urgent need to clarify the authority of Northern Command (which includes the United States) in the event of an emergency. Although the National Response Plan apparently assigns decision-making authority to DHS, Kitfield believes that without further clarification confusion likely will arise regarding the role of Northern Command. In the event of a terrorist incident, which is intrinsically ambiguous in form, the burden of responsibility is supposed to fall on DHS, with Northern Command acting in a support role.[100]

Chris Hornbarger argues that the Defense Department must authorize Northern Command to interact directly with DHS in order to develop federal and national (intergovernmental) domestic incident contingency plans under the supervision of the assistant secretary of defense for Homeland Defense. Unlike some authors, Hornbarger also believes that the legal authority for the commitment of DOD assets to domestic incidents exists under current federal law, despite the DOD's strict interpretation of *posse comitatus*.[101] As part of an effort to address the unclear relationship and differing missions of DHS and DOD, Michael Pitts proposes that the two departments strive to merge their disparate missions into one all-encompassing strategy to achieve national security and defense.[102]

IN THE WAKE OF KATRINA

On the domestic front, natural disasters have tested the efficacy of various interagency reform efforts, highlighting the need for greater coordination and planning. Hurricane Katrina, the greatest natural disaster to hit America in the twenty-first century, served to underscore some of the problems inherent in post-crisis relief efforts. Prior to its landfall, natural disasters were sparsely discussed in much of the literature pertaining to interagency reform, overshadowed by the growing threats of terrorism and failed states. In the wake of the event, however, numerous recommendations were made in an effort to analyze and solve some of the problems plaguing interagency cooperation with regard to natural disasters.

Before Hurricane Katrina hit on August 23, 2005, most of the interagency reform literature focused on man-made security issues such as terrorist attacks and postconflict peacekeeping missions. Some of these reports, however, did make recommendations on improving interagency cooperation for natural disasters. For example, one of the recommendations in the 1993 final report of the National Performance Review—made for the purpose of "creating a government that works better and costs less"—called for the creation of an interagency Ecosystem Management Task Force to minimize future risks posed by natural disasters.[103] Similarly, the National Defense Panel, in a report released in 1997, recommended the creation of a national crisis center with employees from various government agencies to deal with future security vulnerabilities, particularly natural disasters.[104]

President Clinton's Presidential Decision Directive 56 created an executive committee tasked with planning and organizing seamless interagency cooperative missions in "complex contingency operations," including natural disasters. Mark Walsh and Michael Harewood, however, express doubts about this committee's potential for success, citing the need for extensive support from the executive and legislative branches, which PDD-56 sometimes lacked.[105]

After the advent of Hurricane Katrina, the issue of interagency reform for improving the national response to natural disasters gained additional attention. As a result of problems mobilizing interagency coordination during and after the hurricane, contentious debates emerged regarding which agency should lead such efforts and what changes in organization or policy are needed to improve the national response in this area.

Although observers of the U.S. government's reaction to Katrina rapidly concluded that it was a failure, they differ over how to improve the government's performance during future disasters. Christopher Clayton argues that a federalized response to the relief effort should have occurred later, following the implementation of FEMA plans.[106] In his view, the National Guard was the only agency with the de facto ability to achieve tangible results. At the time, however, it lacked adequate guidance from federal authorities. In the future, Clayton argues, FEMA should devise plans that would be implemented immediately by other agencies. To facilitate interagency cooperation, he advocates holding more joint training sessions.

Gregg Gross also cites a lack of leadership as the reason for the Hurricane Katrina response's initial failure.[107] According to his analysis, the military lacked proper guidance, which led to subsequent inefficiencies. To remedy this problem, Gross recommends the creation of additional regional interagency groups, each led by a regional ambassador, who would form a close relationship with his national counterparts. If endowed with greater authority and responsibility, regional groups could help direct the efficient usage of federal human resources.

John O'Neil takes this idea a step further, claiming that the internal structure of these regional groups is as important as their existence. Although he complains about poor leadership during the response to Katrina, O'Neil also complains about the weak skills of many midlevel agency employees. In his assessment, if these managers do not understand the procedures of their own agency, they cannot provide guidance to their subordinates. He recommends that planning agencies invest more capital in their midlevel managers.[108]

INTELLIGENCE ANALYSIS
AND INFORMATION SHARING

Analysis of how to improve the efficiency and effectiveness of the intelligence community has also become more common during the last decade. Furthermore, whereas reports on the community from the 1970s and 1980s focused largely on legality and propriety, the last decade has seen the spotlight shift to issues of coordination, particularly how to improve information sharing for the purposes of national security.[109]

Loch K. Johnson reviews problems associated with the now disabled position of the director of central intelligence (DCI). He concludes that the DCI lacks sufficient resources and authority and is hobbled by widespread interagency rivalry. Though Johnson hopes to avoid creating an overly centralized intelligence community, he recommends better integrating the DCI into the intelligence community, requiring DCI concurrence for the appointment of all intelligence program directors, expanding DCI involvement in the intelligence budget preparation, endowing the DCI with the power to redirect intelligence community funding, and institutionalizing the process whereby intelligence officers complete rotations in different agencies.[110]

The events of 9/11 set in motion a concerted effort to remedy the intelligence community's perceived weaknesses. In order to evaluate opportunities for reform, a number of national-level commissions produced studies examining the state of interagency intelligence cooperation. In one such study, the Joint Inquiry Staff put forth a number of recommendations to improve the sharing of intelligence. The staff proposes creating a director of national intelligence (DNI) who would serve as the president's principal advisor on intelligence, integrating the collection and analytic capacities of the NSA, FBI, and CIA, institutionalizing joint training and interagency responsibilities for employees within individual agencies, and improving congressional oversight.[111]

Similarly, the *Final Report of the 9/11 Commission* cites a lack of resources and poor incentives for cooperation between agencies as major obstacles to an effective intelligence community. Its authors note that while individual actions, such as the creation of the position of DNI and the establishment of the National Counterterrorism Center (NCTC), have provided the government with new tools, cooperation between these bodies remains deficient. The 9/11 report also rated the performances of the federal government and its congressional overseers as distressingly weak.[112] The authors of the report urge clear information-sharing procedures and performance evaluations as potential means of encouraging the necessary cooperation.[113]

The Commission on the Intelligence Capabilities of the United States Regarding Weapons of Mass Destruction presented its final report to the president in 2005. Among its findings, the Commission concludes that the intelligence community "has too little integration and too little innovation to succeed in the 21st century. It rarely adopts integrated strategies for penetrating high-priority targets; decision makers lack authority to resolve agency disputes; and it develops too few innovative ways of gathering intelligence." Echoing the recommendations of other commissions, it proposes the creation of an integrated intelligence community structure under the DNI, the organization of the intelligence community toward specific missions, and the expansion of the Information Sharing environment to include all intelligence information. The report's comprehensive analysis stresses the importance of addressing interagency issues, as well as department-specific concerns.[114]

Gaps in congressional oversight are the dominant focus of the *Investigation into the Lack of Coordination between Federal Agencies*, compiled in the 2003 Congressional Record. The study criticizes the Department of Justice (DOJ) for its perceived unwillingness to provide information to the Senate Committee on Governmental Affairs, which Congress believes has hampered the committee's investigations concerning national security. At the time, the Congress also objects to the DOJ's practice of denying committee requests for information on persons who are the subject of terrorism investigations, in accordance with its policy of "not providing Congress with information about people who have been investigated but not prosecuted."[115]

Flows of information within the intelligence community are another matter of concern. In his guide to reorganizing the structure and roles within government, Thomas Stanton stresses the need to assure information flows to the proper level of government for consideration and possible action. Combining related government programs to provide an organization focus, clear prioritization, and accountability can help facilitate the collection and exchange of intelligence.[116] Both 9/11 and the war in Iraq are commonly cited as instances where poor quality information resulted in major setbacks. Christopher Cox notes that failures in these cases highlight the flaws in cooperation between the fifteen separate intelligence agencies, and underscore the need to improve the quality of information gathering resources to better meet national and homeland security objectives. Cox promotes improved communication and interoperability between domestic law enforcement and intelligence collectors, a union opposed by many experts of national security, as one solution to this problem.[117]

Even among agencies that have shown marked progress in interagency coordination, the problem of poor information sharing persists. In his article on interagency operations, Matthew Bogdanos presents the case of the Central Command's Joint Interagency Coordination Group (JIACG) as an example of this situation. While the Joint Staff found that JIACG "integrated U.S. government objectives, creating a forum for interagency operational planning and coordination," the absence of information sharing standards hindered efficient communication within the intelligence community. Bogdanos believes that establishing a protocol within individual agencies for the sharing of information will not only encourage the necessary communication but also offer incentives for other agencies to follow suit.[118]

Most observers believe that one of the greatest requirements for achieving effective interagency coordination in the war on terror is effective communication and information sharing, and yet they identify recurring problems in this area. In 2002 Richard B. Myers, then chairman of the Joint Chiefs of Staff, stressed that the imperatives of countering terrorist threats required discarding the Cold War "need-to-know" approach toward information sharing, and instead advocated relying on a more inclusive "need-to-share" principle. In his assessment, this strategy would improve agency integration and allow for rapid decision making.[119]

The Homeland Security and Advisory Council (HASC), a DHS body that provides independent policy advice and recommendations to the Homeland Security secretary, reaffirms General Myers's recommendation in its 2007 *Report of the Future of Terrorism Task Force*. The council recommends combining foreign and domestic intelligence into one National Intelligence Estimate (NIE). It also offers other proposals to enhance information sharing and cooperation between local, state, federal, and international agencies. In its authors' assessment, restructuring the intelligence community, including integrating it better into the work of DHS and the NSC, should be a priority for intelligence reform.[120]

According to Michael Warner and J. Kenneth McDonald, President Bush's signing of Executive Order 13355 ("Strengthened Management of the Intelligence Community") gave the DCI marginally more authority. This consolidation was enhanced through the signing of Executive Order 12333, which increased the DCI's autonomy, and the passage of the Intelligence Reform and Terrorism Prevention Act, which helped redefine "national" intelligence. In their review of existing intelligence studies, Warner and McDonald find several recurring themes: the need to sustain intelligence capabilities in peacetime, keep the intelligence community responsive to the Congress and the president, and hold a single individual responsible for the coordination of intelligence efforts. Warner and McDonald argue that many of the 9/11 Commission Report's recommendations have been successfully implemented. They attribute this result to strong political leadership on behalf of intelligence reform.[121]

More effective utilization of resources for national security purposes constitutes another strong argument for intelligence community integration. In a contribution to *Joint Force Quarterly*, Marine Corps general and chairman of the Joint Chiefs of Staff, Peter Pace, makes the case for "resource leveraging" by both enhancing the sharing of intelligence among government agencies and incorporating information from sources outside the intelligence agency. General Pace suggests that making this type of cooperation issue-specific produces more precise solutions to national security problems, and makes more efficient use of resources both inside and outside the intelligence community.[122]

G. Gregg Webb seeks to draw lessons for contemporary policy debates in his case study of the effective intelligence liaison between the FBI and the State Department from 1940 to 1944. Webb argues that President Roosevelt's creation of the Special Intelligence Services, which were located within the FBI but required DOS approval to conduct foreign intelligence tasks, forced collaboration between the agencies and an effective (though temporary) sharing of information. Webb encourages further analysis of this partnership and the integration of its more advantageous aspects into the structure of the modern day intelligence community.[123]

Despite the recurrence of more flexible information sharing in intelligence reform proposals, some analysts downplay the importance of such adjustments. In his remarks at the Johns Hopkins University School of Advanced International Studies, former CIA director James Woolsey rebuffs claims that the events of 9/11 indicate a serious coordination problem within the U.S. foreign intelligence community or that existing problems require a major reorganization of the intelligence community. Rather, he argues that specific weaknesses should be addressed on an agency-by-agency basis.[124]

Outdated information technology is viewed by many as a technical obstacle hindering intelligence gathering and sharing. While updating this technology should be an easy step to improving information networks, and a move which should spark little controversy, critics of the intelligence community find themselves frustrated by the persistence of this problem. In an assessment of the State Department, the Foreign Affairs Council Task Force explains how a lack of funding and resources has resulted in a reliance on ineffective technology, which in turn makes communication within the DOS and between other agencies very difficult.[125] In his book *Securing America's Future: National Strategy in the Information Age*, Daniel Gerstein echoes the call for updated technology systems. Claiming that U.S. methods and procedures remain anchored in the Industrial Age, he suggests U.S. national security strategy will suffer due to an inability to reap the full benefits of the Information Age. Gerstein argues that the lack of emphasis on improved technology stems from U.S. national security strategies that lean toward the use of military and political hard power, while neglecting soft power methods. He argues that these soft power methods—which rely primarily on economic, social, and cultural tools—depend on advanced information technologies.[126]

Many technological advances—such as digital cameras for reconnaissance purposes—have already improved intelligence-gathering capabilities. Nevertheless, these innovations tend to be mission specific, may be of limited availability, and are best suited for intelligence gathering, not information-sharing purposes.[127] Some observers, such as Eric Chabrow, suggest that the creation of a website gateway for technology-related information resources could foster interagency cooperation. These databases would provide easy access to a store of valuable information, including technical reports, journal citations, and federal websites.[128] These opinions are expanded upon by Kurt Fuller in his book, *Leading at the Speed of Light: New Strategies for U.S. Security in the Information Age*. Fuller emphasizes the need for leadership to evolve alongside the technology it wields. He contends that skills must adapt to ensure that leaders are capable of performing in a constantly changing data- and information-rich environment.[129]

Information operations (IO), a key component of national security and military strategy, is commonly cited as an area in need of modernization. In his assessment of the current status of IO, Brad Ward describes the IO goal of "information superiority" as "the capability to collect, process, and disseminate an uninterrupted flow of information, while exploiting or denying an adversary's ability to do the same." However, limited approval authorities, restricted influence over operations and tactics, constraining security procedures, and confusion over various agencies' responsibilities have resulted in debilitating coordination and dissemination problems. Accordingly, Ward emphasizes the need for the United States to capitalize on its technological advantages to achieve "information superiority" and an integrated IO system.[130]

A study by Robert David Steele likewise finds that the thrust of IO-related issues has shifted over the years from protecting critical infrastructures and preventing electronic espionage toward improving the analysis of collected information and enhancing interagency information sharing. Steele stresses the importance of achieving further improvements in the use of three elements: strategic communication, open source intelligence, and joint information operations centers. Advanced technologies are again deemed essential in innovation. Unlike most recommendations for intelligence reform, which typically advocate top-down restructuring, Steele's proposals can be implemented through a less comprehensive approach.[131]

A final section of study looks beyond the internal gaps in the intelligence community, to analyze the effects of intelligence gathering on institutions outside the intelligence community and on individual American citizens. In this sense, Richard Best suggests that collaboration between law enforcement and intelligence agencies has raised significant legal and administrative difficulties, particularly since 9/11. Furthermore, concerns have emerged that the increased use of information derived from intelligence sources in judicial proceedings sets a standard for obtaining information through underhanded means, potentially undermining civil liberties.[132]

THE LONG WAR

Perhaps no single issue has generated more discussion in recent years on interagency effort and coordination than the execution of the global war on terrorism (GWOT). From September 11, 2001, to the present, a myriad of U.S. public entities have redefined their missions and refocused their policies and priorities toward addressing the threat of terrorism at home and abroad. Analysts generally agree that "a new scale of extra-military cooperation beyond existing expectations or plans" is necessary to achieve success in countering terrorism.[133] Unfortunately, authors also generally concur that the current U.S. interagency system is not optimized for this task.

The National Commission on Terrorist Attacks upon the United States offers a series of recommendations on U.S. foreign policy, homeland security, and intelligence reform. With respect to this last subject, its members call for creating a National Counterterrorism Center (NCTC) that would consciously draw on the Goldwater-Nichols' model by combining a joint intelligence function with joint operational planning, thus serving as "a civilian-led unified joint command for counterterrorism."[134] The Commission also advocates establishing a Senate-confirmed National Intelligence Director (NID) in order to oversee both the national intelligence agencies and the newly proposed national intelligence centers. These bodies would integrate experts from a collection of disciplines against common targets such as terrorism and nuclear proliferation. The Commission also emphasizes the importance of strengthening congressional oversight of intelligence and homeland security.

The 9/11 Public Discourse Project, which succeeded the 9/11 Commission in an unofficial capacity, gives overall government progress in the area of information-sharing a "D" grade in its final assessment of how well the U.S. government has implemented the recommendations of the original commission. It assessed U.S. government performance according to such criteria as providing incentives for information sharing, developing a government-wide "trusted information sharing" network for interagency activities, and using performance evaluations to encourage more effective communication. The authors of the Public Discourse Project's Final Report on the 9/11 Commission reaffirm the 9/11 Commission's earlier criticisms regarding insufficient resources, minimal incentives, poor presidential backing for creating an improved information-sharing environment, and the existence of numerous complaints regarding information sharing.[135] The HASC also identifies continuing problems in this area, while reaffirming increased information sharing between federal, state, and local law enforcement and intelligence agencies as critical to the success of future interagency counterterrorism efforts.[136]

Pace argues that the lack of a figure below the level of president with the authority to direct agencies to work together in countering terrorism was yet another hindrance to the U.S. government's prosecution of the war on terror. In his assessment, this problem leads to faltering policy execution due to "stovepiping" and poor coordination.[137]

Analysts also believe that bureaucratic cultures plague interagency coordination in the GWOT. Martin Gorman and Alexander Krongard maintain that the current national security structure is not conducive to interagency operations, because government culture rewards "bureaucratic self-interest" instead of agency sacrifices for a common goal.[138] In their assessment, without a new culture of cooperation, U.S. GWOT-related efforts will suffer from bureaucratic wastefulness and operational redundancies, because they are conducted in a "piecemeal" fashion that prevents any long-term planning or progress.

In "Solving the Interagency Puzzle," Sunil Desai concludes that while most of the necessary tools for successful U.S. execution of the war on terror exist, "the essence of the problem is that the entire interagency community is dominated by individual agency cultures rather than a common interagency culture."[139] Desai sees the lack of a coordinated interagency doctrine, personnel policies that reward dedication to the home agency, and disparate values, polices, and goals as serious obstructions to developing an interagency system more effective at fighting the war on terrorism.

In contrast, Tim Lannan, in his article "Interagency Coordination within the National Security Community: Improving the Response to Terrorism," does not consider cultural differences to be a major problem. Instead, Lannan believes that a "common threat-oriented objective" is often sufficient to overcome bureaucratic cultural differences.[140]

A small contingent of authors raises questions surrounding the role of strategic information campaigns in the war on terrorism. Rather than complaining about inadequate interagency information sharing, these authors focus on insufficient coordination among those U.S. agencies involved in public diplomacy. Jeffrey Jones argues in his paper, "Strategic Communications: A Mandate for the U.S.," that the resources currently allocated to information campaigns targeting terrorism are "insufficient by a factor of ten."[141] He believes that with the dissolution of the U.S. Information Agency and the increase in propaganda by groups like al-Qaeda, more effective interagency coordination is needed to ensure that the United States can counter its terrorist adversaries in the battle for "hearts and minds."

Similarly, Jeryl Ludowese questions why, given the importance of the battle of ideas, the U.S. government has not substantially increased its funding for strategic communication and information campaigns in the same way that it has for other political, diplomatic, economic, and military efforts related to the GWOT.[142] In Ludowese's view, the United States has not developed a coherent strategy to communicate effectively with foreign audiences.

To improve coordination of interagency activities and unity of effort, Pace suggests creating a "joint interagency task force," where designated cabinet or agency heads would take the lead on individual counterterrorism initiatives and direct personnel from different agencies. General Pace believes that the creation of his "joint interagency task force" structure would help overcome cultural problems, because it would improve interagency trust, and allow personnel to become acquainted with agencies other than their own. He also proposes better connecting incentives and promotions to interagency work. Making promotion contingent on interagency service is likely to quickly increase the level of interest in interagency cooperation and education about other agencies.[143]

Desai urges greater integration, education, and interagency initiatives to overcome cultural differences. Before the creation of any joint interagency headquarters, Desai suggests merging NSC and HSC and creating a national interagency "university" to provide a similar education to all personnel, but particularly to senior-level officials, across all agencies.[144]

Gorman and Krongard believe that nothing short of a legislative mandate will solve the cultural woes of the current interagency national security system. In their analysis, reform legislation should mandate structural and cultural changes to the system, while providing for low-level strategy development, an interagency approach to policy implementation, and an interagency governing board similar to the Joint Chiefs of Staff that would evaluate interagency progress on a variety of national security efforts.[145]

Colonel Lucynski also considers aggressive and robust legislation that completely restructures institutions and doctrine necessary in order to effectuate meaningful change.[146] Desai argues, however, that congressional intervention is not necessary and that swift presidential action in the form of an internal directive or executive order could achieve sweeping results. "By executive order, the president can establish the basic doctrine, create—within his executive office—an office with the authority to develop it, and direct all executive branch agencies to submit proposals for aligning their regional structures and implementing personnel exchange programs such as those described here."[147]

Jones calls for creating an integrated interagency national strategic information policy that would unite the plethora of U.S. agencies concerned with public diplomacy and give them a common task and vision in the GWOT. To help achieve this objective, he favors creating regular interagency discussion forums that would involve representatives from various federal agencies and public diplomacy branches of the White House Office of Global Communications (OGC).[148]

A 2005 congressional report on the lack of a national communications strategy also advises the president to "revitalize the position of Director of the Office of Global Communications and provide clear direction to the OGC to form a unified approach." In addition, the report suggests that in order to achieve a truly integrative approach to strategic communication efforts, the OGC should coordinate not only with DOS but also with DOD and the Broadcasting Board of Governors.[149]

One unique proposition for improving unity of effort comes from Ashton Carter's *International Security* essay on "The Architecture of Government in the Face of Terrorism." Carter deems solutions such as designating a lead agency, creating the Department of Homeland Security, and appointing a "terrorism czar" largely ineffective and inefficient.[150] Instead, he favors dividing up counterterrorism and antiterrorism duties according to a timeline. Agencies would be assigned discrete tasks such as detection, prevention, protection, interdiction, containment, attribution, and analysis. After performing its assigned task, an agency would not be involved in any later functions. According to Carter, this approach would streamline efforts by reducing the excessive breadth of activities currently undertaken by each U.S. government agency.

AFGHANISTAN, IRAQ, AND POSTCONFLICT STABILITY OPERATIONS

The current postconflict stability and reconstruction operations in Afghanistan and Iraq have stimulated debate on the function of interagency operations overseas as well. Several authors identify major problems in the preparation and execution of both operations. Nevertheless, analysts also identify several key successes achieved in Iraq and Afghanistan and attempt to use these accomplishments as the basis for timely recommendations on improving interagency coordination across several fields.

In the assessment of many authors, the problems in Iraq, Afghanistan, and other postconflict operations derive from a lack of "unity of effort"—a broad criticism that encompasses communication failures, bureaucratic clashes, poor leadership, and the absence of interagency doctrine. For example, Peter Roman underlines the failure of military and civilian institutions to cooperate effectively in the operation when assessing the need for an effort resembling Goldwater-Nichols at the interagency level.[151] Donald Dreschler of the School for Advanced Air and Space Studies, describes Operation Iraqi Freedom as but the most recent example of "the failure associated with inadequate interagency planning."[152] According to the Beyond Goldwater-Nichols Project at the Center for Strategic and International Studies, "Interagency planning for Operation Iraqi Freedom may be the best example of a need for revolutionary interagency reform."[153]

Analysts are particularly critical of collaboration between the Departments of Defense and State. They detail several causes for this poor interagency coordination, including a lack of dialogue between the two agencies, competing priorities and philosophies, and a general state of interdepartmental conflict. For example, Robert Mendenhall points to a failure of the Departments of State and Defense to create an effective interagency working environment to plan for postwar efforts in Iraq ahead of time. Whereas DOS spent nine months planning for the postwar situation, DOD allocated only two months for such planning before the invasion and comprehensively disregarded the suggestions offered by the State Department.[154]

According to Donald Dreschler, the Defense Department virtually ignored the State Department during preparations for the Iraq war. More surprisingly, when the Pentagon finally consulted with State, the latter failed to properly involve its own Contingency Planning and Peacekeeping Office in the Political-Military Bureau—renowned for its successes in Kosovo. Due to "internal bureaucratic politics," the regional and functional bureaus did not integrate their planning activities.[155]

Though James Hearn highlights President Bush's creation of the Office of the Coordinator for Reconstruction and Stabilization (S/CRS) at State as a possible means to avoid these prewar planning problems in the future, he expresses concern that the office's prospects for success will remain questionable as long as it ignores the need to work with Defense in providing security.[156]

Interagency problems in Afghanistan and Iraq extend beyond Pentagon-Foggy Bottom rivalries. Christopher Briem's examination of military-NGO (nongovernmental organizations such as the Red Cross) relationships in Iraq and Afghanistan leads him to conclude that "an inability or unwillingness" on the part of the military to "leverage these [NGO] resources can only promote mission failure." In addition to civil-military cultural clashes, the military in both Afghanistan and Iraq has found dealing with the plethora of NGOs operating in their region to be overwhelming.[157] Craig Currey also finds that a failure to address and organize military-civilian-NGO coordination effectively has led to redundant efforts, misunderstandings, and an over reliance on the military for humanitarian assistance.[158]

Outside the realm of "unity of effort," the United States has experienced other major problems during the postconflict phases of Operation Iraqi Freedom and Operation Enduring Freedom. Craig Currey attributes many of these problems to the reactive, ad hoc nature of stability and reconstruction efforts in both areas. The military planners and combatant commanders responsible for an operation typically respond with whatever help from nearby NGOs or civilian agencies they can muster. Similarly, Gregg Gross, in his report on interagency reform in the twenty-first century, deems the ad hoc nature of postconflict reconstruction planning (as executed in Iraq and Afghanistan) to be the main problem with the current interagency structure.[159] The nature of this planning prevents agencies from proceeding beyond "crisis mode," and impedes their ability to create preventative, long-term plans for dealing with postconflict stability operations. Yet, a lack of "sound doctrine" at the national level often lies behind the ad hoc nature of U.S. management of stability operations.

Christopher Schnaubelt's article, "After the Fight: Interagency Operations," focuses on the difficulties of establishing and maintaining clear authority in Iraqi postconflict interagency operations. The lack of an unambiguous leader to guide the two main organizations concerned with the planning and execution of Iraqi reconstruction, the Congressional Provisional Authority and the Combined Joint Task Force-7, as well as questions surrounding their respective authorities, engenders problems relating to synchronizing efforts and executing orders.[160]

Opinions diverge among authors on whether interagency coordination problems in Iraq and Afghanistan derive mostly from difficulties at the operational level, or whether strategic-level failures are largely to blame. Alan Mangan cites the latter issue as the underlying obstacle to effective interagency coordination. He claims that all recent efforts to plan, organize, and build resources for stability and reconstruction operations have been hampered by the absence of a grand strategy to guide operations.[161]

Authors who take the "operational-level view" highlight a perceived lack of direction from the president and NSC, bureaucratic infighting in Washington and overseas, cultural differences between agencies, and an inherent aversion in many civilian agencies to the execution of long-term planning. Thomas LaFleur suggests that if the Bush administration had implemented Presidential Decision Directive 56, a directive adopted during the Clinton administration to ensure effective interagency cooperation, then some departmental-level friction in Iraq might have been averted.[162] Major General Henry Stratman cites "philosophical and operational" differences as the major hurdles to overcome in creating effective interagency initiatives for the steady reconstruction of Iraq.[163]

Although the authors agree that the United States needs more effective interagency coordination in Iraq, Afghanistan, and future stability and reconstruction efforts, analysts disagree on the extent of the reforms necessary to solve this problem. Some authors favor creating new agency structures, whereas others want to adjust existing bodies.

Several analysts conclude that only congressionally mandated change, implemented through binding legislation, will correct operational-level interagency deficiencies. For example, Christopher Naler advocates legislation to create an Interagency Combatant Command that would harness all the diplomatic, military, economic, and informational elements of national power to institutionalize interagency cooperation. The command would have a number of directorates, each with a commander and two deputies (one civilian and one military) that would organize coordination between agencies.[164] Similarly, Robert Morris's examination of the military-NGO interagency relationship leads him to call for an "NGO coordination center" that could streamline NGO efforts to assist State and Defense and develop interoperability guidelines and strategies.[165] A 2005 Congressional Research Service Report calls for a permanent mechanism for joint civil-military operations to rectify the current ad hoc nature of the system, though the report does not elaborate on what form such a mechanism should take.[166]

Schnaubelt and Bogdanos prefer a less radical solution. They endorse giving greater authority and roles to Joint Interagency Coordination Groups (JIACGs, such as those employed in Afghanistan) in future stability and reconstruction efforts. According to Bogdanos, JIACGs "avoid the insular pitfalls of individual agencies by maintaining an unprecedented flow of information."[167] He also maintains that such bodies work through the "honest broker" principle and allow all agencies involved in an operation to participate in its planning.

Another approach would entail realigning the geographic responsibilities of military and civilian agencies. John Pulliam, in *Lines on a Map: Regional Orientations and US Interagency Cooperation*, thinks that one problem arises from the fact that regional divisions within DOD and DOS do not match up. He believes that realigning each bureau and denying each agency the ability to "draw its own map" would enhance interagency coordination.[168]

Some authors recommend instituting a national-level interagency doctrine to strengthen coordination at the strategic level. For example, James Jay Carafano favors enacting legislation obligating the executive branch to implement a distinct postconflict doctrine that is developed in theater with military personnel and regional interagency teams. Of this project, he writes that "experience and knowledge about peace operations have never been incorporated into mainstream military thinking in any major, systematic way."[169] Creating doctrine to guide interagency efforts in Iraq and Afghanistan in this fashion would require strong presidential leadership.

Other authors downplay the need for such a doctrine. Stratman acknowledges that no doctrine was in place to guide the transition from the CPA to the U.S. embassy in Baghdad, or to military commands. Nevertheless, he claims that constantly reassessing and redefining the situation on the ground, and molding actions to reflect changing conditions—which requires a degree of flexibility that an excessively rigid doctrine might prevent—along with a high commitment to teamwork and a shared vision would be more than sufficient for successful interagency operations.[170]

Despite this difference most authors agree that presidential leadership can play a critical role in ensuring the success of postconflict reconstruction efforts. Without presidential engagement and the promotion of a shared long-term vision for interagency projects, the potential for failure rises significantly. LaFleur advocates presidential "supra-departmental" control over the interagency process to ensure adequate coordination.[171] Vicki Rast, in *Interagency Fratricide*, echoes this sentiment by emphasizing that leaders in the executive branch must ensure that the interagency process functions smoothly. To this end, the president must energize the interagency process if it stalls, and establish a clear strategic vision for the overall project.[172]

More generally, authors make a plea for educating civilian and military leaders on the importance of interagency cooperation and how to function in an interagency setting. Such education can include simulations and exercises that provide opportunities to practice interagency operations in a controlled environment. In addition, lower-level employees at both civilian and military agencies would benefit from more short-term rotations in different agencies. Such exchanges would help them develop personal contacts that transcend agency barriers as well as promote mutual understanding of agency procedures, philosophies, and bureaucratic cultures. The creation of an interagency esprit de corps could help break down departmental parochialism and interagency barriers to communication and information sharing.[173]

NOTES

1. The editors wish to thank the following individuals for making especially significant contributions to this chapter: Elie Biel, Peter Campbell, Christine Gilbert, Therin Jones, Elizabeth Kerley, Greg Kismak, Elizabeth Kwicinski, Philip Lee, Dylan Lehrke, Chris Martin, Rachel Schnittman, Elizabeth Zolotukhina, and Casey Zuber.

2. Bert B. Tussing and Kent H. Butts, "Annual Collins Center Senior Symposium: Aligning the Interagency Process for the War on Terrorism," *Center for Strategic Leadership Issue Paper*, Vol. 11-05 (June 2005).

3. I. M. Destler, "National Security Advice to U.S. Presidents: Some Lessons from Thirty Years," *World Politics* 29, no. 2 (January 1977): 143–76.

4. Alfred D. Sander, "Truman and the National Security Council, 1945–1947," *Journal of American History* (September 1972): 369–88.

5. Paul Y. Hammond, "The National Security Council as a Device for Interdepartmental Coordination: An Interpretation and Appraisal," *American Political Science Review* (December 1960).

6. Edward A. Kolodziej, "The National Security Council Innovations and Implications," *Public Administration Review* (November/December 1969): 573–85.

7. U.S. Congress, Senate, Committee on Government Operations, Subcommittee on National Security and International Operations, "The National Security Council: Comment by Henry Kissinger" March 3, 1970 (Washington, DC: Government Printing Office, 1970).

8. Zbigniew Brzezinski, "The NSC's Midlife Crisis," *Foreign Policy* 69 (Winter, 1987–88): 80–89.

9. Zbigniew Brzezinski, *Power and Principle: Memoirs of the National Security Advisor, 1977–1981* (New York: Farrar, Straus, Giroux, 1983).

10. Arthur Schlesinger Jr., "Effective National Security Advising: A Most Dubious Precedent," *Political Science Quarterly* (Fall 2000): 347–51.

11. Charles W. Yost, "The Instruments of American Foreign Policy," *Foreign Affairs* (October 1971): 59–68.

12. I. M. Destler, *Presidents, Bureaucrats and Foreign Policy: The Politics of Organization* (Princeton, NJ: Princeton University Press, 1972).

13. Brzezinski, *Power and Principle.*

14. Flora Lewis, "Foreign Affairs: The Policy Blind," *New York Times*, September 18, 1981, A35.

15. Brzezinski, "The NSC's Midlife Crisis."

16. David Hoffman, "President Scales Back National Security Council," *Washington Post*, February 3, 1989, A08.

17. Brzezinski, *Power and Principle.*

18. John P. Burke "The Contemporary Presidency: Condoleezza Rice as NSC Advisor: A Case Study of the Honest Broker Role," *Presidential Studies Quarterly* 35, no. 3 (2005): 554–75.

19. John Deutch, Arnold Kanter, and Brent Scowcroft, "Strengthening the National Security Interagency Process," in Ashton B. Carter and John P. White, eds., *Keeping the Edge: Managing Defense for the Future* (Cambridge, MA: MIT Press), 265–83, at http://bcsia.ksg.harvard.edu/BCSIA_content/documents/KTE_ch10.pdf.

20. Gregory M. Martin, *Enhancing American Interagency Integration for the Global War on Terrorism* (Carlisle Barracks, PA: U.S. Army War College, 2006) at http://handle.dtic.mil/100.2/ADA449233.

21. Sidney W. Souers, "Policy Formulation for National Security," *American Political Science Review* (June 1949): 534–43.

22. Paul Y. Hammond, "The National Security Council as a Device for Interdepartmental Coordination: An Interpretation and Appraisal," *American Political Science Review* (December 1960): 899–910.

23. I. M. Destler, Leslie H. Gelb, and Anthony Lake, "Our Own Worst Enemy: The Unmaking of American Foreign Policy," *The American Political Science Review* 79, no. 2 (June 1985): 576.

24. James Kitfield, *Prodigal Soldiers: How the Generation of Officers Born of Vietnam Revolutionized the American Style of War* (Washington and London: Brassey's, 1995).

25. Committee on Armed Services (Staff), "Defense Organization: The Need for Change," Staff Report to the Committee on Armed Services, U.S. Senate (Washington, DC U.S. Government Printing Office, 1985).

26. Commission on Roles and Missions (CORM) of the Armed Forces Report to Congress, the Secretary of Defense, and the Chairman of the Joint Chiefs of Staff, *Directions for Defense* (May 24, 1995), at http://www.fas.org/man/docs/corm95/corm_pr.htm.

27. John E. Lange, "Civilian-Military Cooperation and Humanitarian Assistance: Lessons from Rwanda," *Parameters* (Summer 1998): 106–22.

28. Eugene Bardach, *Getting Agencies to Work Together* (Washington, DC: Brookings Institution, 1998).

29. *Managing for Results: Barriers to Interagency Coordination* (Washington, DC: U.S. General Accounting Office, 2000).

30. Richard A. Best Jr., *Intelligence and Law Enforcement: Countering Transnational Threats to the U.S.* (Washington, DC: Congressional Research Service, Library of Congress, 2001).

31. Robert W. Taylor, "Managing Terrorist Incidents," *The Bureaucrat* 12, no. 4 (Winter 1983–84): 53.

32. Dan Carney and Chuck McCutcheon, "Who's in Charge When Terror Strikes?" *CQ Weekly* 56, no. 29 (July 1998): 18, 1921.

33. Raymond J. Decker, *Combating Terrorism: Federal Response Teams Provide Varied Capabilities; Opportunities Remain to Improve Coordination: GAO-01-14* (Washington, DC: U.S. General Accounting Office, 2000).

34. Kevin C. Colyer, *Command and Control Structure for Joint Interagency Counterterrorism Operations Involving Weapons of Mass Destruction within a Regional Commander-in-Chief's Area of Responsibility* (Fort Leavenworth, KS: U.S. Army Command and General Staff College, 2001), at http://cgsc.cdmhost.com/u?/p4013coll2,413.

35. Neyla Arnas, Charles Barry, and Robert B. Oakley, "Harnessing the Interagency for Complex Operations," Center for Technology and National Security Policy, National Defense University, August 2005, at http://www.ndu.edu/ctnsp/Def_Tech/DTP%2016%20Harnessing%20the%20Interagency.pdf.

36. Douglas T. Stuart, *Organizing for National Security*, November 2000, Strategic Studies Institute of the National War College, at http://www.strategicstudiesinstitute.army.mil/pubs/display.cfm?pubID=299. See also General Edward C. Meyer and Thomas R. Pickering, "Forward Strategic Empowerment: Synergies Between CINCs, the State Department, and Other Agencies," *A Panel Report from the Center for the Study of the Presidency*," August 2001, at http://www.thepresidency.org/pubs/ForwardStrategic.pdf.

37. Margaret Daly Hayes, "Interagency and Political-Military Dimensions of Peace Operations: Haiti—A Case Study," National Defense University, at http://dodccrp.org/publications/pdf/Hayes_Interagency.pdf.

38. Donald Dreschler, "Reconstructing the Interagency Process after Iraq," *Journal of Strategic Studies* 28, no. 1 (February 2005): 3–30.

39. Ronald N. Light, "Joint Vision 2020's Achilles Heel: Interagency Cooperation between the Departments of Defense and State," May 2004, Naval War College, at http://stinet.dtic.mil/cgi-bin/GetTRDoc?AD=ADA426040&Location=U2&doc=GetTRDoc.pdf.

40. Stuart, *Organizing for National Security*.

41. Michelle Flournoy and Shawn Brimley, "In Search of Harmony: Orchestrating 'the Interagency' for the Long War," *Armed Forces Journal* (July 2006) at

http://www.armedforcesjournal.com/2006/07/1857934; Margaret Daly Hayes, "Interagency and Political-Military Dimensions of Peace Operations: Haiti—A Case Study," National Defense University, at http://dodccrp.org/publications/pdf/Hayes_Interagency.pdf.

42. Margaret Daly Hayes, "Interagency and Political-Military Dimensions of Peace Operations: Haiti—A Case Study," National Defense University, at http://dodccrp.org/publications/pdf/Hayes_Interagency.pdf.

43. Morton Halperin, "Reform for Its Own Sake: Two Blue-Ribbon Commissions Offer Some Sound Advice, Some Serious Omissions, and One Real Clunker," *American Foreign Service Association*, http://www.afsa.org/fsj/may01/halperinmay01.cfm.

44. Scott Feil, "Building Better Foundations: Security in Postconflict Reconstruction," *Washington Quarterly* 25, no. 4 (Autumn 2002): 97–109; Sunil B. Desai, "Solving the Interagency Puzzle," *Hoover Institution Policy Review* (February/March 2005), http://www.hoover.org/publications/policyreview/3431461.html.

45. Sunil B. Desai, "Solving the Interagency Puzzle."

46. Meyer and Pickering, "Forward Strategic Empowerment."

47. Deutch, Kanter, and Scowcroft, "Strengthening the National Security Interagency Process."

48. Thomas Gibbings, Donald Hurley, and Scott Moore, "Interagency Operations Centers: An Opportunity We Can't Ignore," *Parameters* (Winter 1998).

49. Sharon S. Dawes, "Interagency Information Sharing: Expected Benefits, Manageable Risks," *Journal of Policy Analysis and Management* 15, no. 3 (Summer 1996): 377–94.

50. Carnes Lord, "NSC Reform for the Post-Cold War Era," *Orbis* 44, no. 3 (Summer 2000): 433–50.

51. Anthony C. Zinni, *A Military for the 21st Century: Lessons from the Recent Past* (Institute for National Strategic Studies, National Defense University, July 2001).

52. Philip A. Odeen, "Organizing for National Security," *International Security* 5, no. 1 (Summer 1980): 111–29.

53. Robert E. Smith, *Interagency Operations: Coordination through Education* (Fort Leavenworth, KS: U.S. Army Command and General Staff College, 2001).

54. Mark R. Walsh, "Complex Emergencies: Under New Management," *Parameters*, 28, no. 4 (Winter 1998–99): 39–50.

55. Stuart, *Organizing for National Security*.

56. Michele Flournoy and Shawn Brimley, "Strategic Planning for National Security—A New Project Solarium," *Joint Forces Quarterly* 41, no. 1 (2006), at http://www.dtic.mil/doctrine/jel/jfq_pubs/4119.pdf; Desai, "Solving the Interagency Puzzle."

57. Clark A. Murdock. et al., "Beyond Goldwater-Nichols: Defense Reform for a New Strategic Era—Phase I Report," *Center for Strategic and International Studies*, March 2004, at http://www.ndu.edu/library/docs/0403BGN.pdf.

58. Margret Hayes, "Interagency and Political-Military Dimensions of Peace Operations: Haiti—A Case Study," National Defense University at http://ndu.org/publications/pdf/Hayes_Interagency.pdf.

59. Albert Zaccor, "Security Cooperation and Non-state Threats: A Call for an Integrated Strategy," *Occasional Paper—Atlantic Council* (August 2005).

60. Desai, "Solving the Interagency Puzzle."

61. Mark R. Walsh, "Complex Emergencies: Under New Management," *Parameters* 28, no. 4 (Winter 1998–99): 39–50.

62. Tonya Langford, "Orchestrating Peace Operations: The PDD-56 Process," *Security Dialogue* 30, no. 2 (June 1999): 137–49.

63. U.S. Commission on National Security/21st Century, *Road Map for National Security: Imperative for Change* (Washington, DC: U.S. Commission on National Security/21st Century, February 2001) at http://govinfo.library.unt.edu/nssg/PhaseIIIFR.pdf.

64. Joseph R. Cerami et al., *U.S. Army War College Guide to Strategy* (2001), at http://purl.access.gpo.gov/GPO/LPS11754.

65. Kitfield, *Prodigal Soldiers*; Arthur Schlesinger Jr., "Effective National Security Advising: A Most Dubious Precedent," *Political Science Quarterly* (Fall 2000): 347–51.

66. U.S. Commission on National Security/21st Century, *Road Map for National Security.*

67. Destler, *Presidents, Bureaucrats and Foreign Policy.*

68. John P. Kotter, "Leading Change: Why Transformation Efforts Fail," *Harvard Business Review* (March–April 1995): 61.

69. David Tucker, "The RMA and the Interagency: Knowledge and Speed vs. Ignorance and Sloth?" *Parameters* 30, no. 3 (Autumn 2000): 66, at http://carlisle-www.army.mil/usawc/Parameters/00autumn/tucker.htm.

70. John Schall, ed., "Equipped for the Future: Managing U.S. Foreign Affairs in the 21st Century" The Henry L. Stimson Center (1998) at http://www.stimson.org/pdf/ausr1.pdf.

71. Philip A. Odeen, "Organizing for National Security," *International Security* 5, no. 1 (Summer 1980): 11–129.

72. Zbigniew Brzezinski, "The NSC's Midlife Crisis," *Foreign Policy* 69 (Winter 1987–88): 80–89.

73. Mathew F. Bogdanos, "Interagency Operations: The Marine Specialty of This Century," *Marine Corps Gazette* 90, no. 3 (March 2006): 60–66.

74. Robert Cutler, "The Development of the National Security Council," *Foreign Affairs* (April 1956): 441–58.

75. Paul Y. Hammond, "The National Security Council as a Device for Interdepartmental Coordination: An Interpretation and Appraisal," *American Political Science Review* (December 1960).

76. Ibid.

77. Fred I. Greenstein and Richard H. Immerman, "Effective National Security Advising: Recovering the Eisenhower Legacy," *Political Science Quarterly* (Fall 2000): 335–45.

78. Gregory M. Martin, *Enhancing American Interagency Integration for the Global War on Terrorism* (Carlisle Barracks, PA: U.S. Army War College, 2006).

79. John A. Lucynski III, "An Interagency Reform Act: Preparing for Post-conflict Operations in the 21st Century," USAWC Strategy Research Project, March 2005, at http://stinet.dtic.mil/cgi-bin/GetTRDoc?AD=ADA432527&Location=U2&doc=GetTRDoc.pdf.

80. Desai, "Solving the Interagency Puzzle."

81. W. Henry Lambright, "The Rise and Fall of Interagency Cooperation: The U.S. Global Change Research Program," *Public Administration Review* 57, no. 1 (January–February 1997): 36–44.

82. Robert W. Taylor, "Managing Terrorist Incidents," *The Bureaucrat* 12, no. 4 (Winter 1983–84): 53.

83. Carney and McCutcheon, "Who's in Charge When Terror Strikes?", 1921.

84. Ashton Carter and J. P. White, eds., *Keeping the Edge: Managing Defense for the Future* (Cambridge, MA: MIT Press, 2000) at http://bcsia.ksg.harvard.edu/BCSIA_content/documents/KTE_ch10.pdf.

85. Ashton B. Carter, "The Architecture of Government in the Face of Terrorism," *International Security* 26 (Winter 2001–2): 5–23.

86. Clarke, *Against All Enemies*, 90.

87. Desai, "Solving the Interagency Puzzle"; Lynn Davis, "Organizing for Homeland Security," RAND Issue Paper, 2002, http://192.5.14.110/congress/terrorism/phase2/organizing.pdf.

88. Carter, "The Architecture of Government in the Face of Terrorism," 5–23.

89. Lynn Davis, "Organizing for Homeland Security."

90. William Newmann, "Reorganizing for National Security and Homeland Security," *Public Administration Review* 62 (September 2002).

91. Stephen Sloan, ed., "Organizing for National Security: The Challenge of Bureaucratic Innovation in the War against Terrorism," *Public Administration Review* 62 (September 2002).

92. Ivo Daalder and I. M. Destler, "Advisors, Czars and Councils: Organizing for Homeland Security," *National Interest* 68 (Summer 2002): 66.

93. Stephen M. Brummond, *Restructuring for Homeland Security: What Is Really Necessary?* (Carlisle Barracks, PA: U.S. Army War College, 2003) at http://handle.dtic.mil/100.2/ADA415078.

94. Schall, *Equipped for the Future*, 11.

95. J. R. Barnes, "Reorganizing for Homeland Security: Lessons from 50 years of Organizing and Reorganizing the Department of Defense," *Journal of Homeland Security* (June 2002) at http://www.homelandsecurity.org/journal/Commentary/barnes26June2002.html.

96. Katherine McIntire Peters, "The Challenge," *Government Executive* 34, no. 10 (July 2002): 10–14.

97. Joint Inquiry Staff Proposals for Reform within the Intelligence Community, *Final Report. The Context: Part One: Findings and Conclusions*, December 10, 2002.

98. Christopher M. Clayton, *National Emergency Preparedness and Response: Improving for Incidents of National Significance* (Carlisle Barracks, PA: U.S. Army War College, 2006) at http://handle.dtic.mil/100.2/ADA448938.

99. Commission on the National Guard and Reserves, Hearing on Homeland Defense/Homeland Security, May 4, 2006, Federal News Service, Washington, DC.

100. James Kitfield, "Military's Northern Command Steps Up Response Efforts," *National Journal*, September 2, 2005.

101. Chris Hornbarger, "Katrina Lessons-Learned: National Contingency Planning for Domestic Incidents," at http://www.dean.usma.edu/sosh/Academic%20Program/Courses/ss493/LESSONS/Military%20Role%20in%20Homeland%20Security/Katrina_Lsns_Contingncy_Planning.pdf.

102. Michael J. Pitts, *A Road Map for National Security: The Intersection of the Departments of Homeland Security and Defense* (Carlisle Barracks, PA: U.S. Army War College, 2006) at http://dtic.mil/100.2/ADA448441.

103. National Partnership for Reinventing Government (formerly the National Performance Review) (1993) at http://govinfo.library.unt.edu/npr/library/nprrpt/annrpt/redtpe93/index.html.

104. National Defense Panel (1997) at http://www.dtic.mil/ndp/FullDoc2.pdf.

105. Mark R. Walsh and Michael J. Harwood, "Complex Emergencies: Under New Management," *Parameters* (Winter 1998).

106. Clayton, *National Emergency Preparedness*.

107. Gregg E. Gross, *Interagency Reform for the 21st Century* (Carlisle: U.S. Army War College, 2000).

108. John E. O'Neil, *The Interagency Process: Analysis and Reform Recommendations* (Carlisle Barracks, PA: U.S. Army War College, 2006) at http://handle.dtic.mil/100.2/ADA449658.

109. Eleanor Hill, "Joint Inquiry Staff Statement: Proposals for Reform within the Intelligence Community" (October 3, 2002) at http://www.fas.org/irp/congress/2002_hr/100302hill.html.

110. Loch K. Johnson, "The DCI and the Eight-Hundred Pound Gorilla," *International Journal of Intelligence and Counterintelligence* 13 (Spring 2000): 35–48.

111. Joint Inquiry Staff Proposals for Reform within the Intelligence Community, "Final Report. The Context: Part One: Findings and Conclusions," December 10, 2002, at http://www.globalsecurity.org/intell/library/congress/2002_rpt/intelfindings.pdf.

112. 9-11 Public Discourse Project, "Final Report on 9/11 Commission Recommendations" (Washington, DC: 2005), at http://www.9-11pdp.org/press/2005-12-05_report.pdf.

113. "The Final Report of the 9/11 Commission," (2004) at http://www.9-11commission.gov/report/911Report.pdf.

114. "Commission on the Intelligence Capabilities of the United States Regarding Weapons of Mass Destruction Report to the President: Overview of the Report," Commission on the Intelligence Capabilities of the United States regarding Weapons of Mass Destruction (May 31, 2005), at http://www.wmd.gov/report/overview_fm.pdf.

115. *Investigation into the Lack of Coordination between Federal Agencies*, Congressional Record—Senate, 108th Congress, 1st Session, 149 Cong Rec S 15948 (November 25, 2003).

116. Thomas H. Stanton "Moving toward More Capable Government: A Guide to Organizational Design," IBM Center for the Business of Government (2002), at http://www.businessofgovernment.org/pdfs/StantonReport.pdf.

117. Christopher Cox, "Change Is Now Inevitable," *Wall Street Journal*, July 22, 2004, A12.

118. Matthew F. Bogdanos, "Interagency Operations."

119. Richard B. Myers, "A Word from the Chairman," *Joint Force Quarterly* 33 (Winter 2002–3): 1.

120. U.S. Department of Homeland Security, Homeland Security and Advisory Council, *Report of the Future of Terrorism Task Force* (2007).

121. Michael Warner and J. Kenneth McDonald, "U.S. Intelligence Community Reform Studies since 1947," Center for the Study of Intelligence (April 2005) at http://www.cia.gov/library/center-for-the-study-of-intelligence/csi-publications/books-and-monographs/US%20Intelligence%20Community%20Reform%20Studies%20Since%201947.pdf.

122. "A Word from the Chairman," *Joint Force Quarterly*, no. 41 (April 2006): 1–4.

123. G. Gregg Webb, "Intelligence Liaison between the FBI and State, 1940–44," *Studies in Intelligence* 49, no. 3 (2005): 25–38.

124. James R. Woolsey, "Remarks at the Johns Hopkins University School of Advanced International Studies" (Washington, DC: January 30, 2006), at http://blueskybroadcast.com/client/sycoleman/eisenhower/docs/trans.pdf.

125. Foreign Affairs Council Task Force, "Secretary Colin Powell's State Department: An Independent Assessment" (2004), at http://www.unc.edu/depts/diplomat/archives_roll/2003_04-06/fac/fac_task.html.

126. Daniel M. Gerstein, *Securing America's Future: National Strategy in the Information Age* (Westport, CT: Praeger Security International, 2005).

127. Dewey G. Jordan, "Operation Unified Assistance," *Marine Corps Gazette* 90, no. 5 (May 2006): 57–58.

128. Eric Chabrow, "Interagency Cooperation," *InformationWeek* 920 (December 23, 2002): 14.

129. Kurt Fuller, *Leading at the Speed of Light: New Strategies for U.S. Security in the Information Age (Issues in Twenty-First Century Warfare)* (Washington, DC: Potomac Books, 2006).

130. Brad M. Ward, *Strategic Influence Operations: The Information Connection* (Carlisle Barracks, PA: U.S. Army War College, 2003) at http://handle.dtic.mil/100.2/ADA415825.

131. Robert David Steele, *Information Operations: Putting the "I" Back into DIME* (Carlisle Barracks, PA: Strategic Studies Institute, U.S. Army War College, 2006), at http://www.strategicstudiesinstitute.army.mil/pdffiles/PUB642.pdf.

132. Richard A. Best, Jr., "Intelligence and Law Enforcement: Countering Transnational Threats to the U.S.," Congressional Research Service (2001).

133. Briem, "Joint Is Dead," 56.

134. *The 9/11 Report*, 403.

135. 9-11 Public Discourse Project, *Final Report on 9/11 Commission Recommendations* (December 5, 2005), at http://www.9-11pdp.org/press/2005-12-05_report.pdf.

136. U.S. Department of Homeland Security, Homeland Security and Advisory Council (HSAC), *Report of the Future of Terrorism Task Force* (January 2007).

137. Jim Garamone, "Discussion Needed to Change Interagency Process, Pace Says," *American Forces Information Service* (September 17, 2004) at http://www.au.af.mil/au/awc/awcgate/dod/n09172004_2004091704.htm.

138. Martin J. Gorman, and Alexander Krongard, "A Goldwater-Nichols Act for the U.S. Government: Institutionalizing the Interagency Process," *Joint Force Quarterly* 39 (Autumn 2005): 51–58.

139. Desai, "Solving the Interagency Puzzle."

140. Tim Lannan, "Interagency Coordination within the National Security Community: Improving the Response to Terrorism," *Canadian Military Journal* 5, no. 3 (Autumn 2004): 49–56.

141. Jeffrey B. Jones, "Strategic Communication: A Mandate for the United States," *Joint Force Quarterly* 39 (Autumn 2005): 108–14.

142. Jeryl C. Ludowese, *Strategic Communication: Who Should Lead the Long War of Ideas?* (Carlisle Barracks, PA: U.S. Army War College, 2006) at http://handle.dtic.mil/100.2/ADA449416.

143. Jim Garamone, "Discussion Needed to Change Interagency Process, Pace Says," *American Forces Information Service* (September 17, 2004) at http://www.au.af.mil/au/awc/awcgate/dod/n09172004_2004091704.htm

144. Desai, "Solving the Interagency Puzzle."

145. Gorman and Krongard, "A Goldwater-Nichols Act for the U.S. Government."

146. Lucynski, "An Interagency Reform Act."

147. Desai, "Solving the Interagency Puzzle."

148. Jones, "Strategic Communication."

149. U.S. Government Accountability Office, "U.S. Public Diplomacy: Interagency Coordination Efforts Hampered by the Lack of a National Communication Strategy" (2005) at http://www.gao.gov/new.items/d05323.pdf.

150. Carter, "The Architecture of Government in the Face of Terrorism."

151. Peter Roman, "Can Goldwater-Nichols Reforms for the Interagency Succeed?" The Henry L. Stimson Center (April 19, 2007) at http://www.stimson.org/pub.cfm?id=431.

152. Donald Dreschler, "Reconstructing the Interagency Process after Iraq," *Journal of Strategic Studies* 28, no. 1 (February 2005): 3–30.

153. Murdock, "Beyond Goldwater-Nichols."

154. Robert K. Mendenhall, *Pre-war Planning for a Post-war Iraq* (Carlisle Barracks, PA: U.S. Army War College, 2005).

155. Drechsler, "Reconstructing the Interagency Process after Iraq."

156. James J. Hearn, *Departments of State and Defense: Partners in Post-conflict Operations: Is This the Answer for Past Failures?* (Carlisle Barracks, PA: U.S. Army War College, 2006).

157. Christopher Briem, "Joint Is Dead: What Is Next?," *United States Naval Institute Proceedings* 130, no. 1 (January 2004): 56–59.

158. Craig J. Currey, *A New Model for Military/Non-governmental Organization Relations in Post-conflict Operations* (Carlisle Barracks, PA: U.S. Army War College, 2003).

159. Gross, *Interagency Reform.*

160. Christopher M. Schnaubelt, "After the Fight: Interagency Operations," *Parameters* (Winter 2005–6).

161. Alan F. Mangan, *Planning for Stabilization and Reconstruction Operations without a Grand Strategy* (Carlisle Barracks, PA: U.S. Army War College, 2005).

162. Thomas M. Lafleur, *Interagency Efficacy at the Operational Level* (Fort Leavenworth, KS: School of Advanced Military Studies, 2005) at http://handle.dtic.mil/100.2/ADA435932.

163. Henry W. Stratman, "Orchestrating Instruments of Power for Nationbuilding," *Joint Force Quarterly* 41(Spring 2006): 32–37.

164. Christopher L. Naler, "Are We Ready for an Interagency Combatant Command?", *Joint Forces Quarterly* 41(Spring 2006): 41.

165. Robert. Morris, "Train Like We'll Fight," *Armed Forces Journal* 142, no. 9 (April 2005): 36.

166. Nina M. Serafino and Martin A. Weiss, "Peacekeeping and Post-conflict Capabilities: The State Department's Office for Reconstruction and Stabilization," Congressional Research Service (2005). At http://digital.library.unt.edu/govdocs/crs/permalink/meta-crs-7335:1.

167. Bogdanos, "Interagency Operations."

168. John E. Pulliam, *Lines on a Map: Regional Orientations and United States Interagency Cooperation* (Carlisle Barracks, PA: U.S. Army War College, 2005).

169. James Jay Carafano, Ph.D., and Dana R. Dillon, "Winning the Peace: Principles for Post-conflict Operations," *Heritage Foundation Backgrounder* 1859 (June 13, 2005).

170. Stratman, "Orchestrating Instruments of Power for Nationbuilding," 32–37.

171. Lafleur, *Interagency Efficacy.*

172. Vicki J. Rast, *Interagency Fratricide: Policy Failures in the Persian Gulf and Bosnia* (Maxwell AFB, AL: Air University Press, 2004).

173. Kenneth O. McCreedy, *Waging Peace: Operations Eclipse I and II—Some Implications for Future Operations* (Carlisle Barracks, PA: U.S. Army War College, 2004).

Index

9/11 Commission, 252–253, 257
9/11 Public Discourse Project, 257

Administrative support in emergency, 213
Afghanistan
    Soviet invasion of, 138
    U.S. intervention in, 260, 261, 262, 263
AFL-CIO, 57
African Americans in Hurricane Katrina, 231
Agricultural Experiment Station, Alaska, 81
Agriculture Department, U.S. *See* U.S. Department of Agriculture
Aidid, Mohammed Farah, 150, 151
Alaska, statehood and economy of, 66, 69
Alaska Commission. *See* Federal Reconstruction and Development Planning Commission for Alaska
Alaska Field Committee, 74, 79
Alaskan Construction Consultant Committee, 73
Alaskan earthquake, 1964
    impact of, 67, 68–69
    initial response to, 2, 67–68
    post-recovery analysis of, 82–86
    recovery and rebuilding after, 4, 66, 69–82
    statewide evacuation, alternatives to, 2, 69, 75

Alaskan Military Command, 67–68
Albanians, Kosovo purging of, 153, 160
Albright, Madeleine, 161–162
Alfred P. Murrah Federal Building, Oklahoma City, destruction of, 1995, 248
Allen, Thad, 218–219
Alternative energy, 121–122
Ambrose, Stephen E., 34
American Protective League, 12
American Samoa, influenza prevention measure in, 24
Anchorage, Alaska as All American City, 82
Anchorage Daily News, 82, 83
Anderson, Clinton
    Alaska recovery planning commission appointment of, 70
    commission work of, 71, 75
    committee formed by, 73
    leadership of, 84
    priorities of, 80
    public speeches of, 78
Annan, Kofi, 158
Antigen-drift, 10
Antigovernment attitudes, 231
Arab oil embargo, 1973-1974, 114, 119–120, 121, 123
Argentina, devaluation in, 185
Armed crisis, managing, 154–156, 163–164

Armed forces. *See also under individual branch of the military*, e.g.: U.S. Army
    Cold War information operations, role in, 57
    natural disasters, role following, 67–68
    World War II information operations, role in, 29, 30, 35, 36, 37–38, 39, 41–42
Armed Forces Network (AFN), 57
Armed Propaganda Teams (APT) (Vietnam), 98
Armitage, Richard, 143
Arms control, 56
Army facilities, influenza cases at, 7, 18
ARVN (Army of the Republic of Vietnam), 100
Asia, foreign funds flowing into, 180
Asian banks, aiding, closing or merging of, 183
Asian countries, exchange rates of, 174, 184
Asian financial crisis
    economic conditions prior to, 179–180
    impact of, 172–173, 175–177, 184, 185
    lessons learned from, 186–189
    origin of, 172, 180–181, 183, 189
    response to, 2, 177–180, 181–185, 189
Asian Monetary Fund, 182
Assessment role in disaster relief, 197, 199, 206
Associated General Contractors of America, 73
Association of Southeast Asian Nations (ASEAN), 178
Atomic Energy Commission, 70–71
Axis powers as World War II news source, 29–30

Baker, James, 141, 152
Baker, Newton, 19–20, 21
Balance-of-payments crises, 179, 181, 187
Bangkok Bank of Commerce, collapse of, 174, 184

Bank of Indonesia, 183
Bank of Thailand, 183
Bartlett, John, 23–24
Bataan, fall of, 30
Bay of Pigs invasion, 1961, 59
Black, Gregory D., 31
Blackman, Lieutenant General, 203
Blair, Tony, 162
Blue, Rupert, 13, 14, 21, 24
Boland Amendments, 134, 138, 143, 144
Bosnia crisis
    complex contingency operations in, 240
    crisis prevention, prospects for, 163
    interagency squabbling during, 2
    intervention delay, factors in, 150, 151–153, 154–157, 167–168, 169
    intervention, failure, factors in, 4
    leadership void in, 154
    reactive response to, 165–166
Brazil, devaluation in, 185
Broadcasting Board of Governors, 259
Brown, Michael, 218–219, 228, 229
Brzezinski, Zbigniew, 49, 141, 236–237, 246
Bundy, McGeorge, 131
Bureaucracies, understanding and improving, 245–246
Bureaucracy, ballooning, 237
Bureaucratic cultures, differing, 243, 258, 259
Bureau of the Budget (BOB), 72, 85
Bush, George H.W., 149, 152, 155, 156, 214, 238
Bush, George W.
    Department of Homeland Security created by, 248, 249
    Hurricane Katrina response, comments on, 211
    intelligence policies of, 254
    international disaster planning directive rescinded by, 194, 262
    natural disaster planning by, 213
    opponents of, 231
    prewar planning improvement measures of, 260
Business owners, response to emergency health measures, 23

Camdessus, Michel, 178
Camp Colt, Pennsylvania, 19, 23
Camp Funston, Kansas, 7
Capital account convertibility, 180
Capra, Frank, 37–38, 41, 42
CARE, 198, 200, 206
Carter, Jimmy
    advisors of, 237, 238
    covert action, devaluation by, 51
    energy policy of, 121, 124, 125
    foreign policy of, 49
    problems faced by, 124, 126
Casey, William J., 135, 136, 137–139, 143,
    144, 145
Catastrophic Disaster Response Group, 220
Censorship during World War I, 6, 11, 13,
    14, 15, 22
Censorship during World War II, 34
Center for the Study of the Presidency, 5
Central Intelligence Agency
    in Cold War, 47, 50–51, 62
    Iran-Contra affair, involvement in,
    133, 134, 135, 137–139, 145
    post-Cold War role of, 163
    Vietnam role of, 90, 91, 95, 97, 107
Chavalit Youngchaiyudh, 176
Checks and balances, 2–3
Chernobyl incident, 60
Chertoff, Michael, 218, 228, 229
Chieu Hoi amnesty program, 92, 95, 96,
    98–99
China, stable currency of, 183
Christian Scientists, emergency health
    measures, response to, 23
Christopher, Warren, 155
Chuan Leepai, 176
Church Committee, 138
Civil defense, 213
Civilian-military cooperation
    in disaster response, 194, 208
    in emergency response, 243
    in humanitarian response, 198
    Vietnamese, 94
Civilian–military divide, Cold War era,
    51–52
Civilian–military divide, post-Cold War,
    241, 261

Civil libertarians, emergency health meas-
    ures, response to, 23
Civil rights battle, 67
Clayton, Christopher, 251
Clean Air Act, 118, 119
Clinton, William J.
    Asian financial crisis, response to,
    177, 184
    Bosnia policy of, 155, 156
    emergency response planning by,
    244, 251, 262
    foreign policy of, 150, 154
    impeachment hearings of, 153
    international disaster planning by,
    194, 213
    Kosovo policy of, 159
    leadership style of, 151–154
CNN, 228
Coal as transportation fuel, 121
Coast Guard, 224, 225
Cohen, William, 189
COI. See Office of the Coordinator of
    Information
Colby, William, 97, 106, 107, 108, 109
Cold War
    addressing, 67
    crisis management during, 59–60
    diplomacy during, 46–50, 56–57
    (see also Public diplomacy (Cold
    War strategy))
    information operations during, 54,
    55–57, 59, 62
    political action during, 56–57
    psychological operations during,
    46–50, 47–48, 49, 51–52, 53, 55, 56,
    62
    U.S. criticism during, 2
Collective Action Clauses, 185
Combined Support Force (CSF) 536,
    195–196
Combined Support Groups, 203
Commission on Roles and Missions,
    1995, 239
Commission on the Intelligence Capabil-
    ities of the United States Regard-
    ing Weapons of Mass Destruction,
    253

Committee on Environment and Natural Resources (CENR), 247
Committee on Public Information, 27
Communication role in disaster response, 67–68, 197–198
Competition in disaster relief, 199–200, 201
Complex humanitarian operations, 193–194
Congress for Cultural Freedom, 50
Contingency operations, complex, 240–242, 251
Contingency Planning and Peacekeeping Office in the Political-Military Bureau, 260
CORDS. See Office of Civil Operations and Revolutionary Development Support
Corps of Engineers, 80
Counterinsurgency missions, 89
Counterterrorism, 213, 240
Covert operations, 50, 51, 131, 137–138, 140
Credit, private in Asian banks, 180–181
Creel, George, 13, 27–28, 39, 42, 46
Crisis action planning, 169
Crisis analysis, nature of, 151
Crisis Management Center, 60
Crisis response, budgeting for, 167
Croatia, 153, 165–166
Croat-Moslem war, 155
Cronkite, Walter, 42
Cuban Missile Crisis, 59–60
Cultural awareness role in humanitarian operations, 198–199
Cultural differences between agencies, 243, 258, 259

Darlan, Jean-Francois, 33–34
"Darlan deal," 33–34
DARTs (Disaster Assistance Response Teams), 202, 204
Davis, Elmer, 28, 30, 34, 36, 38, 39, 40, 41, 42
Dayton Accords, 153, 157
DC (Deputies Committee), 164
DCI (director of central intelligence), 252
Deaths during influenza epidemic, 1918, 6, 10, 19, 20

Deaver, Michael, 141
Debt financing, 188–189
Decentralized execution
    doctrine role in, 3
    innovation and flexibility allowed in, 114
    in Katrina aftermath, 219
    key actors in, 22
Deep soil tests, 69
Defense Civil Preparedness Agency, 212
Defense Department, U.S.
    Asian financial crisis response, role in, 177–178, 181
    Bosnia crisis, policy on, 155, 167–168
    in Cold War era, 237
    international disaster relief, participation in, 200
    post-9/11 role of, 250, 259, 260, 262
    post-Cold War role of, 151, 153, 154, 162, 163–164, 165, 241, 244, 245
    post-Vietnam War reform of, 239
Defense industry, influenza cases in, 8
Defense public diplomacy, 52
Department of Agriculture, 118
Department of Energy, 118, 123–125
Department of Homeland Security, 205, 213, 214, 220, 223, 249–250, 259
Department of Interior (DOI), 118, 125, 224
Détente, 48, 49
Deterrence, 56
Deutch, John, 238, 248
Dien Bien Phu (Vietnam), 158–159
Diesel fuel, alternatives to, 121
DiLuzio, Frank, 72
Director of central intelligence (DCI), 252
Disaster Assistance Response Teams (DARTs), 202, 204
Disaster response, domestic, 214–215
Disaster response, international, 193–195, 197–201, 206–209
Disease trends and movement patterns, surveillance and tracking system for, 6, 13
Disease warning system, 13

Disinformation, rejection of, 32
Doctors Without Borders, 198, 206
Doctrine
        for civil-military planning, 243
        during Cold War, 52–53, 62
        for Defense Department, 244
        definition and importance of, 3
        Hurricane Katrina demonstration
        of value of, 212
        during World War II, 31–32, 43
Domestic Policy Council, 123–124
Donovan, William "Wild Bill," 29, 30,
        32–33, 35, 36, 43, 47, 50
"Don't Ask, Don't Tell" policy, 152–153
Dreschler, Donald, 241
Dulles, John Foster, 58

Eagleburger, Lawrence, 152
Earl, Robert, 145
"Earth Day" celebrations, 117
Earthquakes
        recovery complexities of, 68–69
        rescues following, 216
        tsunami-causing, 192
Easter Offensive, 1972, 104, 108
East Timor, U.S. intervention in, 240
Economic Stabilization Act, 1975, 115
Egan, Governor, 74, 78, 82–83
Egeland, Jan, 202
Eisenhower, Dwight
        influenza quarantine organized by,
        19
        as President, 47, 48, 49, 56, 58, 236,
        237, 247
        World War II involvement of, 33,
        34, 42
Eisenhower, Milton, 34
Electric vehicles, 121, 122
Emergencies, complex, responding to,
        243–244
Emergency Highway Energy Conservation
        Act, 1974, 123
Emergency management, phases of,
        212–213
Emergency Petroleum Allocation Act,
        1973, 115
Emergency supplies, distributing, 4

Emergency Support Functions (ESFs),
        215–216, 221, 223
Emerging markets, 185–186
Encounter magazine, 50
Endangered Species Act, 118
Energy conservation, 121, 122–123
Energy Conservation and Production Act,
        1976, 115
Energy crisis, government role in creating,
        2, 114, 115–117, 119–120, 126, 127
Energy Department, 118, 123–125
Energy independence, 120–123
Energy Mobilization Board, 125
Energy policy, 114–117, 120–125, 127–128
Energy Policy and Conservation Act,
        1975, 115, 123
Energy Research and Development
        Administration, 121
Engineering and management practices,
        80
England, influenza cases in, 9
Environmental movement, 117–119
Environmental Protection Agency (EPA),
        118, 125
Environmental regulations, 122, 126
Ethanol, 121
European currency crisis, 1992–1993,
        174
European Recovery Plan, 55
European Union, 240
Exchange rates, 173–174, 180, 186, 187,
        188–189
ExCom (interagency body), 59–60
Executive administration policy making,
        151

Family role in health care, 23
Famine relief, 194
FCO (position), 218, 224
Federal agencies, budgets allocated for,
        166
Federal assistance, restrictions following
        natural disaster, 76–77
Federal Aviation Administration, 68, 70,
        73, 204
Federal Disaster Assistance
        Administration, 212

Federal Emergency Management Agency
    (FEMA)
    Department of Homeland Security,
        merge with, 220
    duties of, 216, 221
    establishment and pre-Katrina
        years, 212–214
    forerunner of, 68, 83
    Hurricane Katrina response of, 2,
        83, 211, 212, 222–223, 224,
        225–226, 227, 228, 229, 230,
        231–232, 251
    management of, 218
    public opinion toward, 231–232
    regional offices of, 250
    Urban Search and Rescue Task
        Forces, 225
Federal Energy Agency (FEA), 115
Federal Energy Regulatory Commission,
    118
Federalism, principle of, 3
Federal Preparedness Agency, 212
Federal Reconstruction and Development
    Planning Commission for Alaska,
    70, 71, 72–74, 77, 79, 80, 81, 82,
    83–84, 85, 86
Federal Reserve, 177, 182, 188
Federal Response Plan (FRP), 214, 215
Federal Trade Commission, 116
FEMA *See* Federal Emergency
    Management Agency
Field activities and operations, 4–5, 72
Film industry during World War II, 31,
    37–38, 41
Final Report of the 9/11 Commission,
    252–253
Financial crises, international
    management and containment of,
    173
    preventing, 185
    U.S. response to, 177–180, 186–189
Financial Sector Assessment Program, 185
Fiscal and monetary austerity, pitfalls of,
    187
Fiscal policy, importance of, 180
Fischer, Stanley, 178
Fitzgerald, Joseph, 74

Floods, search and rescue operations fol-
    lowing, 223
Flu epidemic, 1918. *See* Influenza
    epidemic, 1918
Ford, Gerald, 121, 124
Ford Motor Company, 8
Foreign direct investment, 180
Foreign Information Service (FIS), 28, 29,
    30, 31, 32, 33
Foreign military officers, U.S. education
    and training of, 57
Foreign policy, systems of, 236–237
Foreign policy making, 238–239, 246
Foreign Service Institute, 61–62
Forrestal, James V., 42
Fortier, Don, 137
France, influenza cases in, 9
Free-market energy policy, 114–115, 117
Free trade, 187–188

Gasoline
    alternatives to, 121
    price and availability of, 127
    shortage of, 116, 120
Gates, Robert, 145
Gaulle, Charles de, 33
Gays in military, policy on, 152–153
General Accounting Office (GAO), 82
George, Lloyd, 8–9
German army, influenza cases in, 9
Germany, foreign policy toward, 36
Global capital market, 179, 185
Global War on Terrorism, 185, 186,
    256–260
Goebbels, Joseph, 32
Goldwater-Nichols Act of 1986, 239
Government Accounting Office, 239–240
Government-managed information, pub-
    lic attitudes toward, 46
Government, perception *versus* reality
    concerning, 1
Greek civil war, U.S. Army advisory role
    in, 89
Gross, Gregg, 251
Guadalcanal campaign, 35
Guatemala, CIA-engineered coup in, 50
Guerilla warfare, 89

Habibie, B.J., 176
Haiti, U.S. intervention in, 162, 240, 241, 242
Hakim, Albert, 139, 144
Hamlet Evaluation System (HES) (South Vietnam), 94–95
Hart-Rudman Commission, 244–245, 248
Hart-Rudman Phase III Report (U.S. Commission on National Security), 239
Hasenfus, Eugene, 133, 144
Haskell County, Kansas, 7
Hayes, George, 74
Health officials, public attitude toward, 22
Heating oil, shortage of, 116, 120
Hemagglutin, 10
Hezbollah, 132–133
Holbrooke, Richard, 153, 155, 156, 168
Homeland Security Act, 2002, 218
Homeland Security and Advisory Council (HASC), 254, 257
Homeland Security Council (HSC), 248–249, 259
Homeland Security, Department of. See Department of Homeland Security
Homeland Security Operations Center (HSOC), 219, 220–221, 223
Homeland Security Presidential Directives, 214–215
Homer, Alaska, 67
Home remedies, 15
Hoover, Herbert, 12, 13, 21
Hormutz, Straits of, 127
Host nation support and participation in international disaster relief, 201, 205, 206, 207–208
House Foreign Affairs subcommittee, 60
Housing and Home Finance Agency, 70, 77
Housing, temporary following Alaska earthquake, 75
Huk rebellion, 51
Hull, Cordell, 37
Human capital, interagency operations, role in, 3, 4
Humanitarian operations, 193–194, 208
Hungarian Revolution, 1956, 47, 50, 59

Hurricane Andrew, 1992, 214
Hurricane Katrina, 2005
    Federal Emergency Management Agency response to (see FEMA (Federal Emergency Management Agency): Hurricane Katrina response of)
    local responsibilities in wake of, 249–250
    mass care following, 225–229
    media coverage of, 2, 211, 228, 231
    overview of, 211–212, 216
    public opinion concerning, 231–232
    response, assessment of, 250, 251–252
    response to, 202, 217
    search and rescue operations in, 223–225
Hurricane Rita, 2005, 211–212, 217, 232
Hurricanes, search and rescue operations following, 223
Hussein, Saddam, 149, 162, 167

ICEX. See Intelligence Coordination and Exploitation
ICRC. See International Committee of the Red Cross
IMF. See International Monetary Fund (IMF)
India, British rule in, 33
India, Indian Ocean tsunami impact on, 196–197, 201, 207, 208
Indian Ocean tsunami, 2004
    international response to, 192, 193, 202
    overview of, 192–193
    U.S. response to, 195–197, 202–205, 208–209
Indian Ocean Warning System (IOWS), 201
Individuals, undervaluing of, 3
Indonesia, Indian Ocean tsunami impact on, 196, 201, 203–204
Indonesian Bank Restructuring Agency, 183
Indonesia, riots in, 176

Infectious diseases, inoculations against, 19

Influenza epidemic, 1918
    factors contributing to, 2, 6
    first wave of, 7–10
    government response to, 4, 6, 10–12, 13–14, 16–18, 20–22
    military response to, 7–8, 9, 18–19, 23
    national, state, and local response to, coordinating, 6
    publicizing, delayed of, 15
    second wave of, 10–19
    third wave of, 19–20

Influenza virus
    containing, 19
    movement, tracking, 21, 22
    spread of, conditions enabling, 10

Information operations (IO), 256

Information sharing, 253, 255, 257

Information technology, 255

Ingelsby, Thomas, 23

Ink, Dwight A., 70–71, 73, 78, 80

Innovation, unleashing, 84–85, 86

Institutional culture impact on leadership, 41–42

Intelligence Coordination and Exploitation (ICEX), 96–97

Intelligence, gathering and analysis of, 32, 252–256

Interagency behaviors, 151

Interagency conflict, preventing, 208

Interagency cooperation and coordination
    in financial crisis response, 186
    in Hurricane Katrina, 219–223, 232, 251
    improving, 242–243, 244, 262–263
    in international disaster response, 194, 198, 206–207
    obstacles to, 161–163, 235, 237, 245, 246–247, 260, 261
    on-site mechanisms for, 198
    post-9/11, 248–249, 253–255, 256–258, 259–260, 261, 262–263
    post-Cold War, 240
    in Vietnam War, 108
    in World War II, 38, 41

Interagency crisis management committees, 59–60

Interagency doctrine, 3, 4

Interagency Incident Management Group, 219, 220, 222

Interagency operations
    in Cold War era, 235–239
    defined, 1
    importance of, 20
    management of, 85
    post-9/11, 261
    post-Cold War, 239–242
    in Vietnam War, 106

Interagency policy and policy making, 4, 146, 151, 154, 163–169, 246

Interagency process, 246

Intergovernmental management, 79–80

Interior, Department of (DOI), 118, 125, 224

International Broadcasting Committee, 59

International Committee of the Red Cross (ICRC), 204, 206

"International Information Policy" (National Security Division Directive (NSDD) 130), 55

International investing, 174

International Monetary Fund (IMF), 178–179, 180, 181–182, 183, 184, 185, 188, 189, 240

International monetary system, 173–174

International reserves, 187

International trade and commerce, 174

International Union of Operating Engineers, 73

Intervention operations, 240–242. *See also under specific operation*, e.g.: Somalia: U.S. intervention in

IO. *See* information operations

Iran-Contra affair
    analysis of, 133–139
    circumstances leading to, 130–131, 139
    dissent on, 142
    failure, factors contributing, 4
    impact of, 139–140
    interagency failure role in, 139, 140, 142

National Security Council (NSC)
degradation characterized by, 237
overview of, 132–133
presidency, impact on, 2
uncovering of, 144–146
Iranian Revolution, 1978-1979, 114, 124, 125–126, 127
Iran-Iraq war, 127
Iran, U.S. hostages in, 126, 138
Iraq
army of, 108
war in, 260, 261, 262, 263
Islamic resurgence in Indonesia, 176

Jackson Committee, 47, 58
Johnson, President Lyndon B.
Alaskan Earthquake, 1964, response to, 2, 54, 66, 67, 69–70, 71, 72, 75, 77, 81, 82, 84, 86
domestic policies of, 123–124
National Security Council, dealings with, 236
Vietnam policy of, 91–92, 93, 106
Joint Economic Committee (House), 178
Joint United States Public Affairs Office (JUSPAO), 51
Journalism and public diplomacy, 60
Journal of the American Medical Association, The, influenza epidemic not covered in, 8

KAL 007 shoot-down, 60
Kanter, Arnold, 238, 248
Katrina, Hurricane, 2005. See Hurricane Katrina, 2005
Kennan, George, 46
Kennedy, John F.
administrative style of, 237
assassination of, 66
foreign policy of, 48, 54
national security policy of, 131, 236
Operations Coordinating Board (OCB) demise under, 58
special warfare forces promoted by, 51
words and ideas, importance attached to, 49

Kennedy, S.M., 14
Khomeini, Ruhollah, 125, 138
Kim, Dae-jung, 176
Kissinger, Henry, 48, 123, 131–132, 141, 236
Kitfield, James, 245, 250
Knox, Frank, 42
Komer, Robert W.
Accelerated Pacification Campaign endorsed by, 102
Chieu Hoi program endorsed by, 98
as CORDS (Office of Civil Operations and Revolutionary Development Support) head, 94, 95–96, 97, 105, 106, 109
MACV (Military Assistance Command Vietnam) assignment of, 93
Project Recovery, participation in, 101
Regional and Popular Forces study requested by, 99–100
security promoting measures by, 107, 108
Tet offensive, commentary on, 103
Vietnam pacification role of, 92
Koppes, Clayton R., 31
Korean War, 46, 49
Kosovo crisis
Bosnia conflict spread to, prospective, 156
Bosnia policy, comparison to, 157–159
complex contingency operations in, 240
contingency planning in, 260
interagency squabbling during, 2, 162
intervention delay, factors in, 153, 157–159, 168–169
intervention failure, factors in, 4
leadership void in, 154
reactive response to, 163
U.S. objectives in, 159–161, 165
Kurdistan (Northern Iraq), humanitarian operations in, 198
Kuwait, Iraqi invasion of, 149, 155, 167

LaGuardia, Fiorello, 32
Lake, Anthony, 155, 156, 158
Lansdale, Edward, 51
Latin America, Communist expansion in,
    combating, 132
Laurie, Clay, 32
Lawrence, Chris, 228
Leadership
    importance of, 3–4
    influenza epidemic, 1918, lack dur-
        ing, 15
    in intervention operations, 151,
        169
    in national security, 245
    in natural disaster recovery, 84, 219
    in Vietnam War, 105–106, 108–109
    in World War II, 38–39, 41–42
League of Nations, 28
Lebanon, U.S. hostages in, 132–133, 135,
    136
Ledeen, Michael, 139
Leepai, Chuan. See Chuan Leepai
Lending policies, strengthening of, 185
Lending practices in Asia, 180–181
Lifesaving techniques, 213
Limited government, 3
Local communities, challenges exceeding
    coping capacity of, 5
Local communities, influenza epidemic,
    1918, response to, 15–16, 22–23
Local dimensions of international disas-
    ters, 199–202
Local jurisdictions and individuals,
    authority and autonomy of, 3
Local public health departments,
    influenza, response to, 13
Lodge, Henry Cabot, 18, 91
Logistical support in emergency, 213
Long-term capital, 180

MacAdoo, William Gibbs, 12, 21
Macedonia, Bosnia conflict spread to,
    prospective, 156
MacLeish, Archibald, 28–29, 30, 32, 37, 39
MACV (Military Assistance Command
    Vietnam), 90, 92, 93, 95, 96, 99,
    100, 101, 106, 107, 108
Magsaysay, Ramon, 51

Malaysia, unrest in, 176
Maldives, Indian Ocean tsunami impact
    on, 196, 201
March, Peyton C., 11
Market liberalization, impact of, 184
Marshall, George C., 33, 37, 42, 55
Marshall Plan, 55
McCarthy, Joseph, 58, 60
McDermott, Edward A., 68
McFarlane, Robert, 131, 132, 134–135,
    136–137, 139, 141, 142, 143, 145
McNaughton, John T., 100
Medical emergency, myth in disaster
    aftermath, 197
Meese, Edwin, 133, 140, 141, 144, 145
Mexican peso crisis, 1994-1995, 174, 177,
    179
Meyer, Edward C., 242
Military operations, budgeting for, 167
Military services. See Armed forces; indi-
    vidual branch of the military, e.g.:
    U.S. Army
Milosevic, Slobodan, 153, 158, 159,
    160–161, 162, 167–168
Minier, Loring, 7
Mitigation of emergency, 212
Miyazawa Fund, 182, 183
Mladic, Ratko, 168
Mobile Emergency Response Support
    teams, 221, 222
Montenegro, crisis prevention in, 163
Morgenthau, Henry, Jr., 36, 38
Murrow, Edward R., 48, 54
Muskie, Edmund, 146
Muslim populations, radicalization of,
    186

National Commission on Terrorist
    Attacks, 257
National Commission on Terrorist
    Attacks Upon the United States
    (9/11 Commission), 239
National Counterterrorism Center
    (NCTC), 252, 257
National Defense Panel, 244, 245, 251
National Defense Panel of 1997, 239
National Disaster Medical System, 216
National disaster response, 213

National Endowment for Democracy, 59
National Energy Plan, 121
National Environmental Policy Act, 122
National Flood Insurance Administration,
    212
National Guard, 224, 225, 251
National Homeland Security Agency, 245
National Incident Management System
    (NIMS), 215, 216
National Intelligence Center (NID), 257
Nationalistic self-determination
    movements, post-Cold War, 157
National Logistics Center, 222
National mobilization, 213
National Oceanic and Atmospheric
    Administration, 118
National Response Coordination Center
    (NRCC), 219, 221, 222
National Response Plan (NRP), 212, 214,
    215, 216, 217, 219, 222, 223, 224,
    225, 227, 229–231, 232
National security
    emergency preparedness, 213
    financial crisis impact on, 175–177,
        186–189
    international financial policy
        impact on, 173
    policy on, 163
    post-9/11, 259
    resources for, 254–255
    structure, assessing, 238–239, 240
    structure, enhancing, 245
    system reorganization, 244
National Security Act of 1947, 58, 131,
    235, 236, 247
National security advisor post, 130,
    131–132, 134–136, 141, 142, 143,
    146, 237, 238
National Security Council (NSC)
    Asian financial crisis response, role
        in, 181
    assessment of, 246–247
    Bosnia and Kosovo interventions,
        role in, 152, 156, 157, 160, 162, 163,
        169
    in Cold War era, 235–238
    crisis decision making prior to, 21
    establishment of, 58, 130

    interagency policy, role in, 123
    Iran-Contra affair, role in, 131–132,
        135–136, 136–137, 138, 139, 140,
        142, 143, 144, 145–146
    leadership of, 92
    literature on, 235
    policy making, role in, 151, 154,
        165, 166
    in post-9/11 era, 248–249, 259, 262
    in post-Cold War era, 240, 242
    staffing of, 247
NATO. See North Atlantic Treaty Organi-
    zation
Natural disaster response, 2, 77–78, 198,
    200–201
Natural disasters, literature coverage of,
    pre- and post-Katrina, 250–251
Nazi propaganda, 28, 32
NCTC. See National Counterterrorism
    Center
Neuraminidase, 10
New Orleans, Hurricane Katrina impact
    on, 211, 217, 231
New Orleans, levees, failure at, 211–212
New Orleans Convention Center, shelter
    at, 211, 227–229, 231
Ngo Dinh Diem, 89
NGOs (nongovernmental organizations).
    See also name of specific
    organization, e.g.: Red Cross
    certification of, 206
    coordination with, 207
    disaster relief efforts by, 197, 198,
        199, 200, 201, 208
    Indian Ocean tsunami response,
        role in, 193, 196, 197, 202, 203, 204
    military, work with, 194, 196,
        204–205, 261, 262
Nguyen Cao Ky, 90
Nguyen Van Thieu, 90
Nicaragua, covert operations in, 138
Nixon, Richard M., 48, 113, 115, 121, 124,
    131, 237
North Africa, allied occupation of, 33–34
North Atlantic Treaty Organization
    (NATO), 150, 156, 157, 159–160,
    160, 169
Northern Command, 250

North, Oliver, 132, 133, 134, 135,
    136–137, 138, 139, 143, 144, 145,
    146
NRCC (National Response Coordination
    Center), 219, 221, 222
NRP. *See* National Response Plan (NRP)
NSC. *See* National Security Council
    (NSC)
Nuclear weapons, 55–56, 67

OCB. *See* Operations Coordinating Board
OCO. *See* Office of Civil Operations
Office of Civilian Defense, 32
Office of Civil Operations (OCO), 92–93
Office of Civil Operations and
    Revolutionary Development Sup-
    port (CORDS)
    advisors requested by, 100
    assessment of, 104–106, 109
    decisions, participation in, 108
    deputy of, 97
    direction of, 101
    function of, 90–91, 93
    growth of, 96
    performance of, 94–95, 98, 99, 102,
        107
Office of Emergency Planning (OEP), 68,
    70, 73, 83
Office of Facts and Figures (OFF), 28–29,
    31, 32, 33
Office of Homeland Security, 248, 249
Office of Strategic Services (OSS), 31, 34,
    35, 36, 41, 46, 50, 51
Office of the Coordinator for Reconstruc-
    tion and Stabilization (S/CRS),
    260–261
Office of the Coordinator of Information
    (COI), 28, 29, 30, 31, 33
Office of War Information (OWI), 31, 32,
    33, 34, 35, 36, 37, 38–39, 40, 41, 46
Oil, domestic, supply and production of,
    113, 115–116, 116, 117–119, 120,
    121, 122, 126, 127
Oil drilling, 118–119, 126
Oil prices, controls for, 115, 116, 118–119,
    126
Oil prices, increase in, 113
O'Neil, John, 252

OPEC (Organization of Petroleum
    Exporting Countries), 113, 114,
    116, 117, 119, 120, 125–126
Open markets, shift toward, 180
Operational activities, 4
Operation Desert Storm, 155, 167
Operation Enduring Freedom, 261
Operation Iraqi Freedom, 231, 246, 260,
    261
Operation Restore Hope, 150
Operations Coordinating Board (OCB),
    58
Operation Sea Angel, 193, 195, 205
OSS. *See* Office of Strategic Services
    (OSS)
Outer Continental Shelf Lands Act, 1953,
    118
Over-institutionalization, 236
Over-personalization, 236
OWI. *See* Office of War Information
    (OWI)
OXFAM, 198, 200, 206

Pacification operations, 89
Pacific Command (PACOM), 194–195, 203
Pahlavi, Mohammad Reza, 125
Panama, psychological operations in, 52
Pandemic, potential, preparation for,
    23–24
Pardew, James, 156
Partisan politics, 231
PC. *See* Principals Committee
PDD. *See* Presidential Decision Directive
Pentagon, combat command structure of,
    4
People and personalities, success or
    failure, role in, 3–4
Peres, Shimon, 139
Perfectionism, 231
Perry, William, 156
Pershing, General, 11
Persian Gulf, psychological operations in,
    52
Persian Gulf War, 166
Philadelphia, influenza cases in, 14–16
Philippines, counterinsurgency operations
    in, 51, 89
Phoenix program, 97, 103–104

Pickering, Thomas R., 242
Poindexter, John, 131, 132, 133, 135–136,
     137, 139, 141, 142, 143, 144, 145, 146
Policy papers, 164–165
Polish Solidarity Movement, 57
Political or cultural activities, clandestine
     support of, 50
Political warfare, 50–51, 62
Powell, Colin, 156, 158, 159, 162
Poyer, John, 24
Preparation for emergency, 212, 214
Presidential Decision Directive (PDD) 56,
     244, 251, 262
Presidential Directives, 214
Presidential leadership
     and armed crisis management, 154
     interagency operations, role in, 3
     postconflict reconstruction, role in,
     263
Presidential system of foreign policy,
     236–237
Prevention of emergency, 212
Principal Federal Official (PFO) position,
     217–218
Principals Committee (PC), 164, 165
Project Independence, 121
Project on National Security Reform, 5
Project Recovery (Vietnam), 101–102
Project Takeoff, 95–96
Propaganda during Cold War, 50
Propaganda during World War II, 28, 30,
     31, 32, 36, 43, 46
Prueher, Joseph W., 175
Psychological warfare
     during Cold War (see under Cold
     War)
     during Vietnam War (see under
     Vietnam War)
     during World War II, 29, 32, 33, 42,
     43, 46, 47, 51
Public Affairs Committee, 58
Public diplomacy (Cold War strategy)
     in Carter administration, 49–50
     core missions of, 54
     description of, 48, 55
     jurisdiction of, 60
     in Reagan administration, 52–53,
     55, 56–57, 58, 60, 61–62

staff involved in, 61–62
Public health crisis, cooperative response
     required to, 20

Quarantine and containment procedures,
     wartime
     examples of, 19, 24
     non-action on, 17
     obstacles to, 24
     opposition to, 6, 14

Radio broadcasting, Cold War era, 50, 52,
     57, 59
Radio Free Afghanistan, 59
Radio Free Europe/Radio Liberty (RFE-
     RL), 47, 50, 59, 61
Radio Marti, 59
Reagan, Ronald
     Cold War psychological operations
     of, 49, 52
     domestic policy of, 141
     energy market deregulation by, 117
     foreign policy of, 55, 58, 60–61,
     130–131, 132, 141
     Iran-Contra affair, involvement in,
     133, 134, 135, 136, 139, 145, 146
     leadership style of, 130, 140–141
     National Security Council (NSC),
     dealings with, 237
     Soviet policy of, 56
     United States Information Agency
     (USIA), relationship with, 54
Rebuilding countries, 2
Recovery after emergency, 213
Red Crescent, 206
Red Cross
     Alaskan Earthquake, 1964, aid fol-
     lowing, 68
     Hurricane Katrina, aid following,
     225, 226
     Indian Ocean tsunami response,
     role in, 193
     influenza epidemic, aid during, 14,
     17, 23
     in Iraq and Afghanistan, 261
     professional NGO standards, role
     in establishing, 206
Refined oil products, problems for, 116

Reforms, implementing, 4
Regan, Don, 135
Regional Forces/Popular Forces (RF/PF), 98, 99–100, 101, 103, 104, 107–108
Regional Response Coordination Centers (RRCCs), 221, 222
Relief organizations, deployment and response capabilities of, 207
Reports on the Observance of Standards and Codes, 185
Response to emergency, 212–213, 214–215
Response to recovery transition in natural disaster, 77–78, 198, 200–201
Revolutionary Development Cadre (South Vietnam), 102–103
RFE-RL. See Radio Free Europe/Radio Liberty
RF/PF. See Regional Forces/Popular Forces
Rice, Condoleeza, 238
Richard, Charles, 18
Risk aversion, 151, 152
Rita, Hurricane, 2005, 211–212, 217, 232
Robert T. Stafford Disaster Relief Act, 1984, 218, 223
Rogers, William, 131
Roosevelt, Franklin D.
    administrative style of, 38, 40, 43, 237
    appointments by, 29
    Office of Facts and Figures (OFF) created by, 28
    Office of War Information (OWI) created by, 31, 34
    postwar policies of, 36
    war information policies of, 35, 42
Roth, Stanley, 175, 177
Rowan, Carl, 54
RRCCs (Regional Response Coordination Centers), 221, 222
Rubin, Robert, 177
Russia, near implosion of, 185
Rwanda refugee humanitarian relief crisis, 1994, 239

Salvation Army, 68
Sandinista National Liberation Front, 138, 144
Santa Barbara oil spill, 1969, 118

Saxton, Jim, 178
SBA. See Small Business Administration
Schlesinger, Arthur, 237, 245
Schlesinger, James, 124
Scowcroft, Brent, 152, 238, 248
S/CRS. See Office of the Coordinator for Reconstruction and Stabilization
Secord, Richard, 138, 139, 144
Secretarial system of foreign policy, 236
Sedition Act of 1918, 12, 22
Senate Foreign Relations Committee, 60, 61
September 11, 2001, terrorist attacks of, 185, 213, 235, 247
Shalikashvili, John, 153, 156, 162
Sherwood, Robert E., 29, 30–31, 32, 39
Short-term capital, 180, 186
Shultz, George, 132, 135, 141, 142, 143, 144–145
Simplicity of disaster recovery structure, 85–86
Single-manager concept, 106–107
Situation awareness and control, 213
Six-Day War of 1967, 119
Slim, William, 206
Slovenia, 165–166
Small Business Administration (SBA), 70, 81
Smallpox, inoculations against, 19
Smith-Mundt Act of 1948, 46
Soldiers, influenza cases among, 7–8, 19
Solidarity Movement (Poland), 57
Somalia
    famine relief effort in, 1992-1993, 194
    humanitarian operations in, 198
    U.S. intervention in, 150–151, 154, 155, 162, 240
"Somalia Syndrome," 2, 151
South Korea, presidential elections in, 176
South Vietnam
    counterinsurgency operations in, 89–90, 96–97
    government of, 94, 101, 102, 104–105
    pacification campaign in, 5, 89–90, 92, 94–95, 97–98, 99, 100, 101, 102, 103, 105–109

territorial security of, 107–108
    U.S. mission in, 90–91
Sovereign Debt Restructuring
    Mechanism, 185
Soviet Union
    fall of, factors contributing to,
        49–50, 52
    insurgencies supported by, 124
    threat, containment of, 48
Space exploration, 56
"Spanish sickness," 11
Special interest politics, 115
Srebrenica massacre and marketplace
    bombing, 157
Sri Lanka, Indian Ocean tsunami impact
    on, 196, 201, 205
Stafford Act (Robert T. Stafford Disaster
    Relief Act), 1984, 218, 223
Stalin, Josef, 47
Stanton Commission, 54–55
Stars and Stripes newspaper, 42
State Department
    Alaskan earthquake, 1964, response
        to, 70
    Asian financial crisis response, role
        in, 177–178, 181
    in Cold War, 46, 47, 52, 54–55,
        57–58, 60, 61, 62, 131, 237
    foreign policy making, role in, 151,
        167–168
    Indian Ocean tsunami response,
        role in, 194, 203
    international disaster relief, partici-
        pation in, 200–201, 208
    post-9/11 role of, 259, 260, 262
    post–Cold War role of, 154,
        161–162, 163, 164, 165, 241, 242,
        245
    Vietnam role of, 90, 92, 93, 107
State of Alaska Reconstruction and Devel-
    opment Planning Commission, 74,
    79
Stettinius, Edward, Jr., 37
Stiglitz, Joseph, 179, 187
Strategic communication and
    information, 258, 259
Strategic leadership, 4, 154
Strategic planning, 245

Strategic vision and planning processes,
    151
"Stripper wells," 116
Structural damage due to earthquakes,
    68–69
Subcommittee on Domestic and Interna-
    tional Monetary Policy (House
    Committee on Banking and Finan-
    cial Services), 178
Suez Canal crisis, 1956, 59
Sukhumbhand Paribatra, 172
Summers, Lawrence, 177, 180
Superdome (New Orleans), shelter at,
    211, 226–227, 231
Synthetic fuels (synfuels), 121, 122

Taft, Howard, 13
Taiwan currency, devaluing of, 175
Taylor, Maxwell, 91
Taylor, Robert, 240, 248
Technological advances, 255–256
Television broadcasting, Cold War era, 57
Tenth Amendment, 3
Terrorism, pre-9/11 measures against,
    213, 240
Terrorist attacks, possible, pre-9/11 warn-
    ings concerning, 247–248
Terrorist attacks, pre-9/11, 248
Tet Offensive, 1968, 98, 100–101, 102, 103,
    104, 108
Thai baht, crash of, 172, 174–175, 182,
    185
Thailand, constitution revised by, 176
Thailand, Indian Ocean tsunami impact
    on, 196, 201, 205, 207–208
Tidal waves. See Indian Ocean tsunami,
    2004; Tsunamis
Timberg, Robert, 136
Tito, Josip Broz, 149
Totalitarian regimes, propaganda of, 46
Tower, John, 146
Tower Commission, 146
Trans-Alaska Pipeline, 120, 126
Transportation role in disaster relief,
    197–198
Treasury Department, 177, 180, 181, 182,
    185, 188
Truman, President, 236

Truth *versus* propaganda, wartime, 28, 30, 31, 32
Tsunamis. *See also* Indian Ocean tsunami, 2004
   in Alaska, 78
   relief, coordinating, 5
   warning systems for, 201, 207
Typhoid, inoculations against, 19

U-2 shoot-down incident, 1960, 59
UNICEF, 193
Unified statescraft (defined), 189
United Nations, 158, 159, 199, 202, 207, 240
United Nations Development Program, 196
United States Information Agency (USIA), 47, 48, 49, 53, 54, 56, 58, 59, 60, 61, 62
Urban renewal projects following natural disaster, 81
Urban Search and Rescue, 224
Urban Search and Rescue Task Force, 216
USAID Assessment Handbook, 199
USAID (U.S. Agency for International Development)
   complex contingency operations, participation in, 240
   Haiti intervention, participation in, 241
   India disaster preparedness, aid for, 192, 196, 197, 201, 208
   Indian Ocean tsunami response, role in, 194, 202, 203, 204
   interagency competencies and competition, reconciling, 200
   Vietnam stabilization, participation in, 90, 91, 95, 97, 107
U.S. Army
   actions and operations of, 89
   civil support role of, 89
   war information, role in, 33, 34
U.S. Coast Guard, 224, 225
U.S. Congress
   Asian financial crisis response, role in, 178, 185, 188
   in Cold War, 60
   Executive Branch, attitude toward, 231

   in Iran-Contra affair, 143–144
   in post-Cold War era, 164, 165, 166, 167
   in World War II, 35, 36, 39, 40
U.S. Department of Agriculture (USDA), 90, 118
U.S. Federal Reserve, 177, 182, 188
U.S. Fire Administration, 212
U.S. Information Service (USIS), 51, 90, 91
U.S. International Communications Agency, 49, 58
U.S. Marine Corps, tsunami relief participation by, 195–196, 203, 204
U.S. Navy
   influenza cases in, 9
   tsunami relief participation by, 204
   war information, role in, 42
U.S. Public Health Service, funding of, 17–18, 19–20
U.S. Public Health Service, influenza epidemic, response to, 7, 13, 14, 16, 22, 23
U.S.–Soviet relations, 134

Vaccines, administering, 4
Valdez, Alaska, relocation and rebuilding of, 75, 77, 78–79, 82
Versailles Treaty, 28
Veterans, returning, influenza cases among, 14
Vichy regime, 33, 34
Viet Cong uprising, 1968, 98
Vietnam War
   attention to, 67
   CIA crippled by, 138
   divisions over, 124
   foreign policy, long-term impact on, 158–159, 239
   heats and minds, battle during, 2
   media criticism of, 48
   psychological operations in, 51, 52, 95, 97
   U.S. involvement ended in, 113
Viruses, mutation of, 10, 19
Voice of America (VOA), 46, 48, 53–54, 55, 59, 60
Volunteer Medical Service Corps, 17

Vulnerability Assessment Framework, 185

Walsh, Lawrence E., 133
War on Terrorism, 185, 186, 256–260
Wars, fighting, 2
Watergate, 50, 113, 121, 124, 138
Weinberger, Caspar, 132, 135, 141, 142, 144, 145, 146
Weinberger Doctrine, 156, 158
Westmore, William C., 93, 106
White, Lee, 71
White House Council on Environmental Quality (CEQ), 118
White House Office of Global Communications (OGC), 259
Why We Fight film series, 37–38, 41, 42
Wick, Charles, 54
Willard Group (Group of 22), 184
Wilson, Woodrow
    appointments by, 12
    influenza response, inadequate of, 16, 20, 21
    information measures undertaken by, 27, 34, 39, 40, 42
    war commentary by, 11
    wartime reinforcements sent by, 9, 18
Wolfensohn, James, 179
Workforce, influenza impact on, 16
World Bank, 177, 178, 179, 188, 189, 197
World Bank Group (WB), 240
World Health Organization (WHO), 240
World Trade Center, attacks on, 1993, 248

Worldviews, impact on policy, 154, 155
World War I
    dissent, suppression during, 12–13
    influenza spread during, 6, 8–9
    information operations during, 27–28, 34, 46
    war effort during, 10–13, 14, 16, 20–21
World War II, information operations during
    agencies involved with, 28–29, 34–36
    effectiveness, evaluating, 42–44
    evolution of, 46
    media role in, 40–41, 42
    overview of, 27
    political battles surrounding, 2, 30–31, 35, 36–37, 38, 39–40
    psychological operations (*see* Psychological warfare: during World War II)
    purpose of, 31–33, 34–36
    war news, public demand for, 28, 29–30

Yom Kippur War, 1973, 113, 119, 120
Youngchaiyudh, Chavalit. *See* Chavalit Youngchaiyudh
Yugoslavia, disintegration of, 149–150, 167

Zinni, Anthony, 194

About the Editors and Contributors

GARY W. ANDERSON is a vice president at Hicks and Associates, a wholly owned subsidiary of SAIC. Mr. Anderson was formerly a fellow with the Potomac Institute for Policy Studies and remains on their Board of Visitors. He served as the first director of the Marine Corps' Center for Emerging Threats and Opportunities and then led Potomac's National Center for Unconventional Thought. He did pioneering work in the areas of military robotics, nonlethal weapons, urban operations, and humanitarian operations. He has served as a special advisor to the deputy secretary of defense on matters concerning constabulary and counterinsurgency operations. He also teaches a graduate-level course on the Revolution in Military Affairs at George Washington University. Before joining the Potomac Institute, Mr. Anderson served for twenty-nine years in the Marine Corps, retiring as a colonel. He commanded troop formations at every rank serving in combat in Somalia and as a United Nations military observer in Lebanon and the Gaza Strip. He was the J-3 (Operations Officer) for the highly successful 1991 Operation Sea Angel humanitarian operation in Bangladesh. Upon retirement, he was chief of staff of the Marine Corps Warfighting Lab at Quantico.

Mr. Anderson is a graduate of Embry-Riddle Aeronautical University and received his master's degree in public administration from Pepperdine University. He also attended the National Security Studies course at the Maxwell School of Public Administration at Syracuse University. He is a member of the Marine Corps Association and serves on the executive committee of the National Institute for Urban Search and Rescue.

JOHN R. BRINKERHOFF is a consultant on national security affairs, with broad experience in mobilization, emergency management, force development, strategic planning, and manpower programming. He has been a national security consultant for twenty-five years and has been associated with the Institute for Defense

Analyses for over half that time. Mr. Brinkerhoff served for seven years as a career senior executive in the Office of the Secretary of Defense as director of manpower programs, director of intergovernmental affairs, special assistant to the deputy assistant secretary of defense for reserve affairs, and deputy assistant secretary of defense for reserve affairs. After leaving the Office of the Secretary of Defense, he was for two years the acting associate director of the Federal Emergency Management Agency for National Preparedness Programs and concurrently the deputy executive secretary of the Emergency Mobilization Preparedness Board.

Mr. Brinkerhoff served twenty-nine years in the United States Army, retiring as a colonel. During his twenty-four years of commissioned service, he commanded engineer units in Korea, Germany, and Vietnam and served two tours of duty on the Army Staff and two tours in the Office of the Secretary of Defense. Mr. Brinkerhoff is a graduate of the United States Military Academy and has earned master's degrees from the California Institute of Technology, Columbia University, and George Washington University. He is a graduate of the Army Command and General Staff College and the Army War College. He is author of two books and numerous articles and papers.

JAMES JAY CARAFANO is a leading expert in defense affairs, military operations and strategy, and homeland security at The Heritage Foundation. An accomplished historian and teacher, Carafano was an assistant professor at the U.S. Military Academy in West Point, New York, and served as director of military studies at the Army's Center of Military History. He also taught at Mount Saint Mary College in New York and served as a fleet professor at the U.S. Naval War College. He is a visiting professor at the National Defense University and Georgetown University. Carafano is the author of *GI Ingenuity: Improvisation, Technology and Winning World War II* (2006); coauthor of *Winning the Long War: Lessons from the Cold War for Defeating Terrorism and Preserving Freedom* (2005); and coauthor of *Homeland Security* (2005). His other works include *Waltzing into the Cold War* (2002) and *After D-Day*, a Military Book Club main selection (2000).

Carafano joined Heritage in 2003 as a senior research fellow after serving as a senior fellow at the Center for Strategic and Budgetary Assessments, a Washington policy institute dedicated to defense issues. In 2006, Carafano became assistant director of Heritage's Kathryn and Shelby Cullom Davis Institute for International Studies. Before becoming a policy expert, he served twenty-five years in the army. Before retiring, he was executive editor of *Joint Force Quarterly*, the Defense Department's premier professional military journal. Carafano is a member of the National Academy's Board on Army Science and Technology and the Department of the Army Historical Advisory Committee, and he is a senior fellow at the George Washington University's Homeland Security Policy Institute. A graduate of West Point, Carafano also has a master's degree and a doctorate from Georgetown University and a master's degree in strategy from the U.S. Army War College.

ALEX DOUVILLE is director of policy studies at the Center for the Study of the Presidency. He joined the Center in October 2004 as a research assistant to the director of homeland security projects. He has coordinated the Center's homeland security initiatives on strengthening NATO's role in the global war on terror, enhancing defenses against the threat of smuggled nuclear weapons and weapons of mass effect, and examining the impacts of an overstretched Reserve and National Guard. In 2005, Douville became the Center's strategic planning director and special assistant to the president. In this role he assisted Center President David Abshire in his research and speech writing. He also cowrote and edited the Center's brochure and designed and edited the Center's 2005 publication, *Maximizing NATO for the War on Terror*. For the past two years, Douville has also served as a Presidential Fellows Mentor. Each year he assists two fellows as they research and write a paper on an aspect of the American presidency. The Presidential Fellows Program is composed of eighty-five undergraduate and graduate students from across the country who meet in Washington, D.C., twice a year to present their papers and become immersed in public policy.

Douville earned his B.A. in European history from Union College in 1997 and his M.A. in U.S. military history from Temple University in 1999. He received the 1998–99 U.S. Marine Corps' Masters Thesis Fellowship. His thesis on the Pacific War is included in the archives at the Marine Corps Historical Center in Quantico, Virginia.

ROZLYN C. ENGEL is an assistant professor of economics at the United States Military Academy at West Point. Dr. Engel is the founder and director of the department's faculty research seminar. She has published a number of scholarly papers and served as an editor and legislative correspondent in the U.S. Senate.

She has a bachelor's degree from Smith College, has master's degrees from the London School of Economics and Columbia University, and was Bradley Research Fellow. Dr. Engel also holds a Ph.D. from Columbia University. Prior to receiving her doctorate in economics, she worked as an editor and writer for several public policy groups, including the Brookings Institution, the International Monetary Fund, and the Russell Sage Foundation. Dr. Engel has held leadership positions in several community nonprofits.

DWIGHT A. INK served in policy roles under seven U.S. presidents, including service as vice president of two government corporations. As assistant general manager of the Atomic Energy Commission during the Eisenhower administration, he initiated Washington consideration of the limited nuclear test ban concept that was later negotiated under President Kennedy. President Johnson appointed him executive director of the cabinet-level commission to lead the recovery of Alaska after the devastating 1964 earthquake in that state. President Johnson also selected him to chair the White House Task Force on Education and assistant secretary of HUD. Mr. Ink headed the Office of Executive Management for President Nixon where he led the president's reorganization efforts such as the establishment of OMB and EPA. He led President Ford's drive to reduce the government's use of energy during the Arab oil embargo. President Carter appointed him executive director of his 1978 Civil Service Reform. He then headed the Community Services Administration, which he closed down for President Reagan. Mr. Ink concluded his federal service as assistant USAID administrator for Latin America and the Caribbean for Reagan.

After retiring from government service, Mr. Ink was then appointed president of the New York Institute of Public Administration, where he led efforts to help the leadership of the People's Republic of China in their reforms, as well as the central governments of central and eastern Europe in making their transition to democratic institutions and market economies. Mr. Ink received a B.S. from Iowa State University and an M.A. in public administration from the University of Minnesota.

BEN LIEBERMAN is a senior policy analyst at The Heritage Foundation's Roe Institute for Economic Policy Studies. He specializes in energy and environmental issues, including the Clean Air Act, climate change, and the impact of environmental policy on energy prices. His commentaries on environmental and energy issues have been published in the *Baltimore Sun*, *BusinessWeek*, the *Chicago Sun-Times*, FOXNews.com, and the *Washington Times*. He has also appeared in interviews on CNBC and FOX News Channel. He has testified before Congress on several occasions.

Before joining Heritage in 2005, Lieberman served as associate counsel and director of air quality policy at the Competitive Enterprise Institute in Washington. Lieberman earned a law degree from George Washington University in 1993 and is a member of both the Maryland and District of Columbia bar associations. He also earned a bachelor's degree in accounting from the University of Maryland in 1988 and became a certified public accountant in 1989.

CARNES LORD, professor of military and naval strategy in the Strategic Research Department of the Center for Naval Warfare Studies, U.S. Naval War College, is a political scientist with broad interests in international and strategic studies, national security organization and management, and political philosophy. He has held a number of positions in the U.S. government, including director of international communications and information policy on the National Security Council staff (1981–83), assistant to the vice president for national security affairs (1989–91), and distinguished fellow at the National Defense University (1991–93).

Dr. Lord has taught political science at Yale University, the University of Virginia, and the Fletcher School of Law and Diplomacy and was director of international studies at the National Institute for Public Policy. He is the author among other works of *The Presidency and the Management of National Security* (1988) and *The Modern Prince* (2003).

VICKI J. RAST is a serving Air Force officer. She is the author of *Interagency Fratricide: Policy Failures in the Persian Gulf and Bosnia* (2004). The book is based on interviews with 135 people who were involved in the decision-making process in the administrations of George H. W. Bush and Bill Clinton. These include H. Norman Schwarzkopf, Brent Scowcroft, John M. Shalikashvili, Condoleezza Rice, Lawrence S. Eagleburger, Richard B. Cheney, and other prominent individuals. Her other works include "Airpower's Effectiveness in a Changing World Destabilized by Asymmetric Threats," "National Fragmentation, Ethnicity, and the New World Order," and "The Iraq-Kuwait Crisis: Structural Deprivation Leads to Revolution." Colonel Rast previously served as assistant professor of national security studies, Air University, and associate professor of political science, USAF Academy. She is currently the special assistant to the director, Plans and Programs, Headquarters United States Air Force Academy.

Colonel Rast is a 1988 graduate of the United States Air Force Academy. She received a master's degree in public administration from Troy State University. She is also a graduate of the U.S. Air and Staff College, and a PhD from George Mason University.

NICHOLAS EVAN SARANTAKES is an associate professor of joint and international operations at the U.S. Army Command and General Staff College. He has a Ph.D. in history from the University of Southern California. He also holds the M.A. degree in history from the University of Kentucky. He did his undergraduate work at the University of Texas. He is the author of *Keystone: The American Occupation of Okinawa and U.S.-Japanese Relations* (2000) and *Seven Stars: The Okinawa Battle Diaries of Simon Bolivar Buckner, Jr. and Joseph Stilwell* (2004). He is currently finishing a book that examines allied strategy and joint international operations at the end of World War II tentatively titled *Allies to the Very End: The United States, the British Nations, and the Defeat of Imperial Japan.* He has published a number of articles that have been appeared in outlets like the *Journal of Military History*, the *Royal United Services Institute Journal*, and ESPN.com. He received two writing awards for the best article published in the *Southwestern Historical Quarterly*, another for his work in *Joint Force Quarterly*, and two from the Command and General Staff College.

Dr. Sarantakes is a fellow of the Royal Historical Society and has previously taught at Texas A&M University–Commerce, the Air War College, and the University of Southern Mississippi.

JOHN SHORTAL is the assistant chief of the U.S. Army Center of Military History. Dr. Shortal is a graduate of the United States Military Academy and has earned master's degrees from the University of Southern California and Temple University. He received his Ph.D. in history from Temple University in 1985. He is a graduate of the Army Command and General Staff College and the National War College. Before coming to the Center of Military History he served thirty-two years in the United States Army, retiring as a brigadier general.

Dr. Shortal served five tours overseas, taught history at West Point, served on the Army Staff, and commanded infantry units in the United States and Korea. His last assignments in the army were as the assistant division commander of the 2nd Infantry Division, in the Republic of Korea, and as the deputy commanding general of the U.S. Army Recruiting Command. He is the author of *Forged by Fire* (1987) and has written a number of articles and papers.

RICHARD W. STEWART is the chief historian of the U.S. Army Center of Military History. Prior to assuming his new post, he was the chief of Histories Division at the Center from 1998 to 2006. Dr. Stewart received a bachelor's degree in history from Stetson University (1972) and a master's degree in history from the University of Florida (1980). He earned his Ph.D. in history from Yale University in 1986. Dr. Stewart is also a graduate of the U.S. Army Command and General Staff College and the National War College. Before coming to the Center, he was the command historian, U.S. Army Special Operations Command, Fort Bragg, North Carolina, and the historian for the Center for Army Lessons Learned at Fort Leavenworth, Kansas.

A retired colonel in military intelligence, United States Army Reserve, with thirty years of commissioned service, Dr. Stewart has deployed as a combat historian for Operation Desert Storm (Saudi Arabia and Kuwait), Operations Continue Hope/Support Hope in support of UNOSOM II (Somalia), Maintain/Restore Democracy (Haiti), Joint Guard/Joint Force (Bosnia), DESERT SPRING (Kuwait and Bahrain), and after 9/11 to Afghanistan in support of Operation Enduring Freedom.

RICHARD WEITZ is a senior fellow and director of program management at the Hudson Institute. He analyzes mid- and long-term national and international political-military issues, including by employing scenario-based planning. From 2003 to 2005, Dr. Weitz was a senior staff member at the Institute for Foreign Policy Analysis (IFPA). From 2002 to 2004, Dr. Weitz was a consultant for the Center for Strategic and International Studies, the Defense Science Board, and DFI International, Inc. He also has held positions with the Center for Strategic Studies, the Belfer Center for Science and International Affairs (BCSIA) at Harvard University's Kennedy School of Government, and the U.S. Department of Defense.

Dr. Weitz is a graduate of Harvard College (B.A. with highest honors in government), the London School of Economics (M.Sc. in international relations), Oxford University (M.Phil. in politics), and Harvard University (Ph.D. in political science). He speaks some German, French, and Russian. Dr. Weitz recently published a book for the Strategic Studies Institute of the U.S. Army War College, *The Reserve Policies of Nations: A Comparative Analysis*. In 2005, the International Institute for Strategic Studies published his study, *Revitalising US–Russian Security Cooperation: Practical Measures* (Routledge, 2005), as part of its Adelphi Paper series. He has written extensively in such journals as the *National Interest,* the *Washington Quarterly, NATO Review, Studies in Conflict and Terrorism, Defense Concepts,* and the *Journal of Strategic Studies.* His commentaries have appeared in the *International Herald Tribune*, the *Washington Times*, the *Wall Street Journal* (Europe), *Aviation Week & Space Technology*, and many Internet-based publications such as Washingtonpost.com.